INTIMACY UNDONE

INTIMACY UNDONE

MARRIAGE, DIVORCE AND FAMILY LAW IN INDIA

Malavika Rajkotia

SPEAKING TIGER

SPEAKING TIGER BOOKS LLP
125A, Ground Floor, Shahpur Jat, near Asiad Village,
New Delhi 110049

First published in hardback by Speaking Tiger 2017
This revised paperback edition published by Speaking Tiger 2022

ISBN: 978-93-5447-297-8
eISBN: 978-93-86050-57-1

10 9 8 7 6 5 4 3 2 1

Typeset in Sabon Roman by SÜRYA, New Delhi
Printed at SBM Industries Pvt Ltd, Rai (www.sbmprints.com)

To my parents:
my father, the Late Sardar Jitinder Singh who wanted the very first copy off the press, and even now and always remains present with me
and
my mother, Gurdarshan Kaur.

I learned about family from them and the lessons were all good.

CONTENTS

PREFACE TO THE REVISED PAPERBACK EDITION

It has been five years since the first publication of this book which was conceived five years before that. I enjoyed the writing process and obtained some satisfaction in watching the book on its quiet but steady journey. The last year seems to have seen a surge of interest in the book and much to my delight I even saw a copy at the Bangalore Airport that I sneaked to the top of the pile. I suspect it was the title, *Intimacy Undone*, that gave it entry there, and some readers may have been disappointed that it wasn't the pulpy airport read they had expected.

But I also like to think that at least some of those who bought the book found it engaging and useful. Because family law, especially seen from the perspective of gender, impacts our lives deeply, and often in ways we may not imagine.

In this preface to the paperback edition, I focus on an overview of how the law has developed since 2017, the year the first edition of this book was published. I primarily deal with four areas:

i) Three judgements that are predicated on the concept of privacy and their impact on family law.
ii) The issue of the 'fault theory' for divorce, which needs to be urgently resolved for efficient management of the heavy boards of family courts and overworked judges.
iii) Developments in the law of maintenance and alimony amounts.
iv) International child custody disputes.

Privacy and Family Law

Three particular judgements by the Supreme Court after 2017, though not directly on family law, have a strong impact on the 'fault theory' for divorce. They are: *Puttaswamy v. Union of India,*[1] dealing with privacy; *Navtej Singh Johar v. Union of India,*[2] decriminalising consensual same-sex intercourse; and *Joseph Shine v. Union of India,*[3] decriminalising

1. (2017) 10 SCC 1
2. 2018 10 SCC 1
3. (2019) 3 SCC 39

adultery. The true, meaningful reading of these judgements that recognise the right to privacy and autonomy should also recognise the right to exit bad marriages. But unfortunately that effect has not been felt and will not be felt as long as the 'fault theory' rather than the principle of the irretrievable breakdown of a marriage is given primacy as a ground for divorce. (The genesis of the fault theory and its effect have been dealt with in detail in the book.)

The core issues of divorce, as I have said in the book, are finance and custody of children, which tend to get sidelined as 'ancillary' to the long trials on proving 'fault', thus clogging the system. Judicial time would be better spent on adjudicating matters of finance and custody and releasing people from toxic bonds.

Despite clear rulings that cruelty is as the person says it is,[4] and that judges should not impose their own standards of what amounts to cruelty, divorce is still difficult due to a lack of appreciation of—indeed, even a refusal to understand—the nuances of unhappiness. The spouse who says she is unhappy must suffer the indignity of her condition being belittled or dismissed. Can we in our regular life imagine ourselves saying: 'You are not unhappy enough. Because I would not be if I were in your place. You have not suffered enough to deserve a divorce'?

In *Manish Kumar v. Sandhya Kumari*,[5] the Delhi High Court ruled for an approach of reducing the rigour of the fault theory by recognising that divorce petitions are filed really as a last resort because the marriage has broken down and thus the statutory requirement of 'fault' needs to be diluted with the more humane approach that the marriage has broken down and the person asking for divorce has a right to move on with his/her life and have issues of custody and finance dealt with efficiently. Unfortunately, this judgement remains a rare bold approach.

The trajectory of precedents is meandering this way and that with uncertainty about the next one (largely dependent on the judge, who is drawn by luck). If there are Supreme Court rulings for easier divorce[6] there are as many rulings that go the other way, even as recently as August 2022.[7]

4. See V. Bhagat v. D. Bhagat (1994) 1 SCC 337, ¶16 and Raj Talreja v. Kavita Talreja (2017) 14 SCC 194, ¶11;

5. Manish Kumar v. Sandhya Kumari 2016 SCC OnLine Del 5642.

6. See Samar Ghosh vs. Jaya Ghosh 2007 SCC 4 511

7. See Sulekha vs Pradeep Pachouri SLP(C) No. 5726/2021 IV-C onn 22nd August, 2022

Given this uncertainty, lower courts tend to be cautious by interpreting the statute with a high bar for proof of cruelty. They also tend to champion the idea of the 'sanctity' of marriage—without considering that refusing a divorce does not serve the purpose of preserving a marriage in any case. There isn't a single case that I know of where parties resumed their marriage because their divorce was disallowed. Most chose to live with their new partner.

The divorce jurisprudence has thus not travelled much further from the 1970s, when my *mamaji* was refused his divorce and so was lumbered with a legal marriage to a spouse he never saw after the first year of marriage. Divorce was relatively rare back then, but now with the flood of divorces this almost default approach of refusing rather than allowing divorces has made the law that was problematic fifty years ago positively regressive now.

Those who are anxious about modern societies destroying the old order and undermining 'sacred' institutions like marriage, need to understand that most people want a divorce to marry another partner who they think is more suitable to their personalities and needs. It is a search for greater fulfilment—which the privacy judgements, referred to above, guarantee—and thus easier divorces are in fact better for the preservation of marriage (if that is needed at all).

The anxiety of the conservatives seems to be more about preserving the traditional structure of the institution of marriage, which means its patriarchal dominance. This overrides and deflects from the true values of a marriage: those of equality, mutual respect, empathy and healthy intimacy.

It is time to focus on these inner values of a marriage rather than the fossilised structure of traditional patriarchy.

Financial Remedies

Here too there is not much development. The law on the principle of sharing has not seen any noteworthy movement and maintenance and alimony figures continue to be inadequate, measured out reluctantly in small containers. The debate is about the maintenance rights of a working woman (who does paid work, since housework is unpaid labour) in contrast to those of a 'non-working' woman. The debate is also about what a 'non-working woman' should be awarded as maintenance and the expectation that she should do 'something' to enable herself.

Each case must be considered on its own merits. Maintenance claims of qualified non-earning spouses who make no effort to earn is rightly perceived as diluting their claim.[8] However, in *Ruchi Rai Sehmbey v. Simon Jason Sehmbey*, J. Ravindra Bhat makes a distinction between employment and employability.[9] The judgement also appreciates the fact that given the job markets, late entrants to jobs—which is what a previously 'non-working' woman would be—will obviously be severely handicapped.

Moreover, there is always the high probability of men remarrying easily compared to women. A 2021 judgement of the Supreme Court in *Rajnesh vs. Neha*[10] gives an overview on maintenance but the principles are only reiterated rather than developed. It has also prescribed disclosures made under oath by parties stating their financial details and assets, in order to allow for a better analysis of financial worth. This was only a Delhi High Court requirement after the *Kusum Sharma*[11] *and Puneet Kaur*[12] rulings (mentioned in the book). With *Rajnesh vs. Neha* it becomes an all India requirement and will certainly allow for more meaningful maintenance orders.

Wife's Residence

Since *B.P. Achala Anand v. S. Appi Reddy,*[13] where Justice Lahoti noted the gap in the matter of the wife's residence, the law has developed in satisfying leaps and bounds with the passing of the Protection of Women from Domestic Violence Act 2005. Section 17 of this Act recognises the woman's right to continue to reside in the shared household, regardless of title. This includes women living in relationships 'like' a marriage. The impact of this section was diluted considerably by the 2007 *Taruna Batra* judgement[14] but has now been rectified by the Supreme Court in the *Satish Chander Ahuja vs. Sneha Ahuja*[15] judgement of 2021.

However, this right of residence of the wife is qualified by the right of

8. Rupali Gupta v. Rajat Gupta, 2016 SCC OnLine Del 5009

9. Ruchi Rai Sehmbey v. Simon Jason Sehmbey, 2013 SCC OnLine Del 4657

10. Rajnesh vs. Neha (2021) 2 SCC 324

11. Kusum Sharma (1) v. Mahinder Kumar Sharma, 2014 SCC OnLine Del 7672

12. Puneet Kaur vs Inderjit Singh Sawhney 2011 SCC OnLine Del 3841

13. B.P. Achala Anand v. S. Appi Reddy (2005) 3 SCC 313

14. S.R Batra vs. Taruna Batra (2007) 3 SCC 169

15. Satish Chander Ahuja vs. Sneha Ahuja (2021) 1 SCC 414

the husband and the family to provide her with an alternative residence in the same segment. Two Delhi High Court judgements[16] lay down that the wife has a right to a residence but cannot insist on which one. But this, according to me, would obviously not be applicable to women who have other legal interests in family properties developed by various legal transactions, for example trust and coparcenary rights of husbands in case of partition or improvements to the properties. Further, this approach does not deal with the fact that while a wife may not have made monetary contributions in the purchase of a house, it is her work in the home and rearing of children that gave the man the freedom and ability to earn the wealth to buy that house. Thus, it is important to give a monetary value to a woman's work in the house. One such judgement is of Justice Prabha Sridevan, albeit in the context of an insurance claim.[17]

Daughter vs. Wife

In the property section of the book, I briefly address the matter of the 2005 amendment to the Hindu Succession Act that recognises a daughter as coparcener in the Hindu Undivided Family (HUF). Several conflicting judgements, and now the recent *Vineeta Sharma* case[18], hold that the daughter's rights are retrospective to the very inception of the Act. The judgement has also held that in some facts and circumstances unregistered family partitions can also be looked into while adjudicating whether the daughter can claim partition under the amended act. The judgement is problematic on many counts, apart from making difficult reading on account of the inherent contradictions of appreciating and agreeing with legal principles and then reaching a conclusion against such settled law on rules for interpretations of statutes, coparcenary properties and the law on the principle of retrospectivity.

The reach of this issue is wide and the potential damage is huge, given the possibly thousands of estates that will be unsettled by this ruling. Here I recommend H.M. Seervai[19] on the care that is required on holding laws to be retrospective and disturbing estates well settled under the regime of the earlier law.

---

16. Sunil Madan vs. Rachna Madan 2012 SCC OnLine Del 3265 and Ajay Kumar Jain vs. Baljit Kaur Jain 160(2009) DLT 401 (DB)

17. National Insurance Co. Ltd. v. Minor Deepika 2009 SCC OnLine Mad 828

18. Vineeta Sharma v. Rakesh Sharma, (2020) 9 SCC 1

19. Constitutional Law of India 4th Edition Volume 1 Law & Justice Publishing Co. (1 January 2021)

The case of *Phulavati*[20] settled the controversy that the amendment was prospective (rather than retrospective), with some exceptions such as pending *lis*, which was aligned with the well-established and settled first principle that a statute is to be read prospectively since no new law should disturb settled estates and rights. It also aligned with the interpretation of the Supreme Court in a series of judgements as to the meaning of notional partition on the death of a coparcener wherein the shares of the heirs immediately become fixed and a new coparcenary may be formed without disturbing what is already fixed.

Both these settled principles have been drastically disturbed by the *Vineeta Sharma* ruling that ends bewilderingly with an ancient irish adage that 'a son is a son till he takes him a wife but a daughter is a daughter all of her life'. This is archaic and patriarchal, displaying a dislike and suspicion of daughters-in-law while burdening daughters with an extra duty of care even at the cost of their personal lives.

The point is that the wife has not been given equal statutory rights in matrimonial property to balance the rights that a daughter has in her parental property. The other point is that wives become vulnerable yet again to dowry pressures to claim their shares of property from fathers and brothers.

I am told that nowadays many families have started obtaining relinquishment deeds from their daughters and sons-in-law at the time of their marriage in *lieu* of giving them dowry.

None of the judgements on the 2005 amendment have looked at the aspect of the custom of dowry which often constituted a daughter's inheritance in gold as equal to that of the son in land. Further, no judgment deals with the consequences of this legislation: First, a daughter is a coparcener in her parental HUF but if there is a partition in the marital HUF, she gets a share there too. Secondly, a poor daughter married into a rich family suffers because her maintenance rights from her husband remain insubstantial. Thirdly, a rich daughter could still be pressured by a greedy family-in-law to ask her parents for her right in the ancestral property as a coparcener and she thus ends up isolating herself from both her marital and parental families.

One can't argue with the worthy intent, but retrospectivity is wreaking havoc in settled estates. Women's rights will be better addressed if legislations are brought in to address all aspects of gender imbalance

---

20. Prakash v. Phulavati, (2016) 2 SCC 36

and inequality. Meaning thereby that the wife and mother should not get marginalised while enabling the daughter.

Custody

After fault and finance, we come to arguably the most important aspect of a divorce law, custody.

Here, there is a sharp difference in intra-country and international matters. In intra-country, even if it is inter-state or inter-city, the courts have tried co-parenting plans with varying degrees of success, largely dependent on the willingness of parents to make the plans work. However, the starkness of the gender battle is best brought out in conflicting international jurisdictions.

At the time of the first publication of this book in 2017, the last word on the matter was the deeply problematic *Surya Vadanan*[21] case that jettisoned the welfare principle as the primary concern, to be dealt with by the court to which the child would be returned—in this case, a court in the UK. The judgement was critiqued by me as lacking nuance and doing what the Hague Convention envisages without considering that India is not a signatory to the Convention for good reasons.[22] The judgment ignored even the margin of discretion that the Convention retained for judges, to refuse to return children removed from one jurisdiction to the other.

Surya Vadanan was overruled by two successive three-bench rulings in the *Nithya Raghavan*[23] and *Kanika Goel*[24] cases. The Supreme court restored the welfare of the child as the central concern and aligned it with the maternal preference rule, holding in the Kanika case that a nanny was no substitute for the mother.[25]

The trend seemed to be to understand that mothers fleeing foreign jurisdictions needed the protection of their home countries and that it was easier for the fathers to litigate custody issues here than it was for women to undertake expensive litigation in the foreign countries where they had no jobs and family support.

---

21. Surya Vadanan v. State of T.N., (2015) 5 SCC 450

22. See The Many Legal Complexities Around Cross Border 'Parental Abductions', *The Wire*. May, 2022

23. Nithya Anand Raghavan vs. State (NCT of Delhi) (2017) 8 SCC 454

24. Kanika Goel vs. State of NCT of Delhi (2018) 9 SCC 578

25. P 33.

However, this consideration was again sidelined in *Lahiri Sakhamuri* v. *Sobhan Kodali*,[26] where the children were ordered to be returned (and of course the mother followed) on the ground that the US jurisdiction had been invoked by Lahari herself and the summons issued had restrained her from changing the custody arrangement. This was followed by the *Yashita Sahu*[27] case that followed the reasoning of Lahiri to the same conclusion. In *Yashita,* the court still relied on the principle of comity of courts even while acknowledging the child's need for the mother.

Even after the above-mentioned cases, one could advise that the return to foreign jurisdiction orders were only when the wives had submitted to the foreign jurisdiction, which of course is a settled good principle of private international law.

However, the *Vasudha Sethi*[28] judgement—on facts similar to *Nithya* and *Kanika*, in that there were no foreign proceedings—ordered the return of the child holding that this was in the welfare of the child. Thus it seems that return orders are made on the ground that the opportunities for the child are better in the developed world than in India. This approach tramples on the value of the mother in the child's life, in whose care the child had been from birth, indeed, even before birth. It also devalues the mother who has birthed and looked after the child at considerable personal cost, and making a number sacrifices of varying degrees.

In Vasudha's case we had cited Professor Eekelar on a new approach to the welfare principle that intertwines with parental rights but is balanced with due consideration to the primary caregiver, who is invariably the mother. The court discarded this approach by holding that the welfare of the child alone is to be considered, but the court did not define the criterion to assess welfare. And clearly the child's emotional distress due to separation from the primary caregiver was no concern. I suspect this is because invariably the courts presume that the mothers are committed to their children and will follow them anyway. Thus the system takes the woman for granted just as the husband does. Mothers are reduced to chattel in the family.

I recently read an article in *The Leaflet* critiquing the Vasudha judgment[29] and I was happy that at least discussions about the problems

---

26. Lahari Sakhamuri v. Sobhan Kodali, (2019) 7 SCC 311

27. Yashita Sahu v. State of Rajasthan, (2020) 3 SCC 67

28. Vasudha Sethi v. Kiran V. Bhaskar 2022 SCC OnLine SC 43

29. 'Supreme Court rules parental rights irrelevant in custody battles: why the decision may backfire', *The Leaflet*, (31st January, 2022)

with the welfare principle when the mother's rights are ignored are being injected into the developing jurisprudence. Hopefully, Indian jurisprudence will evolve and become sensitive to the predicament of women who flee their matrimonial homes due to domestic violence which is exercised in a variety of ways, including coercive control.

Part of the reasoning, in these 'return' orders, is that the child is a foreign citizen. Yet citizenship is not a factor in any Indian statute dealing with children or in any other statute or convention worldwide. This is because citizenship can be obtained without permanent residence; foreigners can be domiciled in one country while being citizens of another: citizenship of a Caribbean island country can be purchased without even a visit.

The term used in all Indian statutes dealing with children has been 'ordinary residence' of the child. The Hindu Marriage Act uses 'domicile' of the parties. Most common law statutes use 'habitual residence'. The Indian statute requirement of 'ordinary residence' is in fact a lower threshold than 'habitual residence'. Even so the term has been fraught with uncertainty and ambiguity due to various conflicting judgements.[30]

My argument is that a child cannot have an independent residence but with a parent, and of the two parents it is naturally with the parent who is the primary caregiver. For instance, what is the habitual residence of a breastfeeding child but at the breast; what is the residence of a two-year-old but on her mother's lap; what is the residence of a five-year-old but a home run by her mother? It is for this reason that the Hindu Minority and Guardianship Act, 1956[31] has the maternal preference rule for children under five years of age.

It would of course be different for a teenage child whose habitual residence would be the unique eco-system of school, friends, a particular routine and so on.

Having said which, it is noteworthy that in none of the international custody cases I have cited have the children been older. In all cases the mother was the primary caregiver and brought the child/children away with her to escape a marriage that was intolerable due to 'domestic violence' in its widest definition, including coercive control. I need to stress the definition of domestic violence in its widest amplitude because

30. See Ruchi Majoo v. Sanjeev Majoo (2011) 6 SCC 479 and Lahari Sakhamuri vs. Sobhan Kodali 2019 SCC OnLine SC 395 and Nithya Anand Raghavan vs. State (NCT of Delhi) (2017) 8 SCC 454

31. Section 6(a)

the default tendency is still to be dismissive of the claim unless there is blood and gore. In one case,[32] the Delhi High Court was dismissive of the woman's claim of domestic violence, saying something to the effect that all women say that. In another case,[33] the Delhi High Court called the marital home in the foreign jurisdiction the woman's '*karmabhoomi*', again ignoring her claim of domestic violence of coercive control. In one case where I represented the woman, she had to submit grocery bills and even take permission to buy a new mattress; how can this not be considered domestic violence? The expectation seems to be that these are no reasons to exit a marriage and a woman must be patient and adjusting. As one trial judge said to me, '*Yeh sab toh har ghar mein hota hai* (But this sort of thing happens in every home)'—in other words, what's the big deal?

A deep unhappiness caused by oppression and coercive control exercised through finance, and emotional and psychological manipulation has not been considered seriously by our courts even though in *Dastane vs. Dastane*[34] the Supreme Court warned against the imposition of the standard of the reasonable person for cruelty in a claim under contract law.

In custody battles, another useful method of assessment would be to see whether the parent is fighting for the love of the child who is being unfairly withheld from him or whether the litigation is being used to assert power. The problem with such 'return orders' has also been that our courts send the children out with the mother in what they hope will be a 'soft landing', and trusting that the courts of the other country will abide by the principle of 'comity of courts'. This has unfortunately not worked well in any of the return cases as far as I know, although I have not examined each case. But of the above mentioned cases, I know that in two the women and children have returned to a situation of being locked in another legal battle and none of the undertakings to the Indian court have been complied with.

This problem is most starkly demonstrated in *Perry Kansagra v. Smriti Madan Kansagra*,[35] where the custody of an eleven-year-old boy was handed over to the father with the condition that he would bring the child back annually to meet the mother. The order was to be 'mirrored'

32. 2013 SCC OnLine Del 1262

33. Kanika Goel vs. State of NCT of Delhi (2018) 9 SCC 578

34. Dr. N.G Dastane vs. Mrs. S. Dastane (1975) 2 SCC 326

35. (2019) 20 SCC 753

in the foreign court but this did not happen due to technicalities. It has now been three years since the mother had any contact with her son.

I must mention two cases that I believe are unprecedented and could have serious consequences. In 2018, a seven-month-old child was abducted by her father to a Middle Eastern country. A habeas corpus petition was filed and the child was eventually returned and a generous visitation order given to the father, subject to the child's passport being deposited in court.

A year later, the child was abducted again using a new passport obtained from a Caribbean country. We filed another habeas corpus petition that resulted in a robust judgment authored by J. Manmohan[36] of the Delhi High Court. The matter eventually reached the Supreme Court where the father's egregious conduct was not given full import. When a passport is deposited and then the child is abducted it becomes more than a custody matter. It is fraud on the court that needs to be addressed. Yet, the Supreme Court, ignoring this aspect, remanded the matter for a rehearing on custody.

The matter was eventually settled with custody and guardianship to the mother and fair visitation to the father. Thus the High Court ruling on the matter remains good law so far since it was not set aside on account of the settlement.

Another case was the abduction by the father (a US citizen) of the child (also a US citizen). Here the Supreme Court had ruled that the child should remain with the mother. This abduction was effected by using two passports: one deposited in court as security and the other used to exit the country with the child across the Nepal border. The habeas corpus case here is pending.

~

In conclusion, all of this should and can be easier. The fault theory is an unnecessary burden and clogs up the system. Adjudication of financial remedies by the principle of sharing and compensation rather than the general lifestyle rule would be better for women and children and also help reduce litigation since the settlements would be larger and women would not want to litigate for basic financial needs. Co-parenting is a good arrangement but co-sharing of finances would be fair, too, and is needed just as much. Children would also be better placed between parents more or less financially equal or at least less unequal. In matters of custody, certainly the children must be the focus, but not at the expense of one

36. Kiran Lohia v. State Govt. (NCT of Delhi) 2018 SCC OnLine Del 8686

parent's persona and right to dignity, by expecting her to trail the child back to the country she had fled.

The matter of easier divorces was considered by the UPA (1) government when it introduced a marriage reform bill.[37] It passed the Rajya Sabha but then lapsed. This Bill had also mirrored contemporary English law and had other problems, that are now rendered moot.

A meaningful development of family law jurisprudence is that it be humane, which in turn means that it should address separate rights within the institutional vessel. Any other approach is weighing the ship down with the toxicity of anger and bitterness.

The issues surrounding acrimonious battles in fault divorce, gendered division of labour within households, financial settlement on divorce and child custody are by no means discrete. The patriarchal construct of the role of women within the house and in society is at the core of all of them. The division of responsibilities within the house impacts the role of women within the workplace, determines their financial status and their responsibilities as the primary caregiver. On the breakdown of a marriage, women face the dual challenge of having to deal with financial insecurity and also fighting for custody. The current legal framework is not designed to accurately attach value to the contributions of care made by the wife within the familial set up. These contributions are often made at the cost of professional opportunities since the marketplace still finds it difficult to accommodate the needs of the primary caregiver. The intersectionality of these issues tells us that the goal of achieving an egalitarian society cannot be attained through reform in silos—the family, the division of responsibilities within the family, the setup of the workplace as well as structures of childcare need to be examined in a more holistic manner.

To retrieve the purpose of marriage from this weighed-down vessel we need a new set of rules wherein all work in the marriage, including housework and rearing of children, is given a financial value to allow for a more equitable distribution of wealth generated in the marriage. Also, the adjudicating approach has to be to a perspective of justice that is not shaped by the expectations of traditional patriarchal morality. We need a jurisprudence that demonstrates an empathetic respect for the suffering and pain that is a divorce process.

MALAVIKA RAJKOTIA
New Delhi, August 2022

37. The Marriage Laws Amendment Bill, 2010

INTRODUCTION

This book grew from a judicial barb that lodged in my heart. A judge in open court remarked to me that it is lawyers who are largely responsible for prolonging divorce litigation. My stung reaction was to write an open letter to the Chief Justice of the Delhi High Court—which I never sent because, to my surprise, it grew into this book.

~

The letter was in defence of family lawyers. The suggestion that lawyers are mainly responsible for obstructing settlements exposes a lack of understanding of the dynamics of the matrimonial conflict, which is much deeper and broader than what can be seen in court. A discussion of finance and parenting styles can get acrimonious even in intact marriages, but such disagreements are distorted to grotesque proportions in divorce situations. Since it is an emotive argument for the couple, a lawyer can never completely control a case and judges can never grasp the complete matter.

It is the litigants who decide on how far and how long they want to battle. We lawyers try to ensure that their decision is based on sound advice about the strengths and weaknesses of their cases, usually with the counsel that settling helps in achieving emotional closure—the value of which is never completely grasped, even by those who give such advice. Emotional closure can be achieved only at the pace of the suffering persons involved.

Divorce litigation is exhausting because the endeavour is to achieve in divorce that which does not exist in many intact marriages: equality in matters of finance and parenting. Fair and equal sharing is an emotionally fraught exercise, because the dynamics of most marriages are unequal. Even seemingly equal partnerships have an undertow of traditional gender equations, which essentially cause the dynamics to be unbalanced.

We lawyers risk seeming disruptive to the judge's bench, as we struggle to obtain for our clients the closest semblance to the equality that the law promises, even while knowing that the outcome can never be entirely fair. Since the social reality is inherently unequal, we have to protect our clients from being intimidated or daunted by a legal system that may compel them to give up substantial rights.

Family lawyers are also always advised by courts to avoid getting personally involved. As officers of the court, we maintain a distance from the client. Due to that quality called empathy, however, we are vulnerable to 'translating' our client's troubles into our own. Schopenhauer asked: 'How is it possible that suffering that is neither my own nor of my concern should immediately affect me as though it were my own, and with such force that it moves me to action?'[1] Every family lawyer suffers this to some extent and it need not always be bad, as long as it is checked by constant self-awareness about boundaries.

I have watched with a sense of pain as my clients' hope for a speedy resolution dries up under the rigour of procedure. It is here that litigants draw strength and reassurance from the support of their partisan lawyer. I take providing that to be an integral part of my brief.

~

Every family unit is a microcosm of a certain part of society. Divorce litigation is an opportunity to study social change: it is like looking under the bonnet of a car when it has stalled. While you are fixing what is wrong in your particular car, you learn about cars generally. The legal history of family law is also the history of our collective movement towards civilized society, one with meaningful gender equality, fair distribution of material wealth and tender treatment of children.

Family law is treated as 'soft' because, according to many people, it is more about common sense than 'hard-core' law. It is to correct this perception that I begin the book with a chapter on the complicated history of family laws in India, as well as the careful advocacy required in establishing a case or defending it.

Divorce cannot be completely understood without an understanding of the history of marriage. The second and third chapters cover this, along with the changes that the institution of marriage has undergone, as moral values with regard to family, sex and gender have evolved.

~

I visualize the architecture of this book as a large pavilion in a forest of complex social realities. From the foundations, which are the history of marriage and family law, arises the super-structure of marriage and divorce law; custody law; laws on privacy within a marriage; concerns about the morality of adultery, pre-marital sex and sex within marriage; the ethics of litigation; the remedy of mediation and so on. Yet, the structure of the pavilion is dynamic and reflects social change.

1. Schopenhauer, *On the Foundations of Morality*

The matter of children is interesting because even though they are a part of the structure of family law, they are also separate living beings, housed with their parents till they strike out on their own. Kahlil Gibran explains it beautifully in his poem, 'On Children':

> *Your children are not your children. They are the sons and daughters of Life's longing for itself. They come through you but not from you. And though they are with you yet they belong not to you.*

~

Then comes the matter of the integrity of the structure, which is bolstered with reference to our Constitution, from which emanate the concepts of gender equality and the current burning topic of the uniform civil code, vis-à-vis the right of each community to have a personal law in traction with the move towards gender equality.[2] I have argued against imposing a uniform civil code, preferring the moderate route of reform within each community: otherwise, the topic tends to get hijacked by the majority into minority-bashing and brings to the fore identity politics, deflecting from the true purpose of achieving gender equality. We are currently in the midst of such a conflict on the validity of triple talaq in Islamic Law.

Family law has evolved alongside women's rights movements within and beyond each community. Since personal laws are rooted in patriarchy, a family law judge has to harmonize the principle of equality with the social reality that each community is different and change must not be perceived as a threat to its identity.

A characteristic of family law is its wide margins of discretion. Thus the emerging jurisprudence sometimes seems confused, because the exercise of judicial discretion will obviously be coloured by the socialization of each judge. Parliament is also responsible for the confusion, because it enacts various welfare legislations for populist reasons without careful debate, and the judiciary is left to fill the gaps in inept legislative drafting. It is this fluidity in family law that is misunderstood as the absence of 'positive law', requiring only logic and common sense.

---

2. The State of Bombay vs Narasu Appa Mali, AIR 1952 Bom 84 states that 'it is competent either to the State or the Union Legislature to legislate on topics falling within the purview of the personal law and yet the expression "personal law" is not used in Article 13, because, in any opinion, the framers of the Constitution wanted to leave the personal laws outside the ambit of Part III of the Constitution'; See also: Sri Krishna Singh vs Mathura Ahir, 1980 SCR (2) 660: 'In our opinion, the learned Judge failed to appreciate that Part III of the Constitution does not touch upon the personal laws of the parties.'

The evolution of family law has also given an opportunity for thoughtful and active judges to espouse opinions that nudge the nation towards the constitutional ideals of gender equality, secularism and pluralism, even while negotiating territory mined with the raw nerves of identity and gender politics. The politics of change in India has revolved around customs that continue to survive even after being declared illegal. Family courts are the arena for this struggle of custom versus law. It requires a judiciary that furthers the law, but not too far away from social change as a ground reality. This the judges do by exhorting, even pontificating (not always unduly, we hope) while stating their opinions. We Indians are talkative and as Amartya Sen writes, argumentative. The downside to this is when judges expose their personal biases and prejudices and create precedents that spiral us away from, rather than further along, the road to a sharper delineation of rights.

~

As my letter in response to the judge expanded into a book, the first section I wrote was 'my advice to clients' which now comes in the Epilogue. I tried to understand a person whose life was unravelling and the frustration of a litigant dealing with the seeming lethargy of a clogged legal system without any immediate remedy in sight.

The book is sprinkled with anecdotes about legal proceedings and cases. However, facts that may identify specific cases have been withheld, and details have been changed to protect the identities of the people involved. Only those cases where the facts are already in the public domain have been discussed at length.

The judgments cited are mostly from the Supreme Court, as being representative of the law of the land, as well as from some High Courts to describe various trends of thought in law. However, of the High Courts, the Delhi High Court is most frequently cited, since it has passed many important rulings that could be said to reflect various crucial social trends, and is the court I am most familiar with.

A common thread through the chapters is the story of my maternal uncle (Mamaji), whose personal life was shrouded in the divorce battle he lost and his gallant attempt to reclaim his life despite the law.

The last chapter discusses the future of marriage. I argue that marriage is still the most important rite of passage: but divorce is also crucial because it is a chance to undo a mistake in choice of life partner and try again. Remarriages indicate that the institution of marriage is still robust. Nevertheless, the social bias against divorce is also apparent from the fact that divorcees are not part of mainstream marriage portals, but form a separate class, sometimes literally, as a website named secondshaadi.com shows.

A limitation of the book is that it deals with a predominantly middle- to upper-class and North Indian context. This book is also largely in the context of Hindu law, though other personal laws are mentioned to aid in perspective on gender and political issues. Confining myself to these parameters is how I could make such a sprawling subject manageable for *this* book.

~

In recent years, commercial possibilities and the growing volume of litigation has generated more interest in family law, even though most lawyers and judges still claim that they cannot deal with the emotional impact of intensely adversarial gender and social battles.

The core and traction of family law is the conflict between men and women, society and law, conservative and liberal, change and the resistance to it. It is about the mismatch of expectations from marriage and family. The law has to negotiate the investment of general society in the ideal of marriage, in addition to what specific families might need to resolve their disputes. Conservatives argue that Indian culture is fading because the institution of marriage is under threat. So, they feel they have a bounden duty to hold tightly to an idea of marriage known to 'Indian culture.' While doing so, there is no thought of the patriarchal roots of marriage, from which have grown other civil and public institutions also tainted by skewed gender dynamics.

My argument is that a basic cause of divorce is the growing challenge to patriarchal power. Much of the confusion around divorce is due to the present flux, while we as a society settle into new roles in marriage and new ideas of family. Till then, we must deal with the violent backlash of a seething patriarchy that draws support from powerful men. Politicians, parliamentarians, national leaders, lawyers, judges, academics, so-called 'civil society', have supported the backlash, some vociferously and many others by silent inaction. The dissenters are few but feminists are foremost amongst them.

Even so, I have tried to warn that feminist perspectives do not endorse misuse of beneficial legislation by women or their families and advisers. Thus, cases have to be contextualized in the human instinct to exploit—present when dealing with any other law—but that does not justify the removal of beneficial legislation—just as no other law can be removed from the statute books because it is misused.

I highlight these issues for the benefit of all stakeholders in the legal system: judges, lawyers and litigants. I hope I can also reach students and others who are interested in a comment on legal perspectives to the social issues arising in our burgeoning middle class.

MALAVIKA RAJKOTIA
New Delhi, 2016

1. MARRIAGE AND DIVORCE CONSTRUCT

DIVORCE AND THE LAW

In 1934, A.P. Herbert wrote a novel called *The Holy Deadlock*[1] about the tragedy of a marriage with no exit: 'A bad bargain that must be stuck to as long as life lasted. Was there any other lifelong bargain in which a mistake was irrevocable, from which the law provided no honorable escape at all?'

At the time UK law subscribed to the fault theory. A person petitioning for divorce (petitioner) had to support the claim with reasons that the other (respondent) suffers one or all of the 'faults' enumerated in the divorce law. The defense against this was two-pronged: first, that the case made out was false and the respondent did not suffer the faults alleged, and second, that the petitioner was, in fact, taking advantage of his/her own fault and the court should not reward such reprehensible marital and litigation conduct.

In 1934, English law allowed adultery as the only fault that could be a ground for divorce. Thus, many couples who agreed that they wanted a divorce would cooperate in creating a case for adultery. A lucrative industry arose to support collusive divorces. The services of women (not necessarily disreputable) could be engaged by husbands, to enable them to be 'caught' by any person willing to depose in court, thus bearing witness to an inappropriate proximity of the married man with another woman.

In Herbert's novel, Mr Adams is a quiet, unassuming man who often wondered, as did every one who met them, why his wife married him in the first place. Mrs Adams seems to have come to the same realization and falls in love with someone else. She asks her compliant, loving husband to arrange for a divorce. Mr Adams goes through the charade of manufacturing evidence of adultery because he loves Mrs Adams and will do anything for her, including giving her a divorce if that is what she wants. He arranges to be caught in a hotel bedroom with a lady who is experienced in such matters and, much to Mr Adam's relief, takes charge of the matter: they must be seen dining by candlelight: then they must be seen to retire together to their bedroom where they have checked in as Mr and Mrs Adams. The next morning, they must be seen together by the waiter who serves them their bed-tea. Mr Adams sends his wife

1. A.P. Herbert, *The Holy Deadlock*

the details of his fabricated rendezvous: hotel bills, names of the hotel manager and waiter etc. Mrs Adams files her petition on the ground of Mr Adams' adultery. She calls upon the waiter and hotel manager who are willing witnesses.

Now comes the twist: Mrs Adams is a glamorous newsmaker and the press picks up the story of her love affair with a co-actor. The judge is a zealot who loses sleep worrying about social anarchy being unleashed if divorce becomes easy. So, the Adams are denied their divorce because the judge finds that Mrs Adams is not without fault either, since she is having an affair with another man.

Mrs Adams and her lover walk out of the courtroom hand in hand: they can never be married. Some look at them with disapproval but many think of them as brave and beautiful with their difficult love.

Mr Adams walks out of the courtroom, heavy with the knowledge that he is tied in law to a woman who does not love him. He will never see her again. His walk into the sunset is going to be lonely. In 1934, how many women would agree to be with him, knowing that he can never marry? He decides to take charge of his life to the extent he can: he writes to the woman whose 'services' he had retained for the hotel room charade. Till he receives her reply, there are evenings to go through: he slows down and smiles at a woman standing on a corner: 'Good evening. Coming any place with me?' The girl is nineteen and Irish, and says 'Be jabers! it's a free country—if you are not found out...come on then!... I'm married myself.'

This novel sparked off the first divorce law reform movement in England, which led to the passing of the Matrimonial Causes Act 1937.

Divorce law in the UK

The history of divorce law in England is the stuff of romance. It has been created by kings, poets, writers and philosophers. It began with King Henry VIII's desire to annul his marriage with Queen Catherine of Aragon to free himself to marry Anne Boleyn. The Pope refused and so the English Parliament broke away from the Catholic Church in 1533.[2]

Even so, Christian England could not bring itself to find divorce palatable and so it was available on very limited grounds, and only by special dispensation of the ecclesiastical courts or an Act of Parliament. Neither of the options were available to an ordinary or even a highly

2. See http://www.bbc.co.uk/history/people/catherine_of_aragon/

ranked person for that matter. Divorce was governed by canon law in the ecclesiastic courts, which still held a Christian view of marriage. They granted divorce *a mensa a thoro* (separate bed and board) which, however, did not free a person to remarry.

~

In 1643, the poet John Milton addressed Parliament on the matter of divorce. The speech was from his document titled 'Doctrine and Discipline of Divorce' written as a letter to Parliament to satisfy them that Christ was not against divorce and did not 'meddle in matters judicial'. The reason for his campaign was his anger, humiliation and loneliness when his wife left him. He spoke for the 'right of man' (gender specific) to divorce his wife if she was unpleasant and unsatisfactory and they were incompatible. The divorce, he said, should free both to remarry.

Milton poured an acid torrent of words on the clergy that interpreted the bible to deny divorce to 'man' (still gender specific). He called them man-haters who collectively formed a prelacy that was the 'great whore'. Given our present times, it would interest the reader to know that he was not censured for his language against the church and clergy.

Milton's battle was successful and the assembly that acted for Parliament in matters clerical, allowed for divorce in the 'confession of faith treatise'[3] in cases of infidelity or abandonment.

~

The next call for reform was by a woman, to create rights where there were none. Caroline Norton left her husband, George Chappel Norton, in 1836 and subsisted on her earnings as a writer. Mr Norton claimed for himself the money earned by his wife, as under English law, she had no right to any independent property. Mrs Norton had her revenge by running up huge bills to be paid by her husband.

Mr Norton then mounted a case against the then Prime Minister, Lord Melbourne, for 'criminal conversation' or 'crim con' with his wife. The trial nearly brought down the government but eventually the jury threw Mr Norton's case out. Lord Melbourne survived the scandal but Caroline Norton lost her reputation and the friendship of Lord Melbourne.

Norton had also abducted their children and allowed Caroline no access till one died of negligent treatment of an injury. After that Caroline was allowed minimal supervised access. Having lost everything, Caroline Norton fought desperately and obtained three legislative reforms: the

3. George G. Perry, *History of Reformation in England*

Matrimonial Causes Act 1857, the Married Women's Property Act 1870 and the Custody of Infants Act 1839.[4] The first of these allowed for divorce on the ground of adultery for a husband, while for a wife, it required adultery combined with other offenses such as incest, cruelty, bigamy or desertion. In 1857, adultery as a criminal offense (crim. con.) in England was also removed from the statute books.

~

In 1929, Bertrand Russell rounded up the history and social context of divorce in a brilliant treatise titled *Marriage and Morals*. Marriage was maintained by combining it with morality. He was only moderately in favour of divorce: 'the conclusion seems to be that, while divorce is too difficult in many countries, England is one, easy divorce does not afford a genuine solution of the marriage problem.'[5] His solution was to free marriage from morals by distinguishing marriage from sexual relations. Men, he advises, should be free to have extra-marital relations because that will help save marriages. He does not talk about women.

Four years later, Herbert highlighted the problem of divorce in his novel *The Holy Deadlock*. As a Member of Parliament, he moved a private bill for marriage reform soon after his book was published. And so was passed the Matrimonial Causes Act 1937. This act gave both parties the right to file for divorce on the ground of adultery simpliciter;[6] and three more grounds were added: desertion, cruelty and incurable insanity.

Subsequent divorce reforms in 1969 and 1973 moved toward making divorces easier by diluting the fault theory while strengthening the rules of equitable distribution of marital property.

Family Law in India

While English divorce law developed over 400 years, women in far-away India dealt with the law differently. Child marriage, sati and such evil customs notwithstanding, women in India had a different position than that of Mrs Norton. They had rights of maintenance and alimony and could own immovable property, besides their jewellery as stridhan. Even

---

4. Caroline Norton, *Caroline Norton's Defense: English Laws for Women in the Nineteenth Century*

5. Bertrand Russell, *Marriage and Morals*

6. The legal definition of simpliciter is 'in or by itself'. The significance of introducing adultery simpliciter as a ground for divorce meant that neither party had to couple adultery with another offense in their divorce petition.

though both Britain and much of India shared patriarchy as a social order, some matrilineal societies could be found in the South and Northeast of India (though control was exercised by the maternal uncle). Men practiced bigamy. Divorce was possible amongst the lower castes. Indian law was rooted in custom derived from religious texts interpreted differently by the Brahmins and maulvis of different regions.

After the Queen's Proclamation in 1858, making India her direct dominion, the English made a better effort to understand the legal systems of the country they were to rule. Many Orientalists became deeply interested in matters of Dharmashatric and Islamic law. The first Chief Justice of the Supreme Court in India in 1783, Sir William Jones, studied Sanskrit and spent time with shastris and maulvis to grasp the finer points of the customary laws followed by various communities, while Sir Henry Mayne's extensive research earned him the status of an authority on Hindu law. The country thus came to be ruled by Indian law as interpreted by the British.

In 1881, a District Judge in Madras, James Henry Nelson, published a prospectus of the scientific study of Hindu law.[7] It was, he said, his attempt to clear many misconceptions of the British understanding of Hindu law. He highlighted fifteen popular misconceptions and framed specific inquiries, the answers to which would give a more precise and scientific answer to 'what is Hindu law'. Nelson suffered severe criticism for what was seen as his challenge and criticism of more influential English scholars of Hindu law. His career was deflected into the wilderness and his views find no mention in books of classical Hindu law, except in the exhaustive critiques and research by J.D.M. Derrett.

Some of the many questions and inquiries Nelson framed are worth reading because they continue to be relevant and many of them remain unanswered: 'Who is a Hindoo?'; 'When were the Dharmashastras written?'; 'How do they differ from one another?'; 'What is the source of Mitakshara and Vijneshawara?'; 'What is meant by and included in the terms Dravida? What portion of the population in the south can be said to be Dravida? How have Brahmanism and Dravidism acted and reacted on one another?'; 'What was the authority of the heads of panchayats mukhiyas to punish crimes and settle disputes before the British came to power?'

What Nelson called popular misconceptions in 1881 continue till date;

7. James Henry Nelson, *A Prospectus of the Scientific Study of the Hindu Law*

for example: so-called Hindu law is applicable to 'all persons vulgarly styled Hindus' and 'to their descendants however remote'; 'that a state of union is to be presumed amongst the Hindus'; 'that a son or a grandson may compel a partition of ancestral property'.[8] His comment on the parochialism of the northern and southern regions holds true as a modern problem in independent India.

Those misconceptions in Hindu law that found their way into being considered good law must now remain. And that brings us to the principle that the British used often while grappling with their perception of the law and a custom quite contrary to it: *factum valet quid fieri non debuit*—what ought not to be done becomes valid when done.[9] The Dharmashastras also have the same principle to deal with—the problem of long custom that obtains the sanction of law because of its tenure in time, or with any act that is better left alone rather than undone: 'that what is done cannot be undone by a hundred texts'.[10] The purpose of this principle was not to make legal an act that was patently illegal, but to institute a distinction that acts in violation of laws that were directory in nature were to be let alone, while violation of mandatory law had legal consequences.

The principle of *factum valet* has particular relevance in marriage, inheritance, alienation of family property by the karta or patriarch and such matters. For example, a marriage of cousins not permitted by the law of a community would not be illegal once it was done. Similarly with child marriages: they are illegal and must be prevented, but once the ceremony is complete, it is treated as a valid marriage.[11] Along the same lines, the sale of property by a karta, even in violation of the parameters that allowed it, would not be invalidated.

Our present day understanding of Hindu law is largely imported from the British understanding of the Dharmashastras and custom to form a unique amalgam of Indian and English common law. This is how English common law came to India as the banks within which flowed the personal

---

8. James Henry Nelson, *Indian Usage and Judge-Made Law in Madras*, p. 12

9. Madhu Kishwar, 'Codified Hindu Law: Myth and Reality' in *Economic and Political Weekly*, Vol. 29, (Aug, 1994), pp. 2145-2161

10. K. Jaishankar. 'Manusmriti: A critique of the criminal justice tenets in the Ancient Indian Hindu Code' in *ERCES Online Quarterly Review*

11. See p. 364: Section 11, Hindu Marriage Act: Nullity of marriage and divorce—Void marriages; See also: Section 5, Hindu Marriage Act: Condition for a Hindu Marriage.

laws of the communities that they thought better to leave alone. Thus marriage, divorce, property, succession, guardianship of children and rights of women were left untouched by them, except for reform that was initiated from within the communities. Indian common law thus became the legacy of independent India.

Judge developed law is an integral part of common law. To develop or 'make' law, judges had to deal with two sources of law: multiple customs in various regions and some statutory laws that had been passed during the colonial reign. This method was obviously patchy and haphazard, so to get closer to achieving justice, they used the common law principle of 'Justice, equity and good conscience' (JEGC). The jurist and Hindu law scholar Derrett considered the JEGC approach to be well intentioned but inept, because it compromised the code and custom of Hindu law.[12]

~

Over the years, though UK law has travelled a different trajectory, it continues to be of interest, allowing us to better understand the origin and context of many legal principles now applied as common law in India.

The movement in favour of divorce began in England because the laws there entailed monogamy. Intellectuals called for divorce to be seen as part of a right to personal fulfillment, and an individual's search for freedom to undo a mistake in their choice of partner. It began with only men wanting the right, as women could not really be free in a man's world and so looked to marriage as their social security. In contrast, as I mentioned earlier, Hindu classical law allowed for divorce amongst some lower castes, but in practice, men mainly used it to discard a woman and marry again. Upper-caste men traditionally did not need to avail of divorce because they were often wealthy enough to support any number of wives. Muslim men also practiced polygamy.

The first divorce act in India thus owed its origin to the British. The Indian Divorce Act 1869 was passed for Christian colonial officers living in India. It was the same as the English Matrimonial Causes Act 1857 and it was skewed in favour of men. A man could obtain a divorce on the ground of adultery, while a woman had to prove incestuous or bigamous adultery, or rape, sodomy or bestiality. She could also try to prove adultery with cruelty, if the cruelty was of such a nature as would entitle her to divorce *a mensa et thoro*. This Act became the default personal law for Christians in India and remained unchanged till 2001, when it was

12. J.D.M. Derrett, *Essays in Classical and Modern Hindu Law*, Vol. 4, p. 8

amended to include more grounds for divorce, as well as a provision for no fault divorce by mutual consent.[13]

~

The Shariat Act 1937 was passed to ensure that Islamic personal law was dispensed according to the principles of Shariat without the custom and regional variations that had crept in.

Superficial knowledge of Islamic marriage law focuses on the possibility of four wives and on the husband's right to divorce by pronouncing talaq; but, of course, the law is more complex and often more progressive than the stereotypes imply. A few misconceptions should be cleared up. Most modern Muslims are as monogamous as any other community. Under Islamic law, men have limited rights of property disposition and no person with a vested right of succession can be disinherited. Finally, the right of dower (mehr) was essentially a prenuptial maintenance arrangement that was reduced to a nominal sum by overbearing and oppressive patriarchs.

~

Hindu customary personal law remained untouched till 1951, when divorce surfaced to popular Hindu consciousness with talk of the Hindu Code Bill.[14] The 1955 film *Mr. & Mrs. 55* reflects the social anxiety the Bill from its very onset.

The film opens with a newspaper boy shouting, '*Parliament mein talaq par jordar bahas.*' Madhubala is an orphan who lives with an aunt and a governess. She is heir to a considerable legacy which, according to her father's will, she can realise only when she marries. A girlish, plaited, bespectacled Madhubala excitedly tells her governess, 'Nanny, nanny, the divorce bill will surely be passed!' Nanny, a motherly figure, symbolizes mass disapproval of westernization: '*Sab key sab Angrez ho gaye ho*,' she says sarcastically mimicking strident feminist slogans, such as 'Freedom of women from violence by men'.

The film cuts to a stern, bespectacled, sari-clad Lalita Pawar (Madhubala's aunt) lecturing a group of women on self-esteem and their legal rights, while they, sotto voce, are discussing the benefits of milk

13. The Indian Divorce Act, 1869 was applicable to all Christians in India till 2001 when it was amended and renamed the Divorce Act, 2001. It is still applicable only to Indian Christians.

14. Customary divorce existed prior to Hindu Code Bill: See R. Naga Raja Sarma, 'Ethics of Divorce in Ancient India', *International Journal of Ethics*, Vol. 41, No. 3 (April, 1931), pp. 329-342; The Hindu Marriage Act, 1955, Special Marriage Act, 1954

and gram paste for a sparkling complexion. The film tells us that women libbers are unattractive villains who devour other women—those who 'naturally' are more interested in sparkling skins than 'women's issues'.

The strident aunt is portrayed as a scheming villain who draws up a plan to realize Madhubala's legacy by misusing the new divorce law. She decides to bribe a poor cartoonist (Guru Dutt) to marry her niece, provided he will divorce her once she gets her money under the will. The Hindu Code Bill is passed and Madhubala and Guru Dutt go through the marriage charade. The couple then fall in love and want to stay married. Lalita Pawar is upset by their primal behavior, which has endangered her money-making scheme.

Marriage has matured Madhubala and she is now a serene, calm woman who challenges her aunt with the conviction of love. 'I do not understand,' says Lalita Pawar, with her iconic single raised-eyebrow look. 'I have been to Europe, England and US—I understand men's oppression of women and true liberation.' Marriage is about mutual love, respect and equality, replies Madhubala.

Sixty years later the film is still charming. Its limitation is the unkind portrayal of the feminist represented by Lalita Pawar. Tight-lipped and desexed, she wears her sleeveless blouse as a badge of liberation rather than sartorial elegance. Madhubala begins well as a bold heroine for the times, chasing a tennis-playing dude in her figure-hugging trousers, but marriage tames her into the classic, modest, sari-clad, head-covered Indian nari. The message is clear: Marriage is a good thing because it transforms women into serene beauties.

Given Guru Dutt's own difficult marriages in real life, I was surprised at the film but the subject was topical and reflected the anxieties of a powerful lobby that ranged from intellectuals to ordinary persons and even to President of India at the time, Dr Rajendra Prasad.

~

In September 1951, Dr Prasad wrote to then-Prime Minister, Jawarhalal Nehru about the bill, calling it a revolutionary change being imposed upon a reluctant people:

> 'The proposal to give share to female heirs in the family property has caused much controversy. It is wrong to suppose that the Hindu Law does not confer property rights on women. It does confer such rights, and in the case of what is known as Stridhan the right is absolute having its own separate line of inheritance, giving, generally speaking, preference to female over male heirs.... What [the old law] seeks to avoid is the intrusion

of anyone who is likely to be a complete stranger into the family home and thus avoid disruption of the joint family...'

The President then writes his understanding of the old law: 'If two brothers separate, the daughter of a separate brother inherits his property.' I respectfully disagree: a daughter did not have a legal right of inheritance from her father under Mitakshara Hindu Law.

Dr Prasad continues:

> 'Abrogation of custom as a source for Hindus will have the effect of petrifying that law and the only method left for introducing any change therein will in effect be resort to legislation. This is bound to hamper growth and make reform more difficult.'[15]

This too is a risky proposition: The President does not mention how reform can be effected without legislation. He then says:

> 'The Bill will after all affect...a minority though not an inconsiderable minority of Hindus. Others belonging to the so-called inferior castes enjoy and have always exercised the right under caste customs of ending the marital tie by a very simple, inexpensive and unquestionable method of placing the matter before a caste panchayat and setting it with a caste dinner, thus putting the seal of public approval on it. By abrogating all customs and making it obligatory on all who want the marital tie to be dissolved to take resort to a court of law with all trouble, expense, delay and uncertainty which litigation in this country involves, the majority of the Hindu Community will be deprived of its rough and ready though none-the-less effective and certainly the cheaper method. Its minority will have forced upon it a law which the great bulk of it including both men and women does not want. It seems unnecessary to force such a law on those who do not want it, particularly when it is perfectly easy for those who want to enjoy the benefits of divorce to have it simply by registering their marriage under the existing enactment relating to civil marriage. If there is any defect or deficiency in the effectiveness of the existing enactment that may be amended to the satisfaction of those who want it.'[16]

My critique of the President's argument is that he does not deal with the true purpose of the bill—the improvement of the rights of women under Hindu law. In his approximately two-thousand-word letter, women find a cursory mention in the context of stridhan that I have extracted above.

---

15. S.C. Kashyap, A. Kashyap, *Indian Presidency: Constitution Law & Practice*, p. 81

16. *Ibid*. p. 82

I do agree that the codification of Hindu law did not address the regional diversity of customary laws. Under the Mitakshara system[17] male heirs had rights in property by birth. The Punjab was driven by agrarian customs to ensure that land remained in the family and daughters were not the primary heirs. In contrast, the Dayabhaga system of Bengal and portions of the Northeast gave the patriarch absolute power over property to deal with as he pleased through his life. The Mitakshara of the South gave no rights to women in case of partition but the other schools[18] did. The Marumakatayam, Aliyasantana and Nambudri laws[19] were matriarchal in intent but although property was transmitted through the female line, the maternal uncle was all-powerful. Many customs that were favourable to women were also lost in the process of codifying Hindu law, but the President does not address that because he is concerned about maintaining custom rather than creating legal rights.

As to the President's regret about killing the custom of divorce by panchayat for the option of expensive and oppressive litigation, the statute has a provision for following proven customs, provided it does not reinforce unconstitutional caste and class prejudices. More pertinently, a panchayat may have ordered a divorce over a meal, as the President noted, but how likely is it to have included a fair provision for the wife's maintenance and alimony? It is this uncertainty in the panchayat form of family law that caused the need for statutory law in the first place. Just as well, when you consider that modern khap panchayats are also capable of ruling that a woman be stoned or raped as punishment.[20]

~

In 1954, Nehru had wanted to delay the Hindu Code Bill[21] because he considered the matter to be potentially inflammable but Dr B.R. Ambedkar

---

17. Mitakshara is sub-divided into four schools by region: the Benaras School, the Mithila School, the Bombay School and the Dravida/Madras School.

18. Dinshaw F. Mulla, *Principles of Hindu Law*, p. 504

19. The Marumakatayam and Nambudiri schools of classical Hindu law were practiced in what is today Kerala and the Alliyasthanam school was practiced in Kanara, which is the southern part of coastal Karnataka. These schools are matriarchal in nature.

20. 'Dalit moves SC against khap diktat for her rape' in *The Times of India*, 20 August 2015; 'Khap panchayat's rape order of 2 UP sisters echoes in UK' in *The Times of India*, 31 August 2015.

21. Kishwar, 'Codified Hindu Law: Myth and Reality' in *Economic and Political Weekly*, Vol. 29, (Aug, 1994), pp. 2145-2161

had agreed to be law minister, despite not being a Congress supporter, only to be instrumental in pushing the law that he had drafted through Parliament. His approach was to reach constitutional equality beyond gender and caste[22] by passing a law so that '...custom gets dried up'. Parliament however agreed with the conservative President and rejected the Bill in 1951 as being too radical. Dr Ambedkar resigned.[23]

The hypocrisy and timidity of our leaders then was apparent in that they clearly wanted women to be empowered—but not equal. Absolute gender equality was feared as something that would subvert traditional orders, which remained sacred. This remains true when you consider the actions and statements of our current leaders, behind the lip service to the principle of equality.

~

Eventually Ambedkar's Bill of 1951 and the idea of women's equality was cut into bite-sized pieces and introduced slowly over the years, beginning in 1956. An amendment in 1976 introduced new grounds for divorce. Until then, these were limited to: living in adultery; conversion from Hinduism; incurable insanity lasting for at least three years immediately preceding the filing of the petition; virulent forms of leprosy; venereal disease in a communicable form; renunciation of all worldly pleasures by entering a religious order; presumed dead if not heard of as being alive for a period of seven years; non-resumption of cohabitation after a decree of judicial separation; and non-compliance with a decree for restitution of conjugal rights. The grounds were widened in 1976 and divorce by mutual consent was introduced.

The President's concern about a daughter's share in the family home was dealt with in Section 23 of the Hindu Succession Act, whereby a daughter could not ask for partition of her parents' home though she may have had a right in it. The section was repealed by the amendment of 2005 which brought us full circle to what Ambedkar had suggested in 1950: daughters were free to demand partition of their parental homes in the same way their brothers could and they were equal coparceners in property owned by a Hindu Undivided Family.[24]

---

22. Article 14: Equality before law.

23. Sharmila Rege (ed.), *Against the Madness of Manu: B.R. Ambedkar's Writings on Brahmanical Patriarchy*, pp. 233-243

24. G. Sekar vs. Geetha and Ors., AIR 2009 SC 2649

> The frog hopped into the Princess' lap and said: 'Elegant Lady, I was once a handsome Prince, until an evil witch cast a spell upon me. One kiss from you, however, and I will turn back into the dapper, young Prince that I am and then, my sweet, we can marry and set up housekeeping in yon castle with my Mother, where you can prepare my meals, clean my clothes, bear my children, and forever feel grateful and happy doing so.'
>
> That night, on a repast of lightly sauteed frog-legs seasoned in a white wine and onion cream sauce, she chuckled to herself and thought: 'I don't fucking think so!!'

~

The fact that marriage is hyped up as necessary by men tellingly reveals that they need marriage for their own social definition and, preferably male heirs. Although a man's bachelor status may be envied by his sedately married peers as the repository of freedom to indulge in sex, high-cholesterol food and drink, I have found that men are less able to deal with singleness than women. Talking to a rare find—a man who remained unmarried till the age of fifty—I was disappointed to know that he would have liked nothing better than to have had a 'normal' family life. 'Just never happened. I missed the bus I guess,' he said, a little sadly. A female friend disagreed, saying: 'If he has reached his fifties and never married, there has to be something wrong'.

Men need marriage to establish and celebrate male success, but women are brought up to believe in marriage as their only validation and escape from the protective prison of being 'respectable' while single. The short story 'Arakhaniya' (The Unprotected) by Sarat Chandra Sen explores the life of an unmarried woman. 'In this manner the unlovely, wretched and unmarried girl continued to pass her days.' The story is universal and still contemporary. *Bridget Jones's Diary* (1996) is about a woman's search for the only two things that can make life worthwhile: the ideal weight and the perfect boyfriend. She finds him and marries him and perhaps she sheds the weight to emerge as an attractive married woman.

Women fear the spinster label, which evokes a dull, dreary woman who is presumed to be non-sexual and so invites pity and malicious laughter. But there are many other equally malicious labels. If she is bold enough to have had sex without marriage, she is a woman of 'easy virtue': a 'hooker' desperate to be married. If she looks self-sufficient and happy in her singledom, she must be frigid or a lesbian, because how can it be conceivable otherwise that she is happy without a man?

~

Notwithstanding Faludi's reassurance to single women, and despite men who say they are commitment-phobic, most people marry—for a wide variety of reasons. A man might say, 'I have a job, enough money so I am ready to marry and "settle down"'. Anyone might say, 'I need to marry' or 'I want to marry'. Another will say, 'Marriage makes me secure'. Most people marry because they want children; for some it is convenient; the timid marry because their parents insist. 'It's the only way in our very conservative family', they say. For others, the reasons to marry can be as mundane as needing a marriage certificate for immigration, a spouse visa or citizenship status. The Hollywood film *Green Card* (1990) is the story of such a marriage of convenience that leads to love. There are also some psychological advantages to marriage, shown by studies to be a validation of self, a state of comfort and a longer life for married people.

The marriage rite

Everyone loves other people's weddings. It is always fun to meet the world at a happy gathering but the bridal couple look horribly stressed and tired. Smothered in their finery, they are reduced to symbolic social statements about clan and kinship. This is particularly true of arranged marriages and marriages amongst the very rich.

In this last year I have attended three weddings of the sons or daughters of rich and influential families. The wedding card is delivered with pomp and splendour, accompanied by mithai or the more fashionable Belgian chocolates. Some of these marriages are for love, but most are arranged to meet the usual criteria of a strategic family alliance to achieve a certain socio-economic status. Arranged marriages do not exist in the West, they like to tell us, but the truth is that the same criteria are also useful for a match where 'love' conveniently emerges.

Weddings are an opportunity to assert and expand areas of influence: to announce the dynamics between rishteydaris by not inviting such and such because of a court case or finally inviting so and so after many years of a feud. It is a social networking device and sometimes there are no criteria other than an opportunity to make a loud statement of wealth. Laxmi Mittal was just another multi-billionaire until he became a household name with the wedding of his daughter at the palace of Versailles.[34] The

34. Claire O'Connor, 'Top Ten Most Outrageous Billionaire Weddings' in *Forbes*: 'The prize for most outrageous wedding in recent years goes to Vanisha Mittal, daughter of India's second richest man, Lakshmi Mittal.'

irony of the need to buy into a palace that had witnessed the gruesome end of an ancient aristocracy was lost in the excitement of an Indian displaying power in Europe. The younger Mittal, Pramod, has outdone his brother with a 503-crore-rupee wedding in Spain.[35]

Most couples are so traumatized by the scale of ceremony that it's no surprise that many divorce petitions start with problems from the wedding day—'she/he was badly behaved and threw a tantrum that day' is a common refrain.

Intimacy Undone

Once the couple are stitched together 'in law', they have to find their own way together. Various types of differences, such as cultural or familial divergence, may make for odd clashes but that does not necessarily mean a higher chance of divorce, just as a seamless coming together from the same background does not guarantee a good marriage. Most of the reasons why a marriage does or does not work are not even in the realm of the rational.

A marriage 'works' when it is structured around a settled intimacy. It may not be happy, or even fulfilled, but just settled. If this inner life in the structure dies, the courts call the standing social and financial structures left around the marriage 'an empty shell'. To force a dead marriage to continue[36] is to keep a corpse, and the modern view is that it would be cruel.

Intimacy, by its definition, means seeing the other unmasked which thus must also include the irrational sides of that other—and of one's own self while dealing with the other. Intimacy is unrefined and true, and thus by its very nature tests marriage, which is a house dressed in material finery. The other major tension in marriages comes from individual aspirations that seek to break away from the stifling constraints of social and family 'bonds'. A related source of tension is the unrealistic expectation that the other partner will be a messiah for continued happiness, including, of course, romance. But romance and marriage are also fundamentally incompatible, because 'it is the very essence of romance to thrive on obstacles, delays, separations and dreams whereas marriage is designed for constant physical proximity to the monotonous

35. 'The Most Expensive Wedding Of This Year' in *Forbes*: Pramod Mittal

36. Naveen Kohli vs. Neelu Kohli (2006) 4 SCC 558

presence'.[37] Incompatibility erodes the relationship daily, bit by bit, till 'the last strands of a relationship can break from a single glance or a moment of silence'.[38]

Dismantling patriarchy, dismantling power

The social, sexual and economic consequences of a marriage are cemented by legal rights to property and the responsibility to manage it for the family's benefit. When only the 'empty shell' of the marriage is left, the court becomes responsible for the distribution of the marriage's assets within the family. Equitable distribution is a delicate and complex exercise, given that the social equations amongst men, women and children are essentially iniquitous. The inequities within the family began when women lost the battle to exist on their own terms in the public sphere and were shut into their homes to fight a losing battle there as well. Over the centuries, her disempowerment was reinforced again and again to ensure and maintain institutional patriarchy.

Some women look for reform by way of better rights within patriarchy. Perhaps they think that society will evolve to gender equality and slough off patriarchal structures. Yet, many powerful, successful women and educated, sophisticated men suffer the prejudices of patriarchal social norms because learning to transcend the male view is a difficult exercise that requires unlearning first. We may have evolved from when a Hindu woman's devotion to her husband was expected to survive his death. She need not be a sati any longer certainly. But many would still prefer if she is devoted to her husband as the personification of the lord (Pati Parmeshwar, Pativrata, Patitva). She may work, but it is still expected that 'graceful' women seeped in 'sanskriti' and 'samskaras' are gentle and subservient. Many men want to retain this comfortable status quo of centuries, but many women want to break through and fly. (Not coincidentally, *usko par lag gaye*—a phrase that means she has grown wings but implies that she is on her way to becoming a slut or, at the very least, an unattractive animal—is used mainly for women who show signs of independence from patriarchy).

Women are now breaking free from patriarchal expectations to fly with brilliantly coloured wings. In the past, this was not an option because

---

37. Laurence Lerner, *Love and Marriage, Literature and its Social Context*, p. 124

38. Vivek Shanbagh, *Ghachar Ghochar*

women living outside a man's protection were considered disreputable. Now it is possible for them to enjoy economic freedom that even the patriarchal conservatives and traditionalists have learnt to grudgingly respect. That divorce rates are increasing exponentially is more an indication of the changing expectations of marriage than a failure of the institution.

There is another social perspective: in India marriages, and hence divorce, are treated differently because of closely-knit extended family, whose lives are intertwined with the nuclear family unit. The legal definition of family comprising husband, wife and their children, for the purpose of divorce excludes families who continue to live jointly. In such cases, the elders (patriarchs and by that age even matriarchs) control the family through finance and influence until things fall apart after their death.

I have seen two divorce proceedings that began upon the death of the patriarch. The wives in both cases thought they had reasonable working marriages and were stunned when their husbands spoke of discontent and revealed extramarital liaisons that they had kept under wraps till their fathers died. In both cases, the daughters-in-law were treated with great affection by the father-in-law. Both women had differences with the mothers-in-law who in both cases, after the death of the patriarch, conspired with their sons to oust the wives.

The law and its lawgivers

The so-called developed economies have many words and phrases to describe India, but the common ones are 'complex' or 'land of contradictions.' This is patronizing, given that all cultures and countries are fraught with inherent contradictions. Even so, one has to agree that our many cultures contain opposite extremes that manage to coexist and thus stand in stark relief against each other. Some parts of Indian society have begun the process of embracing life outside marriage as acceptable, but in other parts, marriage connections that break caste and class barriers lead to murder justified as 'honour killing'.[39] Legal reform by the legislature and judiciary keeps pace with society even while guiding it to the ideal constitutional goal. The judiciary has been a powerful agent of change

39. 'Dalit moves SC against khap diktat for her rape' in *The Times of India*, 20 August 2015

and by and large has lived up to the challenge with some path-breaking judgments.[40]

Initial social reform movements in India brought the law into the home only tentatively. Even by 1983, the Delhi High Court observed that to allow the Constitution to enter homes would be like allowing a bull to enter a china shop.[41] The analogy is unfortunate because to liken the law to a bull is to not see its majesty and refinement, which can be illuminated by justice. And to liken the family to a china shop is to not see the ugly inequities and pain that cannot and must not be carefully maintained like china. The judge ignored that the Constitution is truly alive only when its values enter our homes. It must enter the home not as a bull into a china shop, but as sunlight into its dark grimy recesses. Having said which, changing the analogy is simpler than the monumentally complex task required for us to carefully negotiate our way through the competing narratives of the Constitution and custom, much as we would in a china shop—an impossible task for a bull, but not for justice.

Given human limitations, cultural socialization will inevitably condition individual and professional political views and beliefs. Unravelling a marriage is the work of a legal system that includes judges and family lawyers. Any assessment of their work must factor in that they, too, are a part of their own family structures and that, despite their legal training, they cannot entirely remove themselves from the many societal norms that remain innately unfair. Thus, the patriarchal socialization of lawyers and judges should not surprise us because they too are only human (no matter how many times you may feel otherwise during your brushes with family law). Having said which, we must acknowledge that the present legal system is a form of primitive patriarchy at its worst, and benevolent patriarchal patronage at its best.

The fault lines become the most evident when matters of religion enter the courts. Derrett's passionate call for codification of Hindu law in the 1950s was tempered by 1970,[42] when he advised restraint against too

40. Sukh Ram and Anr. vs. Gauri Shankar & Anr, AIR 1968 SC 365; Punithavalli Ammal vs. Minor Ramalingam & Anr., AIR 1970 SC 1730; Eramma vs. Verrupanna & Ors, AIR 1966 SC 1879; Gummalapura Taggina Matada Kotturswami vs. Setra Veeravva & Ors. AIR 1959 SC 577; Mangal Singh & Ors. vs. Shrimati Rattno & Anr., AIR 1967 SC 1786

41. Harvinder Kaur vs. Harmander Singh Choudhry, AIR 1984 Delhi 66

42. J.D.M. Derrett, authority on Hindu Law

much change because 'traditional Hindu ideas, shorn of the outmoded and obsolete elements, still had a vital role in administration of justice'. This is a problematic position because it does not consider that the residue of Hindu law, after the trimming and shaving, is oppressive and unconstitutional gender and caste inequality. Gender inequality did not seem to have concerned Derrett, because he also said that he found that the Western type of gender equality created unfeminine women.[43] He might be easily dismissed as a product of his time, but his ideas still have currency today. The recent efforts of certain political parties to reclaim for the nation what they think was a glorious past (read pre-Islamic) are dangerous, because they are also a call to return to a patriarchy sanctified by the scriptures that was oppressive to women and the lower castes. By now, the originals are so lost that we are at risk of powerful lobbies 'inventing traditions' for Hinduism and the majority of the populace would be none the wiser[44] because, as Nelson said, 'the living camel of Hindu law, for if it ever lived which is exceedingly improbable, it died centuries ago'.[45]

Conservative elements tied to ideas of religious concepts trumping constitutional ones may be well intentioned, but often underestimate the 'fringe': powerful reactionary elements that are threatened by changes to the traditional order. Though patriarchy is under challenge as never before, the backlash against change is also more intense than it ever was.[46]

Conclusion

We know now that the most powerful social change can be wrought through dialogues in family law. The law is supposed to hack through iniquitous customs that, parasite-like, feed off the traditional social order. The process of getting rid of that parasite is sharp and brutal, but most conservatives who can't visualize a new world fear it will lead to anarchy and so continue to grasp at familiar straws, however unfair.

Hindu myths tell us that Kalyuga is the dark era of no dharma, even though mythological dharma was rooted in unequal caste and gender stereotypes. The description of Kalyuga to me sounds like democracy,

43. See Ch. 2: Decoding Gender, p. 30

44. Eric Hobbshawn, *Inventing Traditions*

45. James Henry Nelson, *Indian Usage and Judge-Made Law in Madras*

46. Engels, *The Origin of the Family, Private Property and the State*

dismantling the traditional order bound in inflexible rules of dharma. Heavens are collapsing only for the Brahmins and for men, who have to deal with the power of the 'rabble' and women who are no longer prepared to 'adjust'.

Tanika Sarkar mentions that marriage reflects social morality.[47] The contemporary moral ethic that flows from the Constitution requires that marriages soaked in the tears of the bride and her family be discarded and the bidai songs not be heart-wrenching. Please indulge me as I relate a unique Punjabi folk song that is my favourite because even while remaining patronizing about women's abilities, it is different:

> The woman sings: *Main pandran murabbian wali,*
> *kutchery vich miloo kursi.*
> I own fifteen murabbas (one murabba is 20 acres).
> I will get to sit on a chair in court (a mark of respect).
> The man replies: *Jey tu pundran murabbian wali,*
> *murabbian tey rakh munshi.*
> If you own that much land, you better get a manager
> (by implication, him).

---

47. Tanika Sarkar, *Hindu Wife, Hindu Nation: Community, Religion, and Cultural Nationalism*

2. DECODING GENDER IN FAMILY AND LAW

Sex is biology and gender is culture[1]

'There is an ancient Persian saying', said our professor with a smile: '*zan* (woman), *zar* (wealth) *aur zameen* (land)' is what drives brothers against brothers. None of us interrupted his lecture to ask how, why and when did women become equated to wealth and property.[2] Brought up in patriarchy, we did not have the equipment to think of these questions, the answers to which would eventually open our minds to alternate power structures in society.

There is no one theory about the events and reasons that brought men to power the world over, but all schools of thought agree that there was a slow insidious growth of male power over women, from becoming the default heads of families to forming patriarchal networks of influence which fanned out into clans, and eventually leading to the state as the ultimate form of patriarchy.

The political explanation for patriarchy, says Engels, is when men took over the tools of production necessary for private property. Agrarian societies needed more labour to farm the land and store surpluses, hence women who could produce children became a resource to be acquired—like land. That, says Engels, was a powerful moment in history.[3] Historian Gerda Lerner, however, argues that patriarchy arose before private property: it was the sexual commodification of women that eventually became the foundation of private property. The earliest law codes institutionalized sexual subordination of women by various means, including by force, creating economic dependency, inducements of privilege for women who conformed to the rules of patriarchy and the treating of non-conformist women as outcastes: witches and/or prostitutes.

Chastity was put forward as the prominent womanly virtue to ensure paternal certainty to regulate matters of inheritance. The izzat of a house, or a community or a nation came to be embodied within the feminine form and thus from sexual subordination to slavery was a short step.[4] As

---

1. Noah Harari Yuval, *Sapien: A Brief History of Humankind*, p. 152

2. Mary Daly, *The Metaethics of Radical Feminism*

3. Engels, *The Origin of the Family, Private Property and the State*, p. 11

4. Gerda Lerner, *The Creation of Patriarchy*, p. 8

chastity was the only required virtue, women became prisoners of their wombs. A woman was tainted if she had been 'had' by any man other than a husband.

This perception of women as sex objects and spoils of war continues into the modern political narrative. Even those who believe that bringing back a Hindu past would benefit the nation, have to deal with the problem of oppression that defines that past. While it is true that at some point in the past, Hindu women had some better rights than English women, for example, these but withered away, not because of the advent of Islamic and British rule, but due to the intensification and then ossification of patriarchal control within Hindu society.

This process of strangling the Hindu woman's persona was in fact a contemporaneous discourse within Hindu society over the ages. While Kautilya and Narada gave her better rights, Manu gave her none and stationed her below a dog. Manu wished to create a society ordered by caste, with the control of women—and of their chastity—as the regulating measure. This obsession with chastity was part of the regulation of society, and any loss of chastity was the fault of the woman, according to Manu's rules of pollution and purity. It is significant that Manu survives in modern discourse as the sole law giver, with Gowalkar wanting the *Manusmriti* to be the source of law for Hindu India, while the others are relegated to history. Apart from academic writers[5] the anti-woman perspective of the 'ideal Hindu past' discourse is generally not discussed.

During the riot-ridden Partition, the Prime Ministers of India and Pakistan met at Lahore in September 1947 and made a joint declaration committing to restore abducted girls and women to their families. Despite the many appeals issued by Gandhi and Nehru, asking that recovered women should not be treated as 'polluted', many families would not accept women who (were) returned to them because of the stigma of loss of chastity unmitigated even in such horrific circumstances. Fearing this, many women who had borne children to their abductors remained where they were, because they could neither bear to leave them behind nor bring them to their villages where they would be viewed as being of 'impure' blood.[6] Such sexualization of not just gender relationships inter se, but also of the relationship of women with society has to be understood to take the next step to women's empowerment. Tanika

5. Cf. Sikata Banerjee, *Make Me a Man!*

6. Urvashi Butalia, *Other Side of Silence: Voices from the Partition of India.*

Sarkar says, '(Hindu) conjugal sexuality and its other—adultery and/or rape—became an important register to test the morality of fundamental social and religious institutions' but the raging immorality of a society that did not—and still does not—try to release women from male ownership cannot be debated enough.[7]

Nevertheless, women's rights movements were begun by crusaders like Raja Ram Mohan Roy and some forward-looking princely states, like Baroda, that had codified Hindu law to protect women from oppressive customs[8] like sati and child marriage.[9] In 1861, the Code of Criminal Procedure was enacted and it provided speedy relief to destitute women. The Women's Right to Property Act was passed in 1937.

Women had separate representation under the Government of India Act of 1935, as did various other separate classes. The Indian National Congress opposed separate electorates as being part of the British policy of 'divide and rule'. That brings us to Gandhi. This is not the place to discuss his close understanding of and complex relationships with women, but it suffices to say that he was a major figure in encouraging women out of the house to be part of the freedom struggle. Yet, he did not forward women's emancipation or Dalit rights because he saw them as potentially distracting from the sole aim of achieving swaraj. This was one reason for his deep differences with Ambedkar who, while speaking for Dalits, also urged women to participate in the Constitution drafting process. He argued that women had participated fearlessly in the freedom movement; why then were their issues not discussed with the same attention as the rights of backward communities and classes, other minorities and different cultural identities? By that time however, women leaders had been co-opted within their religion and caste-based communities and so the separate reservation that women had under the Government of India

---

7. Sarkar, *Hindu Wife, Hindu Nation: Community, Religion, and Cultural Nationalism*, p. 69

8. Government of Baroda passed the Infant Marriage Prevention Act in 1901.

9. Raja Ram Mohan Roy condemned sati and polygamy and spoke in favour of women's property rights. He held the condition of Indian women as one of the factors responsible for the degraded state of Indian society. See: Samita Sen, *Toward a Feminist Politics? The Indian Women's Movement in Historical Perspective*; Policy Research Report On Gender And Development, Working Paper Series No. 9, available at http://unpan1.un.org/intradoc/groups/public/documents/apcity/unpan051009.pdf; Maithreyi Krishnaraj, 'The Women's Movement in India: A Hundred Year History' in *Social Change*, September 2012 vol. 42 no. 3 pp. 325-333

Act of 1935 was ultimately dropped. Indian women had lost the chance to assert themselves as a separate gender beyond class and community.

Eventually, there were fifteen women in a 299-member Constituent Assembly. Reading their speeches you can see that they were all greatly influenced by Gandhi. Sarojini Naidu, with an unfortunate lack of insight, remarked that women did not need 'special treatment' because they were equal. Focus on energy to unite the world in contrast to divisive male energies, she said.[10] Women's task was the 'spiritual reform of the world' according to her, and 'every woman must know her divinity'. Besides distracting from the reality of a woman's social status, this attempt to romanticize her cause ended up obfuscating the urgent need to empower her. Insisting on the exploration of the divine while basic living is a struggle sounds like a desperate sublimation, rather than ensuring that all women have the freedom to be a seeker for the sheer love of the divine. The argument also ignores the right not to be spiritual.

Muthulakshmi Reddy, born to a Devadasi family, understandably had a different perspective: that women required economic independence and a voice to present a 'women's point of view'. But she, too, was against separate electoral rolls for women, saying 'we do not want to form a separate caste, for men and women rise and fall together'.[11] She was apprehensive that separate electoral rolls would enfranchise conservative and hence undeserving women. 'Conservative' here seems to imply home-bound women with more traditional roles—a problematic definition, laced with a modicum of contempt for the 'housewife' and based on unfair assumptions about the intellect and ability of a housewife to represent her gender. I know I learned more about women's liberation from my housewife mother and her conservative home-bound mother and grandmother than any fashionable feminist text could have taught me.

Then there was the lack of any common ground between the conservative and liberal views on women's issues. One reason for this could be due to the fact that for the 'conservative', women's liberation came to be seen as a by-product of westernization. The ordinary woman could not identify with many women leaders who seemed to have a Western-influenced image. Though many women leaders had begun to

---

10. All India Women's Conference (AIWC) at Bombay

11. Mary E. John, 'The Politics of Quotas and Women's Reservation Bill in India', Centre for Women's Developmental Studies, www.cwds.ac.in/Politics%20of%20quotas%20and%20WRB-MJ-Ch.8.pdf

make iconic the image of Western liberal values, with their short hair and perhaps the enjoyment of a cigarette and a drink, while mingling freely in elegant anglicized drawing rooms, free India's popular culture influenced by the Hindu idea of the nationalist cause, relegated this image to a vamp.[12] The 'homely' woman returned as a heroine: she was a quiet 'pativrata' Bharatiya nari with coiffed hair and a modest blouse.

Women's movements have long been limited by this perception of being westernized. Hansa Mehta recognized this anomaly when she said that women in Parliament do not 'give a real picture of the position of Indian women in this country' even though 'it is true that a few women in the past and even today enjoy a high status and have received the highest honour that any man can receive, like our friend, Mrs Sarojini Naidu'.[13] A mixture of such naiveté and misplaced confidence in the status of women being better than it really was resulted in women losing the not inconsiderable advantage they had under the 1935 Act.

~

The mistake was to assume that women's interests would be taken up in the same manner as the interest of any minority community, class or caste. To put women in the same bracket as minority communities and backward classes and castes ignores that they are not a minority and their issues need to be dealt with on a larger and more complex scale than that of any class, caste or community. The next level of tension is between women within and across communities: thus, indigenous women's movements remain hampered at the grassroots because women feel conflicted between their right to a voice and the need to demonstrate loyalty to communities that are grounded in cultural and religious ideas of male superiority. This continues to be a complex issue of women's rights versus community and caste lines.

While these other matters could be seen as divisive, a commitment to the empowerment of women in all communities may have helped transcend patriarchy to a more egalitarian society. The time to do this was when the nation was being formed. While Gandhi could have justified his focus on swaraj to the exclusion of all else prior to Independence, his unwillingness to give priority to the matter afterwards is telling, particularly as he seemed to have communicated an expectation that women would give up in the Constitution what they had under the Government of India Act

12. See the careers and roles of actresses Nadira and Helen for examples of this.

13. http://parliamentofindia.nic.in/ls/debates/vol1p9.htm

1935. However, what was settled for was a constitutional guarantee of equality to all, with special accommodation for women-enabling laws. In contrast to the women of the first world, who had to struggle for their right to participate in public life, the Indian woman began her political life as enfranchised and with a Constitution committed to her freedom and equality.[14] It seemed like more of a head start than it really was.

Social and community limitations on women become apparent when you see that Dr B.R. Ambedkar's Hindu Code Bill (1951) that focused on women's rights, was rejected as too radical for a young nation. Even some women parliamentarians could not find it in themselves to support the bill. In 1952, while addressing a women's organisation in Kolhapur, Ambedkar likened the rejection of the bill to milk spoiled by acid.

Excerpts from the parliamentary debates[15] on women's rights reveal the male banter targeting women. R.K. Chaudhri stated:

> 'I find that Hon'ble members of this house are afraid of speaking out the truth of telling the Hon. lady members of this house that they ought to be told that they are proving themselves far too aggressive. This I respectfully say is not a matter to be laughed over... Sir, I warn this house against the aggressive character of our women. I think it is time we speak out.'

What is surprising is that women parliamentarians dealt with their misogynist parliamentarian brethren but did not think that the real world would be a billion times worse.

Despite such obstacles, women's rights were helped by the Dalit and socialist perspectives of meaningful equality that Ambedkar brought to the framing of the Constitution. Feminists Lotika Sarkar and Vina Mazumadar who had supported the idea of no special reservations and treatments, changed their minds in their essay, 'Dissenting Voices',[16] that expounded the idea of meaningful as opposed to formal equality. But, the idea was developed in the context of weaker and socially backward classes and castes rather than from a gender perspective.[17] Thus, gender was

---

14. See p. 355: Article 14 of the Constitution of India

15. Parliamentary Debates, Vol. VIII, Part II. 6th February 1951, pp. 2473-83

16. Lotika Sarkar and Vina Mazumdar (1974), 'Dissenting Voices: Note of Dissent to *Towards Equality*, Report of the Committee on the Status of Women in India' in *Reservations of Women*, ed. Meena Dhanda.

17. Indira Jaising, 'Gender Justice and the Supreme Court' in *Supreme But Not Infallible: Essays in Honour of the Supreme Court of India*, ed. B.N. Kirpal et.al., pp. 288-320.

ignored even while equality was being discussed and gender insensitivity survived legislation and groundbreaking work on the concept of equality. Many important judgments about equality were passed on petitions filed by women, but gender discrimination within families and gender stereotypes in society continue to hamper meaningful equality for women.

Gender Encrypted through Tradition

The roots of gender discrimination in Indian culture today can be traced back to the distant past. Some of the most important influences pervading social attitudes to gender come from folklore and mythology.

Enormous cultural influence is still wielded by the two great epics, the *Ramayana* and the *Mahabharata*. On a conveniently simplistic reading, they reinforce gender stereotypes, leading to a complicated collective psyche when it comes to gender in the political arena. It is easy to understand why politicians draw from these stories to impact the public imagination, but it is disturbing when judges do the same without the caveat that the gender imbalances in these stories are unconstitutional. Nevertheless, they pervade the psychological subtext of social attitudes to gender and marriage.

In the *Ramayana*, the misogynistic treatment of Saroopnakha is an instance of gender bias: when Rama and Lakshman encounter her, Rama refuses her overtures, gesturing towards Sita, but in light-hearted banter suggests that she approach Lakshman, neglecting to mention that he was married too. The message seems to be that an absent wife is license for a husband's sexual liaison, though in the same epic absent husbands have returned to punish their wives for straying. Lakshman refuses her overtures as well but Saroopnakha's insistence provokes him to cut off her nose.[18] Amorous overtures from a woman continue to drive men to complex disproportionate reactions.

Later, Ravana kidnaps Sita after inducing her to cross the Lakshman Rekha. This has been perverted by politicians to imply that women who break the boundaries ostensibly set for their 'protection' do so at their own peril.[19]

The Uttarakhand in Tulsidas's *Ramayana* tells the additional story of the test of fire that Sita successfully passed to prove that she had not been

18. The phrase *nak kat gai* today expresses shame.

19. 'Don't cross "Lakshman rekha," Minister tells women' in *The Hindu*, 5 January 2013

'defiled' by Ravana during captivity in Lanka. But when her chastity is questioned again, Rama abandons her in the forest, saying a ruler cannot rule even with a perceived blemish on his honour, which lies in his wife's chastity. The Rama-Sita ideal of a monogamous marriage harmonious in its equal balance collapses with her banishment in a pregnant condition. The fact is that Sita is not only Rama's wife, but also his subject, and he did not hold her rights as equal to those of the malicious citizens slandering her.

These stories tell of inflexible commitment to honour and Dharma, regardless of the tragic consequences to wives and children. The forgotten story is Sita's strength and valour, which have made her an Indian feminist icon. She opted to accompany Rama to the forest through her own agency. She suffered her second banishment alone and she refused to return to Rama when he eventually repented. Sita became the first single mother in Hindu cultural memory.[20]

The sum and substance of these stories is that the woman's experience of the world was limited to dealing and negotiating her path within a male domain. Depending on the culture of the times, women were better off sometimes and subjugated at other times, but it has always been about guilty female survival in a man's world. Even Kane, the great Dharmashastri responsible for the most detailed and erudite translation of the Shastras, is influenced by stereotypical gender play when he observes: 'Savitri[21] and Sita have been held by the women of India for thousands of years as the highest ideals of womanly virtue, to which they have always

20. Namita Gokhale, 'Sita was the first single mother' in *The Economic Times*, 7 March 2007. The story is eerily similar to one in the Old Testament where Abraham married a slave girl Hagar, because his wife Sarah could not bear him a child. When Sarah eventually conceived, Abraham abandoned Hagar and their child Ishmael at the edge of the desert with a loaf of bread and a flask of water. For the Abrahamic people, Hagar has become a feminist icon representing the strength and power and commitment of a single mother. The story has special meaning for the Black feminist movement because Hagar was an Egyptian slave.

21. Savitri pleaded with Yama to spare her husband, Satyavan's life, but he would not budge, for every man must die when his time comes. However, Yama was pleased with her devotion to her husband and granted her two boons, except for the life of her husband. She first asked that her father-in-law's kingdom be restored to him. She then asked for a hundred sons. The moment the boon was granted, Yama realized that he had made a blunder, for how could a hundred sons be born to Savitri, who was the soul of virtue, when her husband was dead? He was forced to give back Satyavan, and also bless him with a long and prosperous life.

endeavored to approach and one may say that Indian women generally have most successfully lived up to that high and ennobling ideal set before them.'[22] It is significant that Kane does not mention Draupadi as an ideal. She too accepted, without question, having to share her body amongst five men, she too was loyal, but her unconventional predicament is unpalatable to the average Hindu psyche. It is easier to be dismissive of the virtue of a woman with five lovers or even husbands, than to give her space as Queen to five rulers and uncomfortably outspoken at that. Kane attributes this saying to Draupadi: 'I know the total wealth, the income and expenditure of the Pandavas.' No modern man will share this knowledge with women today for fear of alimony claims or fear of losing financial control.

Kane, in his translations of the Dharmashastras, quotes:[23]

> 'From very ancient times one of the articles of faith was that a man was born with debts, that he owed three debts to sages, gods and pitrs.
>
> The wife helped a man to discharge two of his debts, to the gods by associating with him in sacrifices and to the pitrs by procreating a son or sons. Therefore, the goal of the life of women was declared to be marriage and procreation of male heirs...
>
> It was on account of these ideas about the goal of woman's life and the supreme importance of a son that the smrtis and dharma-sutra allowed and even recommended the husband to marry a second time even when the first wife was living.'

Once her relevance was confined to these purposes, it was easy to reduce the woman to a symbolic presence. For example, after banishing Sita, Rama placed a golden statue of Sita by his side for those religious ceremonies that required her presence by Shastric rules. Marriage thus became about Bhartiya women learning to fit into the husband's life by 'adjusting'. Until relatively recently, women themselves saw their own destiny as going to her husband's house in a doli and leaving as an arthi. Life outside marriage was a non-life.

~

Better status for women, as well as for lower castes, was an important part of the call for Hindu reform that began in the early twentieth century with Raja Ram Mohan Roy, the Arya Samaj and Brahmo Samaj movements. The women's rights movement in India began with protests against sati,

22. P.V. Kane, *History of Dharmashastra*, p. 568

23. Ibid

child marriage and a call for women's education[24] but these calls were for better rights within a male-dominated social construct. Despite these reform movements, we have not been able to jettison the baggage of horrendous ill-treatment of women.

For most Indian women, marriage continues to be the sole security. Sometimes it can become an opportunity to be enriched and empowered, within the construct of the marriage, particularly if she produces a son. For a less fortunate woman, it is the end of her life, having left the safety (and relative freedom) of her father's home. Many others may never feel that they are a complete person, having been powerless and brutalized both in their natal and matrimonial homes.

Within the construct of marriage, the pattern is generally the same in poor and wealthy households. In all situations, control over a woman's body and self is negotiated with the father, brother, husband, brother-in-law, mother-in-law, and later, sons. The woman negotiates protection rather than equal participation in the world. Her opportunities outside marriage are not that many and, in any case, the decision to take them up is beset with complications ranging from familial concern for safety to worry about societal reaction to a bid for independence.

Traditionally, once widowed, marrying another man was not an option: this was a cruel custom because child marriages were common and due to the high mortality rate amongst men who fought wars, there were many child widows. One would imagine that the problem of widowhood is of the past, but widows are still abandoned to live in penury in ashrams in Vrindaban and Benaras. A film about their plight was banned as hurting religious sentiments.[25] Indians are now CEOs of multinationals; they figure in lists of global billionaires; many have earned international accolades as brilliant students, authors and filmmakers...but a newspaper headline in October 2013 announced that an NGO made arrangements for widows to fly from a Vrindavan ashram to Kolkata for Durga Puja celebrations.[26] This was going to be their first celebration since they were

24. Raja Ram Mohan Roy condemned sati and polygamy and spoke in favour of women's property rights. He held the condition of Indian women as one of the factors responsible for the degraded state of Indian society.

25. *Water* dir. Deepa Mehta

26. Initiative taken by Sulabh International Social Service Organisation; See also Kamalendu Bhadra, 'Shunned for years, Vrindavan widows return "home" this Puja', in *The Times of India*, 6 October 2013

widowed and for many it was the first celebration in their life, because they were widowed as children.

Legal constructs about inheritance and lack of fair opportunity of employment have resulted in making 'She is a poor widow' the standard phrase worldwide. The Universal Declaration of Human Rights equates widowhood with unemployment, sickness, disability and old age, requiring special legislation and care.[27] Upon the demise of her husband, the ceremony of breaking the widow's glass bangles and rubbing off her sindoor has become a dramatic symbol of her loss of status rather than of her grief.

In 2013, a television advertisement for jewellery made waves. A woman approaches the wedding mandap with her face uncovered, holding a little girl's hand. She walks around the sacred fire with the groom who picks up the child. This is bold, unique, beautiful and important for three reasons: i) that the bride does not have to be simpering coyly behind her veil, ii) that men can be good fathers to children who are not their 'blood', iii) widows can revel in colour and jewellery. Why am I presuming the woman is a widow? When I tried to visualize her as a divorcee, I could not imagine a new family unit being created so easily without the ex-husband creating a shindy about his 'blood' being brought up in 'another man's house'. In the present social scenario, I also could not visualize an advertisement showing such casual acceptance of a couple with a child born out of wedlock.

The Unfree Woman

While the intensity of patriarchal control may differ between cultures and communities, the subservience of women has an almost homogenous sanction through history. Their history of enslaved and commodified sexuality causes women to continue to suffer 'unfreedom'.[28] Given this, no one with the slightest intellect can publicly deny the need for special enabling laws for women's rights. Yet the conversations of many intellectuals and influential people from the elite class will reveal that

---

27. Article 25, UDHR-(1) Everyone has the right to a standard of living adequate for the health and well-being of himself and of his family, including food, clothing, housing and medical care and necessary social services, and the right to security in the event of unemployment, sickness, disability, widowhood, old age or other lack of livelihood in circumstances beyond his control.

28. Lerner, *The Creation of Patriarchy*, p. 24

their personal situation may be quite contrary to such an outlook. A man may be an outspoken liberal on women's rights to the world, but his wife and daughters may well know otherwise. An activist, outspoken woman may still be timid and uncertain of her position and power in her own home. It is not uncommon to hear these sorts of ideas in the most liberal, seemingly equal settings:

Yes, women must have rights but what do you mean by 'equality'?

They must be treated well: after all, they are gentle: they are the fair sex: they are kind, tender, adjusting, selfless, and we must honour them.

You must work, but you need to take time out to look after the children, no?

Such 'patriarchal patronage', which does not see women as equal actors in any meaningful way, and thinks their rights are 'good conduct prizes' to be awarded and taken away at will, rather than immutable and indispensable, is as retrograde as outright unashamed chauvinism. This is the other side of the anti-feminist lobby, which I believe to be more dangerous: that which rewards the docile, weak, dependent aspects of the feminine, thereby inducing subordination.

Feminists who opt out of male protection are marginalized as 'unfeminine' and laughed at in male bonding bonhomie. Fearing the unflattering label, many women are thus caught in the subtle strategy of the patriarchal backlash and shudder at the thought of being mistaken for feminists. Many intelligent, successful women have also bought into anti-feminist propaganda, on the ground that it is anti-male.[29] This comes from a basic lack of understanding of feminism: it is an active movement to arrive at gender equality. That energetic focus is necessary to be able to work towards an open civilized society which transcends gender stereotypes. Thus, feminism is also for men, because it encourages him to break his gender stereotypes as well.

Many confident, successful career women are anti-feminists and many are reluctant to mentor younger women into sharing their hard-won spaces. That is the reason why men love to say that women are their own worst enemies. The tendency to club women together, who should not disagree and, if they do, are each other's worst enemies, as well as the presumption that all women are bound to have the same political agenda, again tends to diminish their intellect and persona. In contrast, disagreements amongst men are seen as 'active political discourse' and so the patronizing attitudes towards women continue.

29. Faludi, *Backlash: The Undeclared War Against American Women*, p. 4

Family Law and Gender Equality

The early feminist searched for better rights for women within traditional patriarchal structures. Many modern Indian women may want to negotiate equality with their right to work, but baulk at the idea of men as home-makers and care-givers. We think we have travelled some little distance beyond the obvious stereotypes of 'he is not a man because he is not a good provider', but that is not entirely true, as this story of an upper-class westernized couple will show:

The husband of a beautiful and successful businesswoman was laid off from his high-paying, high-flying and high-stress corporate career. The existential crises that ensued resulted in each questioning their gender roles. After much anguished soul-searching, which even led to an emotional breakdown, he found the courage to break out of his macho stereotype role and take pride in his wife's success.

She, on the other hand, resented this change in him. She made him feel inadequate by calling him 'small-time'. In a conversation with me, she said she felt embarrassed when they went out to dinner and she had to pay the bill.

I questioned her biases. 'Are not your earnings his as well', I asked, 'considering that his money when he was earning was equally yours?'

'My earnings are mine,' she said, stressing the last word and shook her head with a grimace as if to say: how can you think otherwise. Stretching her slim body with feline languid grace she said, 'My work is only my personal creative expression.'

'Why not celebrate your financial independence?' I said. 'Your earnings from your "creative expressions" are substantial: you should feel secure about supporting him.'

'I can't be stressed with being a provider and let him chicken out!'

'That is true,' I said. 'Most women are not brought up to be providers in the way men are but why can't that change?'

She slowly articulated as if to a wilfully dense person, 'Because he is the man. That's what men do.'

I pressed on, 'You want to break the stereotype for women and work and earn like a man but the man cannot break the stereotype and be the home-maker?' Her response was to look at me with pity and contempt.

~

Many men may be happy to lighten the burden on themselves of being the sole provider, but are reluctant to do so because it could mean loss of power or loss of respect. Some brave men, as in the story I have told earlier, are opting for less-demanding professions or a more fulfilling personal life, and if their wives are equally brave, they are happy to be equal or primary earners. A friend of mine is quite proud of being the earner, while her husband focuses on research that may (or may not) eventually be of financial benefit. However, gender socialization would label such men as 'not man enough'.

Equally, there are many women who are earning more than the husbands, but remain miserable. The husband, fuelled by his delusion that his gender entitles him to a superior status in every respect, resents her growing financial power. Even a loving man may feel insecure about her success, as this thoughtless advertisement reveals: A woman bids goodbye to her husband as she leaves for work, with her briefcase etc. 'Just a moment,' he says and adjusts her sari pallu so it does not cover her mangal sutra. The mark of marriage and ownership is again shown to be more important than any of the two people's achievements and their relationship to each other.

Even though double incomes are more common than ever before, gender expectations have not changed. Most women still find they have to return from work to cook the evening meal. They will make tiffin for every member of the family before they leave for their own offices. Most women will not have complete control over their earnings; many don't have any control at all. The roles within a household continue to be gender-based and hierarchical. The personality of an individual may influence their experience of the world but there is no getting away from gender expectations within the family.[30] What Simone Beauvoir said about women being made, not born,[31] is also true of men.

~

In this scenario, comes a time when resources have to be allocated upon divorce. If women have to stay at home to care for children, they are not compensated with an equal share in the man's earnings. When it comes to property, no amount of education, or even a liberal political viewpoint seems to have alleviated the reluctance of some men at a visceral level to allow women into the domain of economic resources and opportunities that they see as exclusively theirs.

Thus patriarchal attitudes continue to colour familial ambience. The effort of family law is to dilute the impact of such unfair attitudes, which can and do translate into illegal acts. Ergo, it should follow that the

---

30. Yuval Noah Harari, *Sapien: A Brief History of Humankind*, p. 152

31. Simone de Beauvoir, *The Second Sex*, p. 293

keepers of the law (parliamentarians, bureaucrats, judges and lawyers) are all open-minded intellectuals and the polar opposite of the patriarchal strictures they are supposed to be offsetting. But it is not so. Take the legal fraternity: lawyers are loud, opinionated and like to romanticize their profession and themselves as societal heroes. A legal training is often an onward trajectory to politics and the world's greatest statesmen and powerful politicians have been lawyers. How does this mass of black-clad people seething with ideas and ideals view gender equality amongst themselves? My reply is: with the same resentment and confusion and encouragement and joy as society does. Some are committed to gender equality but for many others, it remains an abstract concept that cannot be envisioned in real life.

Because the gender issue is the crux of a divorce battle, the subjective moralistic values of lawyers, judges and mediators are perforce taken into account, raising decibel levels and reducing the quality of discourse. Because judges believe that they have a latitude to speak their minds, family law proceedings and rulings (more than in other areas of law) expose a judge's view on gender politics, whether egalitarian, patronizing or misogynist. Here, some women judges seem tougher on women, perhaps because they do not want to seem biased in their favour. There has been some study on whether women bring a different perspective to judging, but the bottom line is that under-representation on the bench has made them conservative and careful about being too bold and radical.[32]

We lawyers know how to handle the personal politics of our brethren and judges outside the courtroom, but when conservatism becomes misogyny or outright patriarchy while laying down the law, it is a problem, just as mindlessly anti-male arguments also harm the cause of women's progress towards equality. That examples of male chauvinism abound, and there are limitations and discomfort with an open exchange between men and women even amongst the legal fraternity, is apparent. Below are instances of male chauvinism, along with disagreements amongst women on the issue of female empowerment.

The following story makes apparent the discomfort of the legal fraternity in dealing with women as equals. The Delhi High Court got its first woman judge, Justice Leila Seth in 1991. Because of its traditional context of sexual ownership, many lawyers could not bring themselves

---

32. Sally J. Kenney, 'Choosing Judges: A Bumpy Road to Women's Equality and a Long Way to Go' in *Michigan State Law Review*, 2012, p. 1499; See also Prabha Sridevan, 'Judiciary, an Old Boys' Club' in *The Hindu*, 30 March 2016.

to address her as 'milady'. Judges too did not understand it entirely. A barrister friend of mine addressed the judge as milady.

'She is not your lady', glowered the robust Punjabi brother judge sitting with her on the bench.

'She is as much my lady as milord is my lord,' my friend responded with admirable élan.[33]

On the other hand, at the time of writing this, there is a judge in the Supreme Court who does not like to be called 'milady' because it is she who chooses to limit its meaning to the sexual context.

~

A newspaper reported a judge of the Supreme Court evoking much courtroom laughter when he said to a group of women lawyers complaining of gender discrimination in appointments to the higher judiciary, 'No...no...no...don't say that. We are always looking for women judges',[34] implying that their search had revealed no competent female candidates.

~

Women, having grown up in a male-centric world, can have difficulty in disassociating themselves or their daughters from the traditional patriarchal matrix. For example, a lady judge made the required disclosure of her assets and liabilities on the Supreme Court website. Under the column headed: 'Any other liabilities' she mentioned 'two daughters to be married'.[35] Two weeks after the newspapers picked up the story, she argued that an innocuous statement of accounts could not be held to reflect her views on gender: 'my daughters', she said, 'are my biggest asset'. But her passive or subconscious acceptance of patriarchal norms exemplifies why the requirement that Mahila Courts must have female judges has not proven to be as effective as expected.

Such examples extend into other quasi- and paralegal fields as well. Two women presidents of state commissions for women have observed on different occasions that women should dress modestly to avoid being raped.[36] A president of the National Commission for Women observed

---

33. Sushil Bajaj, Barrister at law

34. Harish V. Nair, 'Supreme Court keen to appoint women judges now' in *The Times of India*, 5 November 2015.

35. http://supremecourtofindia.nic.in/assets/gsmisra.pdf

36. 'Guwahati molestation: NCW chief Mamta Sharma advises women to dress "carefully"' in *India Today*, 18 July 2012

that women should enjoy being called sexy.[37]

When these biases come into the courtroom, they directly affect the way the law is interpreted. There have been cases where lawyers have pleaded for their male clients that the wives spoke for too long and too frequently on their cell phones. I was puzzled by this till I read a report that a Punjab State Commission (headed by a woman) had ordered that married women should not use mobile phones.[38] A panchayat in Suraj village, in Gujarat, also banned unmarried women from using cell phones.[39]

~

In another example, a lower-middle-class woman in a courtroom was telling her story of domestic violence and that now she was ready to fight back. The lady magistrate said, 'You talk too much. If this is the way you are in court, you must be driving him crazy at home.' I saw the woman's brave face collapse and her courage evaporate as the courtroom laughed and her husband struck a pose of mock humility—eyes down, head bowed and hands folded—but his sideways smile at the audience was triumphant and complicit with them in berating her.

~

Lawyers and judges expose their views about women and if I wanted to be kind I could say they do this without meaning to, but then I would be lying. During a heated argument in court between my woman lawyer opponent and myself, a male judge looked exhausted and said, 'It's very difficult to see two women fighting.'

I thought, are men fighting and attacking each other in a courtroom or in Parliament a bearable sight? I said instead, 'Perhaps because our voices are lighter, we could sound shrill! However my lord is surely not troubled?' and I forced myself to smile charmingly.

~

Many years ago I filed a suit for declaration that my client (a woman) did, in fact, marry the defendant and now sought a financial entitlement from him as damages for denying the marriage. The man responded to say that she was only an escort and an ardas in the gurudwara did not constitute a legal and valid marriage. The Delhi High Court judge told

37. 'Don't get offended by "sexy", says chief of National Commission for Women (Mamta Sharma)', on NDTV, 26 February 2012.

38. 'Frequent cellphones use cause marital disputes' on IBN Live, 5 May 2011.

39. Hiral Dave, 'Gujarat village bans mobile phones for unmarried women' in *The Hindustan Times*, 18 February 2016.

the husband that if he called her an escort, he must pay for her services. This mindless fatuous chauvinism made me slide low into my chair with sheer embarrassment for the judge who clearly meant well.

Having said which, the remark did help drive an eventual settlement in a rough justice sort of way though I settled for far less than I had asked for. Apart from cost efficiency for my client, I could not even begin to guess at the figure my client's 'services' would have been priced at by the court.

~

One would expect empathy on gender issues from the refined corridors of the Supreme Court but controversial exceptions have come from there too. One male judge referred to a woman living with a man outside the state of matrimony as a 'keep' if she was financially dependent upon him.[40]

~

The danger of romantic paternalism is apparent in the following story of a judge's scepticism about a woman's argument for complete independence and separate residence. In 2005, I was arguing for an independent residence for a woman to be provided by her estranged husband. The judge asked me whether she really intended to live on her own. Of course, I said, surprised by the question. 'Oh,' he said, 'I had thought she might prefer to stay under the protection of her father or brother.' Yet he was not wrong! Many parents would expect their divorced daughter to stay with them because they cannot imagine her living alone and 'unprotected'.

~

Hearing an appeal by the husband against the family court's dismissal of his divorce plea, a division bench judge of the Bombay High Court asked the wife why she could not live with her husband, 'You should go to him. When Sita could join Ram in vanvas, then why can't you go?'[41] The correct answer is that Sita had refused to return from the forest when Rama repented his ill treatment of her! The gender bias of the legal fraternity reinforces untruths and clichés about mythical and epic heroes who are treated as icons for the collective subconscious. The remarkable thing about these epics is that there are actually no heroes—the authors understood human complexities as a mixture of good and bad, but that

---

40. D. Velusamy vs. D. Patchaiammal, (2010) 10 SCC 469: 'If a man has a "keep" whom he maintains financially and uses mainly for sexual purpose and/or as a servant it would not, in our opinion, be a relationship in the nature of marriage'

41. 'A wife should be like goddess Sita: Bombay HC' in *The Times of India*, 8 May 2012.

is a story for a different book. The point I am making is that the law is struggling and sometimes seems to be fighting a losing battle against patriarchal customs, but I do believe it must eventually prevail.

Women in the Legal Profession

A year ago, I saw a lawyer putting up a notice in the Delhi High Court that said, 'Wanted, a junior advocate (male only)'. Though upset, I had to laugh at his pathetic desperation to avoid dealing with the advent of women in the legal profession. Yet the truth is that from resentment to patriarchal indulgence, most men have now become fearful and suspicious of women.

A few months later in November 2013, a young intern alleged sexual harassment by a former Supreme Court judge. The Special Committee of three judges that investigated her allegations found her story to be prima facie correct. The former judge, who held a prominent post in a State Human Rights Commission, initially refused to resign. While people salivated at the salacious details, it took a lone crusade by the Additional Solicitor General, at the time Indira Jaising, to push for his resignation. She wrote in the newspapers: 'I have put forth the details. Indeed they have shocked and shattered most of us. And they have been prima facie established by three judges of the Supreme Court'.[42] It was only then that the judge resigned from the commission he was heading. The saddest part of the story for me was that extracts from her complaint show the intern just wanted to work, as he circled and stalked and hovered and she avoided and ducked, all while continuing to try and complete her designated tasks.

Another allegation against a judge is currently covered under court protection from being reported on.

After these incidents, a senior lawyer told me that women would not be able to get jobs as interns with judges because of such scandals. He followed it up proudly by saying that he had never had a woman in his chambers 'precisely for this reason'.

These incidents reminded me that the Supreme Court in the Vishaka[43] case had laid down guidelines to set up committees to deal with sexual harassment at the workplace. That was in 1997, but the bar did not set up its own committee till 2013.

42. Indira Jaising, 'Is this not what Section 354 is meant for, My Lord?' in *The Indian Express*, 16 December 2013.

43. Vishaka vs. State of Rajasthan (1997)7 JT(SC)384

As I write this, a woman judge of the Delhi High Court has been targeted by an anonymous person who managed to find space in a newspaper to complain that judge lectures a lot, attends conferences and passes very few orders. I have personal experience that she is open, pleasant, and fair and has a genuine commitment to seeing family matters settled. To do that, yes she takes out a lot of time to talk to litigants and manages to drive that balance between coaxing, persuasion and counselling. To be pleasant, open and conversational is a rare ability and needs to be encouraged. Many members of the bar registered their protest with the concerned newspaper. Indira Jaising commented that it was better that the judge attended conferences on women's issues than cocktail parties thrown by zealous networkers. As per her roster she is to handle family appeals and is doing a remarkably good job. There are male judges who have had all sorts of unsavoury allegations about their work ethic and lack of judicial temperament. This is again an instance of double discrimination: against family law and against a lady judge who takes it seriously.

~

Recognizing gender bias amongst the legal fraternity, in August 2014, women lawyers in Delhi formed a forum called Women In Law and Litigation (WILL). There was a grand inauguration ceremony attended by hundreds of women and a handful of men. The panelists were all women who had been designated senior lawyers in Delhi, the first lady Chief Justice of the Delhi High Court (2014) and a lady judge of the Supreme Court. The speeches were interesting. The Chief Justice[44] of Delhi spoke about the first woman lawyer in India, Cornelia Sorabjee.[45] She was the first woman to have studied law at Oxford. She was denied enrolment in Calcutta High Court, which read the definition of pleaders as persons excluding women. Then the judge from the Supreme Court spoke about her father's resistance to her practicing law, even though she was a third-generation lawyer. Then a panelist commented that women needed to move on from dealing with family law. There it was, I thought, feeling a twinge of anger and then a surge of frustration. The bias against family law disregards and diminishes its practitioners, women or men.

The good thing was, of course, that women lawyers had gathered together. In the legal world, under-representation of women on the bench

---

44. Honourable Chief Justice G. Rohini

45. Richard Sorabji, *Opening Doors: The Untold Story of Cornelia Sorabji.*

and the struggle of women at the bar to find their place in the sun is a symptom of a deep systemic gender bias, a dangerous sign in an institution that is the repository of law.

One way to improve matters is by mentoring women in the legal profession. As Baroness Hale said 'Pioneering women must champion the cause of women generally, otherwise the world will slip back into its masculo-centric way'. Speaking with another feminist, Fiona Woolf, Baroness Hale said, 'we both share Madeline Albrght's view that there is a special place in hell for women who don't help other women.'[46]

Kate Millett's explanation for why women don't really seem to like each other is that they have such low self-esteem and thus do not seem to think much of other women. Millett cites an experiment by Philip Goldberg where he gave two essays amongst a group of women to respond on its scholarship. One was by John Mckay and the other by Joan Mckay. The women generally agreed that John was far superior. Yet the essays were identical.[47] Millett was writing in 1970 and things have changed a lot since then. Even so, the social community values women as less, and so women, who are part of the social fabric, devalue their own worth and the value of their intelligence, hard work, etc. Men may say 'my wife doesn't work', when she may be multitasking and doing more complex managing than most men! But the wife in question will also say 'no, I don't work', and so will her female family members.

Women of generations past have struggled and endured much for me to be able to say and write and live the way I do, and I salute them. But the paths they broke and trails they blazed are still rocky with gender conflict.

The Dualities of Women's Reality Today

The stark fact that cannot be emphasized often enough is that in patriarchy, the only point of reference to engage with a woman is sexual. While she tries to transcend that, she has a dual reality, in which the base is still sexual and the superficial layer is what she tries to create for herself.

Magnified by religious edicts, 'ethical' norms of chastity, virginity and marriage are the most uniform product of this gender divide across the world. Historically, women's bodies were the ownership of men and

46. 'Lady Hale gives the Fiona Woolf Lecture for the Women Lawyer's Division of the Law Society'. *Women in the Judiciary*, 27 June 2014, available at https://www.supremecourt.uk/docs/speech-140627.pdf

47. Kate Millett, *Sexual Politics*, p. 55

society, along with carrying the burden of ensuring male heirs, despite it being scientifically proven that the gender of the child is determined by the man's chromosomes. A 2005 legislation defines verbal and emotional abuse as including 'name calling and insults or ridicule specially with regard to not having a child or a male child'.[48]

~

The success formula of the most powerful Indian women politicians seems to be about projecting an image that transcends all sexualized associations. This they do by maintaining a single status that elevates them to the iconic state of a matriarch. The widow status of Mrs Indira Gandhi and Sonia Gandhi in a Hindu context implies celibacy and thus they are seen as having transcended the sexualized limitation of their gender. In 1975, Mrs Indira Gandhi appealed to the country after her ruthless imposition of Emergency rule to forgive her as they would a daughter. Mrs Sonia Gandhi calls herself the Bahu (daughter-in-law) of the nation. 'Amma' Jayalalitha is also the single matriarch: Mayawati, the leader of the Dalit cause, has also remained single. Didi, Mamta Banerjee, has added to her popularity by a moral bigotry that appeals to patriarchal mindsets: Rape happens because women have no business to be out late, was her statement after a woman was raped coming out of a nightclub in Kolkata.

These appeals work and so the politicians carry on, but any deviation from the norm of wife, mother and sister will still marginalize her into witch, bitch and prostitute. The subtext remains one of male ownership. Upon marriage, she takes his name; once divorced, she is expected to revert to the name of her father.[49] In fact, a woman's decision not to take her husband's name is still viewed with suspicion and discomfort.

Rape

The gender sensitivity of a society can be gauged from its treatment of rape as an offense. By that yardstick, India falls way below even the 'passable' mark. The important thing to remember is that rape is not committed by a man overcome with lust, but one who is asserting power over women whom he senses are slipping away from their subservient positions. Any serious issue that makes waves through the social psyche is bound to

48. Clause (iii)(a) of Explanation to Section 3, Protection of Women from Domestic Violence Act, 2005

49. Shibu Thomas, 'Woman can't use husband's name after divorce: Supreme Court' in *The Times of India*, 17 November 2011.

have a dark comic aspect to it. I did not think it was possible to do that with rape till I saw a spoof PWD traffic sign outside the district courts in Saket with the advisory: STOP RAPING—a horrific trivialization of a terrible crime.

The demonic rape case of December 2012 stung through bone to the collective social marrow, causing an anguished mass uprising calling for women's safety. It led to a path-breaking report on gender by a commission headed by the late Justice Verma. All political parties came together on the issues of gender, violence and abuse. As a result, in 2013, the legal definition of rape and sexual assault was widened by an amendment to the Indian Penal Code (IPC): S.354 IPC (outraging a woman's modesty) was made a non-bailable offence.[50]

While this was happening, the first public comment of RSS chief Bhagwat after the incident was that rape does not happen in Bharat but in India.[51] The statement is not even in the margin of correct. Of the eight forms of marriage in traditional Hindu Law, two allow men carry off a woman forcibly or have sex with her if she is drunk, sleeping or out of her mind. [52] Two others, which enjoin a bride price have been wiped out with the devaluation of women. Marriage rituals have remained largely unchanged from early times except for the relative simplicity brought in by the Arya and Brahmo Samaj movements, which also have not survived. Thus, the early legitimization of rape by marriage, rather than being punished, still lurks in the modern psyche and has made rape a complex subject, with a subtext that trivializes the crime not as a painful, horrendous, humiliating violation but a 'soiling' of 'reputation' because of the disproportionate value that is still attached to chastity. In 2015, the Supreme Court observed that rape was a 'defilement' where the woman loses her 'purest treasure'.[53] Hence, the logic becomes that pre-marital sex with a promise to marry is all right, but it becomes rape when the marriage promise is not followed through. The woman's lack of agency over her body is reinforced by the fact that under the Indian

---

50. See p. 375: Section 375 & Section 354 of the Indian Penal Code Pre and Post the 2013 amendment.

51. 'Rapes happen in India, not Bharat, says RSS chief Mohan Bhagwat' on IBN Live, 4 January 2013.

52. V. Nagarajan, *Evolution of Social Polity of Ancient India: From Manu to Kautilya*, Book 2, p. 30

53. State of M.P v. Madan Lal, AIR 2015 SC 3003

Penal Code, the rape of a woman is punishable by a minimum of seven years of imprisonment but the rape of another's wife during a period of separation carries a lesser punishment. Moreover, rape within marriage is not an offence.

Any criminal case, as an offence against the state, cannot be settled by consent between the complainant and the accused. Exceptions have been created for cases under Sections 498A and 406 to help the speedy resolution of family matters, even at the cost of making offences under this section almost quasi-civil, except in cases of extreme violence or murder. But for rape cases to be treated in the same way amounts to obfuscating the gravity of the crime. Consider Gresta Kujur's case in 2012[54] where the High Court, despite the objections of the prosecution, chose to quash proceedings against a rapist, because he had married the victim. The judge observed that to send the rapist to jail would leave the 'prosecutrix in the lurch'. No questions were asked as to the circumstances of the alleged marriage and whether it was of her free will.

Recently, a man accused of raping his niece was acquitted by a Delhi District Court because the victim married him after the incident, allegedly of her free will.[55] I have also been told by a mediator that he was instrumental in settling a rape case where the victim married the rapist.[56] In 2005,[57] Varkala Radhakrishanan raised concerns about the practice of rape victims marrying their rapists, but his speech was interrupted and the House adjourned without sensible debate.

The exception to the offence of rape in cases of marriage is a significant indicator of a woman's place in society. It is the 'Bharat culture' that views a raped woman as 'tainted'. This is the cause of the deep irrational guilt felt by women about being in the wrong place at the wrong time, which prevents her from speaking up. She, too, feels she has become a dirty secret.

~

Rape is an important matter for discussion because it gauges a person's point of view on matters of gender. Some view it as a crime against

---

54. Gresta Kujur & Anr vs State, MANU/DE/6454/2011

55. State vs. Aslam Mohd, SC. No. 252; See also 'Delhi court acquits man in rape case' on Zee News, 20 January 2014

56. The Supreme Court recently in the case of State of M.P. vs. Madan Lal, AIR 2015 SC 3003 has stated the following on the issue of compromise in rape cases: 'We would like to clearly state that in a case of rape or attempt of rape, the conception of compromise under no circumstances can really be thought of.'

57. Lok Sabha Debates, 6 May 2005.

'honour' which misses the point because to view a woman's chastity as her 'honour' reinforces a patriarchal mindset that is important to break away from if we are serious about gender equality. Rape needs to be viewed as a sexual offence that violates a woman's agency over her body.

The disappointment in those who do not respect this simple premise cuts very deep. To cite an instance, may I refer to a recent controversial judgment that resulted in an acquittal due to the difference in semantics between forcible sex (that is rape) and forceful sex. The judgment may even be correct, as far as appreciation of evidence is concerned, since the court held that the offence could not be established beyond reasonable doubt.[58] To acquit is judicial prerogative but the writing of the judgment could surely have been more sensitive. The court accepted medical evidence that there were injuries around the vaginal orifice because of 'forceful penetration' but then made the extraneous observation that the victim was 65 to 70 years of age and beyond menopause. I could not understand the import of the victim's age, unless perhaps the judge was trying to say that older women have a problem of vaginal dryness. Also, there seemed to be an underlying presumption of consent because the deceased had consumed alcohol.

The treatment of rape in Indian law has been arbitrary for many years, with everything from the victim's caste, class, religion, clothing, personal history and recreational habits affecting the outcome of otherwise entirely straightforward cases. Lotika Sarkar, a leading law scholar, freedom fighter and feminist, said in 1980, 'A provision in criminal law I am ashamed of is the one pertaining to rape. The only excuse I have today is to say that somehow at that stage it had not occurred to us that rape was such a major problem in our society.'[59]

In 1979, Lotika Sarkar, along with three other prominent public intellectuals[60], wrote an open letter to the Chief Justice of the Supreme Court of India protesting the reasoning in Tukaram v. State of Maharashtra[61] that became notorious as the Mathura rape case. The

---

58. Achey Lal v. State of NCT, 2014 (4) JCC 2796

59. Lotika Sarkar, *Towards Equality: The Report of the Committee on the Status of Women in India*, (CSWI)

60. Upendra Baxi, Vasudha Dhagamwar, Raghunath Kelkar, Lotika Sarkar, 'Open Letter to the CJI', available at http://pldindia.org/wp-content/uploads/2013/03/Open-Letter-to-CJI-in-the-Mathura-Rape-Case.pdf; also at Baxi Upendra, Reghunath Kelkar and Lotika Sarkar, 'Notes on the Reform of Rape Allied Offence', *Supreme Court Journal*, 4 SCC 1979

61. AIR 1979 SC 185

reasoning in the case is skewed by unquestioned patriarchal norms that are at the core of insensitivity to women. The case highlights my point that many members of the judiciary, despite their training in law, are not able to transcend patriarchal socialization.

Mathura, a girl aged between 14 and 16 was an orphan who lived with her brother, Gama. They were labourers. Mathura developed a relationship with a man named Ashok. He was the cousin of a woman called Nushi. Mathura worked at Nushi's house. Ashok and Mathura decided to get married. Gama filed a police report that his sister Mathura had been kidnapped by Ashok, Nushi and her husband. They were all brought to the police station at 9 p.m. and their statements were recorded. When they were about to leave the police station at about 10:30 p.m., the head constable, Tukaram, directed that Mathura should remain at the police station.

The subsequent events are recorded by the Supreme Court that acquitted Tukaram and Ganpat: 'Immediately thereafter Ganpat...took Mathura...into latrine...pulled off her salwar...then dragged her to the chhapri...and raped her despite her protests and stiff resistance on her part...he departed after satisfying his lust and then Tukaram...fondled her private parts...wanted to rape her but was unable to do so for the reason that he was in a highly intoxicated condition.'

Ashok and Gama were concerned about the bolted doors and lights out at the police station with Mathura inside and a crowd gathered to support their cry of concern. Eventually Mathura emerged to say that she had been raped by Ganpat. The Sessions Court did not hold the sexual intercourse between Mathura and Ganpat to be rape.

The Nagpur bench of the Bombay (as it was then) High Court overturned the order and said that it was highly unlikely that Mathura 'would make any overtures or invite the accused to satisfy her sexual desires...nor could she have resisted her assailant.'

The Supreme Court *reversed* the finding of the High Court after recording the undisputed facts above. It held that there was no injury to show resistance to intercourse and it was probable that 'the alleged intercourse was a peaceful affair.'

The open letter expresses its outrage at the judgment in the following words: 'Your lordship, this is an extraordinary decision sacrificing human rights of women under the law and the Constitution'. Proceeding to challenge the reasoning of the Supreme Court as unsound and against all settled principles of appreciating evidence and inference of circumstance, the authors of the letter said,

> 'there is not a single word condemning the very act of calling Mathura and detaining her at the police station in gross violation of the law of the land...nor is there a single word in the judgment condemning the use of the police station as a theatre of rape and or submission to sexual intercourse. There is no direction to the administration to follow the law. There are no strictures of any kind...a case like this with its cold-blooded legalism snuffs out all aspirations for the protection of human rights of millions of Mathuras in the countryside. Why so?.... The court under your leadership, has taken great strides for civil liberties in cases involving affluent urban women (Maneka Gandhi; Nandini Satpathy). Must illiterate, labouring, politically mute Mathuras of India be continually condemned to their pre-constitutional fate?... What more can we say? We can only appeal, in conclusion to have the case reheard, as an unusual situation, by a larger bench, and if necessary by even the full court. This may appear to your lordship as a startlingly unconventional, and even a naïve suggestion. But nothing short of protection of human rights and constitutionalism is at stake. Surely the plight of millions of Mathuras in this country is as important as that of Golak Nath and his holiness Kesavananda Bharti challenging the validity of the restriction on the right to property as a fundamental right, whose cases were heard by a full court.'

The letter, as far as I know, was never responded to.

A consequence of outrage at the Mathura case was that it led to some crucial amendments in the law where the presumption of innocence was reversed in cases of custodial rape.[62]

~

In all family laws and issues such as gender, judgments swing wildly in all directions because they are influenced by personal views on values and morals. There is no getting away from a personal viewpoint, but a judge who suffers patrilocal vision is not acceptable. Justice Krishna Iyer called upon an imaginary judge, saying, 'we feel convinced that a socially sensitized judge is a better statutory armor against gender outrage than long clauses of a complex section with all the protections writ into it.'[63]

---

62. The Criminal Law (Second Amendment) Act 1983 (No. 46); Section 114 A of the Evidence Act now presumes that if the victim says that she has not consented, it becomes a rebuttable presumption. Section 376 of the Indian Penal Code was amended and Sections 376(A), (B), (C) and (D) were enacted, which made custodial rape punishable. The amendment also added provisions for in-camera trials and prohibition on disclosure of the victim's identity. See also: Leela Fernandes, *Routledge Handbook of Gender in South Asia*

63. Krishna Lal vs. State of Haryana, AIR 1980 SC 1252

Such a judge was not the norm at the time, and it seems unlikely that it will be so today. The margin for personal influence could certainly be reduced if there were clear parameters for the exercise of personal discretion or filters to minimize the colouring of a judgment by a personal view.

Some subsequent rulings showed that the judicial mindset remained unchanged while others were remarkably progressive. As to the former, the Supreme Court reduced the sentence of a rape conviction from seven years to three, giving the following reasons:

> 'So far as the sentence of seven years' rigorous imprisonment on both the accused persons is concerned, it appears to us that it may not be unlikely that the accused persons at the beginning had a genuine desire to help the prosecutrix in reaching her brother's place quickly. But later on, when she agreed to share the same room at night in the hotel, the two young men became victim of sexual lust and against the consent and protest of the prosecutrix, committed rape on her. **Considering the very young age of the accused persons and considering the circumstances under which there was very likelihood that they could not overcome the fit of passion and lost all sense of decency and morality and ultimately committed the offence of rape and also considering the fact that the incident had taken place long back** and during the course of the proceedings upto this Court, both of them had suffered disrepute and mental agony, we think that the ends of justice would be met if both the accused persons are awarded a lesser sentence. We, therefore, direct that both the accused persons should suffer rigorous imprisonment for three years'.[64] [emphasis mine]

Justice Iyer also suffered from the same patriarchal patronage that women's causes need to cease being grateful for. This is what he had to say on the offence of rape and sentencing:

> 'A philanderer of 22 overpowered by sex stress in excess...overpowered the temptingly lonely prosecutrix of 24...raped her in hurried heat and made an urgent exit having fulfilled his erotic sortie... He is barely 22 with no criminal antecedents save this offence. He has a young wife and a farm to look after. Given correctional courses through meditational therapy and other measures, his erotic aberration may wither away'.[65]

The unquestionably great judge, looking to reform jurisprudence that he was a passionate proponent of, reduced the sentence from four years to two years.

64. Raju vs. State of Karnataka, 1993 SCALE (4)220

65. Phul Singh vs State of Haryana, AIR 1980 SC 249

On the other hand, despite our having to suffer the personal limitations of the socialisations of judges, the law of rape has progressed robustly and reassuringly. Thus, the same great judge, Krishna Iyer held in the Krishan Lal case[66] that the statement of a rape victim, if credible could be accepted without corroboration. Justice Thakkar in another case says: 'In the Indian setting, refusal to act on the testimony of a victim of sexual assault in the absence of corroboration as a rule, is adding insult to injury. Why should the evidence of the girl or the woman who complains of rape or sexual molestation be viewed with the aid of spectacles fitted with lenses tinged with doubt, disbelief or suspicion? To do so is to justify the charge of male chauvinism in a male dominated society'.[67]

This sounds good, but then the same court denigrated Western women who file false rape charges because they may be vindictive, gold diggers and so on. It argues that Indian women are chaste and virtuous and never make an allegation of rape that would 'taint' them for the rest of their lives[68]—a complicated reasoning suffering from perverse patriarchal patronage that has been severely criticized in the Verma Commission report.

In the Karnel Singh case,[69] the delay in filing an FIR was held not to be a circumstance against the prosecutrix. 'The reluctance to go to the police is because of society's attitude towards such women; it casts doubt and shame upon her rather than comfort and sympathize with her: therefore delay in lodging complaints in such cases does not necessarily indicate that her version is false.'

Until 2003, the Evidence Act allowed for a rape accused to impeach the credit of a witness by 'showing' that she was of 'generally immoral character'. Fortunately this was deleted by an amendment in that year. Yet, it is significant that till then, the Supreme Court on no occasion ruled on a challenge to this grossly unfair and unjust provision.

---

66. Krishan Lal vs State of Haryana, AIR 1980 SC 1252

67. Bharwada Bhoginbhai Hirjibhai vs. State of Gujarat, AIR 1983 SC 753

68. Bharwada Bhoginbhai Hirjibhai vs. State of Gujarat, AIR 1983 SC 753; See also Wahid Khan vs. State of Madhya Pradesh, (2010) 2 SCC 9 where the SC has stated, 'It is also a matter of common law that in Indian society any girl or woman would not make such allegations against a person as she is fully aware of the repercussions flowing therefrom... For an unmarried girl, it will be difficult to find a suitable groom'

69. Karnel Singh v. State of M.P., AIR 1995 SC 2472

Rape as backlash

Historically, as her subordination was sexual it is not surprising that the patriarchal backlash to women's bid for freedom is also sexual: rape, violence or sexual harassment perpetrated to diminish her persona both at home and in the workplace. In recent decades, reaction to women-enabling legislation has increased patriarchal oppression. The backlash is not just restricted to less educated rural areas. It is apparent even in Delhi's backyard. The Khap Panchayats have ruled that women are to cover their heads; wear only traditional clothes; not carry mobiles. A couple daring to marry outside caste risk their own lives and that of their families.[70] A woman suffers the risk of being punished for perceived transgressions by a panchayat ordering her to be gang-raped.[71]

Since ownership of a woman is tied to patriarchal honour, a woman without a man is seen as anybody's. Hence the common defense for rape is that the rape complainant was of 'easy virtue'. Nowhere was this brought out with greater chilling effect than when a lawyer defending a rape accused in the gruesome Delhi rape case of 2012 said: 'Everyone is responsible for their own safety. If someone roams around irresponsibly then they have only themselves to blame if something bad happens to them...The circumstances for rape are created by you. And then when something bad happens, you become the victim—when in fact you're equally responsible for it.'[72]

Since sexual submission is what constituted being a 'woman', it is no surprise that her revenge and rebellion is also sexual freedom: thus to judge women who choose this form of rebellion is also undemocratic. The increasingly sexual 'item' dances have become a controversial subject amongst feminists, some of whom disapprove of short skirts and pouting lips in a way that borders on zealously puritanical. A perspective, given the times, that I believe needs to be carefully avoided by every public intellectual.

~

70. 'UP Khap Panchayat bans women from stepping out and the minister endorses it' in *DNA*, 14 July 2012; 'Now, khap panchayats ban cell phones for unmarried girls' in *The Indian Express*, 23 November 2010; 'Haryana Khap asks girls above 10 years to stop wearing jeans, using mobile phones' in *The Hindustan Times*, 23 September 2013.

71. '20-year-old tied to tree, gang-raped on orders of village council, say police' on NDTV, 3 January 2014.

72. *India's Daughter*, BBC documentary.

Equality is absence of exploitation because no one can be the means for another: an individual is an end in itself. Erich Fromm says equality for women is sameness rather than oneness[73] but it should be full freedom to be what you are. Thus, women might have a different approach to who they are and want to be. This was beautifully enunciated by the Supreme Court in the case of Anuj Garg.[74] The subject of the challenge was certain types of jobs in the hospitality industry being denied to women on the grounds of their safety being compromised. Striking down such exclusion, the court said 'the...law ends up victimizing its subject in the name of protection...(women's) empowerment should reflect in the law enforcement strategies of the state as well as law modeling done in this behalf.' Talking of women, the court says, 'It is their life; subject to constitutional, statutory and social interdicts, a citizen of India should be allowed to live her life on her own terms.'

Conclusion

On gender, I suspect that Sardar B.S Mann's[75] words in Parliament in 1952 echoed what many men wanted to say but dared not:

> 'Sir...in your kindness you show certain concessions to lady members here. Now when we are going to discuss this Bill may I request that henceforward you will treat hon. lady members and men members on an equal footing and no concessions will be shown to lady members? It is high time for them to make up their mind either to have the concessions or to have the Hindu Code Bill'.[76]

That 'concessions' of chivalry were in lieu of property rights is a travesty. Will the etiquette of good manners be lost when men have to share their property with women and the genders become equal? The answer lies in a story told to me as true. This is about a gallant Bengali student at Cambridge for whom I feel affection without knowing him. He chivalrously opened the door for a young feminist activist. She railed against his chauvinism. The Bengali blinked a few times behind his round glasses and then unfazed by her tirade said, 'Ma'am I would have opened the door for you even if you had been a polar bear.'

---

73. Erich Fromm, *Art of Loving*, 2006.

74. Anuj Garg v. Hotel Association of India, (2008) 3 SCC 1

75. Chacha of General M.P.S. Mann and my granduncle

76. http://www.ambedkar.org/ambcd/64B2.On%20the%20Hindu%20Code%20 Bill.htm

3. LOVE, SEX AND MARRIAGE

The Tricky Trinity

> *'There is hardly any activity, any enterprise, which is started with such tremendous hopes & expectations, and yet, which fails so regularly as love.'*
>
> —Erich Fromm, philosopher and psychologist

But what about marriages arranged before love can find its way to the couple? 'Good matches' arranged by families sometimes further the interest of the allying family more than the couple. They may work as much or as little as those marriages where 'love' visits before marriage.

Fromm and Campbell[1] describe love as an act of will committing to caring for another, or as the act of sacrificing the self, not to the other, but to the relationship, instead of asking and expecting only to receive love. Such love could be parental or friendly. But the love of couples is celebrated by the sexual act. There can be sex without love, but can the love shared by couples survive no sex? In other words, how important is the sexual component in love between a couple?

The law recognizes the importance of sex, which is why it is not the wedding ceremony but consummation that validates a marriage. An unconsummated marriage is treated as void in law. Various courts have observed that sex is an important ingredient of marriage and a sexless marriage is anathema; they have granted divorces to those pleading that there is no sex in their marriages.[2]

But is sex all that is required to make a marriage? This legal position was taken literally by the Madras High Court, leading to a problematic judgment:

> 'However, if any couple, subject to their attaining the mandatory age of freedom, who indulge in sexual gratification, then that would be considered as valid marriage and they could be termed as "husband and wife", as a

---

1. Erich Fromm, *The Art of Loving*; See also Joseph Campbell, *The Power of Myth*

2. Mrs Rita Nijhawan v. Mr Bal Kishan Nijhawan, AIR 1973 Delhi 2000 reiterated in Vinita Saxena v. Pankaj Pandit, AIR 2006 SC 1662; Smt. Shashi Bala v. Shri Rajiv Arora, 188 (2012) DLT 1

> result of their choice of freedom... Hence, the main legal aspect for valid marriage is consummation or sexual interaction.'[3]

This reduction of marriage to a sexual act diminishes an institution that has survived robustly and even elegantly over the centuries. It ignores that marriage is about raising families; it is a team effort of survival through tumultuous careers and child-rearing. If it works, it creates a safe haven away from the world. It becomes an intimate friendship that may not continue to be actively sexual, but is unique because of a shared past of unashamed nakedness. Eekelaar calls it 'friendship plus'.[4] The Delhi High Court observed that marriage is companionship and consortium at many levels beyond the sexual.[5]

Thus, some courts say that sex is central, while others disagree. There are no complete and clear answers, but it can safely be said that a marriage is made robust when its sexual component is strong. The absence of sex is only a symptom of a deeper malaise in the marriage.

~

The Dharmashastras, recognizing the complexity of the issue, treated sex seriously enough to dedicate a sutra to it. Human endeavour (purushartha), the shashtris said, comprises three broad aims (trivarga) that are discussed in separate sutras: dharma (duty), artha (material engagement) and kama (love).[6] The *Kamasutra* is misunderstood as being limited to positions for sexual intercourse. This second-century sutra is actually a commentary on the aesthetics of eroticism and sensuality.[7] Its treatment of women's sexuality is remarkably liberated, even for present times. Vatsyayana's woman is sexually active and demands pleasure. Even so, Vatsyayana's advice is pragmatic: although a love marriage is desirable, to maintain caste purity is a primary duty.[8]

3.Aysha vs. Ozir Hassan, (2013)5 MLJ 31: On a petition filed against the judgment by an advocate, the Supreme Court clarified : 'In fact, what the learned Judge wanted to say is that if a man and woman are living together for a long time as husband and wife, though never married, there would be a presumption of marriage and their children could not be called to be illegitimate': Uday Gupta vs. Aysha, 2014 STPL(Web) 299 SC.

4. J. Eekelaar, *Family Law and Personal Life*, p. 49

5. Harvinder Kaur vs. Harmander Singh Choudhry, AIR 1984 Delhi 66

6. Wendy Doniger, *On Hinduism*, p. 22; See also: Wendy Doniger and Sudhir Kakar, *Kamasutra: a new, complete English translation of the Sanskrit Text*, p. xiii

7. Wendy Doniger and Sudhir Kakar, *Kamasutra: a new, complete English translation of the Sanskrit Text*, p. xxxix

8. *Ibid* p. 178

We have not been able to dismantle class and caste structures over the centuries since the *Kamasutra*. The barriers are protected as a matter of maryada, the breach of which may be at pain of death. Later centuries (tenth century onwards) saw the rise of communal barriers. By this I do not mean only the divisions that arose with the advent of Islam and Christianity, but the challenges to Brahminical Hinduism by Buddhists, Jains and later, the Sikhs. Unlike in the West, in India there have been no basic structural changes to the concept of marriage because we remained an essentially agrarian society. Arranged marriages remain popular to further alliances that serve socio-economic or political purposes and love receives approval only within prescribed social barriers. Now, as we transition to an industrialized society, the washes of change have begun.

The ensuing conservative resistance exposes, through the violence it employs, its inability to engage with the politics around family structures. Its preoccupation with arranging marriages to maintain caste and cultural purity, and the disapproval of premarital sex as not 'Indian', has led to a sex-absorbed society, ready to manipulate, confine and burden with cultural baggage, until the natural flow of this most basic desire is perverted. The courts are flooded with habeas corpus petitions, literally demanding that the bodies of runaway couples be produced. The stories follow a common pattern: parents say their daughter has been abducted, while the daughter says she has run away for love. The judge counsels the parents to allow the children their happiness.

Even so, it is not always a simple story of the couple presenting their families with a *fait accompli*. A husband moved a habeas corpus petition, saying that his wife had been abducted by her parents. The wife was summoned to court. Without a glance at her husband, she told the judge that she did not want to be with this man and had been forced to marry him. The husband, broken and betrayed, asked that he be allowed to speak to her just once, but the parents refused and hustled the girl out of court.

~

Of the many reasons to marry, legitimized sexual gratification remains an incentive, even though premarital sex is not viewed as a life-shattering scandal any longer. A sexual mismatch complicates and highlights innate differences that are in danger of becoming insurmountable. If the couple survive the first sexual contact—which could well have been a disaster, or disappointing at the very least, with the messiness and awkwardness outweighing any possible pleasure—they will find how to balance their sexual energy and truly embark on a marriage.

Of course, there are pitfalls to this. There may be an expectation of intense romance, fuelled by romance novels. The adrenalin rush of a new love can be addictive. Then there is the other side: sexual desire wanes. 'I love her, but I am not "in love" with her', he may say miserably. 'He is a good man, but I can't explain it; I am not happy', she may say.

On the other hand, the comfort of a relationship that is non-sexual cannot be underrated. Many couples live in that happy groove. But what cannot be argued with is that the chances of success in either a love or an arranged marriage are largely influenced by sexual chemistry.

Conjugal Intimacy

A young man married for just a year visited my office with his father. He complained that his wife fights relentlessly, always wants her way and his parents are not made to feel welcome when they visit. When I asked about her parents and their visits, he looked nonplussed, saying they don't visit either. Many men would find that a perfect state of affairs, I joked, but he was too stressed to smile back. I cleared my throat, wondering where to begin, when a thought struck me. I asked him, 'How is your conjugal intimacy?'

To me, the phrase enfolds the meaning of marriage. The first word describes the relationship of marriage and the second, its desired outcome. Given that they were newly married, my question was about sexual intimacy, though intimacy is not limited to sex alone.

'It's all right', he said, looking embarrassedly at his father.

I pressed on: 'How are you when you go on holidays together?'

'We are fine.'

I breathed in, enjoying the prospect of telling a client something completely different from my usual spiel. I began, 'Marriages are important. To marry is a difficult decision,' and then I stopped. In fact, I thought, for the majority in the country, it is not a difficult decision. Marriages are arranged on seemingly superficial criteria. Once the first test of caste, height, fairness, good looks and bank balance is passed, there are a few supervised meetings to explore common interests. The more liberal families may allow a short few months for a courtship. I am not scoffing at the idea of arranged marriages. They work, at least as much as 'love' marriages. I simply have no idea why.

I am often moved and impressed by the foolhardy courage of a young couple from sheltered backgrounds, resigned to embarking on the inevitable marital journey. They have yet to learn how constrained is the freedom to disembark. Even so, the decision to jump on board still has to have an element of instinct, as too much thinking may be a deterrent from ever boarding. This young man sitting before me and his new wife had jobs, an independent apartment, and, by his account, a reasonably active sexual life. They were definitely luckier than most. I cleared my throat and began again, 'I believe that sexual intimacy, particularly in a new marriage, drives a marriage past many a rough road. So if you are good with each other on holidays, then your core attraction is healthy and any strain in the marriage is external. Give this careful thought. I do think you will be all right. Will she go to a marriage counsellor?' Both father and son agreed that she would. 'In that case,' I said, 'she is probably as shocked and bewildered as you are by the intensity of the change: step with care but do relax.' I recommended a counsellor and sent them off, hoping I would not see them again.

~

As natural as the presence of sex in a new marriage is the leakage of sexual desire in an older one. So we enter the dangerous territory of the time when the sexual fires within marriage have cooled. It is quite common: one person does not want that much sex any longer, while the other continues to be sexually active. Who is to decide on how much sex and how often?

A couple had been married for fifty years. After the children grew up, the couple drifted to separate bedrooms and an independent coexistence that was neither sullen nor harmonious. They were wealthy, and their house had two distinct portions that reflected their different personalities. She was a homemaker who was beautiful and flamboyant. He was rich and not outgoing.

Eventually, when he asked for a divorce, her shock and near collapse seemed excessive, considering she knew about his intimate life. I got a faint glimmer of understanding when I realised that though she often complained of his absence from her life, she had learned to draw comfort even from his silent presence next door. To the outsider, they seemed to be in a sexless marriage of socio-economic convenience, but judging by her reaction, I could not call it loveless. It was a friendship that he had betrayed, she said. What compounded her bitterness was the timing: he was moving on to a new life while she was unlikely to find an age-appropriate male companion.

Invincible Repugnance

In law school, when we studied Mamaji's case, I decided that his marriage never took off because it lacked sexual chemistry. Lawyers would call my interpretation of Mamaji's predicament 'invincible repugnance'. This phrase is not used in Indian courts but English law has dealt with it in the context of repugnance that may arise from consent having been obtained under duress or fear of some sort.

The celebrated case is Szechter vs. Szechter.[9] The facts are the stuff of a good film. In 1940, a girl, N, was born in Poland to Jewish parents. When she was still a baby, the Germans despatched her along with her mother to an extermination camp. While on the train to the camp, the mother threw her out of the train window, so she might have a better chance to live. The baby survived, but her spine was broken. She was looked after by a Jewish woman called Mrs K. N's real mother died in the camp and her father committed suicide.

In 1949, Mrs K was arrested as a member of the Polish resistance and sentenced to ten years in jail. N survived and eventually even found her way to university. There she worked as a secretary to Professor L, and became friendly with him and his wife, both also of Jewish origin. Both L and N were arrested. He was released but, due to various legal technicalities, under Polish law the only way for N to leave Poland was to renounce Polish citizenship by marriage. Professor L hatched a scheme with his wife—he would divorce her and marry N, and once she was safely out of the country, divorce N and marry his wife again.

L followed through with his scheme and the newly married couple, L and N, found their way to England, where they applied for divorce. The judge grappled with the law and decided that the correct legal position was this: in order to show that N was incapable of consummating the marriage, it was necessary to show that she suffered an invincible psychological repugnance that made her unable to have intercourse with L. The fact that she did not wish to be married or to have intercourse with him fell far short of establishing invincible repugnance on her part.

The other point was the matter of N's consent to the marriage. Had it been induced by an external fear? The judge found that it had, because of the threat to life, liberty and limb posed in the political environment of Poland at the time of the marriage. The divorce was granted on the ground that consent was vitiated by the external circumstances.

9. [1970] 3 All ER 905, (see pp. 831, 832, 834).

A year later, in 1971, Singh v. Singh[10] was filed in the context of an Indian arranged marriage in England. Mrs Singh sought a divorce claiming repugnance because the marriage had been arranged without her consent. She had not seen Mr Singh till the marriage and when she did, she found him unattractive. The court denied her petition holding that:

> 'in order to prove duress sufficient to vitiate an otherwise valid marriage it must be shown that the will of one of the parties thereto had been overborne by genuine and reasonably held fear caused by threat of immediate danger, for which the party was not himself responsible, to life, limb or liberty, so that the constraint destroyed the reality of consent to ordinary wedlock.'

The court found that though she may have consented to the marriage solely to please her parents, there was no evidence that her will had been overborne by fear.

The law seems tough in yoking two people together: after all a person cannot be faulted for feeling repugnance and the other is not at fault for being perceived as repugnant. This is a real possibility in arranged marriages. Where repugnance is not respected, we are left with conjugal rights and corresponding duties that would be non-consensual and thus would constitute marital rape. That could be the reason why the urban intellectual is repulsed by a minister's comment that India was not ready for marital rape to be a criminal offense but we will come to that later.[11]

The introduction of irretrievable breakdown of marriage as a cause for divorce has made this discussion moot in the UK but not so in India. The approach of the Indian courts on marital sex is as problematic as was that of the UK in the fault regime. Courts have granted divorces dissolving sexless marriages, because they say sex is vital to a person's life;[12] yet, there is no indication on how evidence is to be appreciated to establish the negative of absence of sex.

Also the courts have stressed on absence of sex rather than willful refusal which might in certain circumstances be considered cruel.

---

10. [1971]2 All ER 828; B. Hale et al, *Family Law and Society Cases and Materials: Invincible Repugnance*, p. 27

11. Rajyasree Sen, 'Maneka Gandhi tells us marital rape isn't rape after all' in *LiveMint* 14 March 2016.

12. Shashi Bala vs. Rajiv Arora, (2012) 188 DLT 1; Vidhya Viswanathan v. Kartik Balakrishnan 2014 (11) SCALE 71

By holding that absence of sexual intercourse is a marital fault of cruelty, the courts are expounding conjugal duty over sexual repugnance: the courts do not seem to have considered that refusal of sexual intercourse may be due to a deeper problem that is exacerbated by the person demanding sex. If sex is a measure of the health of the marriage, then no sex is often a symptom of a deeper malaise. The revulsion from cruel, irrational or unaesthetic behavior is bound to lead to diminished or no sexual activity. The ground for divorce would then be cruelty, then not the consequent lack of sex. In fact, to insist upon sex in a tumultuous marriage would also be cruel.

The courts do not seem to have dealt with the argument of repugnance as a reasonable defense even while accepting that refusal of sex is cruel.

An example

H filed for divorce pleading, as one amongst many other grounds, denial of sex as a cause. That a baby had been born less than a year ago should have been enough to neutralize the no-sex plea, as well as the fact that H had not even bothered to support his plea by proof of medical intervention or therapy. W's case was that all was well till the birth of the child who had a congenital defect.

In his rejoinder, H reiterated his original case with a significant addition that W 'never easily consented for sex', thus implying that there was sex, but just not enough.

W, in her response, also hinted that H's attitude to sex was very feudal and unattractive. Though they did have sex she said, it may not always be as per his demand. The judge asked me the meaning of the 'feudal' plea, which I explained as H disregarding W's need for sexual fulfillment as unworthy of his time and attention. I put on my clinical straight face to say this but the judge's fair skin reddened to a point that made me alarmed for his health.

A normal sex life can only be seen from the surrounding circumstances. In this case a baby, shared bedroom, a common social life and holidays together should be adequate. How often and how good, I argued, could not be for the courts to decide.

The judge allowed the divorce, saying that W had not been able to prove that there was sex. The good judge ignored the principle of evidence relating to preponderance of probabilities: it was highly improbable that a couple with a small child had not recently had sex. Willful denial and cruel refusal of sexual intercourse is a negative that is difficult to prove in any case. It is also a delicate matter and a plea of no sex or inadequate sex in the face of an otherwise normal situation is specious.[13]

To make sexual intimacy the subject of a trial without taking the surrounding circumstances into account, as was done in this case, is intrusive and unjust and trivializes the tragedy of a family falling apart.

~

There is another problem with the proposition that absence of sex amounts to cruelty.[14] It makes sex a marital duty, and obligatory marital sex is not consensual. The law is that marital rape is not a criminal offence.[15] These judgments compound the vulnerability of women because they cannot plead marital rape as cruelty, since the absence of sex is also cruelty.

Adultery

A marriage may survive the absence or refusal of sex because of its socio-economic investments and advantages. But then we come to the moral question: is it reasonable to punish those who seek sex outside marriage because they have no sexual life within it, and do not want to rock the marriage boat either? Thus, as important as sex within marriage is, the matter of sex outside it. Is it cruel to punish for adultery when there is no sex in the marriage?

There are no clear boundaries here: extra-marital sex as a substitute for a sexless marriage is one thing, but there could also be very little sex in the marriage, and the extra-marital sex would be supplementary to it. Adulterers may not think of extra-marital sex as a reason to disrupt an otherwise friendly and comfortable home. For them, it is a practical arrangement leading to legal problems only when found out. The cuckold also may choose to look the other way for the same reason: there are other advantages in the marriage.

So we deal with extramarital sex on three bases: its morality; as a marital fault; and as a criminal offense.

~

---

13. Shakuntala Kumari vs. Om Prakash Ghai 19 (1981) DLT64, Smt. Linda Constance Edwards vs. Shri William Edwards & Anr. 91(2001)DLT 355, Praveen Mehta vs. Inderjit Mehta, AIR 2002 SC 2582, P vs. P, (1964) 3 All ER 923, Sheldon vs. Sheldon, (1966) 2 All ER 257, Lennie vs. Lennie, [1949] UKHL 4

14. Shashi Bala vs. Rajiv Arora, 188(2012)DLT1; Rita Nijhawan vs. Balakishan Nijhawan, AIR 1973 Delhi 200

15. Exceptions to Section 375: Exception 2: 'Sexual intercourse or sexual acts by a man with his own wife, the wife not being under fifteen years of age, is not rape.'

The law of adultery is as follows: *Whoever has sexual intercourse with a person who is and whom he knows or has reason to believe to be the wife of another man, without the consent or connivance of that man, such sexual intercourse not amounting to the offence of rape, is guilty of the offence of adultery, and shall be punished with imprisonment of either description for a term which may extend to five years, or with a fine, or with both. In such a case, the wife shall not be punishable as an abettor.*[16]

This definition, along with the husband's right to 'consent' and 'connivance', was imported from UK law which, in turn, draws from the Hebrew commandment of 'Thou shalt not commit adultery'. Here we have the difference between the Abrahamic and Hindu cultures. The former tried to impose order via commands. Adultery had serious and devastating consequences.

There is no similar parallel in classical Hindu law. On the contrary, the iconized romantic Krishna was in a passionate relationship with the married Radha. The morality of Krishna's love for the married Radha is explained through the spiritual analogy of an atma seeking to completely merge with paramatma, leaving no sense of self. The dangerous consequences of flouting social norms are likened to the difficulties that every true spiritual seeker has had to face. There is a tacit acceptance of human failings such as adultery, gambling, drunkenness, that even devtas may suffer from. It is also believed that a privileged life wasted on sexual pleasures (sambhog) depletes the good karma bank and requires a fresh start on the ladder of karmic evolution.

Spiritual and other explanations and reasons for this treatment of adultery notwithstanding, there are several literary references to extra-marital love as a joyous addiction. Sanskrit scholar J. Moussaief Masson[17] writes, 'Contrary to all the law books and ethical treatises in Sanskrit, the love poetry rarely, as here, praises the quality of faithfulness. Most love poems in Sanskrit literature are about illicit love.' The pleasure of adultery is described by a poet as follows:[18]

...but who in this world can
fill one with joy
like another man's wife
loving with naked breast[19]

16. Section 497, Indian Penal Code

17. W.S. Merwin and J. Moussaief Masson, *Sanskrit Love Poetry*, p. 30

18. Translated from Krsnakavi's *Tarasasankam*

19. *Ibid* p. 169

A bold mother tells her daughter not to cry about marrying an old man because the village is beautiful and there is a temple hidden in an arbour visited by youthful boys. *The stigma of chastity, has never touched our family with blessings from gods, And Brahmins, Until this day.*[20]

All that is very well, as long as one remembers that stories of such licentiousness were limited to poetry and literature and about the lives of the kings and queens. Folklore and epics are full of stories of devtas committing adultery because, believed the ordinary folk, they had earned these pleasures on account of their past good karmas. The common man is counselled restraint and warned that the consequences of transgressions will invite serious punishment, but simultaneously, the *Kamasutra* gives advice on how not to get caught. In any case, even for these powerful persons, the consequences of being caught were serious. Indra, as the first adulterer, was cursed by several rishis at various times for fornicating with their wives. The modern-day equivalent of the heroes of folklore are the very rich and powerful, cine stars and politicians, whose promiscuity is indulged by the middle class as something that is only for 'badey log' and not for the aam admi who carries the social burden of maintaining morality.

Licentiousness of the bold and beautiful notwithstanding, any man reacts severely to his wife's adultery because therein lies the issue of proprietorship over the womb. The rationale for the origin of the law of adultery that punished only the wife's lover was to ensure paternal certainty: birth control and DNA tests should eliminate that problem. Yet, chastity remains a womanly virtue because men continue to have a sense of proprietorial ownership over women, and her adultery makes a woman automatically a prostitute. Punishment could be financial abuse and removing her children. Punishment by village panchayats could range from ostracism to shaving of a woman's head[21] to even rape.[22] On the other hand, a man's marital infidelity is indulged, and even admired as an attractive trait, particularly amongst the rich and powerful. As Lord

20. E.D. Souza, M. Silgardo, 'These my words,' in *The Penguin Book of Indian Poetry*, p. 332

21. Across the globe, a woman was punished for sexual misconduct by stamping at the symbols of her sexuality. Traditionally hair represents sexuality hence 'good' women kept it tightly knotted and covered and only wanton women cut their hair or let it loose.

22. Vasudha Dhagamvar, 'Invasion of Criminal Law by Religion, Custom and Family Law' in *Economic and Political Weekly* 15, 13 April 2002

Goldsmith (father of Jemimah Khan, ex-wife of Pakistani cricketer-turned-politician, Imran Khan) famously said, 'when a man marries his mistress, there is a vacancy'.

Modern western intellectuals have also challenged the commandment against adultery, arguing that extra-marital affairs help a marriage by making the couple happier in other dimensions of their interaction—bringing up children, running a home and presenting a united social unit. In the 1800s, Dumas had noted: 'it takes two to make a marriage work: sometimes three'. But as in India, this licence and discussion was limited amongst the rich, who were above the constraints of middle-class morality.

Given the moral baggage around a woman's adultery, I was heartened to read the views of a sitting judge in the Mahila Court. Her comments viewed it with compassion. She empathizes with the lonely woman who seeks pleasure and companionship with a married man, but warns against it as impractical rather than as something morally abhorrent.[23]

~

Adultery as a ground for divorce is dealt with later. The criminal law aspect of adultery is now unique to India amongst the nations that call themselves secular and liberal.

First, let us see the strangeness of the law: it is a crime for a man to have sex with a married woman, but she is not to be punished under the IPC. The person who can call for a charge of adultery is the husband, and only the lover can be prosecuted, not the wife. The woman's lover who commits the crime of adulterating the conjugal bed—a euphemism for the womb. The punishment for a lover of a married woman is imprisonment up to five years, or a fine, or both.[24] A single woman, on the other hand, is not punished for having sex with a married man. Thus his adultery with a single woman has no serious consequences, except that it gives his wife grounds for a divorce—which she may not want to avail.

The gender bias of this law was challenged in the Supreme Court. The petitioner was a husband who wanted that the law find his adulterous wife as culpable as her paramour, because otherwise, he said, the law amounted to a licence to women to commit adultery. The court held that protection of wives from prosecution under criminal law did not amount to a licence to commit adultery.[25] In this case, the court was not called

23. Swarna Kanta Sharma, *Divorce: Don't Break After Break Up*, p. 90

24. See p. 382: Section 497 of the Indian Penal Code

25. Yusuf Abdul Aziz vs. the State of Bombay, AIR 1954 SC 321

to consider that the law was unequal in giving husbands the right to sue their wives' paramours, while the wives did not have a corresponding right against lovers that their husbands might take.

Thirty years later, the Court reaffirmed[26] this asymmetrical form of adultery as a criminal offence. The petitioner here was a woman who demanded the same right to proceed against her husband's lover for adultery. The court observed:

> '*Incidentally*, the demand of the petitioner that sexual relationship of a husband with an unmarried woman should also be comprehended within the definition of adultery is a crusade by a woman against a woman. If a paramour of a married woman can be guilty of adultery, why can an unmarried girl who has sexual relations with a married man not be guilty of adultery? That is the grievance of the petitioner'.[27] [emphasis mine]

This 'incidental' observation reiterates my earlier argument about patronizing male humour about 'crusading women', with no understanding that women too have personal and political differences amongst themselves, just as men do.

After pointing out what they thought was the argument of a schizoid woman in intellectual disarray, the fond avuncular bench made some quaint observations: 'It is commonly accepted that it is the man who is the seducer and not the women', it claimed.[28] It also commented:

> 'Mrs X's lawyer says women, both married and unmarried, have changed their lifestyles over the years and there are cases where they have wrecked the peace and happiness of other matrimonial homes. We hope this is not too right but, an under-inclusive definition is not necessarily discriminatory'.[29]

The judges rounded up their legal opinion with the advice: 'stability of marriages is not an ideal to be scorned',[30] but made no comment on why marriage is not similarly threatened when a married man has a love affair with a single woman.

---

26. Smt. Sowmithri Vishnu vs. Union of India & Anr, 1985 AIR 1618

27. *Ibid*, para 9

28. *Ibid*, para 7

29. *Ibid*, para 9

30. *Ibid*, para 12

The lawyer would have been able to make a better gendered argument if she had brought the court's attention to the second portion of Section 497 of the Indian Penal Code. This allows for a wife's adultery with the consent of the husband. Given the reality of women's social position, it is quite likely that a husband would 'give' his wife for monetary advantage. Recently a magistrate's court disbelieved a woman's plea of being forced into prostitution saying the plea was proffered 'in order to hide her illicit relations with her paramour'. The sessions court reviewing the order in appeal was 'disappointed' with this 'complete disconnect from a harsh social reality'.[31]

I have moved the discussion to a level deeper than the imbalance in the adultery law. It is really about the husband's ownership of his wife. In Hardy's beautifully sad novel,[32] the Mayor of Casterbridge repented having auctioned his wife for the price of a drink. I have no equivalent Indian story, except for the following horrific one that I gathered from Pratiksha Baxi's book on rape: In 1957, a few lawyers gathered for post-dinner entertainment and commanded the cook to deliver his nineteen-year-old wife for their sexual pleasure.[33] She died. Baxi found no reported outcome of the case, but one of the arguments of the defence lawyers was that their clients had the consent of the dead woman's husband and so the act did not amount to rape.[34]

I have brought in what should be a straightforward case of rape in this section on adultery, only to highlight the defence of the main accused, himself an additional public prosecutor for the state. The views of the legal fraternity on gender issues have already been dealt with in the previous chapter.

---

31. 'Man forces wife into 'relationship', magistrate denies relief, before court steps in' in *The Indian Express* 13 February, 2012.

32. Thomas Hardy, *The Mayor of Casterbridge*

33. Though the outcome of the case is unknown, the details of the cases pertaining to the rejection of bail and definition of consent can be found in the bail case: Rao Harnarain Singh Sheoji Singh and Ors. vs. the State, AIR 1958 P&H 123

34. Pratiksha Baxi, *Public Secrets of Law: Rape Trials in India*; See also newspaper reports of men forcing their wives into prostitution: 'Mumbai man rapes wife forces her into prostitution' on NDTV, 26 March 2011; 'Husband arrested for pushing wife into prostitution' in *DNA*, 12 January 2013; 'Man held for forcing wife into prostitution' in *The Times of India*, 22 August 2013.

The Implacable Assertion

A wife had fled her marital home one night to save herself from continual, intense, and finally intolerable violence. Her husband did not allow her to take their two small boys with her. He filed a petition for restitution of conjugal rights.[35] She was advised to hoist the husband on the petard of his own petition and go back into the house, even if only to leave again—but this time with the children. It was very unlikely that he would be violent after having started legal proceedings, and protection orders within the marital home could be obtained. She refused, saying she was very scared and that her family-in-law would have no compunction in getting her killed. This is small-town feudal India, she said, and the police will not help me, given my husband's influence.

~

Till 1923, the method of enforcing a decree of restitution of conjugal rights was the same as enforcing a money decree or court injunction—either imprisonment or attachment of property or both. In that year, the law was amended to attachment of property as the only method of enforcing a decree of restitution of conjugal rights.[36]

Traditional Hindu law had no provision of restitution of conjugal rights. It was imported from English law and one of the earliest reported cases is that of Rukhmabai in 1884.[37] Rukhmabai inherited vast wealth from her father. Her widowed mother remarried one Dr Sakha Ram Arjun. When Rukhmabai was still a child, Dr Arjun arranged her marriage with his own cousin, Dadaji Bhikaji, but he did not allow an early consummation. When Rukhmabai was about eighteen, Dadaji, through a lawyer's notice, called for satisfaction of his conjugal rights. By then, Rukhmabai had evolved beyond Dadaji's intellectual and cultural capabilities into a vibrant and educated woman who would not submit to his crude demand. She wrote on her life situation and her marriage in *The Times of India*:

> 'I am one of those unfortunate Hindu women whose hard lot it is to suffer the un-nameable miseries entailed by the custom of early marriage. This wicked practice has destroyed the happiness of my life. It comes between me and the thing which I prize above all others—study and mental

---

35. See p. 364: Section 9 of the Hindu Marriage Act, 1955

36. Code of Civil Procedure, Amendment Act 29 of 1923; See also: Inderjit Kaur v. Rajinder Singh, 18(1980)DLT197

37. S. Chandra, *Enslaved Daughters: Colonialism, Law and Women's Rights*; See also Dadaji Bhikaji vs. Rukhmabai, (1885) ILR 9 Bom 529

> cultivation. Without the least fault of mine I am doomed to seclusion; every aspiration of mine to rise above my ignorant sisters is looked down upon with suspicion and is interpreted in the most uncharitable manner.'

Her lawyers argued that as Rukhmabai was not the age of discretion when she married, so she could repudiate it as an adult. This argument was radical for that time and became the law later to deal with the problem of child marriage.[38] They also argued that such a suit could not be maintained under classical Hindu law. They also cited a US precedent that had done away with restitution of conjugal rights. In any case, they said, a legal action for restitution was possible only to restore to a state that existed earlier. Rukhmabai had never been in a conjugal relationship and thus there was nothing to restore. There was no law that could insist upon commencement of cohabitation.

Judge Pinhey met Rukhmabai and wrote:

> 'She is a most intellectual person, as educated as an English lady, while this man a little better than a coolie. It is no secret that the defendant (Rukhmabai) is a writer of some eminence; and it is altogether revolting to one's sense of decency to think that she should give up her person to such a man as this... It seems to be that it would be barbarous, a cruel, a revolting thing to do to compel a young lady under those circumstances to go to a man whom she dislikes, in order that he may cohabit with her against her will.'

While *The Times of India* called him a Daniel to judgment, saying:[39]

> 'With the use of a little firmness and common sense Mr Justice Pinhey has, in the course of a morning's work, probably done more for the amelioration of the wretched condition of Indian Womanhood than has yet ever been accomplished'

Hindu conservatives worried about the ruling as a challenge to Hindu culture. But their real worry was the subservience of women as part of Hindu culture. The newspaper *Native Opinion* worried about the problem of westernization: 'Any Hindu Wife could now any day refuse to accompany her husband only because she did not like him.' There was no acknowledgement that legal action to force cohabitation was not a part of Hindu culture either.

38. See p. 383: Section 3 of the Prohibition of Child Marriage Act, 2006

39. S. Chandra, *Enslaved Daughters: Colonialism, Law and Women's Rights*; See also Dadaji Bhikaji vs. Rukhmabai, (1885) ILR 9 Bom 529

Dadaji appealed. Justice Melvill of the appeal court held that the courts had 'no discretion in the matter'. He ruled that the distinction between no consummation and restitution of consummation was a semantic exercise since child marriages were legal in this country. The only discretion the courts could exercise, said Judge Melville, was to refrain from ordering an infant wife to join her husband, but since Rukhmabai was a child no longer, she must join her husband.

Rukhmabai reflected, 'The Hindus are now fully assured that under no circumstances can the British government act adversely to the Hindu law.' She faced imprisonment for her refusal to abide by the court decree, but the matter was eventually settled with Dadaji receiving money.

~

When the Hindu Code Bill was debated in 1954, the restitution provision was retained. The Hindu law expert, J.D.M. Derrett, advised that the law of restitution of conjugal rights was relevant in the Indian culture of arranged marriages, since it allowed for a period for reconciliation.[40]

In 1983, the Andhra High Court considered and rejected this opinion.[41] In a well-written, sensitive and progressive opinion, Justice Choudhary ruled that the method of enforcing compliance of a decree for restitution of conjugal rights detailed in the Civil Procedure Code was the same as for the specific performance of a contract and pointed out the problems with this in a matrimonial context:

> 'to call for a party to do something that they were obliged to do in a binding contract and not just a gratuitous promise...but it is difficult to believe that the goal of fostering mutuality and trust in a marriage and of strengthening the marital relationship and the marriage institution, will be achieved by giving the husband a veto power exercisable for any reason whatsoever or for no reason at all.'[42]

As to Derrett's advice, that the restitution remedy was good for India, the court said,

> 'With respect I am unable to agree with this recommendation. Firstly, Derrett did not examine the matter from the constitutional point of view of right to privacy guaranteed by Article 21of the Constitution. Restitution of conjugal rights is an instance of punishing a criminal without a victim.

40. J.D.M. Derrett, *Introduction to Modern Hindu Law*, p. 308

41. T. Sareetha vs. T. Venkata Subbaiah, AIR 1983 AP 356

42. Missouri vs. Danforth (1976-49 L Ed 2d 788)

> Secondly, his remedy of restitution of conjugal rights is not only excessive but is also inappropriate.'

It then proceeded to observe that restitution of conjugal rights included a right to intercourse:

> 'There can be no doubt that a decree of restitution of conjugal rights thus enforced offends the inviolability of the body and the mind subjected to the decree and offends the integrity of such a person and invades the marital privacy and domestic intimacies of such a person... The ancient Hindu system of Matrimonial law never recognized this institution of conjugal rights although it fully upheld the duty of the wife to surrender to her husband. In other words, the ancient Hindu law treated the duty of the Hindu wife to abide by her husband only as an imperfect obligation incapable of being enforced against her will. It left the choice entirely to the free will of the wife.'

The court observed that after the British occupation, Indian legal positions were drastically altered and the British courts thoughtlessly imported restitution of conjugal rights into India. In a passionate recognition of a woman's agency over her body and right to privacy, the Court held that:

> 'the origin of this uncivilized remedy in our ancient country is only recent and is wholly illegitimate...I therefore hold that there are no overwhelming state interests to justify the subordination of the valuable right to privacy to any state interests.'[43]

The Delhi High Court, ruling on another case,[44] was scathing in its criticism of the Andhra judgment, saying, 'In a sensitive space which is at once most intimate and delicate, the introduction of the cold principles of constitutional law will have the effect of weakening the marriage bond.'

The Delhi judgment ordered the wife to return to her marital home, even whilst acknowledging that sexual intercourse could not be enforced by order of court. The good judge seems to have ignored that the dictionary meaning of the word 'conjugal' used in the statute, includes sexual intercourse. He preferred instead to use the more ambiguous and asexual 'consortium', defining it as:

> '(10) Consortium means "companionship, love, affection, comfort, mutual services, sexual intercourse. All these belong to the married state. Taken

---

43. T. Sareetha vs. T. Venkata Subbaiah, AIR 1983 AP 356, para 30

44. Harvinder Kaur vs. Harmander Singh Choudhry, AIR 1984 Delhi 66. See also: Sudha Gupta vs. Harprasad Gupta, MANU/DE/2750/2016

> together they make up consortium." Consortium has been defined as "a partnership or association"; but in the matrimonial sense it implies much more than these rather cold words suggest. It involves a sharing of two lives, a sharing of joys and sorrows of each party, of their successes and disappointments. In its fullest sense it implies a companionship between each of them, entertainment of mutual friends, sexual intercourse, all those elements which, when combined justify the old common law dictum that a man and his wife are one person.'

The judge does not tell us how to ensure that his order to return the wife to the marital home would keep her safe from being forced on to the marital bed.

He seems to have drawn comfort from the line of reasoning that, if the wife did not comply with the order to return to the marital home, the husband could file for divorce. On the other hand, if the husband sought to enforce her return by asserting the legal remedy of attachment of her property, the judge seemed to be relying on the fact that such an order of attachment was dependent upon judicial discretion. Yet, in an age of systemic misogyny, how could he be certain that the discretion would be exercised in her favour? After all, the law is clear and the statute has to be complied with, as the judge himself says.

This approach of leaving too much to chance as far as the welfare of the wife is concerned precisely illustrates my point about the insidious nature of patriarchy. Despite the principles of equality learned in law school and perhaps even believed in, the woman's insistence on leaving her marriage is viewed as morally abhorrent.

The conflict between patriarchy and gender equality that emerged in the Rukhmabai case remained unresolved a hundred years later. No middle path emerged between the extremes of Judge Pinhey and Judge Melville in 1884. In 1983, the Andhra High Court was in tandem with Judge Pinhey and the Delhi High Court with Judge Melville.

In Saroj Rani's case, the Supreme Court sealed the conservative view by agreeing with the Delhi High Court. It lost a valuable opportunity to comment on the manipulation of the law by the dominant partner in the marriage.[45] The court had to consider the misuse of Section 13 (1A) (ii) of the Hindu Marriage Act, the law wherein a divorce may be granted if a decree for restitution of conjugal rights is not complied with and cohabitation is not resumed within one year.[46] Saroj Rani filed for

45. Smt. Saroj Rani vs. Sudarshan Kumar Chadha, AIR 1984 SC 1562

46. See p. 365: Section 13(1A)(ii) of the Hindu Marriage Act, 1955.

restitution of conjugal rights in the trial court. Her husband Sudarshan appeared in court and told the judge that his wife's petition should be allowed and he was willing to resume cohabitation. A consent decree was accordingly passed.

Subsequent events reveal that the husband never had any intention of honouring the consent decree. He filed for divorce a year later, saying cohabitation had not been resumed. The trial court saw through this ploy and dismissed the husband's petition saying that the husband could not take advantage of his lack of good intentions and could not be rewarded for his duplicitous conduct in consenting in court to do something that he never had any intention of doing.

The High Court disagreed and said that intention could not bypass the clear mandate that if there is no cohabitation after the passing of a decree for restitution of conjugal rights, a divorce must follow.[47] The Supreme Court agreed with the High Court. It made no comment on the blatant misuse of this law by a wily husband or even on the issue of restitution being repugnant to the idea of modern civilization. In 2013, the Supreme Court affirmed this position as good law.[48]

Restitution of conjugal rights remains a primitive law in the statute book, used mostly by men who are badly advised to ask for restitution to preempt any action that the wife may file, once out of the house. As a legal strategy, it seems to insult the intelligence of the court. *Main rakhna chahata hoon*, he will say, insincerity oozing from every pore of his poker face. We have not even got to the era where he will say, *main iskey saath rehna chahata hoon.*

By upholding the provision, the courts have denied a woman's agency over her body. And that returns us to the topic of marital rape. The problem is this inability to perceive and respect a woman as a separate, equal person and body. Two-thirds of the world has made marital rape a criminal offence. The Verma Commission Report recommends its criminalization. But, Parliament is reluctant, because it claims that

---

47. See p. 367: Section 23(1)(a) of the Hindu Marriage Act, 1956

48. Kollam Chandra Sekhar vs. Kollam Padma Latha, 2013(11)SCALE617: In this case the restitution of conjugal rights was allowed where the wife was suffering from schizophrenia and the court held that 'When schizophrenia is not of such a serious nature and particularly when it is treatable, it cannot be a ground for divorce under Section 13(1)(iii) of the Act' and held that the respondent had no right to withdraw from her society and demand divorce and that she was entitled to restitution of conjugal rights.

marriage is 'sacred', without clarifying what remains sacred when rape is institutionalized.[49]

Another argument against criminalization of marital rape is that it is difficult to prove, unlike rape by a stranger. The argument is specious, because difficulty in proving them has not deterred the legislature from bringing several other offences into the statute books as criminal offenses.

The feudal hierarchy may be changing with the empowerment of different castes and classes, but the control of a man even at the bottom of the social heap over 'his' woman remains the same. The depth of this mindless indoctrination was revealed to me when a respectable and articulate designated senior lawyer of the Supreme Court said, during a television debate on the issue: 'If marital rape is brought under the ambit of law, then you are inviting the police and law into the bedroom. *Every time a man is thinking of having sex, he will think whether this is consensual or not.*'[50] [emphasis mine] This obtuseness about the matter makes good McKinnon's (many may say extreme) opinion that in patriarchy, all sex is about control, leaving women no real choice, since her power in the patriarchy is her desirability and she is conditioned to receptivity. Thus, McKinnon says, all sex in a patriarchy amounts to rape and 'in marital rape cases, courts look to even greater atrocities than usual to undermine their assumption that if sex happened, she wanted it'.[51]

As mentioned earlier, since the courts find absence of sex as amounting to cruelty, a woman may feel constrained to have obligatory sex to protect marriage. Such reluctant/resigned sex would not amount to rape for the purposes of criminal law, notwithstanding McKinnon's very powerful perception on the matter. But flouting a clear unequivocal 'No!' to assert a conjugal 'right' must be seen by law to be marital rape if women are to be respected in the matrimonial home.

When a minister says that culturally India is not ready for laws on marital rape, she establishes that culturally, once married, an Indian woman gives up her right to sexual ownership of her body. Her view is disappointing in its opaque obtuseness, given her claimed experience of being treated as a non-person in a powerful family. Her culture argument nourishes a view that demeans women. She does not say what has she

49. Rajyasree Sen, 'Maneka Gandhi tells us marital rape isn't rape after all' in *LiveMint*, 14 March 2016.

50. 'Marriage in India is "Sacred", so Marital Rape Doesn't Apply: Govt' on *The Quint*, 30 April 2015.

51. Catherine A. Mckinnon, *Toward a Feminist Theory of the State*, p. 176

done or what she proposes to do to contribute to changing this 'culture', given her experience and leadership position. In fact, she does not even comment on whether it should change.

To make 'culture' and 'conservative' societies the reason not to criminalize marital rape is to send the message that not only does the law allow for marital rape but, in fact, the state encourages it. It is also a missed opportunity to educate a growing new generation in India, which, we hope, will have a modern secular culture that treats women as equal to men.

However, for anyone extolling the haloed virtues of 'Indian culture' and 'sanskriti', this is a good point to stop and rearticulate their argument.

'Open Marriage'

Open marriages are certainly not 'sanskriti' according to the traditionalists, but need to be discussed because they may be uncomfortably close to a subtextual reality. Adultery as an offence is as old as marriage, regardless of its illicitness and the fear of dreadful punishments. Another way to look at it may be that extra-marital sex is condoned by a spouse so that the everyday working of the marriage is not undermined.

Many women and men have come to see me to say that they don't want a divorce, but do want the freedom to explore their sexuality outside marriage. Other men and women come to me outraged at the immorality of their partners asking for this sexual license. What are the parameters of any sexual freedom, if possible, within marriage?

In 1927, this was the subject of a book called *The Companionate Marriage*[52] by Judge Lindsey of the family division and juvenile court in Denver, USA. He argued that the advent of birth control calls for a change in marriage norms and its dynamics to allow for a 'companionate marriage'. He recommended that couples enter into an agreement to refrain from having children till they were certain of their relationship. If they were incompatible during the trial period, they should agree to a divorce by mutual consent, but once the children arrived, divorce should not be allowed except in the most extreme circumstances.

Judge Lindsey did not suggest an open marriage, but a contract for easy divorce if there were no children. Even so, he was hounded and vilified by right-wing fundamentalists and lesser conservatives for his 'immoral' views, and was eventually forced to resign.

52. Ben B. Lindsey, Wainwright Evans, *The Companionate Marriage*

Fifty years later, America, experimenting with birth control, drugs and sexual liberalism enthusiastically received the idea of an 'open marriage'[53] propounded in a book by that name.

The term has come to be misunderstood. The authors did not advise promiscuity, but that a truly fulfilling life within marriage was possible only when the couple had a chance to explore and fulfill various parts of their individual personas. To do this, free private time was necessary. This personal growth, the authors said, is essential for good health. It may require social interactions as individuals rather than as a couple. Such an open marriage strengthened the relationship of the married couple.

Though the philosophy was not sex-centered, sexual and other possibilities could not be ruled out. The book opposes the closed marriage calling it a 'threesome' of love, sex and jealousy which suffocates and kills the partners.[54] Thus, the authors did make a covert case for sexual openness in their argument that exclusive sex within a marriage limited the marriage to a contract for sex, which surely was not the reality of a marriage.

The bottom line, for me, from this discussion is that adultery is tumultuous in its pain, pleasure, joy and grief, and the couples that survive the emotional storms of jealousy and infidelity seem to drift quite charmingly into the calm harbours of companionable old age.

Conclusion

Should adultery be a criminal offence? Unequivocally not!

The first reason for this is the moral argument. To be forced to stay in a marriage for fear of criminal consequences smells of a totalitarian society, and not of the modern liberal tenets that inform our Constitution. The freedom to search for and pursue your happiness includes the right to undo mistakes in choice of partner. Whether you do that by demanding a divorce, or by maintaining a secret intimate life, or an intimacy outside via 'open' marriage is an individual decision, based on your priorities and commitments. The pain and disturbance that the perpetrator of this marital wrong has to live with is punishment enough.

The second reason is legal. The present law is gender-biased and subconsciously reinforces patriarchal principles that are inherently unconstitutional. It is abhorrent that a married man has the right to have

53. N.O. Neil & G.O. Neil, *Open Marriage*

54. *Ibid* p. 257

proprietary control over his wife while there is no deterrent to his engaging in a romantic relationship with an unmarried woman.

Hindu lore respected the power of sex and sought to regulate it as part of an ordered life. The sexual and the sensual was to be explored by the householder as an important part of a life well lived. According to Puranic lore and most religious cultures in India, one must pass the neighbourhood of sex on the road to self-realization.

While moderation and ethical sexual conduct is the ideal path for the virtuous, it is equally true that the sexual impulse cannot be ordered and regulated; its intensity is likened to fever, burning, obsession, wasting away. This conflict has fuelled the power of sex to mythical proportions. The *Kamasutra* and Khajuraho are celebrations of the pleasure of sex, which has the power to elevate sensation to mystical levels of experience.

Today, the upper class enjoys the freedom to retain this cultural memory, but the middle class is gripped by a repressive silence that surrounds sex. The contrast is apparent when you consider that while the writings of Wendy Doniger are disapproved of as being too sexually absorbed, a television talk show has the host asking two lady guests which other women they would like to 'experiment' with.

If sex is one of the barometers of the health of a marriage, society's response to it is a measure of its health as well. In India today, a diagnosis of sickness is returned each day, with stories of rape, sex-related murders, acid attacks and child sexual abuse crawling out of the newspapers like maggots from carrion.

4. THE FAULT GROUNDS FOR DIVORCE

The advent of the right to file for divorce in 1956 did not mean that it was going to be easy to get.[1] Divorce was still based on the fault theory. The petitioner for divorce had to establish that s/he was not at fault in the marriage and that the fault lay with the respondent. The defence, in turn, had to establish that the respondent was blameless and could include that the petitioner was in fact taking advantage of his/her own wrong by filing for the divorce. An obvious example of such a defence is that a petition for divorce on the ground of desertion should be dismissed if it is found that the respondent was forced to flee the marriage due to the cruel conduct of the petitioner.

~

Going back to my Mamaji's story—he was quite certain that he did not want to marry Kulwant Kaur. He was not attracted to her. These were things that could not be discussed with his formal and severe father who would have found this to be foolish talk. So he wrote to his uncle,[2] pleading for help to break the engagement.

Mamaji was a general when he met M. She was married to a junior officer with whom she had two children. When their love affair began, Mamaji resigned from the army since he had violated the rule 'thou shalt not steal the affections of the wife of a brother officer'. The brother officer, Colonel X, was also a gentleman like Mamaji and never bore him a grudge. It was M's decision to leavc her husband and be with Mamaji.

In 2009, when Mamaji was dying of cancer; Colonel X came to see him with his very beautiful second wife, S. Charmed by the general's gallant and gentle courtesy, she smiled at her husband, 'I understand how the General ran off with your wife.' Our silence erupted into a forced false laugh. We knew, as did Mamaji, that he would not survive the cancer. He was beaten again but, as when he lost his divorce case, he took it bravely on the chin.

Kulwant Kaur remained a wife. She never claimed maintenance from him. She was better educated than he, with a fine foreign education. As far as I know, she spent her life alone and became a well-respected

---

1. The original act allowed divorce on the limited grounds of living in adultery, conversion to another religion, renunciation of the world, incurable leprosy or venereal disease, and if the person hasn't been heard of as alive for seven years.

2. B.S. Mann, Member of Parliament; See also Ch. 10: Uniform Civil Code, p. 286, 291

academic. Why did Kulwant Kaur resist Mamaji's divorce petition? Anger, I think, also bitterness and perhaps fear of the stigma attached to being a 'divorcee'. Mutual dealings between her family and ours continue to be impeccable in protocol. Both families attend major events in the other family with dignified cordiality. Her two brothers attended Mamaji's cremation.

The fault theory rendered Mamaji's life incomplete and I do not know that it served Kulwant Kaur any better.[3] 'Hell hath no fury like a woman scorned', will smile some men smugly upon hearing such stories. The full text from which the popular phrase about a woman's fury is extracted from begins with: 'Heaven has no rage like love to hatred turned'.[4] The reality is that some men resist divorce for the same reasons—disbelief, anger and denial that his wife would dare leave him—and either gender can hate with the passion of love.

~

The retention of the fault theory and the limited grounds available for divorce in 1956 show the social anxiety of the time to preserve the institution of marriage. The amendments of 1976 widened the grounds for divorce,[5] but it was not easy (and still is not). The misery of the couple is compounded by the physical, emotional and financial wrangle of the legal process, making many question the wisdom of filing for divorce in the first place.

This chapter will lay out the grounds for divorce recognized currently in Indian law—adultery, bigamy, cruelty, desertion, mental disorder and fraud. The latter is grounds for annulling a marriage, not for divorce per se, though it can help to make a case for it.

ADULTERY

Adultery as a marital fault is a ground for divorce in civil law and either party can file against the other on this ground. Thus, the gender bias in adultery as a criminal offence does not exist in civil law.[6] Even so, the

3. This case was filed just a few years after the Hindu Marriage Act of 1956 that made possible a judicial separation but not a divorce. Legal niceties apart, as far as my uncle was concerned, he had filed for divorce.

4. William Congreve, *The Mourning Bride*

5. Marriage Laws (Amendment) Act, 1976

6. The basis for adultery as a criminal offence has a gendered aspect, which has been discussed in Ch. 3: Love, Sex and Marriage, pp. 66-7, 69-71

remedy is not easily available. The adulterer may actually want the other party to file for divorce and use this as a way to be free of a cumbersome marriage—but the betrayed spouse may not want to make it easy for the adulterer and so will not file for divorce. The adulterer, in any case, cannot file because it would amount to taking advantage of his/her own wrong.

Why then are adultery petitions fought so fiercely? The answer may lie in the financial compensation awarded for marital fault. A husband might resist an adultery petition because he fears that he will have to pay a huge compensation.[7] A wife's claim for alimony will suffer if she is found to be in an adulterous relationship.[8] For her, the answer may also lie in the fear of an adverse ruling on the custody of children. She might have reasonable cause to fear that a court might find her to be of 'loose morals' and rule that her child must not be exposed to her. Even if the court does not pass such a judgment, the husband may not want his child to grow up in the house of 'the other man', and so her safest course of action is not to admit to adultery.

Even under UK law, divorce on the ground of adultery was harder to get for women than men. This can be seen from the Matrimonial Causes Act 1857, which provided that divorce could be obtained only by a private Act of Parliament, effectively reserving it only for the rich, at a time when women had no legal right to their own property. In addition, a wife's single act of adultery gave enough cause to a husband for divorce, but adultery could form the basis for the wife's divorce petition only if it occurred along with incest, bigamy, cruelty or two years of desertion.

The Hindu Marriage Act 1955, following the UK law to some extent, did not allow a woman to divorce her husband if he was found to have committed a single act of adultery. For adultery to be a marital fault, he had to be 'living in adultery', meaning thereby a habitual and continuous course of conduct. Only after the amendment in 1976, did a proven isolated act of adultery become cause for either party to obtain a divorce.[9]

The standard of proof of adultery is only circumstantial and is premised on evident inclination and opportunity, because it is very difficult for

7. See Ch. 6: Maintenance and Alimony

8. See Ch. 6: Maintenance and Alimony, p. 192, for the relevance of conduct in maintenance claims.

9. See p. 365: Section 13 of the Hindu Marriage Act, 1955, pre and post the Marriage Laws (Amendment) Act, 1976

obvious reasons to prove the actual act of intercourse that constitutes adultery.[10]

Extramarital Sex During Divorce Proceedings

An important question that arises, considering that divorces take years to come through: what is the legal consequence of 'seeing' someone else once divorce proceedings have been filed? Given that the courts recognize the importance of sex, do they expect litigants to be celibate while they take years to resolve their lives?

~

Consider the case below:

W, a very attractive, vivacious girl from a premier public school had a traditionally arranged marriage with a person from the same caste and community. Horrendous abuse drove W away and out of the marriage. She filed for divorce on the ground of cruelty. Her husband also filed for divorce, but on the ground of adultery.

He had not been able to make out a case for opportunity and association to prove such adultery while they were living together. He claimed that he had heard her with another man while he was in the neighbouring room, and other such egregious averments that invited no confidence. The husband claimed custody of their daughter saying she needed to be protected from her mother's immoral values.

I advised W to concede the divorce, and fight for custody on the grounds that an adulterous woman need not be an unfit mother. However, she was nervous about risking anything that might jeopardize her access to her child. I then told her that if she wanted the divorce quickly, we could settle the matter by offering to give up financial claims and only seek custody. She agreed. The husband refused, because he said he wanted his daughter. The daughter by now had become utterly hostile to the father as she was aware that he was getting W followed, and had filed frivolous and false cases against her to instigate police investigation.

During the course of this litigation (over more than five years!) W met someone else. She worried that she was not getting any younger and wanted to have another child. Another client of mine had died (the police had closed the case as suicide) just a few months before W asked me this question. I was haunted by the philosophical issue of a protracted

10. Earnest John White vs. Mrs Kathleen Olive White & Ors., AIR 1958 SC 441; Dr (Mrs) Kiran Robinson vs. Ajeet Malcolm Robinson and Ors., AIR 2003 Delhi 44

divorce having the power not just to kill the quality of a person's life, but to kill life itself. I could say nothing other than that life is too transient and precious to allow a case to influence what she really wanted to do, provided her conscience was clear. It was a conversation of platitudes and we left it at that.

In W's case, eventually an exhausted judge told the husband that she thought absolutely nothing of him. She saw nothing in his case. His conduct amounted to cruelty and she would thus allow W's petition. He could not bear another loss of face to a woman and finally agreed to a divorce by mutual consent with no ancillary relief to either side with regard to the custody or finances.

What about platonic relationships?

In another divorce case, I acted for a woman who was always accompanied by a man when she visited me. I knew that their relationship would be bandied about and the 'other man' could face the threat of a criminal prosecution.

In my pleadings I stated at the outset that she drew a lot of emotional succour from this man whose presence in her life had empowered her to file for divorce from an abusive marriage. It was a risk that I regretted when the other side claimed the plea implied an illicit relationship since it needed to be mentioned at all. Yet, I argued that non-sexual friendships with the opposite sex need not necessarily be inappropriately close—the office friend, or a movie companion, for example. The judges were sceptical and in a non-verbal smiling way told me I was too forward for them. I lost sleep over the risk I had taken.

Then happened one of those about-turns that lift doom and gloom and make life fun for a while at least. My client managed to access the Facebook page of a woman whose relationship status claimed that she was married to my client's husband. Our arguments about his bigamy moved the focus away from my client's platonic relationship and the matter eventually settled.

~

In the case I have mentioned above, we were saved by the Internet, but many spouses are threatened by this technology, which allows for a complex virtual intimacy. In fact, the possibilities of the Internet make a simple straightforward extra-marital affair sound quite charming in an old-fashioned way. Virtual intimacy that obviously cannot constitute adultery may still be deemed 'inappropriate' if it could harm the harmony of an intimate life. Pornography, too, is feared as polluting our 'pure' culture and many divorce petitions cite addiction to pornographic sites as a symptom of depravity. Though not illegal, it is certainly not something to be done at home, they say, despite instances of Members of Parliament being caught watching porn on their mobile phones in the House. In the divorce petition, these virtual matters could be dealt with as cruelty if the time spent on the internet is disproportionately high and affects normal life, which is certainly both possible and probable.

BIGAMY

Bigamy was an offence under Christian law, as Christian scriptural authority saw marriage as irrevocably monogamous: 'So they are no longer two, but one flesh. Therefore, what God has joined together, man must not separate'. Divorce continued to be difficult and expensive under the independent Church of England even as late as the nineteenth century, leading a law lord to pronounce a judgment that is a masterly understatement of the anomalies of law. I quote it because it continues to be apposite in India, given our overburdened and close-to-breaking-point legal system:

> 'Prisoner at the bar, you have been convicted before me of (bigamy).
>
> ...Had you taken the other female to lie with you as your concubine you would never have been interfered with by the law. But your crime consists in having—to use your own language—preferred to make an honest woman of her.
>
> Another of your irrational excuses is that your wife had committed adultery... (but you did not take the legal remedy of divorce).
>
> I will tell you what the process is (for divorce). You ought first to have brought an action against your wife's seducer...that might have cost you money, and you say you are a poor working man, but that is not the fault of the law.
>
> You (should have gone with the verdict of adultery) and petitioned the House of Lords for a divorce. It would cost you perhaps five or six hundred pounds, and you do not seem to be worth as many pence. But it is the boast of the law that it is impartial, and makes no difference between the rich and the poor...so...you would have no reason to complain. ...you **might** [emphasis mine] obtain a divorce, which would enable you legally to do what you have thought proper to do without it.
>
> You have thus willfully rejected the (law) and it is my duty to pass

> upon you such sentence as I think your offence deserves...that you be imprisoned for one day; and inasmuch as the present assizes are three days old, the result is that you will be immediately discharged.'[11]

Jewish law is also monogamous[12] although it allows for divorce.[13] The rest of the world was steeped in polygamy, apart from some exceptions in matriarchal societies. Many prophets of the Old Testament had several wives,[14] a practice which was common in pre-Islamic Arab society as well.[15] Islamic law allows up to four wives.

Hindu law was polygamous without limit, until the introduction of monogamy with the Hindu Marriage Act 1956. Having said which, even during its polygamous phase, a second wife was allowed only if conditions, like barrenness and so on, justified taking another wife. Unsurprisingly, these conditions were often ignored by rich men who could afford to be polygamous.[16]

Parliamentary debates on the Hindu Code Bill exposed the reluctance of the parliamentarians to relinquish polygamy. The discussion on the number of wives was as intense as that on woman's property rights. Many were resentful of Muslims being left out of the reform umbrella. Dr S.P. Mookherjee opened his speech saying that there was everything praiseworthy about monogamy, but the government would never pass a separate law about it because it 'dare not touch the Muslim community'.[17] He said, 'So far as monogamy is concerned, I shall support it with one reservation. Make it applicable to all citizens of India.'

Pandit Thakur Das Bhargava supported bigamy through the custom of Kareva in Punjab, where a widow is married to the brother of her dead husband, saying, 'So the custom now is that even if the younger brother of the deceased has a wife living, he will have to marry the widow of his

11. R. vs. Hall, (1845) 1 Cox CC 241.

12. Although polygamy was allowed in ancient Jewish law, monogamy became legally binding on Ashkenazi Jews as early as 900 BCE, according to *The Oxford Dictionary of the Jewish Religion, Divorce*, p. 473

13. Adele Berlin, *The Oxford Dictionary of the Jewish Religion, Divorce*, p. 217

14. For example, Abraham and Moses.

15. Asaf A.A. Fyzee, *Outlines of Muhammadan Law*, p. 74

16. P.V. Kane, *History Of Dharmasastra* Vol II Part I, Chapter XI, p. 1281

17. Hindu Code Bill Debate available at http://www.ambedkar.org/ambcd/64B2.On%20the%20Hindu%20Code%20Bill.htm, See also: Christophe Jaffrelot, 'Nehru and the Hindu Code Bill' in *Outlook*, 8 August 2003.

elder brother and they live as husband and wife. This is practically a case of bigamy according to the Hindu Code...' While explaining the concept of the Kareva tradition, he said, 'the final result of this practice is that neither the property nor the woman goes out of the family and also the children from the previous husband are properly looked after.' He went on to argue, 'If we want to codify our usages and customs, I would like to point out that the most important of our customs is that we should not allow divorce. But we are going to give our women the liberty of divorce, because the Constitution and the sense of justice do not allow that women should lack this liberty. Go ahead and give them this right, but bigamy is an established custom. It has been in vogue for many centuries and it is prevalent in some sections of our society...'[18]

~

The Hindu Marriage Act, 1956[19] and the Special Marriage Act, 1954[20] protect persons from fraudulent marriages by requiring a disclosure that neither has a living spouse at the time of marriage. If one of the couple finds that there is in fact a prior living spouse s/he can seek a legal declaration that their marriage is bigamous and thus void. In most cases, the second spouse knows of the first marriage and so obviously does not file for their own marriage to be void. This is problematic, because it means that the second marriage is valid until a declaration is made about it being a nullity. The available remedy is for the first spouse: s/he can seek divorce on the ground of cruelty and move that the bigamous spouse be tried for the criminal offence of bigamy.[21]

However, this does not address the vulnerability of the first spouse who may not want a divorce and also does not want the other parent of his or her children to go to jail for bigamy. In such a case, the first spouse has no choice but to live with the problem of the second marriage.

Religious marriages that allow bigamy

For those married under the Special Marriage Act, the route to bypass difficult first wives was to have a religious ceremony in the eyes of society, which would be safe from prosecution for bigamy because the marriage

18. Hindu Code Bill debate available at http://www.ambedkar.org/ambcd/64B4.On%20the%20Hindu%20Code%20Bill.htm

19. See p. 364, 367: Section 11 and Section 17 of the Hindu Marriage Act, 1955

20. See p. 390: Section 44 of the Special Marriage Act, 1954

21. See p. 381, 382: Section 494 and 495 of the Indian Penal Code, 1860

rituals were not completed. If you have six pheras instead of seven, who is counting? Everyone is there for the party anyway. And the bigamous couple slip through the eye of the social needle: married twice but safe from legal prosecution.

The textbook case for such sham marriages is the Bhau Rao case.[22] He and his paramour performed the Gandharva form of marriage. The prosecution sought to prove bigamy by saying that as Gandharva marriages were customary in Bhau Rao's region and community, the second marriage was a valid ceremony and hence bigamous. The court found that though the custom did exist, Bhau Rao's ceremony was not performed with full customary rites because the bride's father did not join the foreheads of the bridal couple. So the second marriage was not a valid marriage in custom: ergo, there was no bigamy and the accused was acquitted.

One could make a vague guess at trying to understand this ruling by considering that male polygamy and rites for concubinage were legal till less than a decade before the Bhau Rao case. The husband's bigamy was just not viewed as a serious matter.

~

The second method to marry again without a divorce was to convert to a religion that allowed more than one wife: namely Islam. This route of conversion is not available to those married under the secular law of the Special Marriage Act,[23] wherein 'any other' second marriage also includes marriage under any other personal law. The freedom to marry without a divorce thus boiled down to be applicable only to Hindu men in Hindu marriages converting to Islam to marry again without divorcing their Hindu wives.

Here is a story: A man could not marry his lady friend because his wife refused to divorce him. The lady friend wanted that elusive something called permanence. He decided to publicly demonstrate his love for her by having a social ceremony of commitment (whatever that means!). Her parents (quite rightly) objected to this as inadequate. They wanted, as any sensible parent would, for their daughter to have a marriage with legal consequences of maintenance and inheritance.

At that time, the gossip vine buzzed with stories of celebrity conversions

---

22. Bhaurao Shankar Lokhande & Anr vs. State of Maharashtra, 1965 SCR (2) 837: a secret lovers ceremony of exchanging garlands.

23. See p. 390: Section 44 of the Special Marriage Act, 1954

to Islam. The conversions had nothing to do with religion but with the fact that Islam allowed four wives. Such colourable conversions became rampant, with many respectable cow- and idol-worshipping Hindu men claiming to have converted to an iconoclastic religion. The man also thought this was a good idea.

I advised this man that though he had a fundamental right to practice any religion, his conversion to Islam followed by a second marriage could be questioned as a blatantly dishonest way of bypassing monogamous Hindu law. He visited a mosque anyhow and recounted to me his conversation with the maulvi, who questioned him, saying, 'Islam is not trivial. It is magnificent and powerful and it believes in no God other than Allah. Are you sure you want to do this?' He said yes. The maulvi asked this question a few times and then asked him and the girlfriend to think again. They returned a few days later and were converted to Islam.

The maulvi did not ask the most relevant question: If there were no impediment to your second marriage, would you still convert to Islam?

~

The conversion to Islam route was common until the Sarla Mudgal case.[24] The Supreme Court's judgment on this case dealt with the matter of colourable conversions and declared them illegal.

The newspapers reported it in 1995, on the day my daughter was born. The first conversation I heard as I emerged from the anaesthesia was the doctors saying: 'The courts are tightening the noose around the necks of men. They can't get away with everything. This conversion to Islam to marry again is shameful and the Supreme Court has now said so by calling it bigamy.'

The court dealt with two things: a) It restated the earlier legal position that apostasy did not dissolve a previous marriage automatically,[25] and then b) proceeded to rule that if the apostate married under Islamic law, he could be prosecuted for bigamy.

Since the law was always that apostasy from Hinduism did not dissolve the Hindu marriage, there was never any point in a Hindu woman converting to marry again, because a Muslim woman could not have four husbands. It is only Muslim men who could have four wives. Even prior

24. Smt. Sarla Mudgal vs. Union of India and Others, AIR 1995 SC 1531

25. Budansa Rowther vs. Farma Bibi Air (1914) 26 MLJ 260; John Jiban Chandra Dutta vs. Abinash Chandra Sen, AIR1939 Cal 417; Andal Vaidyanathan vs. Abdul Allam Vaidya, (1946) 1 MLJ 402

to the Sarla Mudgal case, the law was that if the conversion of a Hindu man to Islam could be proven to be colourable, the Islamic marriage by the Hindu man would be bigamous.[26] The sincerity of the conversion could be tested, amongst other methods, by the length of time between the act of conversion and the subsequent marriage. The Sarla Mudgal judgment held that the second marriage made possible by conversion during the subsistence of the first must be held to be bigamous, even without going through the sincerity test.

Although the predicament of the judges is understandable, their judgment has been critiqued for not dealing with the obvious issue that the fundamental right to convert to any religion is rendered meaningless if it is not accompanied by the right to practice it to the fullest extent, which in Islamic law includes polygamy. Different opinions have ranged from Bhattacharjee[27] on the one hand, claiming it unconstitutional to not allow a man to embrace any religion and practice all aspects of it, to Dr Tahir Mehmood on the other, saying that the judgment is correct, as Islam cannot really be called polygamous because of the stringent conditions under which a man can marry again.[28]

The judges were quite clear that they wanted to prevent an easy recourse to bigamy through colourable conversations, which is why their mention of a 1965 Privy Council Judgment from Ceylon[29] without any further comment is strange. That case was on identical facts and the Privy Council concluded that the second marriage was not bigamous, since the pluralistic society of Ceylon allowed for many personal laws and its people had a right to convert to and embrace any religion in its entirety. Had the Privy Council judgment been of an era prior to India's Independence, the Supreme Court in 1995 would have been bound by it and thus would have to attend to it with greater care to distinguish and justify divergence from it. As it happens, the judges chose to ignore the judgment after mentioning it and so furthered no purpose in citing it in the first place.

The Sarla Mudgal case seems to have settled the problem of colourable conversions as none have been reported after it, except the story of a Hindu

---

26. In Re P. Nagesashayya (1988) Mat LR 123; B. Chandra Manikyamma vs. B. Sudarsana Rao alias Saleem Mohammed, 1988 CriLJ 1849.

27. A.M. Bhattacharjee, *Matrimonial Laws and the Constitution*, p. 94

28. See Ch. 10: Uniform Civil Code, p. 289, 300, 310

29. Attorney General Ceylon vs. Reid (1965 All ER 812)

woman lawyer who married an already-married Hindu politician, after they both converted to Islam. To me, this news was more startling than scandalous. How did a lawyer and a politician not know that this was illegal after the well-publicized Supreme Court ruling of 1995?

The Sarla Mudgal ruling helped a client of mine. Hindu H was married to Hindu W. They had two children and lived in an Islamic country. H converted to Islam and married a national of that country. When W learned of his duplicity, he offered her a financial settlement and bullied her into accepting it by obtaining a travel ban restraining their children from leaving the country. She and the children were effectively trapped. The husband then threatened to take the custody of the children, which he could have easily done under the law of that land. The matter was eventually settled only after the Sarla Mudgal precedent helped us to obtain a legal summons to prosecute him for bigamy.

Interestingly, recently the Delhi High Court has ruled that the apostasy of a Muslim woman would automatically dissolve her Muslim marriage.[30] The ruling rescued a woman from an abusive marriage; she had filed for divorce on many grounds under the Dissolution of Muslim Marriages Act and in addition pleaded that her apostasy automatically dissolved her marriage under uncodified Islamic law.

~

It is important to say something about the reasons for polygamy in Islamic marriages here because people who are suspicious of Islam use it as a strawman argument against the religion. Though polygamy allowed a man to have up to four wives, the caveat was that the man must ensure that no wife was discriminated against.[31] Furthermore, historically, women in pre-Islamic Middle Eastern society had been steadily and relentlessly devalued, as was the case in patriarchies around the world. They had no legal rights of maintenance, inheritance or consent to their marriages.[32] The Prophet was also a law reformer and gave women independent legal rights. He propounded marriage as a civil contract that could be terminated by the husband pronouncing 'talaq' thrice, although it was not to be pronounced casually. Triple talaq pronounced in one sitting is still not the approved form of divorce under Muslim law. Many communities within Islam practice the approved form of divorce—talaq al-sunna (revocable form of

30. Munavvar-ul-Islam v. Rishu Arora @ Rukhsar, 210(2014)DLT108

31. S.A. Kadar, *Muslim Law*, p. 29

32. Syed Ameer Ali, *Position Of Women In Islam: A Progressive View*, p. 55

divorce), which requires that each pronouncement be made during three consecutive periods of tuhr,[33] or that each pronouncement is followed by a 'cooling-off period' during which the divorce can be revoked. Under talaq-e-tafwid, the husband could delegate his right of divorce to his wife in the marriage contract. Women could also have the clause of khula or mubarat[34] in the marriage contract that gave them the right to ask for divorce.

~

It is difficult for lawyers, politicians and judges to preach about morality in marriages until there is a more efficient system that allows divorce and for people to settle their lives.

It remains unclear where the morality lies in any given case. If we go by religious rulings, the irony is that Islam practices polygamy up to four wives, but Islam also forbids sex outside marriage as haram. However, this does not hold up in law: the Supreme Court has noted that it is about time that women who live outside marriage have legal rights, along with their children.[35] Similarly, though a Hindu man had no limit to the number of wives he could have before 1956, now he must be monogamous—but he can still have any number of mistresses. Elsewhere, the same Supreme Court ruled recently that a woman cannot claim rights under the Protection of Women from Domestic Violence Act (PWDVA) if she knows that the man she is living with is in fact married.[36] This ruling ignores that the act itself makes no such qualification.

Here is a situation in the Hindu context: despite the hue and cry about the sanctity of marriage; despite the fact that bigamy is illegal; despite social perceptions that live-in relationships outside marriage are immoral, there was an interesting report of a court-sanctioned arrangement between a man and two women: A wife complained that her husband had brought his girlfriend into the matrimonial house. A Lok Adalat court recorded a settlement by which the man, his wife and girlfriend would all live together and the man must alternate fifteen days between the two

33. Period between two menstrual cycles, often referred to as period of purity.

34. The khula form of divorce usually gave the right to the wife to ask to be released from the marriage; it often included giving up the right of dower. Mubarat, on the other hand, is akin to the mutual consent divorce.

35. Uday Gupta vs. Aysha and Anr., 2014(5)SCALE358

36. Indra Sarma vs. V.K.V. Sarma, AIR 2014 SC 309

women.[37] The settlement even recorded that the man's bedroom was to be between those of the two women. Both women would have an equal share in his properties.

No sanctimonious lecture on morality and the purity of the sacred institution called marriage. No concern about children and how they will view this arrangement. No concern that such an agreement could be seen as against public policy under the Contract Act.[38] The resolution clearly favours the man and the arrangement does not disclose whether the wife or the girlfriend were told that this arrangement was not permissible in law. On the other hand, it is possible that they were counselled but thought that even shared male protection is better than nothing at all. For these Indian citizens who do not know and cannot access the law, it is an arrangement of practical security.

Given the confusion that exists between contradictory rulings by law courts, panchayats, khaps and insidious social pressure, politicians, judges and lawyers need to treat family law as a forum for social engineering, rather than settling cases as petty squabbles as the Lok Adalat above did. Till then, the reprehensibly duplicitous conduct and subterfuges that people resort to protect the 'other' relationships from censure by court will only increase.

CRUELTY

'Why do you want to practice criminal law?' asked my professor.

'To study the darkness of human nature,' was my cheeky, trying-to-be-clever answer.

'Ah!' he said, 'then it is family law you want'

At the time, by 'darkness' I meant the problem of evil that was alien to good people. Now, I believe 'darkness' within each of us is inevitable and essential, because it encompasses our complexities, which can be the source of great and luminous creativity. Having said which, evilness and cruelty are symptoms of the same darkness, and thus we all have the capacity to become its instruments.

The 50 BCE Roman stoic, Seneca, wrote all cruelty stems from weakness, while a twentieth-century study on sociopaths defined cruelty as either an erosion of empathy due to circumstance and environment, or no

37. 'Lok Adalat orders man to spend equal time with wife and live-in partner' in *The Hindu*, 2 December, 2013.

38. See p. 373: Section 27 of the Indian Contract Act, 1872.

empathy because of defective brain wiring.[39] Both definitions two thousand years apart are incomplete because they treat cruelty as a pathological defect, while everyday experience shows that it is a pathological essence in each of us that we have to learn to transcend. The effort to transcend it is a journey of learning, humility and understanding of oneness. Spiritual advisers know this when they tell us that an important part of mindful living is to protect ourselves from the consequences of our own cruelty. The Buddha advised that compassion is an inner wellspring that one has to learn to reach, beyond the road of our capacity to be cruel.[40]

Cruelty is also a symptom of unhealthy, delusional righteousness. Stephen Pinker writes of a study by Baumeister who notes that 'the people who perpetrate destructive acts, from every day peccadilloes to serial murders and genocides, never think they are doing anything wrong'. How can there be so much evil in the world with so few evil people doing it, Pinker asks.[41]

The social problem of narcissism emerges from the combination of such righteousness and fear of losing control, possibly due to the rapid pace of social change, accelerated by technology. The cruel person is blinded by what s/he sees as a personal just cause. It is a lack of empathy matched with delusional righteousness that rapes girls and kills children in a communal riot, allowing rioters to go home to lunch with their families before returning to the killing spree.[42]

Although there can be no statistics, media reports seem to indicate that the number of people who are deluded by righteousness and thus intolerant and impatient of opposition is more than is healthy for any society. They are not only on the 'fringe' as politicians are prone to say. Some of it is political and explained as post-colonial trauma, but a lot of it seems to stem from the trauma of fast change that rocks the comforting certainties of custom and habit. We thus stand exposed and shivering as insecure and uncertain people overwhelmed by the times. How strange is our inner development that we still subscribe to the tribalist view of

---

39. Lucius Annaeus Seneca, *Morals: Of a Happy Life, Benefits, Anger and Clemency*; Simon Baron-Cohen, *The Science of Evil: On Empathy and the Origins of Cruelty*

40. Erich Fromm, *Escape from Freedom*

41. Steven Pinker, *The Better Angels of Our Nature: The Decline of Violence In History And Its Causes*

42. Rahul Bedi, 'Indira Gandhi's death remembered' on BBC News available at http://news.bbc.co.uk/2/hi/south_asia/8306420.stm

division by caste, clan and community, and that governments whip up these emotions to benefit from polarized vote banks.

This tribalist inner being is exposed in marriage, which E.M. Forster has described as a process of mutual unmasking.[43] Marriage becomes a lifetime process of removing several masks to reveal various facets of the personality in different situations. When it comes to the point of divorce, almost all my clients tell me that they do not recognize in their partners the person they married. This is a new, horrible and grotesque person, they say.

Besides weakness and emptiness and lack of empathy in family situations, I see cruelty stemming from the desire to control. At every level—emotional, social and financial—the desire is to push the other person to know his/her place as being beneath the aggressor and to not give up any opportunity to say so. The greatest cause for this seems to be fear of losing control or the refusal to recognize that the partner's resentment emanates from a personal sense of inadequacy. The desire to dominate comes from a need to fill your own emptiness: the act of hurting another from dealing with your own feelings of hurt: expressions of rage stem from self-loathing and frustration. Gather all that and the stress manifests into a bandwidth of cruelty, only a part of which is witnessed in a divorce case.

~

Cruelty is expressed by reactions disproportionate to perceived provocation. Consider this: At a mediation meeting, H did not deny hitting his wife but asked me, 'do you know the reason?'

'I don't care', I said. 'The point is that nothing justifies your hitting her.'

'Well, I am going to tell you anyway,' he said shining with zealous virtue. 'She has not filed her tax returns and that is immoral besides being illegal.' And he looked at me smugly as if to say: 'so now tell me I was wrong to hit her.' He could not even register my undisguised disbelief.

This delusional righteousness, say social psychologists, stems from a narcissistic personality disorder which contemporary Indian society seems to suffer from in epidemic proportions.

'What do you think happens in these toxic marriages?' I asked a friend. After a moment's thought, he said that he wondered how the human race has survived. Men and women are two such different beings and their marriage becomes a third living being that needs to be nurtured with care.

---

43. E.M. Forster, *Aspects of the Novel*, p. 43

'Joseph Campbell calls marriage a sacrifice', I said.

'Exactly', said my friend. 'It is a sacrifice to this third living being and that could mean sacrificing your known self. When the stream that nurtures that third living being is poisoned, the results are the toxic marriages that you deal with. Sometimes, you could work on an arduous detoxing process but most people do not seem to have the patience to commit to it.'

~

The most frequently cited cause for a toxic marriage is cruelty, but when you think about it, cruelty is only a symptom of toxicity. Discontent manifests in sarcasm, insecurity, lack of appreciation of the other, complaints and fights, all of which then can escalate to acts of cruelty. Where does the poison begin? Cruelty may begin with rude, unapologetic crassness and self-absorption that a person may not realize they are inflicting and may not even intend. But lack of intent is not a defence against a case of cruelty. The suffering of the other is the only concern. Cruelty could be slow and insidious and by the time you realize it, you have a situation of unmanageable toxicity. The disgruntled and unsatisfied self who is tired of giving and not feeling rewarded, or the curious self who is biting at the restraints of marriage could be the results of this slow poison. Sometimes, of course, the cruelty is obvious and immediate, but still difficult to manage.

Yet marriages trudge along with the weight of cruelty. I have asked clients of both genders why they put up with it for as long as they did and their answers lead me to believe that the social definition that people draw from their marriage is comforting despite the abuse. Their home, however unhappy, shelters them from a world that they find to be even nore alien and fearsome, until it, too, becomes unbearable.

Cruelty is also not necessarily apparent: I am still struck by the strange dichotomy of people who at home are the opposite of what they seem to the world. The family outsider could well find it difficult to believe that so-and-so very worthy person is actually very cruel at home or that such-and-such dreadful person lives in a happy home environment. But it is not the jurisdiction of the law to rationalize cruelty: once proved, it has to protect the victim.

Cruelty all too often carries over into the divorce process. A former victim may turn aggressor. The intense bitterness and misplaced virtue of righteousness erodes mutual empathy and each person thinks of him/ herself as the victim. A husband finds his long-suffering wife's victimized expression unbearable: it makes him feel guilty. He wants to forget what happened and move on but she won't let him, so he suffers her victimhood as an act of aggression. After he files for divorce, there is no unequivocal aggressor and victim, because each turns righteous avenger for their own perception of the suffering they have borne. The matter spirals into vindictive intensity. Stinging retorts from the home come into the courtroom as shrill legal pleadings. The narratives are muddied and bespattered with hate and each suffers from the deluded certainty of their cause. The task of tracing the problem to its beginnings is very, very difficult. In the end, we think it is all best left alone: sever the cord and see how to protect what's left of the persons and the children.

Here is where the legal system along with its support structures of counsellors and mediators is supposed to help but does not always come through. A mediator could suggest a protocol of mutual good conduct to help integrate the stressed home with the outside world and transition to divorce.

~

Since becoming a ground for divorce in 1976,[44] cruelty is now the most common plea in matrimonial litigation. Until then, the law allowed only judicial separation from a cruel spouse: that meant separate bed and board but no divorce. Early judgments limited cruelty to such physical violence or reasonable apprehension of it that would endanger the life, limb or mental health of the complainant.[45] Over the decades the courts have sharpened and refined the definition of cruelty in innumerable judgments to say that cruelty need not be blatant acts of physical violence; words and behaviour that disturb the victim's mental and emotional well-being are also cruel.[46] Mental anguish was recognized only after 1976 and has been developed in the PWDVA. At the risk of a seeming oversimplification, it can be said that a marriage is loving intimacy that exposes and accepts mutual weaknesses and vulnerabilities, but cruelty is the consequence of

---

44. Marriage Laws (Amendment) Act, 1976 (68 of 1976)

45. Binda vs. Kaunsilia and Another (1891) ILR 13All126; Moonshee Buzloor Ruheem and Jodonath Bose vs. Shumsoonnissa Begum, 11M.I.A.338; Narayan Moreshvar Pendse vs. Yamunabai wife of Narayan Moreshvar Pendse and Narayan Jaganath Bhide ILR1876 1 Bom 164; Dular Koer vs. Dwarka Nath Misser (1907) ILR 34Cal971; Kondal Rayar Reddiar vs. Ranganayaki Ammal alias Amirthammal 74Ind. Cas.166 MADRAS HC 1923; Mrs Mary Browne vs. A.N. Browne AIR 1937 Oudh 52; Cowasji Nusserwanji Patuck vs. Shehra Cowasji Patuck AIR 1938 Bom 81

46. Smt. Putul Devi and Anr. vs. Gopi Mandal and Anr. AIR 1963 Pat 93

such intimacy undone. The undoing, after a point, is an uncontrollable process and becomes irrevocable.

Yet there is no exhaustive definition of cruelty. There cannot be one. The courts are careful to warn that while cruelty now includes mental and emotional anguish, the line, however fine, must be maintained to distinguish that from the 'normal wear and tear' of marriage.[47] This is problematic because that definite line between what is cruel and what is not can only be drawn by a rational sensible person, who by this very definition is not a character in a divorce court. Divorce battles cannot follow the yardstick of commercial battles based on the likely actions of reasonable and prudent persons. Divorcing couples are not reasonable or prudent. Moreover, we cannot bring our personal judgments to bear on what we think is cruel. Our innate differences make one person robust while another is not, so we cannot pass judgment based on what we ourselves would feel in the shoes of the other. Even between married people, perceptions can vary widely. A wife said to me, 'I can't understand why he is so angry and calls me cruel; the incidents as he recounts them are true, but I was not vicious.' She actually enjoyed their robust fights, which added a spark for her to their interactions, but she had not reckoned that the tipping point of his tolerance was not the same as hers.

The most recent definition of cruelty by the Supreme Court includes unreasonable and irrational behaviour like a refusal to give a divorce, even though the marriage is otherwise shrivelled and dead.[48] To say that it is cruel to refuse a divorce may seem an anomaly in the fault theory regime, but the court took the deeper view that to punish someone by imprisoning them in a dead marriage when there were no financial and custody issues is indeed cruel.

Many elders complain that the cause of divorce is the low tolerance of people. What they often mean is that women are not that 'adjusting' anymore. I am familiar with both the terms 'tolerance' and 'adjusting' in many of my cases. My mother too says she tided over her early marital difficulties because of the counsel she received from her mother: *chup vat: ghaintey katt: bhaley din awangey.*

Here, in contrast, I have a story about a younger cousin who made me proud: she was expected to dust the rooms and cook in her matrimonial

---

47. Savitri Pandey vs. Prem Chandra Pandey 2002(1)KLJ193; Naveen Kohli vs. Neelu Kohli AIR 2006 SC 1675

48. Samar Ghosh vs. Jaya Ghosh, (2007) 4 SCC 511

home, despite their army of servants. Perhaps it was a drive to domesticate her. Anyhow, she refused and a film of dust gathered on the furniture. The mother-in-law, to make a 'subtle' point, drew a line with her fingertip through the dust and left the room, only to return and see that my feisty cousin had crossed the line with her fingertips. And that was that. Everyone laughed and the mother-in-law bundled up in a disapproving sulk that everyone ignored. She lost her power and my cousin settled into the household with humour and balance.

Who began the battle here? It is not unusual for mothers-in-law to want help in the house. Yet my cousin was entitled to not do unnecessary housework, given the large staff. The line the mother-in-law made may have simply indicated a quiet disapproval that she would have got over with time, but my cousin crossing it could amount to insubordination or sheer cheek as far as the mother-in-law was concerned. In this case, it was all well and the seething subtext settled, but generally it is these undercurrents that heat up and boil over. Then it is difficult to assess who began the battle. Assessment of evidence supported only by verbal testimonies of the warring parties is a tedious task for the court, which is supposed to use the traditional tools of the Evidence Act.

Now the Family Courts Act 1984, permits the court to develop its own procedure to assess evidence[49] but judges do not seem to have boldly taken that challenge. One reason could be that they are unduly intimidated by the scrutiny of the higher court and thus reluctant to do something innovative. The bureaucratization of the lower judiciary is a part of the systemic malaise—an inverted pyramid, with principles of justice applied with greater empathy at the top, and the ends of justice sacrificed to rules of procedure in the lower judiciary.

Cruelty and Class

The Supreme Court has repeatedly said that the definition of cruelty also depends on the individual socialization of the persons involved.[50] This seems reasonable at first but on second thoughts, it is problematic as an over-simplification. Though the courts do not mention rich or poor, the thrust seems to be that such-and-such event is 'unlikely' to happen in 'educated', 'good' (what is that?), 'respectable' families. Does that

49. See p. 361: Section 10(3) of the Family Courts Act, 1984

50. Vishwanath S/O Sitaram Agrawal vs. Sau. Sarla Vishwanath Agrawal, [2012] 7 S.C.R. 607

conversely mean that the less educated, poor or those with 'not good' backgrounds lack social respectability and empathy? Besides being a dangerous generalization, the proposition itself is cruel.

Even when these observations about the nature of individual socialization do not find their way in a judgment, such generalizations and stereotypes almost always cloud the courtroom atmosphere and it is a difficult task to clear the air. I wish it were not so but this is the undeniable experience of working in trial courts—though it also lurks in the higher courts. An experienced senior lawyer, practicing in the High Court of Delhi once told me with visible pride that sexual violence was improbable in our homes because our society and culture respects family. I had nothing to say, apart from asking him to read the newspapers of the last three days: child abuse, rape, dowry deaths, husbands being denied bail by vindictive wives, rape by fathers-in-law, honour killings. I told him he sounded ridiculous unless he was talking of 'people like us' and that too, I said, was not true. I brought up a rape case in the 'good old days' when society was thought to be safer and more civilized than the present. A group of lawyers had called for the cook's nineteen-year-old wife to rape as after-dinner entertainment. Her dying screams could be heard in the neighbourhood. I am sure the lawyers returned home with clear consciences to their own wives and children. In another instance, Jhakhu, of the infamous case[51] by that name, sexually molested his daughter while his friends laughed and watched. They were all under-secretary level government servants.

After this conversation I feel compelled to state here what I thought was obvious but clearly is not: Human perversity lives in luxury as much as in poverty. It is as probable in elegant homes occupied by good-looking, well-mannered, well-dressed people living amongst beautiful things, as in slums and ghettoes where people live like cattle in a pen. In fact, education and money can be tools in the hands of the cruel to refine the forms of cruelty so that they seem less apparent, but are no less intense. When we know that many educated and wealthy people ill-treat their home staff and discriminate on the basis of caste and religion, why should it be difficult to believe that they ill-treat members of their family?

And cruelty does not go by gender—women too are as capable of cruelty. We have all suffered it or inflicted it. The refrain 'You are so mean!' is familiar in playgrounds, carries into classrooms, and is said in

51. Smt. Sudesh Jhaku vs. K.C.J. and Others, 62 (1996) DLT 563

boardrooms as well. It is also common within the confines of a home. When you think about it, it is very likely that someone has called you 'mean' at some time and the accusation may not have been entirely untrue. Most of you will see forms of discrimination and cruelty in your immediate neighbourhood, and with great respect, may I suggest that you look at your families and within yourself as well.

Economic Abuse

The widening definition of cruelty as a ground for divorce, from when cruelty was defined only in physical terms,[52] to when it was expanded to include mental anguish,[53] to now,[54] when it includes economic abuse, which finds specific mention in the PWDVA,[55] is the result of the improving social position of women. Women suffer economic abuse because there is no objective formula to value their work and the value they add to a marriage, apart from symbolic male approval. This is often the case even when women do earn their own money, as they usually do not have complete charge of their finances. A small part of their earnings are doled out to them or they are expected to spend their money on household expenses, while the husbands park their earnings as savings, which the wife eventually loses access to if the marriage ends.

Of course, tightening of money is a common litigation strategy during a divorce case. In a matter where I represented the wife of a millionaire, he decided to reduce her credit card allowance from no limit to Rs. 20,000. He claimed that his generosity was a symbol of his love and now that he did not love her any longer, subsistence was all that she was going to get. He insisted on buying her the cheaper washing machine and refused her the use of a car and driver. Given his financial power, he actually demeaned himself by asking for hisab for money spent on food and groceries. She told me his viciousness was shockingly uncharacteristic, but his anger was childish and stemmed from a thwarted desire for divorce on his terms.

This happens when the man thinks of the money as his alone and sharing it as a privilege he bestows upon his wife if she pleases him.

---

52. Narayan Moreshvar Pendse vs. Yamunabai wife of Narayan Moreshvar Pendse and Narayan Jaganath Bhide ILR1876 1 Bom 164

53. Dastane vs. Dastane, 1975 3 SCR 967

54. Samar Ghosh vs. Jaya Ghosh (2007) 4 SCC 511; K. Srinivas Rao vs. D.A. Deepa, AIR 2013 SC 2176; Ramchander vs. Ananta, 2015 (2) SCALE 634;

55. See p. 384: Section 3, Explanation I (iv) of the PWDVA, 2005

No amount of Ivy League college degrees can remove this socialization ingrained over centuries.

~

Money is the obvious aspect of miserliness. On several occasions I have unsuccessfully tried to persuade judges that a similar expression of power lies in the control of food and rich people are not above this primal instinct. The following are true cases:

A wife had to order meals from outside because she could not access the kitchen.

In another case, the wife ate her meals with the children, leaving no cooked food for the husband. The maids employed by her were tutored to disregard his instructions.

In another instance, a woman married for less than a year into a wealthy family left because they were miserly about food generally. She finally started buying her own food and eating on the sly, in case the family scolded her about wasting money on food.

There is the common expectation that the daughter-in-law will eat only after the entire family has been fed. Tanika Sarkar refers to a Bengali manual giving advice to a young bride on conduct and deportment, but on the issue of food, the good book says, there is no advice because if she served herself, she would be called shameless and if she waited for someone to offer her food, she would go hungry. Sarkar writes that even in the highly educated and enlightened Tagore family, a married woman's meals were disconcertingly uncertain.[56]

I believe these clients because of the tentative trepidation with which they told their stories. They were afraid that I would call them liars, because how can food be a problem in a rich household?

Cruelty Condoned

In 1970, Mr Dastane's divorce petition based on cruelty was dismissed even though the court agreed that Mrs Dastane had been cruel to him.[57] The court found that Mr Dastane had condoned his wife's cruelty by resuming cohabitation, and subsequent to the rapprochement, no act of hers was cruel enough to allow for a revival of the original complaint of cruelty as cause for divorce. In this case, the conservative view against

56. Sarkar, *Hindu Wife, Hindu Nation: Community, Religion, and Cultural Nationalism*, p. 122

57. N.G. Dastane vs. S.N. Dastane, AIR 1970 Bom 312

easy divorces prevailed, despite the undisputed acrimony between the Dastanes. Both were highly qualified government servants, so financial arrangements were no problem and yet both were left miserable.

Interestingly, men now complain of cruelty by women more than they used to. This cannot indicate that women have only now started to become cruel, but only that men no longer have the easy option of discarding inconvenient or cruel wives. They have to take recourse to the law instead.

It is to navigate the male power of discarding, that in the past, women learned to please men. That is the way they obtained protection in a man's world.[58] Besides chastity, their survival kit contained inculcated virtues that I think should be in the following order: skills of cooking and thrifty housekeeping; trained nurturing and restraint to ensure 'adjustment', often mistaken for innate kindness and tenderness; and finally, pleasing looks displayed with the grace and charm of the fashion of the times. This became the feminine stereotype, while the male stereotype is someone hard and angular who takes his pleasure as an entitlement. Strangely enough, the breaking of these gendered stereotypes actually takes us to the mythological idea of Ardhanarishwar, the balance of both genders in the same person—an idea that is absent in the modern versions of the epics that are currently drawn upon as cultural icons.

Evolving gender roles undoubtedly have a place in contemporary Indian society, but even so, the residue of patriarchy and misogyny often lurks, as when the man expects wifely submission and is angry and anguished by her modern questioning and challenging of roles, or when the woman may think suddenly that he is not 'man enough'. A short film by Vinil Mathew has become popular because of its sensitive handling of the male stereotype and the effect of patriarchy on all genders. In it, a baby boy is not allowed to cry when he falls, because boys do not cry. A male teenager is not allowed to cry when he is disappointed or elated at winning a match, because boys do not cry. The young adult does not cry at heartbreak and then the young man is an angry, repressed being, silently arm-twisting to breaking point his new wife. I hope it's making a difference, because it cannot be said better.

Cruelty By Men

The traditional expectations from the modern woman are themselves cruel: she must cook, serve the household and eat last; know and like his

58. Simone de Beauvoir, *The Second Sex*, p. 293

relatives even if he does not; sleep last after cleaning the kitchen; not sleep late in the morning because she has to get the home running; not talk to her parents for too long on the telephone; not visit them too often; patiently put up with anything else that otherwise makes her inadequate; and, if working outside the home, be the subject of cruel teasing, showing her up or running her down for being obsessively career-minded. An instance of residual misogyny is a husband telling the court that his wife was a heartless and cruel woman because she did not breastfeed the child long enough and wanted to return to work as soon as possible.

When a great mind like Aristotle believed that a woman is a cold man, or in any case, less than a man, it is not surprising that ordinary men will not have the courage to differ. How to force this half-person to submit to an all-macho man? The treatment is the same as adopted by many misguided parents to discipline a child. Browbeating literally. They hit her. I fear someone who can hit me, and once the line has been crossed, the probability of his hitting me again is reasonable. The many stories of physical violence range from horrific details to vague generalizations, as the specifics have been lost in the commonness of its occurrence.

A violent situation raises the question of why a person should be driven to violence at all? Provocation is the obvious defence, but the varied yardstick of what constitutes provocation is a social comment too. He may be provoked because she is not submissive enough or, in fact, is assertive. It might also be that she mirrors his hidden confusion and weaknesses, which he then sublimates in violence.

Cruelty By Women

But of course, women hit men for the same reasons, and so men need to protect themselves from physical and mental violence. They also need to be protected from the inevitable presumption against them that it is the man who must have been the aggressor. Most leave the house rather than suffer false charges of violence.

Many men have now begun fearing the stranglehold of a woman's legal power that she may use mercilessly. One of my clients described to me, how his wife (a fraction of his size) follows him around the house goading him with abuse and insults and then says: 'Don't you want to hit me?'

'Have you?' I asked.

'Never,' he said, revolted by the thought. 'I just walk away. At one time, I was so distraught by the effort of my restraint at her goading that

I locked myself in the bathroom and wept like I have not done since my first night in boarding school at age six.'

~

A very dramatic woman, married to my cousin, rang me up shrieking and howling that he was trying to strangle her. Aghast, I called my cousin on his mobile to find that he was out of the house, but yes they did have a fight. I put them on conference call and he asked her when he strangled her. Reply: I meant metaphorically.

~

Stereotypical expectations expressed insensitively are also cruel in impact. A woman is cruel when she belittles and berates him and abandons him at difficult times. A highly educated, rich, 'liberal' businesswoman told her husband that he was not man enough for her since he earned less. It is a difficult job to pass the test of a 'man'. He must be the sole provider. Failure at the workplace is a cause for humiliation at home. If your child was doing badly in school, would you berate him like this or try to support him, I asked. The response was: that's the point—he needs to grow up.

The counter-argument sometimes is that cruel acts by women are to cover their weakness and lack of power in the marriage setup. But the cause is basic—women, like men, can suffer the problem of lack of empathy. It is a human condition, not of gender.

Cruelty As a Criminal Offence

Section 498A IPC was enacted in 1983 to protect women from violence and cruelty and its second limb focuses on protecting women from dowry-related cruelty. The definition of cruelty is being refined and sharpened in law. Its most recent definition under the PWDV Act, 2005, includes economic abuse.[59] Many judgments, directions and notifications have practically dried up the purpose of the first limb[60] and merged it with the second, dowry-specific limb. In practice, the provision has been reduced to stridhan recovery proceedings,[61] despite the various judgments that have held this to be beyond the true scope of the section.[62] Police investigations are limited to raiding lockers and premises to hand over,

59. See p. 384: Section 3, Explanation I (iv) of the PWDVA, 2005

60. Manu Nischal and Ors. vs. State, MANU/DE/0989/2009; Raj Kumar Khanna vs. State, 95 (2002) DLT 147

61. Kapil Sethi vs. State, 184(2011)DLT449;

62. See p. 381: Section 406, The Indian Penal Code, 1860

without verification, expensive clothes and jewellery that she claims as hers. There is a reason why this happened. A sub-inspector at the local police station has no time, patience or understanding to register a complaint for cruelty simpliciter without a dowry allegation. Even if they can be badgered into doing that, the concept of mental cruelty often does not register. The common attitude is: What's wrong with a marriage if she has food to eat, clothes to wear but has to suffer loud words and a whack occasionally? Does he drink and try to beat the life out of her? If he does not, where is the problem?

Special women-enabling legislations should not be seen to imply that the law sees women as incapable of domestic violence; only that it is safe to assume that there are fewer male victims of domestic violence because, besides being physically stronger, they are socially and economically empowered and can avail the common law for redressal of the wrongs suffered by them.[63] The men who criticize these laws are those who are in litigation and find that the judicial system is not as understanding of their moral positions as their extended kin, village, town or even metropolis. Having said which, miscarriage of justice suffered by men is also not uncommon and is the subject of a separate chapter on misuse of due process by women and their lawyers.[64]

Cruel Pleadings

In 1993, the Supreme Court [65] dealt with the problem of shrill and abusive affidavits in bitter court battles and ruled that some type of pleadings could constitute cruelty. Mr Bhagat filed a petition of 160 paragraphs alleging adultery by his wife. Mrs Bhagat filed a lengthier response calling him suspicious, paranoid, insane and saying that his entire family suffered from a streak of lunacy. The trial began and the matter was pending for eight years due to appeals and cross appeals. Mr Bhagat then claimed that his wife's vexatious pleadings entitled him to a divorce without a trial. This is a problematic proposition, because the law entitles a person full freedom to state a case.

In this case, the Supreme Court agreed with Mr Bhagat and granted him the divorce, subject to the cautionary caveat that the Bhagat case not be a precedent. Allegations and counter-allegations were not enough

---

63. Aruna Parmod Shah vs. Union of India (UOI), 2008 (102) DRJ 543

64. See Ch. 9: Misuse of Enabling Laws, p. 266

65. Bhagat vs. Bhagat, AIR 1994 SC 710

for a divorce without a trial, the court said, and avoidance of protracted legal proceedings could not be a valid ground to avoid trial.

Here is an important corollary point. The consequence of a court rejecting some evidence as not adequately proven does not mean that the accusations were false. It is just that they did not meet the standard of proof. This is important in the wake of some recent judgments that are wrongly being read to mean that false criminal cases could be a basis for a divorce.[66] It could well be that facts which cannot stand up to the scrutiny of the standard of proof in a criminal case may pass the much lower standard of proof in a civil case.

Systemic Cruelty

A person traumatized by a bad marriage eventually finds the courage to file for divorce. Often, the shock of subsequently facing systemic sluggishness compounds the trauma of cruelty. The system seems insensitive and converts the matter to legalized cruelty.

Here is an example of cruelty by the husband compounded by systemic cruelty. My client was estranged from her husband who came from a rich and powerful family. In contrast, her own parents were middle-class nonentities. My client was an active stay-at-home mother of two very charming and good-looking daughters, about ten and eight years old. The husband's problem seemed to emanate from self-absorption and more money than wisdom. He was very bored. There was substance abuse, addiction to uppers and downers, long alcohol-flavoured lunches and dinners. The husband, she said, was a violent childish bully. She hated it and hated what her daughters were growing up with. One day she was beaten in their presence and she could stand it no more. She left the beautiful home and rented a flat in an uptown middle-class colony. She said she wanted a divorce and discussions about alimony began. One day her daughters went to visit their grandparents and father in a chauffeur-driven car sent for them and did not return. She went to the local police station but the SHO simply refused to entertain her when he learned whom her parents-in-law were.

It was a Saturday afternoon. I felt her pain and panic and much to the disappointment of my own children, the weekend was spent in preparing

66. V. Bhagat vs. D. Bhagat, 1994 SCC (1) 337; Vijaykumar Ramchandra Bhate v. Neela Vijaykumar Bhate, [2003] 3 SCR 607; K. Srinivas Rao vs. D.A. Deepa, AIR 2013 SC 2176; Samar Ghosh vs. Jaya Ghosh, (2007) 4 SCC 511

the habeas corpus petition for Monday. The case was listed before a conservative lady judge who was inclined to dismiss me, saying that the father taking custody of children did not amount to illegal detention. It took me a while to take her through the precedents and explain that it was reasonable to assume that the children were held back against their will since they had no conversation with their mother about wanting to stay on with their father. Their ordinary residence was with my client and the act of the husband in retaining them amounted to illegal detention. It was important that they be returned immediately, as they had not been in touch with their mother for two days now and would surely be sad and bewildered. The court reluctantly agreed. The children were returned to the mother that afternoon and the matter came up before the High Court again. A leading lawyer from the ruling party appeared opposite me and asked that the father be allowed visitation of the children over weekends. I had no quarrel with that.

Litigation began. We filed for maintenance and divorce on the ground of cruelty. He filed for custody of the children and resisted the divorce, He began delaying the hearing of the maintenance petition.

On the morning of a hearing, my client would reach the house of my associate holding a rosary. Visibly nervous but smiling, she would ask my associate's mother to pray for her. I would collect them both on my way to court.

There was considerable media attention and the husband's lawyer would often drive in just before or behind me in his bottle-green Mercedes. After one of the days in court my client had very excitedly asked me to drop her off at Khan Market where she was going to meet her girls and then they were going in a three-wheeler to the Maruti showroom to collect their basic Maruti 800 without an air conditioner. Later, she told me how the girls had told the salesman that they were taking this small car for now, but their father was going to come back and buy a Pajero because that is what he drove. The dynamics were apparent at the courtroom gate with us emerging from our small cars, contrasting with the husband emerging from the luxury car with his team of posh lawyers.

We were before a very robust and mature lady judge who was entirely unfazed by the unusual sight of this very senior lawyer at a trial court. Arguments were going well. I was certain that we were not going to lose custody and he would have to pay substantial maintenance, but I could not be sure when. Her husband told her that he was damned if he was going to give her money to fight him. My client was in great financial difficulties. She earned a small living as a freelancer.

My client was happy with the children, but the undercurrent was always immensely and intensely sad because the clean break she wanted was receding every day into a remote possibility. Dialogue to settle was impossible because the other side felt they had the upper hand. They had the children for the weekends and the mother was out of their hair without having to be paid any money. I think they hoped that sooner or later she would leave the children and go away, too exhausted to fight.

There were many sinister messages to my client along the lines of *The Godfather* and the horse head on the movie producer's bed. As powerful as a Don, the husband once seriously injured my client's male friend at a public bar. Nothing came of the police complaint. Then, as the tempo of the proceedings mounted, my client was attacked outside her home. This is how she recounted it: 'The doorbell rang. I stepped out and was pulled into the drain just outside the gate, by a woman holding a rough object which she scrubbed against my neck all the while abusing me and saying, "*Aur masti karegi*".' Medical reports confirmed injury from a blunt weapon with iron bristles. We filed a police complaint. I knew that not much would come out of the investigations.

Believing the opposing counsel to be sensible despite his shiny persona, I called him about the attack and asked that we talk settlement. We had a sharp exchange. He accused me of defaming his client with false accusations. I said I was only warning him as counsel to counsel that his client had a history of violence. His client already had the bar attack case reported against him. There could be no reason for my client to be attacked in this way unless instructed specifically. He called me paranoid and slammed the phone down.

A few days later, the car of my client's friend was waylaid while he was driving home at night after a party. He was pulled out and beaten with iron rods. Although we did the usual police complaints, I risked humiliation again by calling the big lawyer hoping that the seriousness of the matter would make him react. Sahibji, I thought I would say to him, it is only a divorce litigation, not a gang war. Once again he hung up on me. It was war after all. The feudal part of the other side could not tolerate a woman standing up for herself and taking them to court. She had brought dishonour to the feudal lord and his family.

I wanted nothing more than some interim maintenance to be organized and for my client to feel safe about the children. The rest could wait. One day I had a conversation with her about filing proceedings under Section 498(A) for mental and physical cruelty and dowry claims. The dowry claim she said was not possible. She had nothing. She brought nothing. She left with nothing. The marriage had been in a temple, against the approval of the parents, and she was given no family jewellery at the time. She did not remember the jewellery that was later given to her because she had never worn it and she could not describe it. It was lying in the common safe in the house.

Typical of his delusional grandeur, the husband had a propensity to play-act as if he was in the movies. One day he called on my mobile. He started the conversation in the oddest way telling me that he loved my client. Somehow, I knew he was taping our conversation. I told him firmly but softly, though I was very angry, that he must never call me again, that he must get his lawyer to communicate with me and that he should know that I was aware he had earlier recorded a meeting at my office when he had come ostensibly to talk settlement. There was a silence and then simply, 'Oh! Okay!' and like a boy found out, he hung up. Another time, he and his junior lawyers came to my office. We started discussing some terms and then he suddenly turned around to say that he was not interested in settling after all. My client was livid and said she could not understand why he wanted to hang on to her for. The husband simply listened with a curious small smile which I found infuriating. Later that evening I found out through the clerk and staff grapevine that he in fact had wired himself up to record the conversation in my office.

I again found his desire to play cops and robbers pathetically childish. He was playing games like little boys do with guns: making noises, as boys do, of gunshots, killing and dying. He had no perspective of the real world. Insulated by power and wealth, all he knew was that this wife was being a nuisance and that did not make him feel good and so he must throw a tantrum. His attitude was scary.

One night at 11 p.m., I got a call from my associate that many friends of my client had been receiving blank calls from her. Some had received text messages saying goodbye. I was out of town. I told her to call the police. I too tried my client's number but got no reply. At 6 a.m., I called my associate who told me that my client's body had been found on a terrace roof of a hotel. Nobody knew why she had gone there.

I reached Delhi airport and went straight to the hotel. My associate told me that the police officer had rung up the husband who arrived at the hotel. He did not want to see the body. He then left for the farmhouse of his lawyer with the green Mercedes. I met him later in the evening at the government hospital where the autopsy was being conducted. The report indicated a fall from a height and concluded suicide. We asked for the autopsy procedure to be repeated. The second autopsy confirmed the first finding.

My client's mother, brother and sister arrived. A powerful political person had called them and they became overwhelmed and too bewildered to grieve. Three lost people from a small town in a far-away state.

After my client died, but before it was confirmed as suicide by the police investigations, I was on a television show to discuss whether the rich and famous get away with murder. I brought up the incident of the earlier attack on my client. The husband's counsel was also on the program and tried to trivialize it by saying that it had nothing to do with his client, but certainly she had no business to be out partying at that hour. 'I always advise young women in my own house against going out at that hour', he said lightly. There was laughter. I did not see the point in a harangue anymore. It just brought out my powerlessness.

I was left with a heavy heart for the children. They had been pulled back into the iron and concrete embrace of the large house of their father and grandfather and the powerful establishment that it stood for.

~

Men suffer systemic cruelty when they are victims of false allegations of child sexual abuse and the courts delay adjudication for so long that the defence becomes merely an academic exercise because the children are gone.[67]

In general, arrogant insensitive judges are part of systemic cruelty. All of us—lawyers, judges, mediators, the media, bureaucrats and politicians—are complicit in our inability to completely understand and master the equipment we work with. I end up being defensive about overloads on the system, a problem that clients do understand because it is becoming a common problem in all institutions, but I have nothing to say when faced with systemic corruption, superficial knowledge and no effort to educate oneself. Some humility and compassion would go a long way in countering this.

DESERTION

'Desertion' in the military is a wartime offence punishable by death.[68] As a marital offence, fortunately it is only a ground for divorce. There are

---

67. See Ch. 7: Children, p. 238

68. John Paul Jones O'Brien, *A Treatise on American Military Laws*, p. 527

two types of desertion. To walk out of the house is simple straightforward physical desertion. The complex version is Constructive Desertion, which can take several forms. For example, the offender may be in the house but performs no marital duty (sex is only one) even while living in the same house.[69] There are two concurrent aspects of Constructive Desertion—Factum Deserendi: the fact of desertion; and Animus Deserendi: the intention to desert. Ill-advised spouses sometimes stay in abusive situations fearing that they will be accused of desertion, but a spouse forced out of a house and marriage by cruel conduct is not guilty of desertion. This is also counted as Constructive Desertion—by the person who has perpetrated the cruelty forcing the spouse to leave.[70]

To constitute a marital offence, the desertion must be continuous for a period of two years. Some clients ask fearfully: if for two years we live separately, are we automatically divorced? Not so. Because it has to be established that the desertion was willful abandonment and not a question of being forced out of the home by deliberately created circumstances.

Desertion as the sole ground for divorce is relatively unusual. This is because it is difficult to prove something so ambivalent and negative as unreasonable withdrawal from marital society, compared with proving a positive act such as cruelty. Of course, desertion is also cruelty in a passive form.

FRAUD

A woman consulted me about getting a divorce. 'You will have to tell me why,' I said.

'Incompatibility,' she said.

'That, I'm afraid, is not a ground for divorce,' I said. 'You have to give me more. Why do you think you are incompatible?'

She looked out of my office window as if she was seeing something very far away. 'It began with my shock when I saw him remove his toupee on our wedding night. I had no idea.'

'But that was years ago! You are reaching the time when most men lose their hair anyway!'

She smiled mechanically to acknowledge the joke but could not laugh easily any longer: 'It's beyond that now. Maybe the problem in our marriage is rooted in my disappointment and his guilt about having

69. Sanjan v. Azara, AIR 2013 Ker 180

70. Ashok Kumar Jain vs. Sumati Jain, (2013) 14 SCC 123

disappointed me with his deception. From guilt it grew to jibes and now I can't bear his cold cruelty any longer. I tried to put my disappointment and compounded misunderstandings behind me and start afresh, but he refused to believe that I really could do it, and so I stopped trying.'

I could not entirely blame the man for his scepticism, as she clearly remained very disturbed by the incident. Anyone may view a toupee as a pathetic cover-up for baldness, but for her to see it as fraud might seem to him to expose a degree of superficiality. She seemed to have forgiven his deception and even felt sorry for him, but should he want to live with her pity? It's a complex matter and the law cannot help here because we have reached the moral component of marriage that is beyond the law.

Legally, we can only ask, does the toupee deception amount to fraud? The law says that it does not. That seems correct, given that otherwise there would be no end to frivolous claims for divorce of the 'I did not see her without makeup' variety. The legal position is that inducements to consent to marriage do not amount to fraud, but actions that prevent a fair consent do. Thus, makeup and toupees that may induce consent are not legal fraud—keep in mind also that fraud is a ground for annulment of marriage, not for divorce per se. Similarly, false representations about educational qualifications, job descriptions and salaries, which are viewed as serious misdeeds in the corporate world, do not have any easy recourse in divorce law.

Now you may say the law is inadequate. The toupee or padded CV are intended to deceive and a layperson would label this as fraud. In law, however, the fraudulent act must attack the root of the marriage. For example, A marrying B, while mistakenly thinking the marriage is with C would certainly constitute fraud. Another type of fraud that indeed affects the root of the marriage would be a spouse concealing that she is unable to conceive or that he is sexually impotent. In the Indian context, the existence of past relationships, or of a current relationship facing parental disapproval, would be deemed relevant information by some for agreeing to a marriage.

People have also complained in court of wrong information given for the matching of horoscopes. The last may sound extreme to many, but for those who believe, it is serious. However, a marriage need not be annulled if information of this type is found to be wrong: one cannot lose sight of the fact that innocent or negligent misrepresentation is not fraud. Some plumping up of all biographical information is bound to happen. It echoes the harmless deception of the traditional teatime ritual where the girl serves delicacies that she 'has made with her own fair hands'.

I suggest that some other ingredients, which may not be grounds for annulling a marriage may still be looked at as grounds for divorce within the framework of cruelty, since fraud is not a separate ground for divorce. The precedent has been set by a California judgment which held that though the facts of that case did not amount to fraud for the purpose of annulment, they could be adequate for dissolution of marriage.[71] Then the toupee (or a wrong horoscope) may find its place in a divorce proceeding. You may call the criterion shallow, but we cannot make moral judgments about the litigant. Divorce is about misplaced expectations and the outrage felt by many who feel they were misled deserves serious consideration.

~

In the law as it stands today, whether the types of deception I have described are fraudulent depends on whether marriage is to be treated as a sacrament or as a contract.

A judicial ruling may take a narrow view, which sees marriage as sacred, and so limits the issue of fraud to the ceremony. Such a view was taken by the Punjab and Haryana court in two matters reported in the 1960s—in one, W thought she was marrying H, but discovered that she married someone else, while in the other, the spouse was drugged during the marriage ceremony.[72] Both marriages were vitiated by fraud.

This narrow view sufficed for the days when shared social networks of kith, kin and class enforced the metaphorical marriage contract, but the broad interpretation is the need of the hour, given that arranged marriages are very popular in our cultural ethos. They are essentially contracts based on mutual representations that influence consent. Decisions to marry are based on information in matrimonial advertisements, which can be difficult to double-check despite due diligence (particularly in NRI marriages). It is only after both parties agree to marry that the marriage will be sanctified.

The broad view is contained in the Special Marriage Act 1956. This view is premised on the contractual nature of marriage and so imports the definition of fraud from The Indian Contract Act.[73] Under the Contract Act, the duty of full disclosure while negotiating out-of-court settlements

---

71. In re Marriage of Johnston (1993)

72. Harbhajan Singh vs. Smt. Brij Balab Kaur, AIR 1964 P&H 359; Surjit Kumar Harichand vs. Smt. Raj Kumari, AIR 1967 P&H 172

73. S. 25(iii)- the consent of either party to the marriage was obtained by coercion or fraud, as defined in the Indian Contract Act, 1872 (9 of 1872)

is governed by the principle of *Uberrima Fides* meaning 'absolute good faith'.[74] According to this perspective, just as false representations and concealment made to induce a person to sign a contract render it null and void, so do false representations to induce consent to marriage.

This is the view taken by the Delhi and the Allahabad High Courts.[75] The Delhi judgment distinguishes between love and arranged marriages on the premise that the latter is contractual because the best match is chosen and arranged based on financial and other relevant disclosures such as educational qualifications. As can be seen by these cases, whether the concealment affects the root of the marriage is the test.[76]

Fraud During Divorce Proceedings

Though not dealt with in any particular statute, fraud in agreements for divorce by mutual consent needs to be addressed. Maintenance or alimony agreements that are settled out of court are generally more influenced by considerations of practical need and efficiency rather than a fair financial sharing after full disclosure of assets. Often, a wife thinks she has a general idea about her husband's wealth only to realize soon after the divorce, that the husband's salary has doubled and he has moved to a posh apartment with another woman with whom he's had a long-standing relationship. Or a husband makes a fair settlement and gives up custody, only to find that she has married again within weeks of the divorce.

The facts of an English case, Jenkins v. Livesey[77] are interesting and deal with what amounts to fraud in such matters. The husband gave substantial assets to his wife, including the major portion of the business they had set up together so that her routine as primary caregiver to their two children would be undisturbed. A month after the divorce, he discovered that she had been conducting a love affair at the time the divorce settlement was being discussed and married her paramour within a year of it being granted. The husband filed legal action for fraud claiming that by concealing her ongoing relationship, she had induced

74. Raghunath Gopal Daftardar v. Sau Vijaya Raghunath Daftardar, AIR 1972 Bom 132

75. Anurag Anand v. Sunita Anand, AIR 1997 Delhi 94; See also Smt. Bindu Sharma vs. Ram Prakash Sharma and others, AIR 1997 All 429

76. Valsa vs. Moore, ILR1991(1) Kerala687; Best Morning Khongthorem vs. Nirmalendu Dev, AIR 1987 Gauhati 63

77. [1985] 1 AC 424

him to arrive at a settlement that was materially different to what he would have done had he known she was going to marry so soon after the divorce. The House of Lords held that by not making full disclosure, the wife was in breach of her duty to the court that had to to check injustice and protect both parties.

In India, divorce by mutual agreement is now not uncommon and one-time settlements have become more common with increased liquidity and prosperity. It is high time that the true transactional nature of pre-nuptial, post-nuptial and separation agreements is recognized and tested under Contract Law. In such an approach, non-compliance of divorce decrees would amount to fraud as a tort and could even be explored as criminal breach of trust. This would go a long way in addressing the scepticism most wives feel about their husbands honouring monthly alimony payments. However, the client will have to be advised that the fraud plea will be available after the final divorce, but not necessarily after the agreement arrived at when the first motion of divorce is filed. The difference is apparent in the case below:

Contempt in Divorce Matters

The Delhi High Court in its contempt jurisdiction had occasion to deal with a case where W reneged from an agreement after the first motion of divorce and refused to sign the second motion of divorce, which she was supposed to after a 'cooling-off' period mandated by the court. The purpose of the cooling-off period (six to eighteen months between the first and second motion) was to allow both persons to think through their life-altering decision. However, she had received part payment of the substantial one-time settlement at the initial motion for divorce. H filed an action asking that she be punished for contempt of court.

W cited a Supreme Court judgment[78] on identical facts, that held that the wife or the husband were within their rights to refuse the second motion for divorce even without cause, as free and voluntary consent was the necessary ingredient at the time of both motions. The Delhi High Court chose to distinguish from the Supreme Court decision and held W for contempt, saying that the first motion divorce petition contained undertakings to court by W that she would proceed with the second motion.

The judgment is a problematic precedent, because its laboured effort to distinguish it from the previous Sureshta Devi case takes away the purpose

78. Sureshta Devi vs. Om Prakash, AIR 1992 SC 1904

of the cooling-off period. Even if the undertakings are held to be valid, the purpose of the cooling-off period is to review such undertakings and promises. There is also her statutory right to change her mind. I understand that the judge was grappling with the moral conundrum of her reneging from the agreement after having received a substantial consideration, but that could have been dealt with by ordering her to return the amount. (It should also be mentioned that at the time of receiving the payment, she had given up substantial and valuable rights of residence in the palatial family home, and hence, the amount was actually very small, relative to her circumstances).

The story of the Delhi High Court case is fraught with disagreement on co-parenting arrangements. The purpose of the cooling-off period is to iron out precisely such issues and the law must allow for complete justice to parties severing marriage ties. The process of doing that can never be simple and needs careful negotiation and supervision while ruling about it.

MENTAL DISORDERS

The author Kay Redfield Jamison writes of her battle with a mental disorder, in this case, depression:

> 'I have found it to be seductively complicated, a distillation both of what is fine in our natures, and of what is most dangerous. In order to contend with it, I first had to know it in all of its moods and infinite disguises, understand its real and imagined powers...
>
> My manias, at least in their early and mild forms, were absolutely intoxicating states that gave rise to great personal pleasure, an incomparable flow of thoughts and a ceaseless energy that allowed the translation of new ideas into papers and projects. Medications not only cut into these fast-flowing, high-flying times, they also bought with them seemingly intolerable side effects. It took me far too long to realize that lost years and relationships cannot be recovered, that damage done to oneself and others cannot always be put right again, and that freedom from the control imposed by medication loses its meaning when the only alternatives are death and insanity.'[79]

Mental disorders have been suffered in silence for the most part. Recently, they are increasingly being talked about, although it has needed film stars and musicians to bring the discussion into the public domain. Legally speaking though, they have had a place in divorce law since 1955.

79. Kay Redfield Jamison, *An Unquiet Mind: A Memoir of Moods and Madness*

The phrase 'mental disorder' occurs twice in the Hindu Marriage Act and the Special Marriage Act. First, to say that sound mental health is necessary for free consent to marriage.[80] Second, that mental disorder is a ground for divorce, if the person 'has been incurably of unsound mind, or has been suffering continuously or intermittently from mental disorder of such a kind and to such an extent that the petitioner cannot reasonably be expected to live with the respondent.' The second has a wider amplitude when you consider that a person may have the ability to consent to marriage and even function in society, yet suffer disorders of a nature that the spouse cannot be reasonably expected to live with.[81] The statute clarifies in an explanation that:

> (a) the expression 'mental disorder' means mental illness, arrested or incomplete development of mind, psychopathic disorder or any other disorder or disability of mind and includes schizophrenia;
> (b) the expression 'psychopathic disorder' means a persistent disorder or disability of mind (whether or not including sub-morality of intelligence) which results in abnormally aggressive or seriously irresponsible conduct on the part of the other party, and whether or not it requires or is susceptible to medical treatment...

Thus the marriage statutes allow for divorce on mental health grounds, with the main factor being the person's behaviour, not merely a diagnosis.

The Supreme Court has warned about the fine line between major mental health disorders and minor psychological issues: 'If the mere existence of any degree of mental abnormality could justify dissolution of a marriage, few marriages would, indeed, survive in law.'[82]

There is no complete mental health formula. Of course, another dimension to the issue is that we need to explore our private mental quirks as part of the journey of self-discovery. Many, if not most of us suffer various degrees of neuroses that we learn to cover for social survival and the line between eccentricity and mental disorder can be narrower than a hair's breadth. There is also ample evidence to show that serious sociopaths and psychopaths can be highly functional at their workplaces for long periods of time; it is often their intimate relations that have to suffer the impact of a person disintegrating into instability. Living with

---

80. See p. 364: Section 5, Hindu Marriage Act, 1956; See also p. 388: Section 4, Special Marriage Act, 1954

81. See p. 366: Section 13(1)(iii) of The Hindu Marriage Act, 1955

82. Ram Narain Gupta vs. Smt. Rameshwari Gupta, AIR 1988 SC 2260

these crumbling persons can be arduous, and is exacerbated by the fact that there are no facilities for medical intervention and family counselling, unlike the ones available for those who have been clinically diagnosed with a mental disorder.

~

The Mental Health Act (1987) deals only with clinically diagnosed patients. Divorce litigation however, daily sees deeply negative personalities who may be highly functional for the world at large, but difficult to live with for reasons known only to the intimate family. Their dysfunctionalities reveal themselves over time as unpleasant and difficult character traits.

It is not uncommon for many divorce petitioners to complain that all was well in the marriage until 'the respondent showed his/her true colours'. Sometimes an illness or event triggers a fundamental character change. Glandular fever, an accident, the death of a loved one: all such events can spark an existential crisis that impacts the family. Such an event could even be a catalyst to personal, spiritual or creative search, but that is still at the cost of the family. Some clients will complain of their spouse and then warn me, 'S/he is very charming and clever so don't let yourself get manipulated'.

Sometimes I sense that it is my client who in fact suffers some obsessive disorders. I then discreetly drop names of therapists that I feel they could benefit from. Many take my advice and I am touched by their humility. Others take away their cases, because they think I have exceeded my brief with my advice, but I have stopped feeling bad about that.

Here, I want to underline that every divorce process requires therapeutic intervention of various types and intensities. I am not embarrassed to admit that I too have felt the need to unburden the baggage of stress and neuroses that the nature of my work compels me to carry. I am uncomfortably close to this leviathan legal system that is unpredictable, slow and arduous, with the people comprising it sometimes quite eccentric. I fear being at its mercy. Not a day passes without me giving thanks for the grace of not having seen my parents in a court of law, like the ageing, harried couples around me, helpless at the mercy of lawyers and judges.

~

Returning to mental health in matrimonial litigation, let's consider the following allegations:

- My spouse suffers from sex addiction/alcoholism/uncontrolled spending.

- S/he has a history of child sexual abuse/incest or inappropriate closeness of an incestuous nature.
- My spouse attacked me violently with scissors and knives/raped me/beat me.
- The husband, in anger and contempt, defecated in the kitchen sink and made her clean up.
- The wife harassed him by hiding the car keys and wallet.
- I face insensitive teasing and ridicule.
- She is rude and the nagging never stops.

Although some of these seem to be primitive expressions of hate and contempt for the partner, they can also stem from something more serious. If the allegations are true, the perpetrator is imbalanced and needs help in the form of therapy or medication. Conversely, if it is a false accusation, the accuser suffers from a complex problem that is equally serious.

At this point, the deeper question of the fine line between the mental imbalances that we all suffer from and major mental disorders is worth discussing in more detail.

~

Recently, a pleasant, articulate, gentle woman came to see me. Her husband had filed a divorce petition on the ground of fraud against her, for not having disclosed that she had been treated for mental disorder and that she had obsessive-compulsive disorder.

As a teenager, she had a habit of imagining a story and then building it to proportions that upset her. The basic therapy and mild medication that was prescribed for a couple of years was stopped, based on doctor's advice that she did not need it any longer as she was cured. The stress of coping with the drastic new situation of her marriage caused the problem to emerge again. The symptoms were anxiety attacks brought on by her imagined fears and worries.

She remained a warm, loving, talented person. Reassuring love from her husband and his family would have coaxed her out of her self-inflicted timidity, but they chose the mental disorder route as an exit from the marriage. Another relevant fact is that when they discovered the problem, the girl's family-in-law asked her father for more money and property to keep the marriage intact. They filed the divorce petition when he refused. We agreed eventually to a divorce, because the hostile environment was exacerbating matters and creating more dysfunctionalities for her.

In this case, the diagnosis of a mental disorder was not matched with unbearable behaviour, though the toll mental illness takes on the families of the patients can be horrific. The problematic question then arises about the legal obligation to care—and hence by extension, to stay in the marriage.

~

John Bayley, in his book about caring for his wife Iris Murdoch,[83] a patient of Alzheimer's disease writes: 'We are accompanied into the millennium, not by the four horsemen of the apocalypse, but by the four cavaliers in white coats. Compassion, caring, counseling, compensation.' Bayley chose to care and that is laudable but everyone does not have the psychological strength to be a good caregiver. We cannot judge them badly in law.

A discussion about mental health in divorce proceedings has to include such persons who are not good caregivers and want to be free of the burden of being in a marriage with someone suffering a mental disorder. It may seem morally reprehensible to allow for the exit, but it is as morally reprehensible to insist that a bad caregiver continue to be one. The legal solution to this conundrum is to ensure the discharge of adequate financial responsibility towards care. The Supreme Court recently ruled on this point in the Kollam Chandra Sekhar case:[84]

> 'Marriage is highly revered in India and we are a Nation that prides itself on the strong foundation of our marriages, come hell or high water, rain or sunshine. Life is made up of good times and bad, and the bad times can bring with it terrible illnesses and extreme hardships. The partners in a marriage must weather these storms and embrace the sunshine with equanimity.... Any person may have bad health and...that is not their fault or within their control, as in the present case, the respondent was unwell and was taking treatment for the same. The illness had its fair share of problems. Can this be a reason for the appellant to abandon her and seek dissolution of marriage after the child is born out of their union? Since the child is now a grown-up girl, her welfare must be the prime consideration for both the parties. In view of the foregoing reasons, we are of the opinion that the two parties in this case must reconcile and if the appellant so feels that the respondent is still suffering, then she must be given the right treatment. The respondent must stick to her treatment plan and make the best attempts to get better. It is not in the best interest of either the respondent or her daughter who is said to be of adolescent age for grant of a decree of dissolution of marriage as prayed for by the appellant. Hence, the appeal is liable to be dismissed.'

83. John Bayley, *Iris: A Memoir of Iris Murdoch*.

84. Kollam Chandra Sekhar vs. Kollam Padma Latha, 2013 (11) SCALE 617

The judgment is problematic because it has intertwined what ought to be (morality) with balancing of rights as they are (law). The moral issue of abandoning the person you live with and loved in good health was the central concern of the court but that moral cannot be an absolute and cannot be imposed by law. A sacrifice for love or duty is an imperfect obligation that cannot be enforced legally and to try and do so could lead to unjust results.

The reasoning of the Kollam Chandra Sekhar case is that modern medicine has dramatically improved the treatment of mental disorders so that it is not unreasonable to expect the petitioner to live with the suffering respondent. The husband is told to ensure that he gives his wife medicine, while she is told to take it dutifully. The matter is wrapped good and tidy and handed down with a generous halo.

One is left to reflect that the sexual relationship of the couple may be impossible or unreliable, given her condition, and it is unjust to incarcerate the couple in a possibly sexless marriage. Particularly so, as the same Court has held on several occasions that sexual intimacy is an integral part of a marriage and has also urged the individual's right to the pursuit of happiness as part of his right to life.[85]

To say that the parties 'must' reconcile is contrary to the legal principle that judges must refrain from passing orders that cannot be complied with or enforced.[86] By dismissing the husband's divorce petition and allowing the wife's petition for restitution of conjugal rights, the judges also rendered ineffective even the moral end they sought to achieve. The husband can still get his divorce by avoiding cohabitation with his wife for two years.[87] Problematic sanctimonious personal views on marriage apart,[88] the judgment has only delayed the inevitable separation by two more tortured years.

Going by this judgment, it would seem that since modern medicine is

---

85. Govind vs. State of M.P, AIR 1975 SC 1378: 'There can be no doubt that the makers of our Constitution wanted to ensure conditions favourable to the pursuit of happiness'

86. Ashok Desai & S. Muralidhar, 'Public Interest Litigation: Potential and Problems' in B.N. Kirpal et. al. (eds.), *Supreme but not Infallible* p. 182

87. As per the law of restitution

88. It may be of interest to the reader that this is the same judge who ruled on the continuing criminalization of homosexuality: Suresh Kumar Koushal & Anr. vs. NAZ Foundation & Ors., 2013(15)SCALE 55.

increasingly effective in managing most mental conditions, mental disorder has ceased to be effective as a single ground for divorce.

~

The legal handling of mental health issues has been inept, to put it mildly. One basic problem is that the trauma of the divorce proceedings further exacerbates the mental problem and the person seeking divorce also suffers appalling mental stress. During the hearings, judges and lawyers either resist dealing with the issue or abdicate responsibility to mental health 'experts'. That is not fair to the litigants either, because the experts are not expected to deliver justice. In addition, in my experience, reports by 'experts' tend to be mechanical and without transparency about the protocol of assessment. For the expert to say that s/he met so-and-so and then recount the interview furthers no purpose.[89]

Conclusion

The evolution of fault theory shows that its application seems to have become less strict by some courts over the years, leading to the sense that if a marriage has clearly broken down irretrievably, it is better to grant the divorce. However, there is no certainty about this approach either: for example in the Family Court at Saket, New Delhi, one judge is anxious about the social stability of society, given the ease with which people ask for divorce. On the other hand, another court has this placard near the witness box:

> Are you holding on to something or someone you need to let go of?
> Why?
> What keeps you from letting go?
> Let go and trust.

89. See Ch. 7: Children, p. 244, for a discussion on experts reporting on matters relating to children.

5. PROPERTY

My great-grandmother from my mother's side, known to us as Beybeyji, was widowed at the age of forty. This was in the early 1900s. Based on the custom of duswand in her clan, a widow was entitled to a tenth of her husband's estate. Even this minimal right was never hers completely because of the other custom of kareva, by which she may have been expected to marry her brother-in-law.[1]

In an era of timid widows, Beybeyji refused the kareva marriage. (I am not even sure that the brother-in-law would have had the courage to offer the marriage, but if he did, I am quite sure that he would have been relieved at her refusal). She also refused to settle for a meagre tenth of her husband's estate. She did not allow her husband's body to leave the house until her four sons obeyed her order to each transfer land to her name, saying, 'I love you all but there is no reason why I should be financially dependent upon you.' The patwari drew up the papers at 10 p.m.

Her eldest son, Major Gurdial Singh Mann, was called Major Sahib and was my maternal grandfather: Nanaji. He fought with the British in the Second World War. He was also deputed as ADC to King George VI. He then met Gandhi and took to khadi. His British commanding officer said that it was a matter of concern that a senior Indian officer like him had visited Gandhi. My grandfather responded that he would probably meet him again but he understood his soldier's duty just as well.

The next son was Sardar B.S. Mann: he became a prominent politician from the Punjab. During the framing of the Constitution he had protested that the Sikhs were not protected enough as a minority. When Independent India debated radical changes in marriage laws, he opposed the equal right of a woman to inherit property and also opposed the Hindu Code Bill in 1951, saying it diluted Sikh identity.[2] His views on women's property rights are telling for the son of a powerful matriarch, and I am told that he had hell to pay when his mother and sister heard of his Parliament speech. 'Beybeyji, it is going to happen anyway,' said the parliamentarian, a confused, scared boy at home.

---

1. Veena Oldenburg, *Dowry Murder: Reinvestigating A Cultural Whodunnit*, p. 149; See also: Rajinder Bedi's beautiful book, *Ek Chadar Maili Si*

2.http://www.ambedkar.org/ambcd/64B3.On%20the%20Hindu%20Code%20Bill.htm

Beybeyji had one other son, whom my father called a 'lovable rogue'. She also had two daughters, one of whom was blind. My blind grand-aunt's story is unusual. She was Bibi Gurbachan Kaur: Bibiji. Bibiji had lost her sight due to a quinine overdose in a suicide attempt as a teenager.

'Why did she try to kill herself?' I asked my mother, who said that she was ashamed because some money that had been entrusted to her was stolen. I did not ask why a fourteen-year-old was entrusted with that kind of money and why she would want to kill herself if it was misplaced, because I knew there was something more to the story, which my mother would never tell me. A few years ago I found two different biographies about Bibiji's life.[3] I have inferred a grimy truth from the gaps in the narrative, but it does not serve this story. All that needs to be told is that the misplaced money was fabricated by the family as a cover-up.

Blind Bibiji became an important activist for women's rights in Punjab and set up one of the first all-women's colleges in Punjab, Mata Gujri College. She set up an ashram to educate orphaned and abandoned girls. I grew up calling her 'Ashram-waley Bibiji'. She travelled from Lahore to Sabarmati to visit Gandhi and returned with five charkhas. One charkha travelled with her after Partition and I remember its sound as part of her meditation and prayer.

This is my translation of a portion of a public speech that she made in Punjabi: 'Women are daughters, sisters, wives and mothers. No mother will allow that someone else's child be killed. Nor will a wife, sister or daughter... But the women of our nation are helpless because they cannot find that one thread on which they can all be connected like beads of a necklace. Nor do they have the awareness to do that. If they did, they would grab the swords, guns and axes from their fathers, brothers and husbands and throw them away.'[4]

The problem of women not being able to form a separate class outside their own communities has been the subject of much study and debate amongst feminists. Ashram-waley Bibiji was a feminist without knowing the term.

Bibiji received a bequest of land from her mother, the widowed Beybeyji.[5] By then, Section 14 of the Hindu Succession Act 1956 gave

3. Jagjivan Singh, *Bibi Gurbachan Kaur Mann: Jeevan Katha*; Sib Nath, *Pulle Visre Lok*

4. Sib Nath, *Pulle Visre Lok*, p. 19

5. See p. 372: Section 14 of the Hindu Succession Act, 1956-Property of a female Hindu to be her absolute Property.

Beybeyji the right to make that will, but the sons refused to respect it. Bibiji was losing heart at the thought of fighting her brothers until she found an ally in her sister-in-law, my Nani, who shamed her husband for grudging a bit of land to their sister after having lost hundreds of acres in Pakistan. He relented and his younger brothers submitted to him. The law could be effectively implemented only with the approval of the patriarch.

The story does not end here. Bibiji died, leaving a will bequeathing most of her property to the ashram she had set up, and some to my mother who had been her travelling companion in the days of her political activity. The 'lovable rogue' brother asked to read the will and when it was trustingly handed to him, tore it up. Those were the days before mistrust and photocopies. My mother did not have the courage to question the destruction of evidence. This time, her own father, the legendary Major Sahib who had implemented Beybeyji's will, was disappointingly silent, as were her own brothers, my elegant beloved Mamajis. They all felt my mother was 'well settled' in her married home and needed no more material wealth.

My mother has not forgotten this: she taught me what she had learned from her days of political activism with Ashram-waley Bibiji: that it is not food, clothes and a lifestyle, but ownership of property that gives a woman context.

Women's Right to Own Property

In 1951, during discussions in Parliament on the Hindu Code Bill, Sardar B.S. Mann[6] suggested that a woman should have a right in her father's property only till she married. But he did not follow this with an argument for better rights for a married woman in her husband's property.

In the same debates, Pandit Thakur Das Bhargava felt that women getting rights in the properties of both the natal family and the husband's family was not entirely workable since, 'At present the son is the pivot of the family'.[7]

Shri M.A. Ayyangar, M.P. was concerned that

> 'the modern woman who is educated in a foreign system who has lost moorings in her own faith wants that she should inherit the property of her father and not her husband. She is indifferent. She wants to have the

6. See Ch. 2: Decoding Gender, p. 57

7. http://www.ambedkar.org/ambcd/64B1.On%20the%20Hindu%20Code%20Bill.htm

> money in her pocket and feel "why should I be subordinate to man?... give me a portion of the property" [...] suppose there is a rich man and his daughter inherits his property. When she is married does it prevent the other man to belabour her and beat her? What prevents him from doing that?'[8]

These debates reveal that despite the lip service, there was deep discomfort with the concept of complete equality for women. Dr Deshmukh in Parliament openly said about women: 'But wife also is property.'[9] There is something unpalatable to men about granting property rights to a species that is viewed as property.

A general statistic estimates that women own about 1 per cent of the land in the world. I don't know about the corresponding figure in India; given that women did have some property rights here, we can assume that it's greater than 1 per cent, but it would still be a low single digit number. As this sobering statistic indicates, reforms to women's right to property remain pending. I would say they are the most important reforms because, to restore that lost 'mother right', as Friedrich Engels,[10] said so poetically, the woman has to be restored to having equal control. Ownership of property will give her the social countenance to negotiate her other rights for herself.

~

In the 1900s oppressive patriarchy was a global problem for women. America had freed its slaves, but women remained chained to their men with no independent property rights. In England, Caroline Sheridan Norton wrote a letter to Queen Victoria:

> '...firstly, because I desire to point out the grotesque anomaly which ordains that married women shall be non-existent in a country governed by a female sovereign... A married woman in England has no legal existence: her being is absorbed in that of her husband... even though she may never see or hear of him'.

Mrs Norton discusses a case where a sailor bequeathed all he was worth to a woman he cohabited with, resulting in the legal wife losing all her income, including what she had from her own parents, since everything

8. http://www.ambedkar.org/ambcd/64B2.On%20the%20Hindu%20Code%20Bill.htm

9. *Ibid*

10. Engels, *The Origin of Family, Private Property and the State*, p. 11

belonged to him. Equity, the hallmark of English justice, did not come to her aid.[11]

Stridhan

Mrs Norton wrote this letter in 1855. It may sound surprising given where we are now, but at the time women in India were actually better off than those in England. Many Indian women owned property and could also inherit a portion of their husband's estate; additionally, they had a lifetime interest in family property for their personal maintenance. They had all rights of ownership to wealth they received at the time of marriage and after. This was their stridhan. Though some daughters of wealthy fathers did receive land, houses and businesses as their stridhan, it was generally considered appropriate to give a bride movable wealth that she could carry to her marital home. However, a woman had no pre-existing legal right to stridhan, meaning that she could not demand it, and her parents and family-in-law had no legal obligation to give it. The giving of stridhan was a voluntary gesture; a gift to fulfill a pious and moral obligation. Once the woman received that gift, her right of complete ownership sprang to life. She dealt with her stridhan as she pleased.[12] Usually it was bequeathed from mother to daughter. Loans given to husbands were expected to be returned with interest.[13]

Three years after Mrs Norton's letter, India became part of the Queen's dominion, requiring English civil servants to begin an exercise to understand the 'native' customs. This was done by recording interviews with the village headmen, local munshis and panchayats, who were probably not even asked about customs relating to women's rights. Usually, women elders have the role of providing cultural continuity and often give advice on custom. Here they were not interviewed, perhaps because of the practice of purdah, or more probably because the English surveyors could not even imagine that the wives of the 'natives' may have better rights for women than the English gave to the 'weaker sex'. It was

11. 'From Caroline Norton, A letter to the Queen on Lord Chancellor Cranworth's Marriage and Divorce Bill', 1855

12. Madhu Purnima Kishwar, 'Destined to Fail: Inherent Flaws in the Anti-dowry Legistlation' in *Manushi* 1988.

13. JAGORI and Monobina Gupta (ed), *Marching Together: Resisting Dowry in India*, 2009.

this skewed understanding obtained by the British that finally[14] stamped Indian women out of society.

Jewellery

Yet, even in the darkest times, the one right the Indian woman managed to retain was the right to own her jewellery. As the exploited gender, she was vulnerable to robbery and appropriation, but her right to the ownership of the jewellery was never in question.

Indian women historically have had a special relationship with jewellery. A report by an English settlement officer around Karnal mentions that Indian women commiserated with the memsahibs for their miserly husbands who gave them no jewellery.[15] Jewellery was important for the men too. Bejewelled maharajas competed with their ranis. The romance and intimacy of a jewel makes for better stories than those found in many monuments and archives.

My maternal grandfather, Major Saab as he was known, was an exception to the rule of this compelling bond between Indians and their jewels. He was rude about jewellery and said it made women look like decked-up prize cows. He particularly hated the nath (nose ring) that symbolizes a married woman. 'It is to allow a man to lead you by the nose, literally', he used to warn me. My mother was his favourite child. Her stridhan was a very small amount of jewellery that her own mother had managed to hide from her austere husband when he sold the family jewels to buy land after Partition.

My mother tells me that two days before her wedding day, she and my Nani went to get her ears pierced because their nerves could not bear the thought of a bride with no earrings, never mind what my grandfather thought. He noticed her pierced ears and exclaimed, '*Acchha ji, tussivi*' (said in an 'Et tu, Brute' type of way), while she ran past him holding her dupatta close around her head. At the wedding reception, my father's family gave my mother a pair of earrings that were dazzling in workmanship but heavy and painful to wear. Her three-day-old pierced earlobes were bleeding, but she was told to endure with her chin up because a bride without earrings was inauspicious. She was told, 'You are a soldier's daughter: you can do it.' My mother bore the pain and smiled

14. Veena Oldenburg, *Dowry Murder: Reinvestigating A Cultural Whodunnit*, p.135

15. Karnal settlement report, 1892 available at http://www.nidanaheights.net/images/Library/books/karnal-gazeetter-1892.pdf

prettily, but her spirit was broken. She would never have tolerated such discomfort at her father's house.

At my own wedding, I excitedly asked my father how I looked as he walked with me to the ceremony. With loving sarcasm he said, 'Lovely! But if there is any jewellery left over, why don't you carry it in either hand?'

And that describes the essence of the Indian woman and her jewels. She is the mannequin to display family wealth. (Though I can't resist mentioning that men also could not bear to part with the greatest jewel of all, the Kohinoor).

~

Then there is jewellery given as appeasement. One way of stopping a child from running riot in the house is to give her some pretty things to keep her quiet while the grown-ups deal with the business of messing up the world. A man is expected to do the same with his woman and the woman is expected to be satisfied with that. The ayyaash zamindaar Rehman in *Sahib Bibi Aur Ghulam* (1962) tells his wife Meena Kumari to leave him with the courtesans and do what all women do. '*Gehney banao, gehney tudvao*'. But Meena Kumari demanded more. She wanted her husband to herself. That was an impossible challenge to his mardangi and zamindaar status.

In modern India today, the father of a young woman who was married into a very rich family told me that his daughter had left her husband because of his serial adultery. But, he told me that the women of his house planned the marriage. They were dazzled by the boy's wealth. 'I never particularly liked him, but he is even more stupid than I realized, openly having affairs. All men have fun', he went on, 'but they make sure their wives are not embarrassed; after all, the wife has to keep the home comfortable and peaceful. Men must buy things for their wives: jewellery, perfume, bags, shoes, clothes. That's all it takes', he told me. 'What more does a woman want? Problem with this foolish boy is that he neither gives her gifts nor does he give her a generous shopping allowance. So she will obviously object!' According to him, the fault was not the boy's adultery but that he did not bribe his wife enough to keep her quiet.

Women, too, grow up with the pressure to display external beauty and being bedecked is seen as essential to feminine beauty. They are also told that a man's true expression of love is when he buys her expensive gifts and so puts his money where his mouth is. In addition, crass commercialism and status anxiety leaves us with a feeling of never having enough of anything.

Munshi Prem Chand described this many decades ago in the classic tale, *Gaban*. A little girl is told that she will marry a man who will love her so much that he will buy her a Chandra haar. So she grows up believing that absolute love is measured by a Chandra haar. At her wedding, her husband sends her gifts of jewellery but not a Chandra haar. She does not think the abject pain of disappointment to be irrational. She had been brought up to believe that the Chandra haar represented happiness and security and she was bereft without one. The husband's deep passionate love for his wife compels him to embezzle money to buy her the haar. The story ends with both cleansed by their travails, wiser and stronger having confronted her childish greed and his weakness.

What is the jewellery really for?

Historically, Indians have hoarded jewellery to meet turbulent times and sold it at the bottom of the pit of financial despair. During the 1990s, when India was liberalized, the Central Bank had to airlift forty-seven tonnes of gold as collateral to get loans from the Bank of England.[16] 'It is like asking a woman to sell jewellery,' said a client of mine, a worried senior navy commander formed by socialist India.

A nineteenth-century British civil servant, Darling, working in the Punjab, gathered from his village encounters that women may pawn their jewellery to tide over a difficult time, but would never sell it because it was their surest defense against widowhood or separation. Jewellery was also used as a collateral for a loan, and actually saved many peasants from mortgaging their land.[17]

Men sometimes used the women's right to enjoy absolute ownership of her jewellery to circumvent the law. Businessmen who were unable to pay their creditors would buy jewellery for their wives and then apply for insolvency. Iravati Karve, the sociologist, claims personal knowledge of a clerk who bought jewellery in his wife's name with money he embezzled from his employer.[18] No money could be recovered from him as his wife's jewellery was her stridhan that the law could not touch.

I will round up this discussion with the note that gold continues to be India's most-imported good, along with oil. Oil for consumption and gold to be hoarded.

16. 'India's Economy: One More Push' in *The Economist*, July 21, 2001.

17. *Ibid*

18. Irawati Karve, *Kinship Organisation in India*

Stridhan vs. dowry

Jewellery given as a woman's stridhan was compensation for the land she could not carry to the marital home. We can see now that this custom metastasized into the pernicious practice of dowry reducing the persona of women to the wealth that they could bring.

However, British sentiment could not differentiate between the two ideas. Veena Talwar Oldenburg[19] writes of the propaganda against dowries undertaken by the civil servant Brayne in the late nineteenth century:

> 'The Punjabi's love for jewellery was, according to him, the worst addiction of all and it is deplorable that men and women bedecked themselves. He made an educated approximate estimate that at the time there was not less than one crore of rupees locked in people's homes in the form of jewellery.'

Brayne tried to persuade the villagers to release that money from its idle state but the villagers were too worried about the loss of peace in their homes if they agreed. 'Allow the ladies half a crore—we must not be too strict or no one will listen to us.'[20]

How did the essentially not bad custom of stridhan become a dowry menace unique to India? How did Indian women who owned jewellery as personal and absolute stridhan become beasts of burden to carry dowry for the husband's family?

I suggest that one of the answers lie in the custom of kanyadaan, the religious duty that makes it a 'need' to earn celestial plus points to marry off one's daughter. This is not simply Jane Austen's Mrs Bennett, who represents the prime preoccupation of mothers across the world to get their daughters married to eligible men. Kanyadaan symbolizes an Indian social attitude, of which Mrs Bennett's anxiety forms only a superficial layer: the deeper and more difficult to rectify foundation of kanyadaan is patriarchy as a religious order. It is the attitude that an unmarried daughter after a particular age is inauspicious, a burden and a matter of shame for her parents (think of common phrases such as '*main ladki ghar pey nahi bitha rakh sakta*'). The exploitation of this deep, almost visceral need to marry off daughters is the reason why Indian women are so vulnerable in the marriage market.

---

19. Veena Talwar Oldenburg, *Dowry Murder: The Imperial Origins of a Cultural Crime* pp.176–180.

20. Half a crore (Rs. 50,00,000) then is approximately equal to Rs. 12,000 crores today

Every wedding story ends with weeping parents, as the miserable bride steps into the doli to leave with her husband. Her girlfriends sing mournful bidai songs, filled with complaints that she must leave her fields and home to her brothers and the jewels she has to carry feel like thorns.[21] In the times when gold was as valuable as land, stridhan seemed fair compensation for a daughter leaving the fields to her brothers. Now that the price of gold no longer compensates for real estate, many grooms have started demanding property as dowry.

Given how vulnerable they feel to the pressure of getting their daughters married, most parents find it difficult to challenge the dowry custom. They only hope to provide enough material satisfaction to the husband's family to act as an insurance policy for their daughters' happiness. The blackmail never stops: for the rest of her married life, every occasion will be celebrated with a monetary transaction between the girl's parental and marital families. Compound this with the customs that dictate the 'girl's side' will not visit their daughter too often; will never spend the night there; will not eat a meal there. It is seen as a sin to take money from the daughter because she is 'parayadhan'.[22] The financial resources depleted by the girl's dowry are replenished through the son's marriage. This is the vicious cycle.

Then there are parents who are too poor to have a dowry for their daughters, but need to marry them off somehow, anyhow. Rahul Bedi reports[23] that dowry demands in Bihar led families to kidnap unmarried men to force them to marry their daughters. The kidnappers charge an extra fee to ensure the continuance of marriage. Eligible bachelors are on the run during the wedding seasons because they do not want to lose the opportunity for a handsome dowry in a properly negotiated marriage.

Currently the distinction between dowry and stridhan lies collapsed, because apart from her personal jewellery the woman is supposed to bring other things, ostensibly for her comfort but really to meet the demands of the groom and his family—in other words, dowry.

Dowry used to be a custom as worldwide as patriarchy, but I am not aware of any part of the world other than India where women are murdered for not bringing enough or for the husband to have a chance

21. Bina Aggarwal, *A Field of One's Own: Gender and Land Rights in South Asia*, p. 1

22. Literally, another's wealth

23. Rahul Bedi, 'Shotgun weddings with a sinister difference', *The Telegraph*, 27 September 2013

to make more wealth by getting a second dowry carried by a fresher bride. The sense of entitlement that comes from being able to draw on the ancient 'riwaj' of dowry precludes grooms and their families from feeling shame about the atrocities they commit. It is socially sanctioned avarice: a consumer sickness of epidemic proportions.

Media reportage of 'dowry deaths'—not even dignified by the term 'murder'—have reduced this foul crime to a statistic, leaving no space to express its full horror. There is no room in public discourse to feel the pain and bewilderment of a young girl killed by the man who was to be her friend and lover. Murderers have to see their victims either as a non-person or assume a grandiose persona to delude themselves into some perverted justification of the murder. The murdered women are either mere shadows because they adhere faithfully to the absolute subservience demanded of them, or are pushed into becoming shadows because of and despite their resistance. The murder is the final step to make her who she should be ideally—someone as good as dead.

My youthful curiosity, cruel in its dispassion, made me wonder why dowry deaths were always by fire. Why not poison or a road accident or stabbing? It took me a while to realize that each murdering family stupidly believes that a kitchen accident is a reasonable alibi. Madhurita Sen has an interesting analogy of the collective subconscious on 'bride burning' emanating from Sita's ordeal by fire.[24] It could also reflect the idea of a Sati.

The method of murder may have changed, but the problem is growing, as ostentatious consumerism becomes the hallmark for status and identity.[25] More than ever before, it is the woman's burden to fulfill the man's wish list. Along with bringing dowry, women are expected to produce sons. The two functions have reduced them to jewel-encrusted wombs.

~

From being a relatively empowered woman compared to her English counterpart in 1858, an Indian woman's social status degraded steadily, leaving her finally with the identity of being a victim of horrific crimes, like child marriage, sati and dowry deaths. The English worked with

---

24. Madhurita Sen, TV discussion on NDTV

25. 'Rising number of dowry deaths in India: NCRB' in *The Hindu*, 6 August 2013. There was a dip and then again there has been a sharp increase in the number of dowry deaths since 1998.

reformist zeal on these matters, but at the same time constructed history from a colonial perspective. Now, so-called 'nationalists' attempt to deconstruct and reverse this history with equal reformist zeal, as Romila Thapar discusses.[26] But to deconstruct law, to start again, could even prove more dangerous. We have to deal with the impact of colonialism on Indian custom, which became law, in the same way we would deal with a boulder that falls on a hillside and crushes all beneath. To blast the hillside to create a new landscape is not an option. You can only encourage growth and life, till the boulder becomes an interesting feature of the landscape. At present, it is cumbersome, baffling, stark, but we have to allow for organic growth of the creatures that emerge from under and around it.

The careless raja

Many years ago, I negotiated a divorce settlement for a raja in a North Indian state. Circumstances had resulted in a lot of his estate jewellery and silver being entrusted to his parents-in-law, themselves also royalty from a neighbouring state. We had to discuss the divorce with another raja who was acting as family arbitrator.

The drive to the arbitrator's town was lovely and my client was good company. We were accompanied by a royal groupie who would keep asking to stop the car, either to pick up another bottle of Coke into which he would pour rum or to relieve himself of the heady cocktail. Despite being a teetotaller, the mild-mannered indulgent raja did not object to this bacchanalia on a Monday morning. When the meeting with the royal arbitrator was over, the raja and groupie left for the palace of the parents-in-law to collect his family jewellery and silver. I remained at the hotel. The groupie gave me the following account:

'We were greeted at the door by the raja's father-in-law, who looked his royal son-in-law in the eye and said, "What jewellery?"

'Raja Sahib, too easy-going to argue, simply turned his back on his soon-to-be ex-father-in-law—and his entire family jewellery—by saying, "Oh, all righty then!"

'The father-in-law, seemingly feeling a twinge of conscience, said "Oh, come back; come back: I won't know what to do with your family jewellery and crest anyhow!"'

The raja collected the jewellery in a large suitcase and left the silver

26. Romila Thapar, *The Past as Present: Forging Contemporary Identities Through History*

packed in steel trunks for another time. The suitcase was brought to the hotel. I was called from my room to the hotel lobby for a cup of tea before we drove back to Delhi. I wanted to see and handle what was bound to be beautiful antique jewellery, but my professional self didn't allow me to articulate such a feminine weakness. We all got into the car and began our drive back to Delhi. Five hours into the drive, night had fallen and I was nervous about our priceless cargo. I suggested we stop at a hotel and carry on the next day; this was not safe. Raja Sahib agreed.

We found a guesthouse in a small town. While the bags were being unloaded, Raja Sahib looked at me, panic-stricken: where was the suitcase with the jewellery? I felt a wave of responsive panic and sweat washed over me till I realized that it was not my responsibility. Curiously, at that moment I wished I had at least seen the jewellery. The raja went into deep meditation, tracing his steps from the moment he had got the jewellery and concluded that he had left the suitcase in the hotel lobby. He wanted to call the hotel, but the telephone lines were down. Raja Sahib and groupie—with bottle intact—got into the car to return to the hotel, five hours away. It was 7 p.m. then.

At noon the next morning, there was a knock at my door. The suitcase had indeed been lying in the lobby and all was well. We carried on our journey after exploring a picturesque small town with many water bodies.

~

Three days later, Raja Sahib called me. 'My mother', he said, 'is very fond of my soon-to-be ex-wife. So when I gave the suitcase to my mother for safe-keeping, she decided on a fun lunch and outing with her soon-to-be ex-daughter-in law: getting the jewellery valued by the family jewellers in Delhi.'

So they spent a pleasant afternoon with the jeweller, talking of the history of each piece and where it came from, followed by lunch at a nice place to moan about how men are, and then back to the jeweller. As the valuation was not over, the jeweller asked them to return the next day.

The daughter-in-law lived close to the jeweller's shop. The mother-in-law told her to carry the jewellery to her house for the night and bring it back to the shop the next day.

The next morning, my client was given the task of collecting his soon-to-be ex-wife and bring her to the shop. He arrived at her house. She was not dressed to go out, but came smiling down the staircase and handed him a small pouch containing gold buttons with the family crest. That's all.

'What happened to the rest?' Raja Sahib asked. He is too well bred to express emotions like astonishment or shock.

She replied, 'It's my stridhan actually. I am keeping it.'

'Oh, all righty then', said Raja Sahib, turning back.

He then called me and recounted the story in short sharp sentences. I could sense his consternation through the stiff upper lip.

'Do you see the irony, Raja Sahib? You nearly don't get this priceless jewellery from your father-in-law. Then you get it. Then you leave the suitcase at the hotel lobby. You go back and recover it. Then your own wife rightly claims it as hers in law.'

He did not laugh with me. 'My estate jewellery is her stridhan?' he asked in sarcastic astonishment.

'The argument could be made', I replied, 'but do you want this to go to court when there is no certain outcome?'

Silence.

I asked: 'If all was well and you were not divorcing, when would you have seen this jewellery?'

'At my children's weddings and some family functions when my wife may have worn it.'

'Is she a caring parent?' I asked

'Undoubtedly', he said.

'Leave it', I said. 'You will see it at your children's wedding and if she wears it till then, Raja Sahib, think about it: so what?'

He thought for a second and then said, 'Oh, all righty.'

The raja trusted his instinct in reading his wife. He did not get angry or malicious and avoided a very ugly pointless legal battle that he may have won in court but would have still not made him feel victorious. I felt a twinge of regret at not having seen the sumptuous cargo that I imagined as having been packed hastily from Aladdin's cave.

Many years later I attended the weddings of both his children. The jewels were magnificent and made by a skill that does not survive.

'It's all there?' I asked him.

'Indeed', he said smiling. 'I had no doubt it would go to my children. She is a good sort, really, with a great sense of family honour. She probably just wanted more wear from it. You know how women are!'

I nodded.

'Or do you?' he asked.

'Why do you say it like that?' I asked, a bit offended.

'Well, I did wonder at the time why you did not open the suitcase.' The raja missed nothing.

~

But this is the story of jewellery; the issue is actually about land. Parliamentarian Sinha commented in the House that the real reason for reform in personal law, as well as the real reason for resistance to it, lay in property: religion and tradition were just the window dressing.[27]

Land and the Law

In Hindu law, historically speaking, the property rights of women were limited to the context of maintenance and alimony. Rights of maintenance were graded according to conduct and an 'unchaste' woman could be reduced to subsistence living.[28] In the early twentieth century, many states had passed woman-friendly legislation[29] as part of the Hindu social reform movement, but other than that, nothing much changed till India became independent.

The constitutional value of gender equality is the promise to restore that lost mother right, and marriage reform is a step in that direction. But no substantial change can be effected until women are given the chance to earn and keep control over immovable property. No amount of baubles can compensate for this right.

---

27. http://www.ambedkar.org/ambcd/64B2.On%20the%20Hindu%20Code%20 Bill.htm.

28. *The Mitakshara* quoting the Yajnyavalkya chapter on marriage: The first text, verse No. 70; Parami Ramayya vs Mahadevi Shankarappa, (1910) 12 BOMLR 196

29. Some states already had codified Hindu law before the advent of the British rule:

- Mysore state had enacted a Hindu Law (Women's Rights) Act, 1933 as cited in the 18th Law Commission of India;
- Hindu law had been codified in the princely state of Baroda under the title 'Baroda Hindu Nibandh 1937'.
- Another matrimonial statute passed during this time was the Hindu Widow's Remarriage Act, 1856. Though it legalized the remarriage of Hindu widows, it also cut off their rights in the properties of the deceased husband in Section 2. However, Section 5 saved the rights of the widow to that property which she would have been otherwise entitled.
- The Indian Divorce Act, 1869 applied to Christians throughout India except in the princely states, Portuguese and the French settlements and certain tribal areas. The purpose was mainly to enable English civil servants to be able to institute divorce proceedings in the colonial territory rather than having to return to England for the purpose. Section 7 stated that the court is to act on principles of an English Divorce Court, assuming that both parties professed to be Christian. This was repealed in 2001 by the Indian Divorce (Amendment) Act, (51 of 2001);

(Contd...)

Women are now not just talking inheritance, alimony or maintenance, but a fair and equal opportunity to earn wealth, and a fair and equal share in the wealth in the home, be it parental or marital. For that, women have to pound through complex social systems that are essentially protection devices to ensure male dominion over every stage that empowers a person to earn. To break into the education domain is only the first step. The more difficult breakthrough is learning to navigate the complicated 'boys networks' that create jobs and influence. And the final stereotype that women can't break from is the expectation that they alone will be the home and child caregivers. The 'working woman' who earns money is still second to men in the work domain but remains miles ahead in the unpaid work of kitchen and child care.[30] The process of empowering women is arduous because it requires reversing a process that began centuries ago when she was the earliest slave.

(Contd...)

- The Special Marriage Act, 1872: The Act as amended in 1923 provides for a civil marriage before a registrar between persons of any religion. It was also to legalize marriages of doubtful validity. All restrictions on marriage imposed by law or custom were removed, except as regards certain prohibited degrees of consanguinity or affinity. Succession to the property of any person professing the Hindu, Buddhist, Sikh or Jain religion who married under this Act was to be regulated by the provisions of the Indian Succession Act, 1925 (Section 24). This Act was repealed by the Special Marriage Act, 43 Of 1954.
- The Hindu Women's Right to Property Act, 1937 was passed to confer greater rights to women than they had regarding coparcenary, partition and alienation. It conferred upon a widow the rights of inheritance to her husband's property even when he left sons as heirs. In all cases, the widows were entitled to claim partition, but their interest in the property was limited to her lifetime for her maintenance alone;
- Finally, after the advent of British rule, the Hindu Married Women's Right to Separate Residence and Maintenance Act, 1946 provided that a Hindu married woman shall be entitled to separate residence and maintenance from her husband on one or more of the following grounds namely; he is suffering from any loathsome disease not contracted from her; he is guilty of cruelty or desertion; he marries again; he ceases to be a Hindu; he keeps a concubine; or for any other justifiable reason, notwithstanding any law or custom to the contrary. Such a married woman would lose her rights if she was unchaste or ceased to be a Hindu. This Act was repealed by the Hindu Adoption and Maintenance Act, 1956.

30. Engels, *The Origin of the Family, Private Property and the State*, p. 11.

What is a woman's right to property?

To study women's rights to property, we need to go back to family property ownership structures and trace what happened to women on the way.

Though Manu is popularly referred to as the lawgiver, he was not the author of either of the two prevailing property right systems amongst Hindus. Jimutavahana authored the Dayabhaga system of Bengal and some parts of eastern India and Vijñāneśvara authored the Mitakshara system for the rest of India. Both systems have regional variations that are so wide that it is safe to assume that there is no one absolute exclusive legal school of Dayabhaga or Mitakshara. That leads to reasonable questions about the authorships of the schools. However, in both the Dayabhaga and Mitakshara systems, with all their variations, the patriarch (karta) has the right and duty to manage property for the benefit of the family.[31]

The Dayabhaga patriarch could not be questioned in his lifetime and succession opened only upon his death.

Under the Mitakshara system, a male child acquired by birth[32] a right in the family property, that he could assert by asking for partition at any time and, if a minor, through his mother. Under the Mitakshara system, upon partition, the wife of the patriarch received a share in the property equal to that of the male coparceners. That is the only time a woman received property in a male domain. This extra share to the patriarch through his wife seems to have been given more as a deterrent to a call for division of property in the lifetime of the karta.

My father would have us, his two daughters, giggling and happy when he would tell us that he thanked God he did not have sons who would embarrass him by pulling his venerable beard (read, claim property rights in his lifetime).

Early law

Hindu societies developed customs other than primogeniture to avoid the fragmentation of land. Very little is known really about pre-colonial law in India apart from that it had a wide and varied custom base. Orientalists like Sir William Jones, Henry Maine and various British civil servants created a picture of what they thought to be Hindu law. Nelson,

31. Hanuman Prasad Panday vs. Mt. Babooee Munraj Koonwaree (1854-57) 6 M.I.A. 393

32. Or even by inception.

as mentioned earlier,[33] challenged their perspective and suffered severe castigation for his criticism.[34]

Over this time and since then, historians and scholars have studied myth, folklore and epics not as fact and history, but to better understand the 'hidden assumptions of society' as Thapar calls it.[35] Based on such a reading, both the *Ramayana* and the *Mahabharata* show that primogeniture was not Hindu law. Rama was the chosen heir not because he was the son of the first wife, but because he was a popular prince. That is why he had to be exiled for fourteen years till his brother was accepted as the heir in the eyes of the praja. In the *Mahabharata,* Bharat had the right to name someone other than his first-born as heir, but he refused to do so because he loved Bhishma. An interesting implication from the *Mahabharata* is that none of the contenders to the throne need to be from the blood lineage of the first ruler, in this case, Bharat.[36] Bhishma was the only true blood-line heir, but he was explicitly barred from being ruler when he gave up his claim to kingship; he also promised to not marry so there would be no children to claim the throne. In fact, even an illegitimate child could have claimed the throne, which is why he took a vow of celibacy. Thus, in life as in epics, in the absence of clear rules of succession, there were multiple claimants whose challenges were settled by wars.

~

Apart from wealth within the family, Hindu social structure monopolized natural resources and access to wealth as the exclusive domain of the upper castes. Thus, the traditional social construct of Hindu societies is not just a straightforward structure flowing from a paterfamilias, but a complicated network of power and influence to serve the upper castes. The patriarchal family structure was used as a strong second rung for male dominance, whereby though all men did not have equal wealth and property, even the poorest man exercised power over his family.

---

33. See Ch. 1: Marriage and Divorce Construct, p. 5

34. J.D.M. Derrett, *J.H. Nelson: A Forgotten Administrator-historian of India, Essays in Classical and Modern Hindu Law*, Vol 2, p.355

35. Thapar, *The Past as Present: Forging Contemporary Identities Through History*

36. Pandu and Dhritshastra were conceived by levirate (niyoga) with the sage, Vyasa. The five Pandavas were sired by devtas because Pandu could not consummate his marriage. The hundred Kaurava boys were born from oil-soaked seeds in earthen pots.

This can be seen from the *Mahabharata*: when Yudhishtra staked and lost the Pandava Queen Draupadi, she had the presence of mind to ask an vital question of great legal importance and insight. If Yudhishtra staked himself and became a slave, how could he then have staked his wife since a slave can own nothing? Bhishma's response is telling: even though a slave could not own property, he said, he still had ownership of his wife.

Power is generated by the control of wealth, particularly land, which has become an exclusive male dominion, albeit with its own internal hierarchies. This hierarchy amongst men makes it difficult for women to break free and unite as a separate class. Simultaneously, with the inception of male control, family identity became rooted in land and business ownership with patrilocal ownership. Great stories were about battles for kingdoms and beautiful women were coveted as valuable commodities. Men could be benevolent to their 'own' women because they were the repositories of their honour (*ghar ki izzat*). But an attack on the enemy included raping 'his' women to attack his honour. So the women of the enemy were 'spoiled' and their children killed, in the same way as his land and wealth was looted and plundered. In the *Ramayana,* Rama's battle with Ravana is for his honour, of which Sita is only a symbol. It is this reduction to a mere symbol that drove Sita into her second exile, because of the cruel perception that, having lived in Ravana's palace, Sita was 'spoiled', despite having passed the ordeal by fire.[37]

Throughout the world, patriarchy reproduced itself through male heirs. The Hindus created another reason to ensure that patriarchy persisted: a deceased man was ensured a place in the other world only if a male heir lit his funeral pyre. Hence arose a custom that became part of classical Hindu law, that four generations of male heirs of a Hindu man had a claim to his property. Since the one closest in bloodline to the original owner was best qualified for the death rites, he received a better share and his male heirs received shares in their father's share and so on. Thus, a great-grandson had a vested right in the land of his great-grandfather but only through his own father's line of succession. To be without a male heir was an adharma that must be avoided by adopting one, said the Brahmins and so Hindu classical law has a well-developed customary law on adoption.

In Hindu law, rights in property were shared amongst coparceners to be used for the welfare and maintenance of dependents. The advent of

37. According to the Tulsidas *Ramayana*

Islam and Christianity in the twelfth century left this unchanged and, in fact, the Hindu idea of familial ownership of property was co-opted as custom into many other communities as well.

In Hindu Mitakshara law, if sons asked for partition, their mother got a separate share equal to those of her husband and sons. However, she hardly ever had control over her land, and most times her interest in land, even as a widow, would revert to the sons after her death. Thus, custom around management and inheritance of land was rooted in the idea that no one person could deal with property arbitrarily and whimsically; every dependent could draw subsistence from the land.[38]

Despite this, the position of women was not equal. A widow's lifetime interest in property or a woman's right to maintenance was dependent on her chastity.[39] Indian law here was different from English law, in which a man's legal rights to absolute ownership and enjoyment of private property diluted his moral obligation to maintain his family. The English reform movement began in 1836 with specific statutes that created different legal rights to land, particularly for women.[40]

While English law became progressive, the rights of Indian women had plateaued due to their imprecise nature, made more amorphous by moral positions about chastity and an increasingly repressive patriarchy. From there, her rights became meaningless symbols, leaving her with no control over what was supposed to be hers in law.[41] Specific legislation to restore the balance was required and the process began in 1937[42] with the Hindu Women's Right to Property Act.

---

38. Kishwar, 'Codified Hindu Law: Myth and Reality' in *Economic and Political Weekly*, Vol. 29, No. 33 (Aug13, 1994) p. 2156: This immobilization of land, says Madhu Kishwar, explains why one of the most powerful proponents of the Hindu Code Bill was the business community, which wanted to release land from the stranglehold of multiple claims and pump it into the economy.

39. Bertrand Russell, *Marriage and Morals*

40. Rajeev Dhavan pointed this out in his brilliant doctoral thesis in 1971. Rajeev Dhavan, *The Supreme Court of India: A Socio-Legal Critique of its Juristic Techniques*, 1977.

41. Agarwal, *A Field of One's Own: Gender and Land Rights in South Asia*, p. 144

42. The Hindu Women's Rights to Property Act, 1937; Hindu Adoption and Maintenance Act, 1956; Hindu Marriage Act, 1956; Hindu Succession Act, 1956.

The evolution of the Hindu Code Bill, 1956

In 1956, when the Hindu Code Bill became law in the form of four acts, each dealing with various aspects of family law, the property rights of women were dealt with minimally.[43] The law brought all non-Abrahamic religions into its fold and, in the process of homogenization of various diverse customs for one common law, many women who enjoyed rights in some regions found them eliminated or, at the very least, substantially diluted. For example, the matrilineal laws of Marumakattayam or Nambudri and the Aliyasantana law of South India allowed women coparceners: they could adopt any number of daughters and had full equal rights of inheritance in ancestral property. Many women had the rights of at least a duswand of their husband's estate.[44] This was a custom that could not be the subject of a will. After the Hindu Acts, the wife and daughter and mother of a Hindu man had rights to his estate only if he died intestate. Thus, what the law gave with one hand, it took with the other.

Beneficial customary laws thus destroyed were restructured into two distinct monoliths of regional patriarchy—the north Indian Mitakshara male coparcenary and the Bengal Dayabhaga system.[45] The parochial politics played out in the course of the parliamentary discussion are telling: Consider what S.P. Mookerjee of West Bengal said:

> 'Somebody said...that South India was specially progressive and many of the laws which we are considering are already in existence there today. I say good luck to South India. Let South India proceed from progress to

---

43. The Hindu Marriage Act (1956) was enacted by the Indian Parliament with the intention to amend and codify the marriage law amongst Hindus. Its purpose was to regulate personal life amongst Hindus, especially the institution of marriage, its validity, conditions for invalidity and applicability.

- The Hindu Adoption and Maintenance Act (1956) dealt specifically with the legal process of adopting children by a Hindu adult, as well as the legal obligations of a Hindu to provide 'maintenance' to various family members including, but not limited to, their wife or wives, parents, and in-laws.
- The Hindu Succession Act, 1956 was passed by the Parliament of India to amend and codify the law relating to intestate succession. The Hindu woman's limited estate is abolished by the Act. This Act made women absolute holders of the land that they received had an earlier limited life interest for the purpose of their maintenance.

44. In Punjab, under the rule of Duswand, a window used to get one-tenth of the husband's share; concubines had a right of maintenance.

45. The Mitakshara system existed in some parts of Southern India too.

> progress, from divorce to divorce... why force it on others who do not want it?'[46]

The same narrow-minded chauvinism prevailed with regard to succession to a Hindu woman's property. Mukut Behari Lal Bhargava argued that no parent would want to inherit a daughter's property.

'Why not?'asked L. Krishnaswami Bharathi from the south.

'Why do you ask?'replied Bhargava. 'Do you not know? Are you not from India?'

'I come from the south of India', responded Bharathi.

As if he had not spoken, Bhargava continued, 'In India no father or mother will ever think of receiving anything from the daughter.'

The North and South parley ends with Bhargava saying, 'That may be a custom or usage prevalent in your part of the country, but in my part of the country, an overwhelming majority will be opposed to the idea... Therefore, the entire fabric of the rules of devolution is based on anti-Hindu ideals.'[47]

No one objected to Bhargava's preposterous suggestion that only the North embodied Hindu ideals. Bharagava's North Indian chauvinism notwithstanding, the states of Andhra Pradesh, Karnataka, Maharashtra and Tamil Nadu had legislated separate enactments giving women equal coparcenary rights[48] decades before the Central Act in 2005 that amended Section 6 of the Hindu Succession Act to make daughters coparceners in their father's joint family property.[49]

~

The Hindu Succession Act 1956 converted a widow's lifetime interest in property into her separate, absolute and exclusive property right.[50] A daughter became entitled to a share in her father's share in joint family property, but only if he died intestate. My family law professor called

---

46. http://www.ambedkar.org/ambcd/64B2.On%20the%20Hindu%20Code%20Bill.htm

47. *Ibid*

48. The Hindu Succession (Andhra Pradesh Amendment) Act, 1986, The Hindu Succession (Tamil Nadu Amendment) Act, 1989, The Hindu Succession (Karnataka Amendment) Act, 1994, The Hindu Succession (Maharashtra Amendment) Act, 1994

49. Prakash v. Phulavati, (2016) 2 SCC 36; See also devolution of property after notional partition: Uttam v. Saubhag Singh, 2016 (3) SCALE 92

50. See p. 372: Section 14 of the Hindu Succession Act, 1956-Property of a female Hindu to be her absolute Property.

this a 'consolation prize' to daughters, because generally fathers began excluding daughters from inheritance by using the device of a will to say that the daughters were 'settled' and had received 'dowry' and thus needed nothing more.[51] Widows generally willed their property back to their sons.

The concept of a will was imported from English law into Hindu law.[52]A written submission to the Hindu Law Committee stated, 'Easy and unquestionable form of wills in favour of sons and against daughters should be suggested'.[53] In the B.N. Rau Committee, a Madras High Court judge said:

> 'It is possible for the Hindu citizen who does not agree with the proposals to get over them. He could make a will and avoid those rules of inheritance by women which may not be to his liking... I, therefore, do not think they are likely to have any serious consequences in general.'[54]

~

The four Hindu acts[55] did not provide for the right of a married woman to reside in her father's home as, according to Ambedkar, 'I think those women who desert their husbands are not likely to be needy women'.[56] His misunderstanding of women's perspective stands revealed in his presumption that a woman who deserts her marriage will do so only if she wants to live with another man or has some other source of maintenance.

As per classical Hindu law, a woman had a right to maintenance from her husband. Under the Right to Property for Women Act, 1937, she had a qualified right to the property for the purpose of her maintenance. Over the years since then, a woman's right in her husband's property has crystallized back to a right to maintenance[57] *from* the property, rather than

51. Kishwar, 'Codified Hindu Law: Myth and Reality', *Economic and Political Weekly*, Vol. 29, No. 33 (Aug 13, 1994) p. 2156

52. Manohar and Chitaley, Volume 1, p. 1359

53. *Ibid*

54. Kishwar, 'Codified Hindu Law: Myth and Reality', *Economic and Political Weekly*, Vol. 29, No. 33 (Aug 13, 1994) p. 2156

55. See pp. 363-72: Hindu Adoption and Maintenance Act, 1956; Hindu Marriage Act, 1956; Hindu Succession Act, 1956; Hindu Minority and Guardianship Act, 1956

56. Lok Sabha Debates, Vol. IV, 1956, Part II, p. 7567; See also Kishwar, 'Codified Hindu Law: Myth and Reality', *Economic and Political Weekly*, 1994.

57. Velamuri Venkata Sivaprasad vs. Kothuri Venkateswarlu, 1999 Supp (4) SCR 522, the court reiterated the classic case of V. Tulasamma & Ors vs. V. Sesha Reddi, AIR 1977 SC 1944

right *in* the property. This is the reality, notwithstanding that the courts have held 'the right to maintenance flows from the social and temporal relationship between the husband and wife by virtue of which the wife becomes a sort of co-owner in the property of her husband though her co-ownership is of a *subordinate* nature.'[58] [emphasis mine]

As to the rights of the silent majority that is without property, the Supreme Court has observed that a man's duty to maintain his wife is a personal obligation, even if he has no property. In a more recent judgment, the Supreme Court reiterates this.[59] In another recent judgment, the Supreme Court[60] has discussed the pre-existing obligation of a husband to look after his wife, making a brilliant analogy with the principle of contract on matters where parties agree to a divorce by mutual consent. It will be an important precedent for fraud and matters of unequal bargaining power and it will also compel the lower judiciary to be less mechanical about divorce by mutual consent. Yet, what is important is that simultaneously in other cases, High Courts are exhorting women to work and learn to become self-sufficient.

~

In 1965, the Supreme Court observed that Hindu law had become irrelevant because the Hindu Succession Act changed the order of succession to property from father to son instead of division amongst male survivors.[61] But women were not discussed. They were not coparceners: they could inherit only if their fathers had not made a testamentary preference for their brothers.

A daughter may have a right to stay in her father's house under some circumstances, but she could not ask for partition of the property.[62] In some regions, (Delhi being one) there were local laws that kept women from inheriting agricultural land, with the reason given that it avoided fragmentation of land.

58. V. Tulasamma & Ors. v. Sesha Reddy (d) by LRs., [1977] 3 SCC 99.

59. Reiterating the position in the Tulasamma v. Reddy case, Jupudy Pardha Sarathy v. Pentapati Rama Krishna, (2016) 2 SCC 56

60. Vennangot Anuradha Samir v. Vennangot Mohandas Samir, 2015(13)SCALE140

61. Mamidi Venkata Satyanarayana vs. Mandela Narasimhaswami, 1966 SCR (1) 628

62. See p. 372: Section 23 of the Hindu Succession Act

Women claiming their rights: two stories

The year was 1965. The widow of my Dadi's brother (her bhabhi) died childless. This opened the question of succession to substantial farmland and the most fabulous jewellery. As per customary law, my Dadi would have got nothing, but under the Hindu Succession Act, 1956, she stood to inherit equally with her two brothers as 'Class II heirs'[63] since the deceased was not survived by a spouse, children or mother (the Class I heirs) and was a Hindu who had died intestate. This story illustrates that the movement from customary law to statute is never smooth.

My Dadi, brought up to cherish her brothers as the family jewels, was initially unwilling to assert her newly acquired legal right. Punjab has a lovely, virtually untranslatable description of a class of relative called 'sharika'. To say someone behaved like a sharika sometimes describes the feeling of envy and jealousy that the 'biradiri' (brotherhood) has, when one amongst them moves ahead in wealth or even happiness. My Dadiji's sharika relatives enjoyed the juicy pleasure and gossip of giving contrary and confusing advice. Finally one cousin prompted my grandmother to make her claim: '*Haq hai Bibiji. Kyu nahin lavoge? Bhra apni thaan. Hun tuhade pote poti haige te tussi riffuggee ho.*' (It's your right Bibiji. Why won't you take it? Brothers are in their place. Now you have grandchildren and you are a refugee.) The advice was sound, but family cynics say it was prompted by the sharika cousin's desire to avoid the further accumulation of wealth in the house of his male cousins, my Dadi's brothers.

As for my Dadi, the fruity 'riffuggee' did it, I am told. Financial uncertainty, combined with her being a widow, gave her the strength to challenge custom and take on her brothers.

She loved both, but the younger brother was a great favourite of hers (as ours). He lived close by. Our second cousins from that house were regular playmates. When the conflict began, the games in each other's gardens stopped. The unfortunate younger brother actually wanted to give his sister her share, but it would have created a dangerous family precedent and it may also have been viewed as emasculating to give in to a woman. On Rakhdee/Rakhi, I am told he wept in his house, as my Dadi did in hers.

Eventually the matter was settled. My grandmother gave up her share of the family jewellery and took her share in the land. The settlement was

63. Class II heirs to a childless intestate widow, as for a Hindu female dying intestate, in the absence of husband and children, the property devolves on the heirs of the husband.

mediated by my jewellery-disliking Nana who said, 'When will you wear this jewellery belonging to that poor woman whose tragic life gave her no occasion to enjoy it?' My Nana's suggestive shrouding of the matter with superstition succeeded.

~

While writing this, in one of those marvellous quirky synchronicities of life, my mobile phone rang. It was a woman who said that she is very poor; she could not afford a lawyer but she saw me on a television debate and found my number online. I wanted to say I was busy, but changed my mind, thinking that really, my true job, more than writing this, was to talk to her.

She spoke to me in Punjabi. 'I and my husband are going to have a divorce, but he has no money. He has recently sold a small piece of land that is his ancestral property and bought a house in his mother's name. Forget about me, but does my son have a right to it?'

'Yes', I said.

'If I talk to him and say this is the law and he must acknowledge my son's right and give him something, do you think he will do it?'

'You can try, but if everyone did what the law expects, the world would be different, would it not? If he was law abiding, you would not feel the desperation to call me like this, would you?'

'Yes... But I can't afford a lawyer. *Vakeelan da koi pata nahi. Bharosa naho hai.*'[64]

We discussed approaching legal aid services or women's groups in her area, but she was dubious about whether they existed. I suggested calling a panchayat of village elders and some family, but they were from different states and had no relatives in common. I gave her the number of a Delhi helpline to find out if they had a branch in Punjab. And that was that.

So much has changed and nothing has. There are women like my upper-class clients who get fine legal settlements, but that is because they or their family can afford lawyers and their husbands and his family have money to give as legal settlements. Then there are women like the one who called me, with no support or access to an efficient justice system. At least technology had made that call possible: there is something in that.

Like my great-grandmother and my grandmother, I too asserted my legal right to some property. As recently as 2013, many persons in my family continued to feel that my demand lacked 'class' and was not in

64. One does not know about lawyers. Can't trust them.

consonance with the feudal grandeur that they still delusionally live by. My so-called sophisticated family in truth does not seem to have been able to get past the patriarchal stereotypes, despite having broken every other social norm.

~

To return to the law: In 1986, the Supreme Court held that the Hindu Succession Act was enacted to 'amend and codify' Hindu law, and thus overrides classical Hindu law.[65] Yet nothing changed in the position of women as the second sex. A fair critique would have to put the obvious gender stereotypes into the context of ground reality. Some feminists and academicians propagate an argument for gender equality without protections, which they see as patriarchal patronage. It is a fair argument, but not practical.

The 2005 Amendment

In 2005, the Hindu Succession Act was amended to make a daughter coparcener along with her father and brothers, bringing us full circle to what Ambedkar had proposed in 1951.[66] This amendment also eliminated the gender bias in the Land Reforms Act wherein a daughter had no share in her father's agricultural property.

On the day the amendment to the Act was approved in Parliament, I was in a dentist's waiting room. A young man there said: 'Now more than ever, we don't want our sisters in our homes. It's a great problem for all of us if their marriages don't work.'

The new law will be a burden to many women, I thought with a sinking heart. It is for the daughters of rich Hindu undivided families.

With equal rights in parental property, many women may feel less resigned to remaining in an abusive marriage. Many others however, will incur the cost of strained relations with their fathers and brothers brought up to believe in the power and entitlement of the Y chromosome.

---

65. Commissioner of Wealth Tax vs. Chander Sen, (1986) 3 SCC 567

66. The Supreme Court has ruled that the act is not retrospective in Prakash and Ors. vs. Phulavati and Ors., 2015(11)SCALE643. The relevant part of Section is quoted as follows '6. Devolution of Interest in Coparcenary Property. (1) on and from the commencement of The Hindu Succession (Amendment) Act, 2005, in a joint Hindu family governed by The Mitakshara Law, the daughter of a coparcener shall, (A) by birth become a coparcener in her own right in the same manner as the son; (B) have the same rights in the coparcenary property as she would have had if she had been a son.'

Recently, a family court order on the matter of a wife's maintenance ruled that since the wife was residing with her parents, where she had a legal right to stay as a member of the Hindu Undivided family under the new law, hence the husband need not provide her with a house. The order effectively allowed husbands to abdicate the responsibility of maintenance and alimony to the fathers of their wives.

Many husbands may also coerce their wives to demand a share in their natal family's property during the lifetime of their parents. This is what the M.P., Shri M.A. Ayyangar, had feared, but of course that is not a reason to not to have the laws. Nevertheless, these changes are meaningful only if women are similarly empowered in the matrimonial home.

Most women do not have rich fathers with enough property to share as a coparcenary. In any case, women are reluctant to monetize their legal shares in parental homes for fear of displacing and alienating their parental families. Most women still need to look to their husbands and their families for financial security. The issue for this majority of ordinary women can be resolved only when their right in marital property is mirrored as clearly as it is in the parental ancestral property under the new law.

The idea of 'community property', with women as equal shareholders in the wealth acquired during the course of the marriage is still not palatable to parliamentarians. A loosely worded bill was submitted by the UPA government: it empowered a judge to factor a husband's 'inheritable property' while awarding maintenance to a wife. The term 'inheritable' is problematic as a legal concept because by its very nature it is uncertain. The bill has lapsed and will someday hopefully be replaced by one premised on solid legal concepts expressed clearly.

~

We have come a long way from 1937, but the sense of entitlement that a boy must have the lion's share of the legacy carries on, not just amongst men, but women; not just amongst the masses, but amongst the rarefied intelligentsia too. Consider the following:

A wealthy man died and his property was divided equally amongst his wife, daughter and son. 'You are both equal', said the educated, sophisticated, upper-class widow. She then proceeded to transfer her one-third share to her son, making him owner of two-thirds of the entire plot. The daughter was hurt, not because she needs more money, but at her devaluation. At an afternoon gossip at our home she complained, 'My mother says she loves me and love is not about money. But then why give it to my brother? She loves me but he is more valuable? Does that make sense?'

The Law and Dowry

The dowry problem always existed but constant reportage and the Indian women's movements made it a topical issue in the 1960s and 1970s. In financially strained times, the husband and his family used marriage as a chance to improve their situation, and in boom times dowry became an opportunity for avarice and vulgar display. In December 1983 a special law reversed the presumption of innocence in criminal cases relating to dowry deaths.

The mechanism was as follows: Sections 113 A[67] and 113 B[68] were added to the Indian Evidence Act and Section 498A to the Indian Penal Code. Section 113 A Evidence Act shifted the burden of proof on the husband to prove his innocence of the crime of abetment of a woman's alleged 'suicide' if the 'suicide' occurs within seven years of marriage. Section 113 B Evidence Act created a presumption of a dowry death if the prosecution could prove that prior to the wife's death, the woman had been tortured mentally or physically for dowry.

Section 498A IPC[69] had two limbs. First, mental and physical cruelty inflicted upon a woman by her husband or his relatives, punishable with imprisonment of up to three years. Cruelty was defined as willful conduct of a nature that would drive her to suicide or cause grave injury or danger to her life, limb or mental or physical health. The second limb makes dowry demands by a husband and/or his relatives a criminal offence. Thus, the presumption of innocence was not available to the accused under Section 498A IPC if the FIR was registered within the first seven years of marriage.

'Dowry death' was defined under Section 304B IPC added in 1986, to say that where the death of a woman is caused by any burns, or bodily injury or in any other type of suspicious circumstances within seven years of marriage and it is established that the woman was being tortured and harassed for dowry, such death will be called a 'dowry death'. However, it must be shown that such torture occured 'soon before her death'.

~

67. See p. 374: 113A. Presumption as to abetment of suicide by a married woman.

68. See p. 374: 113B. Presumption as to dowry death.

69. See p. 382: Section 498A in The Indian Penal Code, 1860-498A. Husband or relative of husband of a woman subjecting her to cruelty

The presumption of innocence is the shining saviour of the innocent. It is the cornerstone of criminal jurisprudence of a civilized world. By the extreme step of killing this presumption, the legislature acknowledged the seriousness of the problem of dowry deaths.

The criticism against this law is that it is as vulnerable to misuse and yet the critics have no argument for why it should be repealed. It is as vulnerable to misuse as any other law and there already exists a deterrent in the law of malicious prosecution.[70] On the subject, Senior Advocate Rebecca John has commented that this legal reform in family law is not as much of a problem as the tendency to cite these laws as precedent while calling for similar reversals of the presumption of innocence in other areas of law like anti-terror acts and even white-collar crimes.

In 1985, the Supreme Court in the Pratibha Rani case ruled that withholding a woman's stridhan amounted to criminal breach of trust punishable under Section 406 IPC.[71] The husband argued that in law, a married couple have a joint status and thus, he could not be said to be taking away *her* jewellery because it was *his* wealth too. Thus, he argued, there can be no breach of trust. I do not know why the judges did not ask the husband whether he would stand by the logical consequence of his own argument: if he was co-owner of her stridhan, she must be an equal owner to all his wealth. His quick backtrack would have been fun to watch, but then judging is not supposed to be amusement and judges should not play cat-and-mouse with arguments in the way we lawyers do.

Regardless, the judgment was clear about the husband's breach of trust, and asserted the wife's legal right to her separate property. This was instrumental in further refining and developing the law reforms of 1983.

The first case under the new legal regime was the widely reported Sudha Goel murder case where the Sessions court convicted the mother-in-law and husband of Sudha Goel for murdering her for dowry[72] and pronounced the death sentence. They were eventually acquitted on the ground of inadequate evidence, and the Supreme Court warned that jingoistic media pitches should be kept out of the courtrooms.

Application of the new law

The 1983 law reform fused with the Pratibha Rani judgment has formed a 498A/406 IPC jurisprudence, making it the most powerful weapon a

70. See Ch. 9: Misuse of Enabling Laws, p. 266, 274

71. Pratibha Rani vs. Suraj Kumar & Anr., 1985 SCC (2) 370

72. State vs. Laxman Kumar, AIR 1986 SC 250

woman has. She may use it in a bona fide manner to protect herself and negotiate a fair settlement from a position of equal bargaining power or misuse it to harass the husband and his family[73] and heighten the pressure on the state machinery to compel extortionist settlement amounts. The latter can be dealt with by imposing penalties and legal consequences on malicious prosecutions.

This fused hybrid of criminal complaints is simply referred to as a 498 case. Sometimes it has been reduced to recovering the woman's stridhan even though many courts have repeatedly said that this is not the true purpose of the section.[74] It has also been used to ensure maintenance payments to counteract the stagnant pace of maintenance orders passed by family courts. Though not legally sound, it has emerged as the systemic response to cases of extreme financial hardship faced by women.

Within the 498A IPC, the first limb of mental and physical cruelty not related to dowry—i.e.: domestic violence simpliciter—is practically a dead letter for two reasons: the first reason is that police take no 498A complaint seriously unless it is an account of horrendous violence and accusations of attempt to murder and/or the words 'cash' and 'jewellery' jump out at them as they speed-read the complaint. They are not sensitized to the nuances of mental cruelty and have no time to be educated about it.

This apathy is the reason that the core truth of bona fide domestic violence is often dressed up in complaints with key words such as jewellery being 'entrusted' to the family-in-law and thus 'illegally detained' by them, dowry demands, and wedding expenses 'beyond the means of my father' incurred 'for my happiness'.

The police has been strengthened in this approach by some High Courts. For example, the Delhi High Court[75] ruled that not every type of cruelty, but only those which relate to 'demands' for dowry should be covered by this section. The judgment however is ambiguous, because at another point, it says that cruelty without such 'demands' is not covered under the second limb of the section, implying thereby that it is covered by the first limb.

Such equivocations have created a lot of confusion. Fortunately, much

---

73. See Ch. 9: Misuse of Enabling Laws, 266

74. Surjit Kaur Chopra v. State and Anr., 2007(98) DRJ 646; Rajesh Chander Bhardwaj vs. State, 125 (2005) DLT 710; Jagdish Thakkar v. State of Delhi, 1993 JCC 177; Ashim Trehan v. State (NCT of Delhi), MANU/DE/4757/2009

75. Raj Kumar Khanna vs. State (NCT of Delhi), 95 (2002) DLT 147

of it was settled by a series of judgments by the Supreme Court, which held that the connection between 498A and 304B IPC[76] was cruelty, but the difference was that 304B was applicable only to dowry death and 498A covered cruelty even without dowry.[77] However, the Supreme Court's clarification still needs to trickle down to the police.

Property Acquired During Marriage

The narrative so far describes legal reforms to empower women by making them economically strong. But their economic independence within the married state has not been addressed. In India, spouses can own their separate property, as opposed to the idea of community property prevailing in the UK, some states in the US, Canada and Australia, where both spouses have an equal interest in any property acquired during the course of the marriage.

In the UK

The rights of Western women have travelled a longer distance from before 1858, when classical Hindu and Islamic laws gave women better rights than English women of the time had.[78] Now, generous orders on alimony and 'property adjustment' have in fact made the UK a haven for divorcing wives.

The Englishwoman embarked on this journey with Lord Denning, her judge in shining armour. In his memoirs, he has likened himself to Don Quixote rescuing damsels in distress when he set about clothing the English wife with principles of equity, as she was bare of all legal rights. Lord Denning's judgments for the cause of the deprived and the weak have made him a legendary judge, even while conservatives have severely criticized his method of judge-made law that rides rough-shod over the legislature.

Denning interpreted the law imaginatively to serve the cause of gender justice. For example, Section 17 of the Married Women's Property Act, 1882 allowed the judge to make such orders as he thought fit in the interests of justice with regard to creating rights for a married woman in

76. See p. 375: Section 304B of the Indian Penal Code, 1860

77. Hira Lal & Ors. vs. State (Govt. of NCT), Delhi, (2003) 8 SCC 80

78. 'From Caroline Norton, A letter to the Queen on Lord Chancellor Cranworth's Marriage and Divorce Bill', 1855

her matrimonial home.[79] Lord Denning took full advantage of what he saw as his power to exercise discretion.

The case was H vs. W.[80] The husband (H) wanted a divorce, which the wife (W) refused to give. He had the title to the house. He sued for ejectment and said that her continuance in the house amounted to trespass. Lord Denning ruled that though the husband had the right to his home, he could not turn her out, as she had a right to stay there, as his wife. This is the principle of the woman's equity to the matrimonial residence. It took twenty years for the issue to be ruled on by the House of Lords.

In 1970, this equity was scotched by Pettitt versus Pettitt.[81] Lord Hodson condemned the principle of equity for the wife in the following manner: 'To use the language of Coke, this would substitute the uncertain and crooked cord of discretion for the golden and straight metawand of the law'. The House of Lords ruled that Section 17 was merely procedural and did not empower judges to make laws that affected legal rights such as title.

Undeterred by the House of Lords curtailing his power to exercise discretion, Lord Denning developed another stream of justice for the wife's equity in the matrimonial home.[82] This was with regard to her subsisting right to the matrimonial home against subsequent purchasers and even a husband's plea of bankruptcy.

A husband guaranteed a bank loan to his own company against the title papers of the house that he owned and lived in with his family. When the company defaulted on the loan, he left the house and abandoned his wife and children. The National Provincial Bank sought to enforce and foreclose the mortgage on the house, even though the four children and wife were residing in it. Lord Denning ruled that justice to the bank had to be tempered with mercy to the wife and children.

This backdoor entry of such a substantial right was strongly opposed by persons such as Lord Megarry, who said:

> 'One of the most lusty infants, to which English law has given birth in recent years is the right of a deserted wife to remain in occupation of the matrimonial home owned by her husband not withstanding his desire to evict her... It may well be that justice requires that the wife's occupation

79. Lord Denning, *The Due Process of Law*, 1980, p. 205

80. (1947) 63 TLR 645

81. [1970] A.C. 777

82. Bendall v. McWhirter 1952 2 QB 466.

> of the home should be protected in some special way: and modern ideas of sex equality may require that the right should not be exclusively feminine in gender. Yet with all respect it may be suggested that legislation and not litigation is the only satisfactory way of delimiting the bounds of so complex a subject. Any protection for the wife should, it is suggested, be provided by statutory amendments of matrimonial law operating on the recognized rights of property, rather than what is (in effect, at all events) the judicial invention of a new proprietary right... Few would suggest that the law as to this newfound right of the wife is at present in a satisfactory state, and some, indeed, may express the hope that the House of Lords will blow away the whole uncertain structure... At least it may be hoped that the right will ultimately be held, not to amount, either in name, or in substance, to any legal or equitable interest in land, and to bind none save the husband.'

The House of Lords agreed with Lord Megarry and in 1964 ruled in favour of the bank and against the wife,[83] saying that the wife did not have the right to stay in the house against subsequent purchasers. Thus, this rule of equity in favour of the wife was also overturned.

The House of Lords did concede though, that while the husband owned the house, he could not drive the wife away. This observation was, of course, of no help to the wife and four children in the case they were ruling in.

Baroness Somerskills, a prominent voice for the feminist cause, led an uproar in Parliament. The protests and agitations of the feminist movement led to the passing of the Matrimonial Home Act 1967. This was followed by the Domestic Violence Act 1976 that empowered a court to order a husband to remove himself and a wife to continue to remain in occupation of a property that she may not have title to and which belonged solely to him. The Matrimonial Homes Act 1983 brought into the realm of law those principles of justice for women that Lord Denning tried to achieve in equity.

Lord Denning's idea of rights of a wife already existed in Indian classical law, but since then the English law has leapt and bounded far ahead of Indian family law as far as gender justice is concerned. Currently the UK is governed by the Family Law Act, which defines the right of occupation of the marital home by a spouse who may not have title to it. The right is subject to the orders of the court that will look at all circumstances, including the conduct of the parties with each other.[84]

---

83. (1964) CH. 665

84. S.33 (6) Family Law Act, 1996

In the US

In the United States, divorce and family law, along with many other legal matters, varies from state to state. The law in California calls for a straight division of all matrimonial property through the middle. The law in New York calls for an 'equitable distribution' of matrimonial property which implies a 50:50 division, but may not really be so. For example, a millionaire's defense is available to a rich spouse to say that the millionaire should be protected from disclosing all assets because s/he (we all know it is mostly 'he' even in the US) has the means to comply with any maintenance/alimony order that the court may make. This is obviously done knowing that the order will be circumscribed within reasonable parameters involving needs and reasonable wants harmonized with the lifestyle of the couple. However, it makes it possible for the total wealth of the marriage to be divided unevenly between the divorcing parties, giving the millionaire the benefit and avoiding disproportionately large assets to a wife who has not directly earned them.

It must be remembered that big alimonies are for the very rich, but the bulk of the divorces even in the West are amongst the middle class and the poor, with little or no property in the kitty to share.

A UK study finds that men are richer by 25 per cent after a divorce, in contrast to women whose lifestyle drops significantly. Separated women have a poverty rate of 27 per cent—almost three times that of their former husbands.[85]

The broadly stated equitable sharing of marital property that prevails across Europe, the UK, the US, Canada and Australia has led many non-resident Indian women (and their relatives and friends) to wrongly believe that a woman under Indian law has a 50 per cent share in the husband's property. Most don't even bother to make the distinction between property that is ancestral and property acquired in the course of the marriage.

Back to India

As in the Western study mentioned earlier,[86] studies in India too have found that in divorce cases, the separate property regime has resulted in making men richer while women lose even what they came into the marriage with. This is because it is very likely that women are compelled to transfer their own assets to the husbands or to spend their earnings

85. Stephen P. Jenkins, *Marital Splits and Income Changes over the Longer Term*, Institute for Social & Economic Research, University of Essex, No. 2008-07, Feb 2008

86. *Ibid*

and personal money while the husband either saves his earnings, or the couple's joint savings are in the husband's name. According to Kirti Singh, advocate, women's rights activist and author, while 23 per cent of women owned land during their marriage, only 6 per cent continued to own it after separation or divorce.[87]

Till today, most women are dependent on the handouts traditionally known as kharcha paandaan, (pocket money for paan and such like) with no control over stridhan and no immovable property to their names. Already vulnerable within the marriage, a wife becomes nakedly so at the time of divorce, now risking unhappiness in her parental home too if she seeks to assert her rights there.

Her rights to maintenance and residence may still not secure a home for her even in cases when it is possible to do so. In fact, she may even stand to lose any property purchased in her name. The Benami Transactions (Prohibition) Act 1998 is an instance of patriarchal bias in laws even when enacted for the ostensible purpose of reform. The Act prohibits claims of ownership of property by those who claim to be the 'true' owners of property, as opposed to the one who is the recorded owner or the benamidar (i.e., the name of the recorded owner who is not the true owner.)

The reform was aimed at the problem of benami transactions where A might not want to disclose ownership of property and so buys it in the name of B but is the true beneficial owner of it. The law is meant to address the problems of corruption, tax avoidance and the general confusion in the real-estate market. It was supposed to do away with opaque transactions and confused ownership rights which made buyers apprehensive about potential litigation if they bought a property only to find that someone else emerged as the 'true' owner.

However, within the blanket ban against further benami transactions and claims on past benami transactions was carved an exception for those husbands who bought property in the names of their wives and daughters. The act allows such transactions as benami, subject to the presumption, (albeit rebuttable) that the property was indeed bought for the benefit of wife and daughters.[88] It is now common for husbands to file suits

---

87. Kirti Singh, *Separated and Divorced Women in India: Economic Rights and Entitlement*, p.32

88. 3. Prohibition of benami transactions: (1) No person shall enter into any benami transaction. (2) Nothing in sub-section (1) shall apply to the purchase of property by any person in the name of his wife or unmarried daughter and it shall be presumed, unless the contrary is proved, that the said property had been purchased for the benefit of the wife of the unmarried daughter.

seeking a declaration that the properties that stood in the name of a wife or daughter were not for her benefit, but were their own investments and tax-saving devices.[89]

The underlying gender bias is clear. Consider this: a property bought in the name of a son is his. The rule of it being a benami transaction cannot be invoked if the property was bought in his name. The benami transaction defense is also not available to a wife who may have bought property in the name of her husband. But a husband or father can still claim ownership of property bought in the name of a wife or daughter by calling it a benami transaction.

The House

Jane Austen's Elinor in eighteenth-century England said, 'Houses go from father to son dearest, not father to daughter, it is the law'.[90]At about the same time, Indian women sang a folk song with playful flirtation: *Nazar laagi Raja tere bangley pey* (Oh my prince, I have an eye on your bungalow).

A good package deal of an eligible bachelor must include a bangla because women are vulnerable on the issue of housing. Most do not earn enough to buy a house and there are very few rich fathers who gift houses to their daughters. It was a single woman struggling with a career and children who told me, 'The day I got my own house, I felt safe. The rest fell in place'.

My mother told me that the unaccustomed simplicity of a village kuchcha home immediately after Partition in 1947 made her most fervent wish to be for a husband who had a big pucca house. This was always followed by a theatrical aside that though she got what she asked for s far as the house went, she wished she had also specified the type of husband in her prayers. I agree with my mother that being married into a beautiful house is not enough. Social context is dependent more upon proprietary rights than access to the lifestyle attached to it. This is what the women's movement has been working towards over the decades.

It is telling that after marriage, the wife is absorbed in the husband's home as 'gharwali', but the first phrase that an inconvenient wife of any class hears is '*ghar se nikalo*'. Many women thus thrown out are compelled to return to their natal homes as guilt-ridden burdens for their

89. Nand Kishore Mehra vs. Sushila Mehra, 1995 SCC (4) 572

90. Jane Austen, *Sense and Sensibility* (dialogue in Ang Lee's 1995 film of the book.)

parents, and after them, as 'poor' relatives entrusted with housekeeping responsibilities in consideration for shelter in a brother's domain.

I personally know children of such women who have suffered low self-esteem due to the lack of a social context and true belonging. One such child told me that she and her mother lived in her maternal grandparents' home, just above the status of servants but below that of the married aunts. After decades of neglect and exploitation as a housekeeper, nurse, and general fetch-and-carry person, her mother returned to her husband in her old age and ironically is now blooming and liberated as a widow who has inherited her husband's house. She is luckier than many in that she could both leave and return, and has finally kindled the fire of independence in her winter years, but many women stay in abusive marriages fearing that they will not receive even cold shelter elsewhere.

My male clients will tell me: 'I can rent her a property. I want her out of the house.' Where he is to stay is almost never a relevant question because from the beginning of the marriage, the option of a husband staying in the wife's maternal home as ghar jamai is generally perceived as emasculating. Hence, social norms collude in ensuring the dependence of women on their husbands.

~

It is reasonable to say that a wife's most basic right is that of residence in the marital home. It is significant that such a basic right was not dealt with by the Supreme Court from its inception in 1950 until 2005. Within these fifty-five years, the Court ruled on every other type of property right and developed the common law principle that even a trespasser cannot be evicted without due process of law. Yet, women who were not tenants and certainly not trespassers remained worried about security in their home.

In classical and later codified Hindu law, the husband was obliged to provide his wife a separate residence if there was reasonable cause for her to live apart.[91]Modern legal opinion, however, reduced the right of residence of a wife to that of a licensee at her husband's pleasure. Divorce lawyers would send legal notices to wives asking that she vacate the 'matrimonial home', as her legal status of license to reside at the husband's pleasure stood revoked due to the estrangement. That no case reached the Supreme Court for it to rule on the matter through these decades is another indication of a woman's lack of social context.

It is only in 2005 that the Supreme Court for the first time, discussed

91. See p. 382: Section 18(2) in The Hindu Adoptions and Maintenance Act, 1956

the 'wife's equity' in the matrimonial home.[92] Noticing the vacuum in rulings on the issue, the court observed, 'Any precedent, much less of a binding authority from any court in India and dealing with a situation as we are called upon to deal with is not available'. In fact a Bombay High Court ruling of 1964[93] was not brought to the attention of the court.

In the absence of any known precedent in Indian law, the Supreme Court discussed various English decisions on the subject. The court observed that a 'matrimonial home' was defined in English law under the Matrimonial Homes Act, 1983[94] which presupposed legal rights of both the husband and wife in the matrimonial home bought during the marriage. The absence of an equivalent Indian act, the court said, meant that in India, a husband and wife did not have equal rights in a home bought during the tenure of the marriage because it would be the separate property of the person who bought it and, more frequently than not, that would be the husband.

The court did mention that Section 18 of the Hindu Adoption and Maintenance Act set out the obligation of the husband to maintain the wife and that maintenance included residence, but, it said, the right was in a subsisting marriage. Once there was a divorce, the relationship of husband and wife ceased, and the wife's rights could only be in terms of the divorce decree.

In the particular case before the Supreme Court at the time, residence did not form part of the decree and thus the former wife had no right of residence. In a general discussion, the court did say that a wife has a right of residence in the matrimonial home and could not be evicted as a licensee at her husband's pleasure. The court thus held that a wife could contest eviction proceedings by a landlord even if her husband chose not to, provided that she could not claim a better right in those premises than her husband had—that of a tenant.[95]

An instance of a problematic interpretation of this judgment is the following ex-parte order passed in a case:

> 'Accordingly, till the next date of hearing, the respondent (husband) is restrained from surrendering the tenancy or handing over possession of the

---

92. B.P. Achala Anand vs. S. Appi Reddy & Anr 2005 3 SCC 313

93. Banoo Jal Daruwalla vs. Jal C. Daruwalla, AIR 1964 Bom 124

94. See also: S.R. Batra and Anr. v. Taruna Batra, AIR 2007 SC 1118

95. B.P. Achala Anand vs. S. Appi Reddy & Anr 2005 3 SCC 313

premises to (landlord). He is also restrained from removing any movable articles which are housed in the premises.'

To keep the status quo till the next date of hearing sounds reasonable, except the truth is, that given our courts, the next date of hearing is so far into the horizon as to be almost invisible. In this case, the matter dragged on for a year. The landlord suffered because the injunction prevented him from filing legal proceedings to recover possession of his property. The husband was restrained from removing even his personal articles from the home. The problem was further intensified because there was no observation as to who was to pay the rent to the landlord.

The wife ended up enjoying for a year precisely that which the Supreme Court had sought to avoid. She ended up with a better right than the tenant because the landlord could not commence legal proceedings to evict her. The clouded fact was that the wife was using the proceedings only as a pressure tactic since she was not living in that house either. Had the court directed the husband to provide reasonable alternative premises within a particular time, justice would have been better served for all concerned.

Coincidentally, while the Supreme Court was dealing with a wife's residence for the first time since Independence, Parliament, just a few months later passed the very powerful and effective Protection of Women from Domestic Violence Act (PWDVA). The statute used the term 'shared household' rather than 'matrimonial home'. It defined a shared household as any home in which the couple lived, regardless of title, which could even be that of a third person. To avoid encumbering other title holders to the property, the statute provides that the husband may arrange an alternative residence for his wife, provided it is of the same standard that she enjoyed while living with him.

This idea of an alternative residence is important. Nowadays many single-storey bungalows owned even by middle- and lower-middle-class families are being rebuilt as flats to form separate residences for each son and his family. A problem arises when the flame of a marital conflict on any of those floors singes the extended family. They also need to be protected and deserve the peaceful enjoyment of their own property. This is done by making arrangements for an alternative residence for the estranged wife.

The Delhi High Court has ruled that the right to residence of an estranged wife does not include her right to insist upon any particular house, as long as the accommodation provided to her is 'more or less' in consonance with the standards of her marital home.[96]

Notwithstanding the legal position that a wife has a right to a residence but not ownership, rich divorce settlements include a house for her. Because such settlements are always good copy, media hype has made them a benchmark for aspirational divorce settlements. An aspiration, let me warn, that is not achieved by the ordinary and is for those who can also quibble about a fashionable address.

The world over, most men cannot afford two homes. A UK newspaper reports that many divorced couples continue to stay together because they can't afford separate homes. Many have a mutual agreement to allow adultery because litigation costs and divorce settlements have become prohibitively expensive.[97] A popular American television series, *Happily Divorced*, explores the humourous aspect of this arrangement to great effect, though here the couple are good friends because the husband discovers his homosexual preference.

Location of the home

A series of rulings about the location of the matrimonial home tell the story of the emerging social status of women. Traditionally, the matrimonial residence followed the husband's location.[98] In 1964, the High Court of Punjab and Haryana[99] quoting Mulla's *Hindu Law* warned women that a wife's duty was to remain with and submit to her husband. A full bench of the same High Court[100] reaffirmed this in 1976.

In 1978, the Delhi High Court[101] ruled that the wife could have a say in the location of the matrimonial home. In that case, the woman was financially better placed than her husband. Interestingly, even then, the court gave the man a 'casting vote' if there were to be a deadlock, with no reasons as to why it should be so.

The issue of alternative residence is admittedly painful for women

---

96. Ajay Kumar Jain vs. Baljit Kaur Jain, 160 (2009) DLT 401; Eveneet Singh vs. Prashant Chaudhri, 177 (2011) DLT 124; Smt. Preeti Satija vs. Smt. Raj Kumari and Anr., 207 (2014) DLT 78

97. Julia Llewellyn Smith, 'Welcome to Maidenhead Britain's Capital of Infidelity' in *The Telegraph*, 13 April 2014

98. B.R. Mehta vs. Smt. Atma Devi & Ors, 1987 SCR (3) 1184

99. Tirath Kaur vs. Kirpal Singh, AIR 1964 P&H 28

100. Kailash Wati v. Ayodhia Parkash, 1977 (79) PLR 216

101. Swaraj Garg vs. K.M. Garg, AIR 1978 Delhi 296

who are resentful at being directed to leave the home in which they have spent more actual time than their husbands. But where men live in family homes with other relatives, it is a sensible resolution for the woman to move out, rather than pushing the entire family into an unhappy huddle.

The wife's right to residence is still hazy when mixed with the claims of an extended family. The Delhi High Court in Taruna Batra's[102] case recognized this problem:

> 'I am of the view that in the context of Indian Society, a pragmatic view has to be taken while attempting to understand what is meant by the matrimonial home of a married couple, because there is no statute in this respect unlike in England where the Matrimonial Homes Act, 1983, would govern the situation. It appears that in England, an innocent spouse who is in occupation of the matrimonial home as a joint owner has a right not to be evicted from there, except by an order of a Court and if that spouse is not in occupation, he or she has a right to obtain a Court order to enter and occupy such a matrimonial home. A spouse who has no proprietary interest in the matrimonial home but is in occupation thereof has a right to remain in occupation of the matrimonial home as against the spouse who has left that matrimonial home...
>
> '12. We all know that the accepted practice in India is that immediately after marriage, the bride resides with the husband, usually in the parental home of the husband and their place of residence then becomes their matrimonial home. Of course, now there are many instances where the couple reside separately since the joint family system is breaking up... In either case, the place of residence of the couple becomes their matrimonial home. A woman, therefore, would have the right to remain in that matrimonial home as long as she is married and if she is "obliged" to leave that matrimonial home, I think she would be entitled to obtain an injunction from an appropriate court protecting her right and preventing her from being thrown out.'

The Supreme Court[103] sweepingly overturned this judgment. While the matter was being argued there, the PWDVA came into force, along with

102. Smt. Taruna Batra vs. S.R. Batra, AIR 2005 Delhi 270: the daughter-in-law asserted residence rights under the PWDVA over a house in the name of her mother-in-law. The daughter-in-law and son had been living there after their marriage. Matrimonial discord led to the daughter-in-law staying at her parents' residence, but when she tried to enter the matrimonial home, the main entrance was locked, restricting her from entering the house.

103. S.R. Batra and Anr. vs. Smt. Taruna Batra, (2007) 3 SCC 169

the clause that protected a woman's right to the 'shared household'[104] regardless of title to the property.[105] The Supreme Court expressed its opinion on the new act as follows:

> '20. If the aforesaid submission (wife's right in a shared household under the PWDVA) is accepted, then it will mean that wherever the husband and wife lived together in the past that property becomes a shared household. It is quite possible that the husband and wife may have lived together in dozens of places e.g. with the husband's father, husband's paternal grand-parents, his maternal parents, uncles, aunts, brothers, sisters, nephews, nieces etc, if the interpretation canvassed by the learned counsel for the respondent is accepted, all these houses of the husband's relatives will be shared households and the wife can well insist in living in all these houses of her husband's relatives merely because she had stayed with her husband for some time in those houses in the past. Such a view would lead to chaos and would be absurd.
>
> 'It is well settled that any interpretation that leads to absurdity should not be accepted.
>
> '22...."shared household" would only mean the house belonging to or taken on rent by the husband, or the house which belongs to the joint family of which the husband is a member.'

The ruling is problematic. According to the Supreme Court, the Delhi High Court had tried to create something out of nothing: there was no legislation on the rights of married women in residences and thus the High Court ruling amounted to 'wishful thinking'. Yet the Supreme Court seems to have done exactly what it accused the Delhi High Court of doing but in reverse: it read down and diluted the clear legislation to a limited meaning of shared household.

The Supreme Court seemed to have tried to draw a balance between competing interests but has created an unhappy precedent on other issues: for example, it ignored the specific provision in the PWDVA that the wife had a right of residence regardless of who had title to the property. It also ignored the fact that clearly, in this case, the husband had moved out of the family home only to defeat the wife's claim of residence. He moved to Ghaziabad, mostly an industrial town, from a leafy colony in Ashok Vihar, Delhi.

---

104. See p. 384: S. 2(s) of the PWDVA which defines 'shared household'

105. See p. 385: S. 17 of the PWDVA—Right to reside in a shared household.

Having said which, the Supreme Court ruling did help one of my clients in the following case:

An example of overreach

My client was H. He and W had lived abroad through their married life. With his funds, H had bought a fabulously expensive apartment in India. He had put his wife's name as an equal owner.

When the apartment was ready to be occupied, W surreptitiously returned to India with the child and occupied it. She filed proceedings under the PWDVA to protect her residence in the apartment and also staked a claim to a bungalow owned and lived in by her father-in-law. She claimed this bungalow to be her matrimonial home because she had spent some time there after she married. (She said it for was a year or so, while he said it was only for a few weeks). She also claimed that a separate floor in this bungalow had been renovated for her at considerable expense incurred by her own father. H denied it. The magistrate did not give an ex-parte relief with regard to any assets but ordered that she not be ousted from the apartment that she had occupied.

After a while, the old gentleman, H's father, decided to sell the bungalow, as it was too large and cumbersome and both his children were settled abroad. The market value was about Rs. 100 crores. Such a high-end real-estate transaction is juicy gossip and W heard about it on the grapevine. The old gentleman had arranged a sale and received some portion of the money; he was to receive the balance by 31st October. In mid-October, the wife obtained an ex-parte injunction from the magistrate restraining the sale of the bungalow. We had two weeks to get this vacated.

We appealed the ex-parte order,[106] since the magistrate had posted the case for hearing much after 31st October. We went back and forth, with the old gentleman pushing for a hearing and the other side doing their best to delay, hoping that he, flush with funds, would pay her a handsome amount to avoid an obstruction to the sale. The buyer of the house told me to persuade my client to settle and pay her a few crores and be done with it, but the old gentleman was jovial and feisty when I spoke to him, and told me he did not mind losing any amount of money, but was not going to succumb to blackmail. 'Won't be able to live with myself. This is wrong and I cannot participate in it,' he said.

W's argument was that the PWDVA provided a single forum for all

106. A court order given in absence of (or without prior notice to) the party against which it is to operate.

claims by a woman including that to any property. H argued that the purpose of the act was to ensure one residence for the wife. Once W had an apartment to live in, H argued, the purpose of the act had been achieved and the magistrate could not usurp the jurisdiction of the civil court to adjudicate on other property disputes. We cited a High Court ruling that title disputes cannot be the subject of proceedings under PWDVA.[107] The stay was vacated and we pushed the transaction full steam ahead to meet the deadline.

Another story: When location matters

W filed a case under the PWDVA.[108] Though there was no order ousting the husband from the shared household, H moved out because he was scared that she would engineer incidents to call the police. He moved to his farm in a small village outside Delhi. It was a lonely life with no neighbours, and his health suffered.

H moved a petition in the High Court seeking that he would provide W with alternative premises so that he could return to his house.[109] The court allowed his petition and the magistrate was directed to ascertain that the alternative residence was commensurate with the matrimonial home that W been occupying.

H has now returned to his house and is paying the rent for her separate residence.

~

In 2014, the Delhi High Court tried to narrow the wide impact of the Taruna Batra Supreme Court ruling by holding that where the families were unarguably living as a joint family, the Taruna Batra ruling does not interfere with the wife's right to residence in that household.[110]

> '43...we are of the view that Taruna Batra's case is only an authority for the proposition that a wife is precluded under the law from claiming "right of residence" in a premises, owned by the relatives of the husband, wherein she has lived with her husband separately, but not as a member of the "joint family" along with the relatives of the husband who own the premises.

---

107. Adil and Ors. vs. State and Anr, 2010(119)DRJ297

108. Sunil Madan vs. Rachna Madan, MANU/DE/2548/2012

109. See Ajay Kumar Jain vs. Baljit Kaur Jain, 160(2009) DLT 401

110. Navneet Arora v. Surender Kaur, 213(2014)DLT611

> '44. However, in the later eventuality, if a couple live as members of "joint family" in a domestic relationship with the relatives of the husband in a premises owned by such relatives of the husband, statutory prescription would indeed enable the wife to claim "right of residence" since it would fall within the realm of "shared household" as contemplated under Section 2(s) of the Act irrespective of whether she or her husband has any right, title or interest in the "shared household".'

Conclusion

In 1951, while debating the Hindu Code Bill, B.K.P. Sinha, a Member of Parliament, said, 'I have had intimate talks with some of these orthodox people. They do not care a grain, an iota, for the Hindu Law or the Hindu principles, or the rishis or the smritis. What rouses them into opposition is the property clause.'[111] We always knew that at bottom, the issue is all about property.

---

111. Dr Deshmukh of Maharashtra responded, 'But wife is also property'. See also, Engels, *The Origin of the Family, Private Property and the State*

6. MAINTENANCE AND ALIMONY

The etymological root for alimony is from the Latin word *alaere*: to nourish; *alimonia*: nutriment.

~

As mentioned earlier, the UK, the US and Australia have the concept of community property in marital relationships whereby property, movable or immovable, acquired in the course of the marriage is equally divided, or equitably apportioned, as Court thinks fit, on the principle of needs, reasonable wants and sharing of community property. In contrast, India is governed by the concept of separate property, whereby each spouse owns their property separately and the financially empowered is supposed to support the weaker.

Financial issues arise in divorce proceedings at two stages: money paid pending litigation (*maintenance pedente lite)* is called interim maintenance, while the final settlement upon divorce is usually called alimony.[1] One reason for delays in contested divorces is the legal mandate that issues of interim maintenance and custody arrangements be dealt with first.

Interim maintenance protects the financially weaker (almost always women) from being being bullied into unfair settlements during the legal battle of rights due to lack of resources. Getting the interim maintenance is itself an intense battle in the midst of the proceedings, since the orders passed then will last through the divorce war. Though interim maintenance includes right of residence,[2] the amounts awarded seldom look after housing needs. They barely look after basic needs, while reasonable wants are an unimagined luxury.

The interim maintenance amount is supposed to be computed from the husband's disposable income, but the propensity of our citizens to have revenue from sources other than the 'known' ones has led to a series of rulings establishing that income tax returns and such documents are not the sole indices of true wealth. The lifestyle enjoyed by the couple is to be looked at to make a true assessment. The court conceded that the

---

1. Chand Dhawan vs. Jawaharlal Dhawan, (1993) 3 SCC 406: permanent alimony can be only granted when the decree of divorce is granted.

2. B.P. Achala Anand vs. S. Appi Reddy & Anr 2005 3 SCC 313; Komalam Amma vs. Kumara Pillai 2008(14)SCC 345

exercise is a 'guesstimate'.[3]

The Delhi High Court has evolved methods of assessing true wealth in a series of judgments, the last two of which, Puneet Kaur and Kusum Sharma, have become a byword in Delhi.[4] They require both husbands and wives to file affidavits stating income over the years of marriage, properties owned, club memberships, holidays, hotels, etc. A picturesque aside is that there is even a column for number of cattle owned! I realized its importance only when a husband told me that his wife makes a substantial cash income by running a small dairy with some Jersey cows tethered in the backyard of their house in the village.

Alimony is the money awarded after the divorce and is premised on the value of the fixed assets, instead of just the disposable income, as in the case of interim maintenance. It is generally financial insecurity that drives many women to contest divorces and because conduct is relevant for alimony awards, they fight tooth and nail to establish their bona fides and the husband's cruelty etc. But the irony is that after a hard battle to establish conduct, the wife often loses the energy to fight for a fair alimony because she is too tired, it is too expensive, takes too long and so on. This failure of the legal system is lightly referred to as 'litigation fatigue' but actually amounts to systemic cruelty. Fear of the emotional and financial costs of multiple proceedings drives litigants to settle 'out of court' and results in the weaker party being constrained to accept far less than the legal entitlement.

This is the reason why there is more case law on interim maintenance, awarded at the onset of legal proceedings, than on alimony, awarded at the conclusion of the proceedings. From 2010 to 2013, the Delhi High Court decided sixty-nine cases on interim maintenance[5] in contrast to a mere fifteen on alimony.[6]

In keeping with the Constitutional guarantee of equality, both husbands

3. Jayant Bhargava v. Priya Bhargava, III(2011)DMC487: 'These are some of the factors, which may be considered by any court in guesstimating or having a rough idea or to guess the income of a spouse'; See also: Gaurav Nagpal vs. Sumedha Nagpal, I (2008) DMC 166

4. Puneet Kaur vs. Inderjeet Singh Sawhney, 183 (2011) DLT 403; Sangeeta Vij vs. Sanjay Vij, 214(2014) DLT 493; Kusum Sharma vs. Mahinder Kumar Sharma, 217 (2015) DLT 706: Cases filed for maintenance under Section 24 of the Hindu Marriage Act, 1955.

5. See p. 368: Section 24 of the Hindu Marriage Act, 1955

6. See p. 368: Section 25 of the Hindu Marriage Act, 1955

and wives can claim maintenance and alimony under the Hindu Marriage Act, but not under the secular Special Marriage Act, where only a woman can claim against her husband. The gender bias in the Special Marriage Act is bewildering, considering it was passed the same time as the Hindu Marriage Act.[7] It has been argued that a gender-neutral maintenance law is irrelevant, since men don't make such claims from women.[8] That may be true for the moment, but gender equality is the law of the future where men are expected to break from their stereotyped roles too. Presently, for a man to ask his wife for maintenance is viewed badly in a machismo-ridden culture, but once men learn to stop defining themselves only in the context of their ability to provide, they will want to claim alimony and maintenance from their wives as well. There is a recent, well-publicized case of the husband of a movie star who claimed alimony.[9]

~

One of the reasons all litigation is time consuming and convoluted is the general propensity of litigants to perjure themselves without fear of consequences. The courts are simply too burdened to impose meaningful consequences for perjury. Applications calling the court's attention to an offense of perjury are treated as secondary and so get ignored in the mill of the primary litigation.

The other reason why litigants perjure themselves is the misplaced zeal of lawyers who fuel the belief of litigants in the righteousness of their private cause, giving them a sense of moral authority that is greater than the law.

The financially empowered (usually men) try to conceal their wealth by methods such as a notice in the newspaper that the son who has or is about to have marital problems has been ostracized from the family and disinherited from all family wealth. They try to veil wealth in a series of

7. Purananda Banerjee v. Sm. Swapan Banerjee, AIR 1981 Cal 123: The constitutionality of The Special Marriage Act was challenged; the court held that it was constitutionally valid and that even if s. 36 did discriminate on the basis of sex, it would be protected by Article 15(3) which allows progressive laws to be made for women and children.

8. Singh, *Separated and Divorced Women in India: Economic Rights and Entitlement*, p. 73: Her all-India survey found only two such cases under the present matrimonial law regime amongst Hindus (one in Delhi and one in Chennai).

9. 'How can Raja demand alimony from me: Shweta Tiwari' in *The Times of India*, 28 June 2012. The properties were in joint names but bought from the actress's earnings. He chose to take one house as sole proprietor and stay away from the daughter, instead of having co-ownership with the daughter.

holding companies, transfer assets by collusive sales of property to friends/family members, or use black money in property transactions to reduce the fair value of their assets.

Women are not averse to such ruses either: They will give up jobs or conceal incomes from cash-generating businesses like catering, tailoring, private consultancies, tuitions, etc. A well-paid designer might call herself an 'artist', conjuring up an image of a casual dilettante to distract from her true monetary worth as a hard-headed businesswoman.

In the UK, the courts have developed various ways of seeing through these tactics. In a recent case,[10] where the husband had bought property in his mother's name in India, the court held that even though the legal and beneficial owner of the property was the husband's mother, the property was bought by the husband and he remained in control of it. In another case, the court lifted the corporate veil to assess the actual assets of the husband.[11]

The Wife's Predicament

Male-centric views emerge here: by and large women are expected to be tough fighters and willing to work to maintain themselves and so maintenance claims may often be thought of as 'excessive' and generally disapproved of. Consider a judge's reaction to the predicament of a woman asking for a hefty alimony from her industrialist husband:

Judge: 'Why do you want maintenance? You are so qualified. Look for a job.'

My client: 'Ma'am I have never worked. I have never had a job. I married straight after graduation.'

Judge: 'There is so much to do: the other day I ate a chocolate cake that cost so much. I asked my cook about the cost of ingredients...the lady who baked the cake is making a 100 per cent profit!'

While I looked at the judge in silent disbelief, Marie Antoinette floated into my brain saying, 'let the helpless wife bake cakes'. To the client I said (in my head), 'You don't need to justify a thing. It is about rights and the opportunity to create a benchmark precedent for many women.'

'Judge Sahib', I wanted to say on behalf of my client, 'I hate cooking, I hate tailoring, I can't make papads and pickles and I can't run a catering business. It is true I am bright, but I was happy bringing up two children

10. Gadhavi v. Gadhavi, [2015] EWCA Civ 520

11. Prest v. Petrodel Resources Limited [2013] UKSC 34

in a charmed life with this very, very, very, rich man. So can we please talk about my legal rights to alimony and maintenance according to the lifestyle rule? We were happy for twenty-five years. That is the investment that needs to compensated for. By the way, he has just returned from a holiday in Tahiti (very far: very, very expensive) with his mistress.

'Judge Sahib, I actually don't need to bake cakes: I can also start a law firm: I have been thinking of starting a rock and roll bar, but that's not the point. Money is also not the only point by the way: it is also important for my son to know that he cannot treat women the way his father does.'

Having said which, my sarcasm makes only a limited point. The bigger point is the noble endeavour of many judges to encourage women to work, even if just to use their degrees and knowledge for public service. The Delhi High Court directed in a matter that not to utilize the professional degree of a woman would be public wastage.[12] This mixture of law and call for social change characterizes the Family Court. Recently, a litigant made an unfair complaint against a judge in the Delhi High court to say that s/he does less work and lectures more. The truth is, the judge works towards resolutions that by their very nature require animated talk, openness and yes, some moral exhortation. The interesting thing is that such talks can lead to mediated settlements, failing which orders will be passed anyway. I am always grateful for the time judges spend in chamber dialogue with litigants and their lawyers because I know they are horribly overworked. It is an unenviable job and every morning when I wake up to the privilege of doing what I like doing, I rejoice that judging is not amongst them. I am also grateful to all judges who make it possible for the rest of us to do what we want to do.

But when we are in court, to the judge in my head I want to say: 'Sahib, though I am not burdened with the privilege of judging, with all due respect, the little time you have for us in court would be better spent listening rather than overwhelming our clients with a flow of your verbosity. As for us lawyers, we love it: it is fodder for our humour and an opportunity for our counter-verbosity. But then do remember that you have given up the privilege of a lawyer's freedom.'

~

To return to male-centric scepticism about alimony: the problem is that the wife's predicament is not completely understood: caught in a divorce situation she will think of financial security and her needs for the future,

12. Kavita Prasad v. Ram Ashray Prasad, CM(M) 1153/2008

which more often than not she will spend alone, because remarriage is a complicated option for many women.

The bottom line is that any man in a divorce situation resents parting with money that he essentially views as 'his.' He does not consider that the wife worked with him to make his earnings possible. He does not want to consider that she did something that entitles her to a share in his wealth. She ran the house (however badly): bore the children (I thought there was no argument about doing that well or badly till a man complained that she did not breast-feed them): brought them up (even if he says she spoilt them): warmed his bed (even if he says she is lousy at it).[13] She did what she could so he could earn, and so at the time of reckoning this long tenure of investment needs to be considered. In any case, his complaints about her at the point of divorce should not retrospectively reduce her value and claim to monetary compensation for the time they lived together as married.

Within the marriage, women rarely have access to the man's wealth or the details of it. When the wife's maintenance claims are processed, apart from obvious needs, some reasonable wants must also be factored in as a basic entitlement. An earning woman's financial claim may be less, but she still needs to be compensated for past investment in the marriage and/or suffering caused to her by domestic violence and so on. And if needs and reasonable wants have been taken care of, the woman should not be encouraged to access the rest of her spouse's wealth as a bonanza. Of course, he too will be compensated from the same kitty if it is established that it is she who caused him enough anguish and maybe consequent loss. The latter type of case has not been seriously pleaded so far, but as we move to better gender neutrality, will probably start to appear in the next few decades.

~

It needs to be remembered that the battle of fair property distribution during divorce is actually not just about man versus woman, but affects children as well. One of my friends told me of her teenage boy and girl holding their stomachs and doubling up in anxiety when they heard that their father had left them. 'Will we be poor now?' An empathetic maintenance ruling would consider children by including comparable holidays for them with both parents to prevent the rich parent from

13. Conjugal duty versus marital rape is a controversial aspect discussed in Ch. 3: Love, Sex and Marriage, p. 64, 66

developing a strategy of inducement to lure the children away from the other.

The life of the housewife and finance is evocatively encapsulated in the kitty party. It is a popular saving device to manage meagre resources and a pleasant escape from household drudgery. It is also another way to tease out some money from otherwise miserly husbands who choose to pay up to avoid the social embarrassment of being called cheap, or to earn social kudos as 'generous'. I remember my mother remarking on a particular woman's luck and power with her husband, since she was a member of every kitty in town.

Women's expenses in a household are rarely for themselves alone. It is from these kitty party savings that they will give alms to a holy man visiting the house or spend an afternoon with women friends at a film. It is how the little bits and bobs that they will buy for their children and grandchildren happen. Sometimes maybe they will buy a bit of jewellery for themselves and try not to feel too guilty about it because it will eventually go to the children anyhow. The tendency is to invest and the joys they earn are often small but savoured well. The micro-finance banking system is based on this ability of women to make a little money go far.

In contrast, as a career woman, I am sometimes shamefully extravagant in my personal indulgences—my mother approves of these as something deliciously wicked. Even so, it seems to me, that the fact I needed to justify my spending on myself indicates a lurking sense of guilt about doing it. That is socialization I guess.

And these are the factors judges need to take into account, by passing meaningful orders of maintenance and alimony that truly take care of a woman's wants besides her needs.

The career woman

Computing maintenance for the dependent housewife is easy because it is predicated on the husband's wealth. However, the principle of sharing wealth and the judge's skill in balancing equities is truly tested while computing the rights of alimony and maintenance of an earning wife.

I believe that women who work with or for their husbands' businesses or professions need special consideration. Their working relationship is governed by the marriage dynamics that typically means male domination, particularly financial control. Generally, she will trust him completely to manage the finances and does not bother to double check them. Even women who are shrewd in their business dealings at work are often socialized to be intimidated by the subject of finance. A friend of mine has set up an NGO focusing on educating women on finance for precisely this reason.

A cautionary case[14]

H and W were equal partners in a business they set up together. Predictably, he was in charge of the finances. He told her that she was an equal shareholder in the company and she never checked. She signed without question any line on any paper that he dotted for her. When they fell out, she realized she had nothing in her name. She set up a case of breach of trust by the husband who, she said, had taken undue advantage of his dominant position in the marriage.[15]

By dismissing her claims as a business partner and relegating the case to a matrimonial dispute, the court exposed its inability to view a couple as business partners and to that extent, vindicated the argument of a systemic gender bias against women. The analogous law is in the realm of contracts between management and labour that are sometimes held to be unconscionable due to the unequal bargaining powers of the two contracting parties.[16]

~

Unfortunately, this is far from unusual. The majority decision[17] of the Canadian Supreme Court in 1975 did not allow a wife's claim of one-half of the interest of her husband's ranching business as she had worked in the ranch with her husband and sometimes managed on her own. The dissenting opinion was in tandem with the Matrimonial Property Act, 1989 that takes into consideration the contribution made by a spouse towards a business asset, and gives the court the power to award a share of the interest in the business.

In 1994, the UK ruled for 'tender treatment'[18] of women who were in business with their husbands because the relationship dynamics of the

---

14. 112 (2004) DLT 544

15. Lord Browne Wilkison: Barclays Bank plc vs. O'Brien ([1994] 1 AC 180, HL)

16. Central Inland Water Transport Corporation Ltd. & Anr. Etc. v. Brojo Nath Ganguly., AIR 1986 SC 1571

17. Murdoch v. Murdoch, [1975] 1 S.C.R. 423

18. Barclays Bank plc v. O'Brien 1994 1 AC 180 (HL)

business partnership was influenced by the dominant positions of their husbands in the marriages.

Wives who can work but choose not to

There are two judgments that, though unhappily worded, are sound in principle on the maintenance claims of working women.[19] The principle in both is the same on the law of mitigating her damages. Thus, women who are qualified to work must do so, and their ability to work will be factored into maintenance rulings, even if they choose not to work.

The Delhi High Court differed from these two judgments somewhat:

> 'In the opinion of the Court, employability and employment ought not to be misunderstood as being the same. That at a particular point of time, a spouse may have enjoyed the benefit of income might be a relevant consideration in the given set of circumstances as for instance the kind of remuneration he or she might have earned and capacity to save, etc.'[20]

Of course women should be encouraged to work, but bear in mind that many are not qualified or equipped to enter the job market. More women than not marry in their twenties, straight after college or a degree course, and so have no earning skills. Others find it heart-stoppingly difficult to enter a fast changing, brutally competitive workforce.

Many earning women may have another disadvantage, in that, relative to their husbands, their salaries are paltry and cannot contribute to their entitlement under the lifestyle rule.

Divorces for Money

The ultra-modern divorce is a product of the economic liberalization. I find many middle-aged men who take that call. The children have grown

19. Mamta Jaiswal vs. Rajesh Jaiswal, II (2000) DMC 170: 'According to me, Section 24 has been enacted for the purpose of providing a monetary assistance to such spouse who is incapable of supporting himself or herself in spite of sincere efforts made by him or herself. A spouse who is well qualified to get the service immediately with less efforts is not expected to remain idle to squeeze out, to milk out the other spouse by relieving him of his or her own purse by a cut in the nature of pendente lite alimony. The law does not expect the increasing number of such idle persons who by remaining in the arena of legal battles, try to squeeze out the adversary by implementing the provisions of law suitable to their purpose.' See also: Damanpreet Kaur vs Indermeet Juneja, 2013(1) Crimes 650 (Del.)

20. Ruchi Rai Sehmbey vs. Simon Jaison Sehmbey, 208 (2014) DLT 455

up and he is bored by his predictable home life. He has the money to buy his independence and in the prime of his career knows that he will earn back the alimony amount and more. He may or may not have another woman waiting in the wings but he wants to opt out of domesticity. He has earned the opportunity to enjoy the bachelor freedom missed in the early desperate years, amongst the sharp stress of his career. These divorce settlements are high, because the man is buying out of marriage and into his own aspirational life of free bachelordom where success has made him attractive.

After the initial shock of 'I don't know what happened' many women are better able to deal with the pain knowing that they will have a comfortable alimony amount. A woman once sent me an SMS to the effect that if she had to cry it might as well be in a BMW instead of an auto rickshaw.

Some women in this situation however, are so bitter that they would do anything rather than let the man embark on his new life: they resist divorce by making 'extortionist' alimony demands, etc.

There are women who also may want out of a long tenure marriage: but then they suffer long battles to realize their claims for maintenance and alimony because the husband sees no reason to part with his wealth if she chooses to exit on what he perceives to be her 'whim'.

I know two women who felt equal to their husbands even though they did not have the same amount of money. Unfortunately they are both in the generation before mine and I do not know any other like them. Both women were devoted wives and mothers till their children reached college. Then they walked out on their husbands. Not for another relationship, but for personal creative satisfaction. One is a writer and another has set up a micro-finance unit. Both are grey, youthful, vibrant and happy. Their husbands are rich—these women are not.

The approach of these women is laudable and I cite them as examples of life's rich possibilities as a single person, but there is no reason for them to be examples to other women to give up or even dilute legitimate financial claims. So far, the financial strength to buy out of a marriage is unique to men, since non-career women in their fifties are usually struggling with empty-nest syndrome. Some may try to make a tentative and nervous return to the workplace but most are ready for some well-deserved leisure after years of household drudgery.

After the grieving, these 'rich' divorces grow quite amicable and the divorced couple may manage to settle into a comfortable friendly existence of co-parenting arrangements.

Whether a divorce will be harmonious or ugly is dependent on many things. A lawyer controls only a fraction of the situation: the rest of it is with the other side's lawyer, both litigants and the judge. Sometimes many things coincide to make some cases smoother than others, while other cases are horrendously rocky and you have to work with the client to negotiate the road with care. In this scenario, bonanza alimonies given by rich men desperate for divorce are an interesting event. This type of moneyed divorce is less stressful, even for us lawyers.

Stridhan has a different meaning for this class. The woman in me loves reading these lists jumping with beautiful things: a Chanel jacket for Rs. 4 lakhs and expensive designer saris and suits worth fabulous sums. It is no longer the traditional gold, silk saris and Kashmiri shawls. The value of a full gold kundan 'set' might be Rs. 20 lakhs. The ring now may be presented in a Judith Leiber jewelled bag worth another couple of lakhs. I asked one of my rich women clients why she thinks she needs so many expensive bags. 'Social status' was the candid reply and to give her a lecture on crass consumerism seemed out of place and boring, even to me.

A story

My client, the wife, lived in the same house in an adjoining bedroom when her husband filed for divorce. She refused to leave, knowing her presence would be effective to push a quick settlement.

We went to the judge's chamber to talk interim maintenance. He said to her: 'Since you are in the same house, your food is taken care of; you have a car, petrol; you don't have to pay electricity bills; so what interim maintenance are you asking for?'

We tried to raise the issue of ill-treatment in the house but were shushed as money-grubbing women; after all such a 'high class' family would not really treat their daughter-in-law so badly. But they did. They were trying to wither her away, by neglect and exclusion even from the kitchen. She was effectively confined to her room.

I then decided to play the upper-class woman's role to the hilt. We submitted expenses for her personal trainer, probiotic food, expensive creams and dermatologist treatments.

'Be reasonable,' I was told.

'I am being reasonable,' I said. 'These expenses are necessary to survive in that social class. Self-indulgent? Maybe. But that's how they lived when they were together; there is no reason why he should get a cheap and cheerful exit with petty cash.'

Eventually the pressure on him to marry again was mounting. Central to the dynamics of Indian families (unchanged since the epics) is the urgent need and pious duty to produce the dynastic heir. We teetered towards a trial and since my client was treating it with robust good cheer, they realized she would not break. The litigation eventually settled at a fair figure as financial settlement for my client.

Her father responded to my beaming congratulations with a quiet, worried and tired 'For what?' I was ashamed of my insensitivity at looking at my client's divorce as my personal success story. It never is. Families suffer a stigma of divorce even more than the daughter does and money is not seen as compensation enough.

Improvements in Interim Maintenance

There is an intense need for immediate attention to clarify the law and make efficient the systems of granting interim maintenance.

There are various reasons why a wife files for interim maintenance:

a) She needs it because she has no money.
b) She needs it because she has some money but not enough.
c) She does not need the money but demands it as compensation for wrongs perpetrated upon her by him.
d) She has a share in the father's wealth but she is angry at having to return to him and upset because her brothers and their wives may resent her. So she needs maintenance from her husband to retain her independence from her parental family.
e) She does not need it but is angry and vengeful at being betrayed.

Women of a) and b) categories are the ones who need money quickly and will suffer the most from litigation exhaustion. They are also vulnerable to predatory men who want to 'help'. Such unsavoury stories are depressingly common. The legal system fails them. They cannot afford sound and reliable help and legal aid is miserably inadequate.

In some cases, it has taken as long as four years to get the first maintenance cheque. The reasons are many: time lost on adjournments; the judge not sitting; the matter not reaching the bench because of a heavy workload; lawyer's strikes in lower courts; hearings lost in endless quibbling about forensic analysis of documents.

Pooja Chauhan[21] walked naked on the road to justice as a desperate

21. Jyotsna Singh, 'Indian woman strips in dowry row' on BBC News, 5 July 2007, http://news.bbc.co.uk/2/hi/south_asia/6274318.stm

protest against this inefficiency. The politics of an inarticulate, unintelligent patriarchy is when men strip, rape or mutilate the wives and daughters of the enemy. Communities strip their own women to punish them for transgressing social norms. Pooja Chauhan's protest was to shame the system by stripping herself.[22] There was no follow-up story in the press.

Women in category c) are in the same category as a) and b) really, but with the difference that these women stay the course, often because they have the emotional and financial support of their parental family. Their claims are taken care of by the PWDVA, which entitles a woman to compensation on several counts,[23] but as mentioned earlier in the absence of any benchmarked parameters of computing compensation, they are mostly always a pitiful travesty.

Those in categories d) and e) suffer low self-esteem in a male-dominated environment. Having declared her assets, it may easily be found that she has no need for interim maintenance, but a trial may find that she has a good alimony claim or in any case can make a financial claim for compensation under the PWDVA.[24]

~

When I began writing this book, I had a list of suggestions to streamline maintenance hearings. Since then, two rulings of the Delhi High Court have delved into the matter deeper than any other rules of procedure. In the Kusum Sharma and Puneet Kaur judgments,[25] the High Court gave practice directions to the family courts requiring both parties to file income affidavits to help a forensic analysis of financial status.

I still have a wish-list: for the courts to have an attitude that reflects market realities on the cost of living etc.;[26] for real and substantial penal

---

22. A similar protest by a group of Northeastern women against AFSPA: Revathi Laul, 'We Stripped And Shouted, "Indian Army, Rape Me!" It Was The Right Thing To Do' in *Tehelka*, 23 February 2013.

23. These are: (a) the loss of earnings; (b) the medical expenses; (c) the loss caused due to the destruction, damage or removal of any property from the control of the aggrieved person; and (d) the maintenance for the aggrieved person as well as her children, if any, including an order under or in addition to an order of maintenance under section 125 of the Code of Criminal Procedure, 1973 (2 of 1974) or any other law for the time being in force.

24. See p. 386: PWDVA Section 22: Compensation orders.

25. Puneet Kaur vs. Inderjeet Singh Sawhney, 183 (2011) DLT 403; Kusum Sharma vs. Mahinder Kumar Sharma, 217 (2015) DLT 706

26. Puneet Kaur vs. Inderjeet Singh Sawhney, 183 (2011) DLT 403

consequences if maintenance payments are not made in a timely manner; for garnishee orders to attach salary at source and ensure its transfer to the claimant's bank account. The Armed Forces have that arrangement to deal with maintenance claims by wives.[27] Courts have been grappling with these mechanism for decades but the problems remain.[28]

The politics of the matrimonial home

W came to see me about a divorce settlement. They had been separated for several years and her husband now wanted to discuss divorce by 'mutual consent'. He wanted her to return some valuable jewellery that had been given to her. She refused.

The Friday following our meeting, I got a panicked call from W that H had abducted their six-year-old child and was now inaccessible. W had left her matrimonial home a few years ago. I could not understand this sudden decision to abduct the child, considering W had never interfered with his meeting her. Clearly he planned to hold the child hostage till W agreed to abandon all property claims.

W decided to go to her matrimonial home and not leave without the child. Dialing 100 and all of that would surely have drawn the predictable police response that a father cannot be held to have kidnapped his own child. She arrived at her old beautiful home in the shaded leafy environs of an exclusive Delhi neighbourhood. Knowing that they would not let her in if she rang the doorbell, she broke a window and climbed into the kitchen. She walked into the drawing room from the kitchen as she must have many times in happier days, but this time the expression of the parents-in-law sitting in the drawing room was one of complete shock and horror.

She parked herself on the sofa and asked that C (the daughter) be brought to her. They said that they did not know where she was. She then

---

27. Section 90(i) of the Army Act,

'90. Deductions from pay and allowances of officers. The following penal deductions may be made from the pay and allowances of an officer: (i) any sum required by order of the Central Government [or any prescribed officers] to be paid for the maintenance of his wife or his legitimate or illegitimate child or towards the cost of any relief given by the said Government to the said wife or child.

'193. Prescribed officer under sections 90(i) and 91(i). The prescribed officer for the purposes of clause (i) of section 90 and clause (i) of section 91 shall be the Chief of the Army Staff or the officer commanding the Army.'

28. Gaurav Sondhi vs. Diya Sondhi, 120 (2005) DLT 426

asked that H be brought. They said they did not know where he was either. She then asked that they call their son from one of their mobiles. They refused. She picked up her mother-in-law's mobile phone and dialed H's number. He took the call. She told him that she was at his house sitting with his parents and was not leaving without her daughter. She could hear her daughter in the jeep screaming and crying for her mother.

While W was in the house, my colleague went to the local police station to report the parental abduction and that W was effectively trapped, as she was not going to leave without her child. The police officer (SHO) called me with the typical spiel that a father was within his rights to take the child and so on. I asked that an officer go to the matrimonial house to record W's statement. The SHO said that W should come to the police station. I said my client would not leave the house till the child was brought there.

The SHO said that he believed that W had not lived in the house for the last five years and her presence there amounted to trespass. I responded that her presence was as much trespass as H's disappearance with the child was kidnapping. Either treat both as offences or neither.

I do believe that the situation required W's physical presence in the house. Once out, any number of complaints would have got lost in the labyrinth of due process. The in-laws threatened to forcibly evict W, so she ran into her former bedroom and locked herself in. It was 8 p.m.

The SHO called me to negotiate a full and final divorce. I did not ask why an SHO was instructed to negotiate with me on their behalf. I said my client had not eaten and was concerned that if she left the bedroom to enter the kitchen they would throw her out. I asked whether the police station could arrange to get food to her. They refused. I then said there would be no talk till the child was brought back

About half-an-hour later, W called me to say that she had been going through some of her husband's papers lying in the bedroom and had discovered the draft of a divorce petition where he had made the most outrageous and scandalous allegations against her.

The pressure mounted with the standoff, and finally a few hours later, H brought home the sleeping child. W carried her out in her arms. She had not eaten dinner, she had not slept, she was exhausted, angry and miserable.

In hindsight, perhaps, I should have asked her not to leave the house and obtained an injunction protecting her right of residence in that house. (The PWDVA had not been passed then.) However, the fact that she had been living away all this while and the contemporaneous accounts even in the police station of her having barged into the house and stayed overnight would have established that W did not have continued residence in the matrimonial home that entitled her to protection. W was also very tired, had not been back in that house for five years, was hated with a vengeance by her parents-in-law and was so humiliated at the way they had treated her that she did not want to stay there a minute longer. She just wanted out and so she left.

We obtained an order protecting W's custody of the child and sought a divorce along with financial relief. We found out that they were planning to sell the matrimonial house. We rushed to the court for an injunction but the sale had been effected a day before we obtained the restraint order. We did manage an order that a sum of Rs. 4 crores be retained by H from the sale proceeds in lieu of W's maintenance claims.

Because of the nature of civil suits, the Rs. 4 crores could not have been handed over to her unless there was a finding in her favour for maintenance of that amount. We then went into the maintenance court under Section 125 Criminal Procedure Code. We told that court about the Rs. 4 crores lying with H as per court order and that we were entitled to a ruling to have the money released. The address spoke for itself, the fact that property had been sold spoke for itself and the fact that a large sum of Rs. 4 crores had been directed by the court to be retained towards her maintenance dues also spoke for itself.

Then began a horrible travesty of justice, made possible for any number of reasons, including complete non-application of mind. The judge made a standard cut-and-paste order using the keywords in such cases: 'keeping in mind the lifestyle' etc., and awarded a monthly maintenance amount of Rs. 20,000 to W and her child. This, against an admitted sale of Rs. 15 crores and a High Court order that Rs. 4 crores be retained for maintenance. The illogicality of this order was shocking and bewildering. W challenged it in appeal. It was dismissed on the ground that as an interim maintenance, Rs. 20,000 was not inadequate. No dispute on the quantum of figures was possible; to do the fractions of her entitlements is simple arithmetic and yet the matter is lost in a procedural labyrinth.

H's contempt for society, people and certainly the court was apparent in his casual walk into a courtroom, hands in pockets, swaying back and forth on the balls of his feet, looking at the judge through half-closed eyes. He walked out with the same insolent leer and winked at me while passing. My face was expressionless as I stared back, but my mind was exploding with violent responses. He did not even honour the order of Rs. 20,000 per month.

We then filed under the Contempt of Court Act and obtained a ruling that the order must be complied in full and the act of contempt would be deemed to continue for each day that he failed to make the payment. Eventually, under contempt law proceedings, the court forced H to pay arrears over several years, which had accrued to a substantial amount.

After the amendment of the Hindu Succession Act in 2005, W filed for partition of the Hindu Undivided Family properties on behalf of the daughter. This suit is what I hope will eventually provide long-term relief and security for the child. But eight years of her growing life have been spent in her aunt's house. She is lucky to have a calm and loving family. More often than not, the woman is crippled completely and would have exited from the battle with nothing.

Anybody reading the story would ask why W did not settle. She wanted to but their offer was not in accordance with even a few of her rights.

W has lost financial benefits from her husband but because of the 2005 amendment to the Hindu Succession Act she has a chance of securing at least her daughter's interests. She has, moreover, gained and enjoyed bringing up her child in a close and loving family. To my mind, H has so far kept his money, but lost a valuable quality of life in litigation.

~

This case typifies the arsenal in the gender war that is divorce. The man has control over the money and the woman of the child. If she has the temerity to ask for more than what he thinks she deserves (if anything at all) he removes the child to force a settlement.

How much maintenance?

W was in her fifties with two grown-up daughters. Though fashionably thin, she looked bleached of blood when her handsome fifty-something husband claimed he wanted a divorce so he could marry a younger woman.

W lived in a farmhouse. She had poured her turmoil into her garden, which responded with a lush green generosity. The only time I saw her face lighten was when she talked of her plants; they too found their way into the battle, with the husband showing perfect *House and Garden* type photos to establish that she was living well and her needs were being met, and the wife showing them to establish lifestyle and thus a commensurate money claim which should be higher than what he was offering.

The High Court judge called us into chambers to discuss settlement. Years of dealing with human misery seem to have given this particular judge a Buddha-like demeanour of dispassionate empathy. Yet even his eyebrows flickered in a small dance step when she named the figure she would settle at. (This case is about a decade ago and financial demands were not high because expectations were not. This lady was breaking the mould.) He then said, 'Don't tell me want you want, tell me what you need.'

And here is the fundamental question. The law provides for maintenance and alimony in the context of a lifestyle enjoyed by the woman in her matrimonial home. It does not distinguish between wants and needs as in English law, though the underlying principle is approximately the same, since lifestyle encompasses wants and needs. Having said which, there is rarely a generous award that will include wants. It covers classes of needs, like housing and food and school expenses, depending upon the economic class. But it will not cover foreign holidays and wardrobe expenses that are reasonable wants, and which she enjoyed in her life with her husband.

Most of the higher judiciary and the seniors amongst the lower judiciary, as also this author, were brought up in the frugal days of pre-liberalization. We are uncomfortable with a definition of want beyond some broad parameters of need, dependent on economic class. Some of us are also the generation that sang with the Rolling Stones, 'you can't have what you want, but you can what you need', but we also protested that we 'ain't got no satisfaction'.

In contrast, the needs of the children who have benefited from economic liberalization are what used to be our wants. 'Lifestyle' in the modern age of liberalization and amongst a certain class can include shopping worth lakhs, luxury travel, membership of exclusive wine and food societies, personal trainers and expensive diet food.

With more Indians on the global rich lists, some maintenance claims seem large, even though they may be only a fraction of the millionaires' income. Even in this class and context, large financial claims by women are viewed as immoral. Society views her as greedy for not demurely accepting a grudging grant to fulfil frugal needs, since a truly feminine 'Indian' persona of self-denial does not allow for her wants. The millionaire's net worth enables him to buy a house on the green and purple of the Monopoly board; she must settle for the red and yellow since that is respectable enough.

The principle of the millionaire's defence was developed in the UK and

US to avoid divorce becoming an opportunity for bonanza gains. 'Pass any order,' the millionaire says, 'because I will cover her reasonable needs and wants but I should not have to make financial disclosures.'

After White v. White in 2000,[29] the courts were reluctant to allow this defence, on the ground that it ran counter to the principle of property division amongst spouses, which was based not just on needs and compensation but also sharing. In 2014, the UK allowed the defense in the special circumstances of one particular case.[30]

In India the defense is not used, I believe due to concern at the unpredictability of the courts if faced with such a defense, and also the confidence that even with full disclosure, the principle of needs and compensation will be applied with conservative circumspection. Sharing is not a principle in our jurisdiction that is based on a separate marital property regime unlike the community of marital property principle that applies in the UK and many states of US. In fact, in White v. White, the court was clear that it wishes to give full play to the principle of sharing.

Court fees

Sometimes wives in maintenance suits file for exemption from payment of court fees on account of being a pauper. It is called Forma Pauperis. The process of establishing a pauper status is a travesty of delays and, in some cases, the most outrageous pleas are made. The problem is that to obtain the benefit of exemption from court fees, she has to show she is a complete pauper with nothing to her name. Usually a claimant may have some money for subsistence, but it does not extend to paying the ad valorem court fees of maintenance suits, which is computed on the monthly amount claimed multiplied by ten years. This is prohibitive.[31]

The wife of a very rich man may be entitled to Rs.15 lakhs a month as commensurate to her lifestyle, but she may not have the funds to pay court fees to the tune of about Rs. 18 lakhs, apart from lawyers' fees, etc. Thus she is denied a fair opportunity of applying for maintenance that is meaningful in the context of her status.

---

29. [2001] 1 AC 596

30. Re A (A Child) [2014] EWCA Civ 1577

31. Delhi High Court fees for maintenance of up to Rs. 4 lakhs are Rs. 6,250, and for every additional lakh, it is another Rs. 976

The states of Maharashtra and Andhra Pradesh have dealt with the problem of this unfair deterrence to a fair claim by fixing an outer limit to the court fees in a maintenance suit by a woman.[32]

Who pays?

The other problem for women is figuring out who is responsible for her maintenance. Section 18 of the Hindu Adoption and Maintenance Act (HAMA)[33] provides that her claim lies against her husband. Yet, many Hindu families live jointly and are dependent on the karta (patriarch) to maintain their lifestyle and social status.

My argument is that Section 18 does not protect properly the legal rights of wives in a Hindu undivided family (HUF) or a joint family, by preventing them from getting their rightful maintenance, because their husbands' claim to be dependent on the karta with little or no personal income (at least on paper). They may not have registered as a HUF for tax purposes but in effect are living in the traditional joint family system. This continues to be very common across all classes.

The court says the wife is entitled to claim only from the husband; the husband now declares he can't afford anything at all, because Daddy owns it all. This reduces the 'lifestyle standard' rule to a farce. As the Delhi High Court observed, 'A person whose parents are well to do in status and owner of a number of immovable properties, their only son can hardly be believed to be employed at a monthly income of Rs. 5,200'.[34]

The sad truth is that women in upper-class joint families are as vulnerable as those of the lower classes. Many wealthy families do not allow 'their' women to work as not befitting their status. At best they will be permitted to attend office with their husbands, subject to his indulgence. This attitude that a working woman is a dishonour is shared by a cook in a household I know. We do not get our women to work, he said to me with pride, even while packing soup and sandwiches for his memsahib's horrendously long day at work.

Section 4 of the Hindu Adoption & Maintenance Act, 1956 provides

32. Since court fees are a state subject under the Constitution, all states have not adopted this welfare measure.

33. Hindu Adoption and Maintenance Act, 1956

34. Deepak Bhushan Gupta v. Reshu Garg, 2013IIAD(Delhi)438

that anything contrary to what has been legislated is no longer law.[35] My argument is that because the Hindu Marriage Act, 1955, or Hindu Adoption and Maintenance Act, 1956, are limited to claims against the husband, claims against a karta continue to be rooted in customary law and thus cannot be excluded as being contrary to any enactment.

The liability and responsibility of a karta and patriarch of a joint family with regard to settling his estranged daughter-in-law must be acknowledged as long as the system of patriarchy and joint families survives. After all, if an HUF receives tax benefits, there must be an equivalent responsibility to look after its members, including the wife, daughters-in-law and daughters. To read it any other way leads to the odd anomaly that under HAMA, a widow will fare better with a claim against her rich father-in-law, but not a wife against her living husband.[36] This rationale is a travesty.

Alimony and the Woman's Conduct

In ancient India, chastity was all that constituted good conduct for women; it needed to survive even the death of the husband.

The stipulation in the Widow Remarriage Act, 1856 that a widow stood to forfeit her husband's property if she remarried, raised the legal question of whether unchaste widows could also lose their rights of maintenance. Tanika Sarkar writes of the great unchastity case,[37] where the court allowed a widow to retain property even though she was 'unchaste' because she had been chaste when she inherited it.[38]

The ruling seems based less on a desire to ameliorate the condition of women than to avoid the confusion of divesting the complicated ownership rights that had accrued over the time that the widow was dealing with the property. The court made no observation on whether an unchaste widow could lose maintenance rights from a husband's estate or from her son's property. The case was about vesting property because there was no male heir.

Today, the relevance of conduct in alimony awards is a complex matter, but the meaning of 'conduct' for women remains wedded to chastity.

---

35. See p. 363: Section 4, Hindu Adoption and Maintenance Act

36. See p. 363: S 19., HAMA: Maintenance of widowed daughter-in-law

37. Moneeram Kolita v. Kery Kolitany, 13 B.L.R. 1

38. Sarkar, *Hindu Wife, Hindu Nation: Community, Religion, and Cultural Nationalism*, p. 83

With a few glaring exceptions,[39] conduct is not given much importance at the stage of awarding interim maintenance claims, because a finding on conduct can only be made after a trial.

Even so, it needs to be noted that since alimony claimants are mostly women, it is their conduct that is measured and not that of the man. The question should be that, if her conduct is a factor in deciding her claim for maintenance and alimony, does he pay more if it is found that it is he who has misconducted himself in the marriage? The distinction between alimony and compensation for misconduct is lost in the wordings of the section on alimony.[40]

A UK ruling, Wachtel v. Wachtel,[41] did away with the relevance of conduct in alimony awards despite a statute enjoining it to be taken into account, with the following words:

> 'When the Judge comes to decide these questions, what place has conduct in it? Parliament still says that the Court has to "have regard to their conduct"—see section 5(1) of the 1970 Act. Does this mean that the Judge in chambers is to hear their mutual recriminations and to go into their petty squabbles for days on end, as he used to do in the old days? Does it mean that, after a marriage has been dissolved, there is to be a post mortem to find out what killed it? We do not think so. In most cases both parties are to blame—or, as we would prefer to say—both parties have contributed to the breakdown. It has been suggested that there should be a "discount" or "reduction" in what the wife is to receive because of her supposed misconduct, guilt or blame (whatever word is used). We cannot accept this argument. In the vast majority of cases it is repugnant to the

---

39. Yogeshwar Prasad v. Jyoti Rani, AIR 1981 Del 99: 'the conduct of the respondent which will include unchastity, has to be taken into consideration not only at the time of making financial provision under Section 25, but it can also be taken into consideration at the time of grant of interim maintenance...The sole question for decision always in such cases is whether the character and gravity of the conduct were such as would be repugnant to justice to ignore them in determining the provision that was to be made by the other party'; See also: Amarjit Kaur vs. Harbhajan Singh, (2003)10 SCC 228: 'Consideration as to the ultimate outcome of the main proceeding after regular trial would be wholly alien to assess the need or necessity for awarding interim maintenance, as long as the marriage, the dissolution of which has been sought, cannot be disputed, and the marital relationship of husband and wife subsisted.'

40. See p. 368: Section 25 of the Hindu Marriage Act; See also p. 390: Section 37 of the Special Marriage Act

41. Wachtel vs Wachtel, [1973] EWCA Civ 10; However, sharing or ouster from the matrimonial home is still based on conduct under the Family Law Act, 1996.

> principles underlying the new legislation, and in particular the 1969 Act... Criminal justice often requires the imposition of financial and indeed custodial penalties. But in the financial adjustments consequent upon the dissolution of a marriage which has irretrievably broken down, the imposition of financial penalties ought seldom to find a place.'

My view on this perspective is that marital assets need to be fairly shared in a divorce, so that a non-earning spouse should not suffer unduly on the material front. However, many people resist divorce because they would then have to establish their own good conduct and the misconduct of the spouse, for the purpose of alimony claims. Even in those cases where conduct is considered to be relevant, some amounts have to be awarded as past contribution to a marriage by way of child rearing and running the household. The Wachtel ruling on conduct is useful in the Indian environment to establish that a husband's divorce may be granted on account of his wife's cruelty, but that should have no bearing on the maintenance claim emanating from her past investment in marriage in better times. Of course, brutal marriages with short tenure require a different perspective. Many courts might be reluctant to reward such misconduct with generous alimony amounts.

Perhaps if parties could agree on the fact of the divorce, alimony claims could be dealt with in detail and lead to quicker resolutions: evidence could be limited to issues of grave misconduct that the court agrees has a bearing on alimony awards.

~

The tenure of a marriage is the investment for which it is reasonable to expect a return. Even committed career women opt for a more flexible career track after childbirth. This has to be factored in for long-tenure marriages where the investment of time should give rise to proportionately higher maintenance and alimony claims. Child-rearing needs separate compensation, and child support is not just about school fees but those needs and wants of the child that the woman, as a primary caregiver, had to provide, as well as the hidden costs of maintaining a lifestyle for the child. Proportionately, maintenance and alimony in short-tenure marriages, particularly when there are no children, could be less.

The most notorious case on short tenure marriage and alimony is McCartney vs. Mills.[42] The Beatles star Paul McCartney married Heather Mills. She was fifty and he sixty-two. The marriage lasted about six years.

---

42. McCartney v. McCartney [2008] EWHC 401 (Fam)

The court observed that when it comes to financial orders in divorce matters, the first principle was that of sharing: meaning thereby that property acquired during the course of the marriage was to be shared. It could be divided equally or with some adjustment after looking at all circumstances. Unfortunately for Mills, McCartney had not acquired any significant wealth during their marriage, which was viewed as of a short tenure by the court.

The next principle is compensation: here, the court did not agree with Mills's claim that she had suffered a financial disadvantage by marrying McCartney on account of her being unable to give priority to her own career. The court eventually ruled on a 'generous interpretation' of her needs as the dominant factor influencing the financial award.

In an essay on the overview of family law, Jonathan Herring commented: 'The message from the case is clear. After a long marriage a wife may well expect half of a wealthy husband's assets. But after a short marriage, needs will often dominate the court's analysis.'[43]

~

The problem in the Indian context is that women extricating themselves even from short-term marriages are viewed as 'spoiled' by their own families, and thus look for compensation for a lifetime. They feel that the chances of a second marriage are now considerably reduced.

A word of caution

The interim maintenance of working or qualified women may be less than for dependent women but this cannot dilute their claim to financial compensation for an abusive marriage or return of their investment in a long tenure marriage. It would be practical to move these claims to the law of compensation where conduct can be weighed in the judicial balance and awards for loss of work, mental and physical abuse, etc. can be more meaningful. The PWDVA makes the distinction between maintenance, alimony and compensation for injury and damage in an abusive marriage.[44] Unfortunately, the law on compensation as a tort—a civil, rather than a criminal wrong—is nascent and ineffective and the amounts awarded are paltry.

It is also important to note that women-enabling legislations do not

43. Jonathan Herring, *Beginning Family Law*

44. See p. 386: Section 20 of the PWDVA

take away the right of men to be compensated as an actionable tort for wrongs suffered by them. No one can deny the existence of violent and vengeful women who make men suffer. The Delhi High Court acknowledged this when it struck down the challenge to PWDVA on the ground of gender bias, but then went on to say that the instances of such vengeful and violent women are rare and few.[45] I agree with the ruling but not the reasoning. Instances of vengeful and violent women are fewer than the domestic violence by men that is almost a social norm, but their low frequency brings no succour to those who suffer cruelty by women. The desperation of the powerless that makes them cruel is as severe as oppression by the powerful. The idea is to empower women so that at some point the domestic violence legislation may become gender-neutral, as it has in some parts of the world.[46] That point regrettably is very far away as yet.

Pre-Nuptial Agreements

Pre-nuptial agreements (pre-nups) existed in the ancient world. The Hebrew law of marriage contract, the Ketubah, gave financial and legal rights to women. Mahar is a type of pre-nuptial contract under Islamic law as well.

Modern pre-nups have evolved slowly in UK common law from the time when a husband and wife could not contract with each other, since they were treated as a single entity in law.[47] Pre-nups have grown as the wife developed an independent legal identity that allowed her to hold property. The UK courts have taken the position that pre-nups have legal force only after an independent judicial enquiry to determine their fairness.[48]

With the increasing rate of divorce and values of financial settlements, the time is ripe for pre-nups to gain a following in India. Section 40 of the Indian Divorce Act recognizes pre- and post-nuptial contracts.[49] The Goa Civil Code provides for them as well. Though I found no cases testing

45. Aruna Prarmod Shah v. Union of India, 102 DRJ 543 (2008)

46. See Serious Crime Act 2015, UK available at http://www.legislation.gov.uk/ukpga/2015/9/section/76/enacted; Swedish Penal Code; The Austrian Code of Criminal Procedure, 2006

47. See Ch. 7: Property, p. 129, for the case of Mrs Catherine Norton

48. Radmacher vs. Granatino, [2010]3 WLR 1367

49. See p. 374: S.40 of Indian Divorce Act

the validity of pre-nup contracts, a discussion about them is necessary because many engaged couples want to explore the idea, particularly if they have been through one divorce.

Like any contract, a pre-nup to be valid, must have valid consideration[50] that, even if not monetary, should not be illusory either. The other important principle is that it should not be against public policy. I can imagine some sort of a loose, baseless vague comment from some quarters that pre-nups could be viewed as against public policy because in India, marriage is a sacrament and to view it as a transaction dilutes the solemnity of the sacred. The argument is ossified and oppressive because it can better be argued that public policy requires pre-nups. Understandably, the engaged couple wrapped in romance don't want to talk about divorce even before the marriage. To them, it may seem inauspicious and unromantic. Yet, think about the time spent in shameless and hectic parleys for extortionist dowry demands; it could be better used to negotiate a pre-nuptial contract. In arranged marriages at least, there is no risk of romance evaporating while families negotiate a pre-nup. Frankly, if romance can survive dowry, passionate love will surely visit the newlywed couple secured in a pre-nup agreement.

A couple embarking on a love marriage could well be squeamish about money talk, but Indians have the advantage of extended family involvements which could be put to good use to negotiate a fair agreement that takes care of needs and wants. Mediators could help draft such agreements with professional neutrality. There can also be financial agreements after marriage (post-nups). All factors considered, pre-nups seem to have the potential to better help an amicable divorce and could prove to be useful to neutralize the uncertainties of embarking on a married life together.

~

Then arises the question of the validity of a contract where the parties do not have equal bargaining power, particularly in the Indian context. Given our socialization, it is rare that a woman will have the bargaining power to match the husband. However, pre-nups can be used to safeguard some of the woman's entitlements. For example, the agreement could include a

50. Section 2(d) in The Indian Contract Act, 1872 states: (d) When, at the desire of the promisor, the promisee or any other person has done or abstained from doing, or does or abstains from doing, or promises to do or to abstain from doing, something, such act or abstinence or promise is called a consideration for the promise

list of stridhan with the clause that she has absolute control over it. This is after all only a reiteration of customary law.

India has a well-developed and sophisticated jurisprudence around 'family agreements'.[51] They are a separate category of contracts, protected from attacks based on legal technicalities.[52] Even though pre-nups are not family settlements since the couple are yet to marry, it might be useful to accord them a special status that could be a baseline for the court to work on. The note of caution is that, given our skewed gender relationships, these agreements will have to be judicially analyzed to check for fairness and that they are not vitiated by unconscionable conduct.

Couples and their families often resolve financial and custody issues at the time of separation, which then becomes the basis of the divorce petition. One such case was tested where H refused to abide by the separation agreement, saying it was unconscionable because it was obtained under false pretenses. W filed for specific performance and the suit was held to be maintainable, using the analogy of the special status of 'family arrangements'. On appeal the division bench upheld the order.[53] The Supreme Court upheld the interim order[54] of payments to be made pending the main suit, but conceded that an important question of law needed to be dealt with and so has left the matter open. H's legal contention is that such an agreement cannot be specifically enforced since there exists a special statute for maintenance. W contends that the special statute is for the time when a suit seeking maintenance is filed but not when an agreement has already been arrived at. The matter has reached the trial stage after fifteen years.

Conclusion

As with every other aspect of the divorce process, the speed (or lack thereof) of the proceedings is always a stumbling block. Maintenance and alimony issues could be streamlined effectively if they were decided

51. Ram Charan Das vs. Girja Nandini Devi and others, 1966 AIR 323; Maturi Pullaiah and Anr. vs. Maturi Narasimham And Ors. AIR 1966 SC 1836; Kale and others vs. Deputy Director of Consolidation and others AIR 1976 SC 807; Smt. Badam v. Bhali AIR 2012 SC 2858

52. See p. 386: Section 17, The Registration Act, 1908 (Documents for which registration is compulsory)

53. Ravi Singhal vs. Manali Singhal, II (2000) DMC 732

54. Ravi Singhal vs. Manali Singhal, 2001(6)SCALE580

within broad parameters of needs, wants and compensations.[55] At present, the lifestyle rule only provides for needs, which vary according to the economic class of the claimant. Equal sharing is not really a factor taken into account in the separate property regime. The margin for the judge's discretion is so wide that it leaves no room for even an approximate guess on the likely outcome of a matter.[56]

---

55. Miller v. Miller; McFarlane v McFarlane [2006] UKHL 24

56. See p. 187 for a case where admittedly a family property was sold for Rs. 15 crores, and admittedly the husband had a Rs. 4 crore share, but the amount awarded to the wife was Rs. 20,000 per month.

7. CHILDREN

A stone tablet from the Sumerian civilization of Mesopotamia in approximately 2,000 BCE, reads:

> 'Arriving at school in the morning I recited my tablet, ate my lunch, prepared my new tablet, wrote it, finished it, then they assigned me my oral work. When school was dismissed I went home, entered the house and found my father sitting there. I told my father of my written work, then recited my tablet to him, and my father was delighted'.[1]

We don't have enough information about that civilization to know whether the tablet reflects the routine of all their children or only those born into privilege. So, while it is fascinating to think that this routine remains familiar to many children more than 4,000 years later, there is also something terribly sad that despite 4,000 years we have not been able to make it the routine of all our children. Dickensian orphans, street children and beggars are the twenty-first-century symbols of an industrializing India who is miserably failing her duty and responsibilities to her children.

~

I did not find an adequate literary examination of the effects of divorce on children, perhaps as it is a relatively modern phenomenon in an India seething with a variety other debates and subjects to explore. Traditional Hindu thought divides human life into four stages: childhood, student life, householding, finally followed by retirement into the ascetic life. However, even though childhood constitutes one-fourth of a life, Hindu legend and lore have very few accounts of children. Baby Krishna's stories are told to showcase his miraculous powers, while the tales of the Kaurava and Pandava children prepare for the politics that led to the Mahabharata war. Nevertheless, Sudhir Kakkar, Indian psychoanalyst, says that unlike in the West, Indian (not just Hindu) children are encouraged to inhabit a mythical, magical world for a long time.[2]

The inner turmoil of children would be better understood and empathized with by us if we recalled our own childhood memories about the things we imagined we would do when we took charge of our life as a

---

1. Cottrell, *Lost Worlds*

2. Sudhir Kakar, *The Inner World: A Psychoanalytic Study of Childhood and Society in India*, p. 105

'grown up'. The disrespect to children caused by not hearing them or not acknowledging their legal persona with rights equal to those of adults was recognized by the Child Rights Convention, Article 12 of which mandates that the wishes of children be given due weight in all decisions concerning them.[3] However, notwithstanding all conventions directing the evolution of law towards greater sensitivity in considering a child's welfare as the most important point in all situations/decisions, the fact is that children's rights are treated as a mere shadow of adult rights.[4]

The rights of the child are premised on their need for a safe home while they cope with 'growing pains'. A childhood remembered as reasonably happy is less about specific events than a sense of safety in ordinary playtime, and familiar routines, with trusted people. That many adult problems are rooted in difficult childhoods is not just pop psychology any longer. A sense of powerlessness is traumatic at any age, but all children at some stage feel that sense more than they deserve to. In the aftermath of divorce, children rebel violently against being misunderstood or ignored. Several studies reveal that children of divorce almost always remember their childhood as a period of loss.[5] They suffer a sense of betrayal mixed with a vague feeling of guilt. Since it is the privilege of children to be self-absorbed, it is not surprising that they may feel responsible for the bad things that happen to them or to people around them. You will understand this if you remember your own bargains with your inner God (or whatever other forces seemed to rule your childhood), promising to give up one thing for something else, or fearing being too happy to avoid the shock of a 'bad' event.

Children in the Divorce Court

From the lead up to and during a divorce, the parents are asked to 'think about the children'. One way to do that is to 'stay together for the sake of the children'—but that is possible only up to a point. Another is for the parents to talk to the children directly, instead of grabbing them while shouting at each other. But that too is easier said than done. There is no

---

3. See Article 12, Convention on the Rights of the Child, available at http://www.ohchr.org/en/professionalinterest/pages/crc.aspx

4. Ashis Nandy, 'Reconstructing Childhood: A critique of the ideology of adulthood' in *Bonfire of Creeds*, p. 423

5. Wallerstein et al, *The Unexpected Legacy of Divorce*, p. 19; See also: Lee & Bax. *Children's Reactions to Parental Separation and Divorce* pp. 217-218.

correct way to communicate something this earth-shattering. There are always consequences. Parents need the grit and patience to teach the child how to live on the portion of ground that s/he is left standing on. It's a tall order, especially in the midst of the grief, rage and other heightened emotions engendered by the divorce. Counsellors can help with this, but the courts often have to step in, in their jurisdiction as *parens patriae*: literally, acting as parent, the court rules on the welfare of the child.

The first question is when does this jurisdiction apply? There has been some argument that the *parens patria* jurisdiction is limited to only to matters involving family courts and custody battles, but I take heart in Justice Sen's observation in ABC vs. State:[6]

> 'We are mindful of the fact that we are presently not confronted with a custody conflict and, therefore, there is no reason whatsoever to even contemplate the competence or otherwise of the Appellant as custodian of the interests and welfare of her child. However, we would be loathe to lose perspective of our *parens patriae* obligations.'[7]

I see this as a signal from the Supreme Court that every court has a *parens patriae* obligation that transcends artificial jurisdictions created for administrative purposes. Recently, however, the Delhi High Court disagreed with me when I suggested that the *parens patriae* jurisdiction was all-encompassing and should also be taken into account in a case of contempt.[8] That judgment, however, passed some supplementary orders to help the child till the ideal resolution was eventually realized.

~

After establishing that the *parens patriae* jurisdiction applies, the court is called to exercise it in a meaningful manner. Mindless repetition has reduced phrases about children and the law to clichés: 'the child is not a chattel/shuttlecock';[9] 'The child cannot be treated as a pawn in the game of litigation';[10] and 'the welfare of the children is the primary consideration/ paramount'.[11]

---

6. ABC vs. State (NCT of Delhi), AIR 2015 SC 2569

7. AIR 2015 SC 2569

8. DKC v. KC, 227 (2016) DLT 1

9. Roxann Sharma vs. Arun Sharma, AIR 2015 SC 2232

10. Om Parkash v. Pushpa, 1975 R L R 29; Hadi Amaan V.R. vs. Union of India and Ors., 2015 (3) KHC 451

11. 2013(135) DRJ 537

The true meaning of 'welfare' leads us to see it as an overarching principle that takes the child above selfish parents and noisy legalese to a place where children are not just heard, but listened to.

The courts are supposed to do what is best for the child beyond any limitations of personal law.[12] The skill of the judge lies in the process of ascertaining what would be the welfare of the child, while knowing that there is hardly ever a completely happy resolution. The commonly used phrase, 'the best interests of the child' could more realistically be replaced by 'the least worst option' as more apposite to a divorce situation.[13] By and large, judges want to do the right thing by children and to give full effective meaning to the welfare principle. There are cases of judicial impatience with intractable parents, but by and large, courts do recognize children as stakeholders[14] in the family.

However, an adversarial legal process tends to expose and even reinforce the vulnerability of children, because parents do not always obtain, or are not willing to listen to, careful advice from lawyers about the needs and welfare of the children over and above their own concerns. That children's welfare is primary has been the legal position since the 1800s, but a sluggish legal system betrays them. There are no protocols on separate case management for children and custody battles are fierce because the custody court is yet another arena for the parents to fight, rather than deal with their children.

Custody Battles

The word 'custody' in the statute is unfortunate because the traditional meaning implies exclusive ownership of the child by one parent. A better word suited to the times would be 'co-parenting', which can have any number of permutations. Parents want 'custody' without fully understanding what it encompasses. Physical custody is different from legal custody. The former includes the basics of caregiving, while the latter includes the right to participate in all matters pertaining to the child in the capacity of a guardian.[15]

---

12. Saif-ul Ismal Habeeb Ali vs. Asma Begum, 2014(1)ALD328; Shama Beg vs. Khawaja Mohiuddin Ahmed, (1972) ILR 2 Delhi 73,

13. Goldstein et al, *Beyond the Best Interests of the Child*, p.53

14. Nandy, 'Reconstructing Childhood: A Critique Of The Ideology Of Adulthood', in *Bonfire of Creeds*; Lloyd de Mause, *History of Childhood*

15. Rayden, *Law and Practice in Divorce and Family Matters in All Courts*, p. 2719

The parent with physical custody is also called the primary caregiver and, given a typical family structure evolved over many centuries, it is usually the mother. Modern fathers and working mothers suffer the deeply ingrained cultural stereotypes that influence judgment by others of what parenting is and who should do it. Since social structures evolve around customary norms, even proactive fathers seem to leave primary caregiving to the mother. The exceptions are too few to be noteworthy (though I have had the privilege of seeing some) and so the 'usual' stereotypes are reinforced and change in perception is very difficult.

A story about stereotypes: My son wanted me to watch his race at the school Sports Day. My case was listed as item one in the High Court, starting at 10:30 a.m. The Sports Day was to begin at 11.30. I thought I would finish my matter and then rush to school. The judge sat at 11.30. I missed my son's race and twenty years on, it still hurts to remember the look on his face when I arrived after the event. I noticed, however, that there was not one father at the Sports Day. When I asked the school principal about it, she said fathers were working and mothers were fine with having the event on weekdays. Ignoring my son's miserable embarrassment, I made many caustic comments about presumed stereotypes, but they obviously found their mark because the following year's Sports Day was on a Saturday—attended by many excited fathers running around in half-pants and sandals. As a divorce lawyer, I could not rid myself of the image of those happy parents ranged against each other in a custody battle. In that case, I thought their children may well prefer to have a single parent attending, as an alternative to both sulking on opposite sides of the field!

~

In custody battles, the problem lies in treating children as divisible assets. Warring parents want equal time with the children, right down to the last hour. As the marriage crumbles, each partner grabs what they see as exclusively theirs. The men genuinely believe (and the system allows and perpetuates that belief) that the money is theirs alone and women say that the children are theirs alone (the system allows and perpetuates that belief as well). Many men resent the mother's influence over the children, just as she may resent his financial power. Men want more quality time with the children and women want a greater share in the finances. The war remains unequal, because she may lose the financial battle, even while he may still get his equal time with the children.

'Finance and children are not related' say judges and lawyers. I have also tentatively suggested so to my clients, but the reality is that they are related more often than not. Thus, the court must quickly rule on financial matters so that custody issues are resolved before the children suffer. Once adequate maintenance orders are passed, the financial strain is reduced and most custody issues fall into place naturally.

Mothers sometimes say. 'Let the matter be completely settled and then you can have access to the children'. This amounts to holding the children hostage. Courts need to confront this problem and deal with it adequately. The other side of the argument is that fathers, too, must discharge meaningful parental responsibility if they want to exercise the parenting privilege.

Finally, apart from all these considerations, the wishes of the children also need to be consulted about what they need, to be able to cope with their unhappiness with divided time between parents. On the other hand, it could be that they don't want to meet one parent at all. If that is the case, the court needs to consider why not. Is it possible that the child has been tutored or brain-washed to dislike one parent? Of course, it is always possible that there are legitimate reasons for children to distrust one parent. To assess tutoring, a good line of questioning for a child refusing to meet one parent is: when did you last love that parent? When were you last together as a family? Who do you talk a lot to now? Who did you used to talk to earlier? and so on. We will return to tutoring later in this chapter.

Sometimes there is a tussle about the amount and quality of time spent with the respective parents. Many fathers want time-share arrangements where the week is divided through the middle, or the child lives alternate months with either parent. I have a deep discomfort with this and always speak against it. In such a scenario, where is home? Where are their computers, books and other personal things, and how much time do they spend there? If living out of a suitcase is unsettling for an adult, how can we expect children to be happy with the arrangement? The Supreme Court has disapproved of such 'split orders' that reduce the child to a 'shuttlecock'.[16]

A strict, technical, 'by the book' and minimalistic approach cannot work here. I thought I was being very imaginative twenty years ago, when I

16. K.S.M. Karthikeya v. G. Renukadevi, SLP No. 4855/2014; See also Dipper v. Dipper, [1980] 2 All E.R. 722: disapproval of split orders; See also J Venkatesan, 'Supreme Court: Child cannot be tossed like shuttlecock' in *The Hindu*, 19 July 2014.

petitioned a court on behalf of the father not for custody but that it develop a suitable 'parenting plan' to achieve the goal of 'shared parenting'. The judge objected to my petition saying that I could not maintain my case as 'shared parenting' was not envisaged in the statute book.[17]

As a lawyer, one has to choose words with care in the Supreme Court and I lost ground for saying carelessly that the 'definition of custody has changed over the decades.' Rather than finding out what I meant, one of the judges laughed and said if what I said is taken to be correct, it amounted to saying that the meaning of the Indian Penal Code as drafted by the great Macaulay would also have changed. I wanted to retort many things: that the problem of S.377 IPC should change, or that Macaulay's English is fast dying and so meanings, unfortunately, are bound to change and not always in a positive meaningful manner. I also felt like saying that I would worry less about Macaulay's Indian Penal Code changing than about changes in our Constitution. Instead, I smiled ingratiatingly and let it go. The exchange however has stayed with me because of the judge's worrying refusal to understand that new meanings could be attached to old words. This is the Supreme Court in 2015,[18] the same year in which it said that 'the law is dynamic and is expected to diligently keep pace with time and the legal conundrums and enigmas it presents'.[19]

You would think that by now we should be inching towards a less technical view on the matter, but the Bombay High Court has recently dismissed a father's plea for access to his child on the ground that to maintain a petition under the statute, he should have asked for custody and not mere access.[20] On appeal, the Supreme Court reinforced this technical and inflexible approach by giving the father leave to file again in the family court asking for custody.[21]

All that is really required is that interpretation of the word 'custody' further the idea of welfare of the children; that allows for a design for shared parenting. Many an anxious mother dreads the loaded meaning of a father's 'custody' petition, which traditionally excludes her from the life of her children: she frantically reattaches the umbilical cord, which, in turn, drives the father to complain of her clinging to the children.

---

17. See Guardians and Wards Act 1890

18. *Ibid*

19. ABC vs. State (NCT of Delhi), AIR 2015 SC 2569

20. W.P. (C) No. 9834 of 2014

21. MANU/SCOR/10268/2015

Over the years of watching this tug of war I have often thought of Brecht's *Caucasian Chalk Circle*, in which the judge Azdak orders that a chalk circle be drawn and the biological mother and the caregiver pull at the contested child within it. The caregiver lets go. The judge orders a second round and again, the caregiver lets go. He awards the child to the caregiver. The biological mother wanted the child only to establish her right to the throne. The modern legal system tugs at our children in the same way that Azdak ordered, but there is no efficient method to reduce the tugging and no Azdak to reward the parent who is brave enough to let the child go.

One gallant father did do so, but only after filing an affidavit that expressed his grief and frustration at a well-meaning but ineffective legal system. The affidavit detailed his suffering over numerous procedural hearings that the child had to attend and spend miserably looking away from the father. I do not want the child to suffer, the father said, but my story needs to be recorded for the child to know the truth someday.

The biblical equivalent of Azdak is Solomon: he ruled that the son under contention must be split in two, each woman receiving half of the child. Solomon found the true mother to be the one who cried out, 'Oh Lord, give the baby to her, just don't kill him!' The other woman, in her bitter jealousy, exclaimed, 'It shall be neither mine nor yours—divide it!' A judge ridiculed my citing these stories as an example of caring, by saying custody tussles were between two parents with equal rights. The fallacy is apparent here: the overriding principle should not be about equal rights but about the welfare of the child. True, parents do have equal rights to the joy of parenting but the problem of managing their competing rights is better understood with examples of such apocryphal tales that establish that caring is inclined to protect rather than possess.

The welfare of the child is central: welfare includes the right to know both parents. A child may be hostile to one parent and his or her wishes are important, but does the child always know its own welfare? After all, there may be reasonable cause for the hostility, but it may also be due to blatant shameless tutoring. The judge cannot make her job easier by simply asking one parent to let go. And though the welfare of the child is paramount, the parents' rights cannot be eliminated either—courts are now required to carefully balance the welfare of the child with the rights of the parent. We will discuss this again and again because there is no clean and tidy resolution. Seemingly inconsistent rulings can be harmonized only when the welfare principle is at the centre of each case. Thus, court orders may seem to vary, but the welfare principle remains consistent on the whole, save for in a few cases of international abduction, where the court seems to have jettisoned it (we will discuss these later in the chapter).

A child's viewpoint

Fortunately we have travelled the distance for these apocryphal tales to have a new dimension: the judge is supposed to ascertain the child's view, something not done by Solomon or Azdak.

To elicit a child's view is a precise and delicate exercise that requires techniques many courts tend to bypass. The first technique is interviewing not just the litigating parents, but the children as well. Yet, for some reason, many judges seem to shy away from it.

This is problematic. Interviewing the child is important, not because the child necessarily knows best, but to give context to her situation. The judge may have been right in his opinion on the hazy or otherwise views of children, but that does not absolve the court from the painful complexity of interviewing the child. The human connection is critical for a true assessment of the situation.

A child under pressure in a divorce court will show various symptoms of trauma. Raging against the helplessness of his situation, one child I knew was monstrously difficult, while another was so broken that he would only speak in whispers as if to silence the tumult around him. To hold that children need not be interviewed because judges are not experts with children would amount to saying that because the judge is not a psychologist he will not note the demeanour of a witness.

Of course, this cannot mean mindless agreement with the child either. Courts have also cautioned against too much interviewing and it may not even be in the best interest of the child to bestow upon her a power she is not equipped to deal with or to burden him with the difficulty of choosing between beloved parents. But all things considered, there is a general consensus by specialists and international conventions relating to children that their view must be given due import while dealing with them.[22] Section 17 (3) of the Guardians and Wards Act, 1890 acknowledges that the child is a person in her own right. This statute from over a hundred years ago envisages interviewing children—why should there be a doubt about the wisdom of that course now?[23]

---

22. See Child Rights Convention, Article 12

23. Sec. 17 (3) of the GAWA states that 'If a minor child is old enough to form an intelligent preference, the court *may* consider that preference.' [emphasis added]

The next question that comes up is the age at which a child can be said to be able to form an intelligent preference. That would be for the judge to decide; the act provides that due weightage to the child's opinion be given in proportion to the child's ability to form an intelligent preference. Thus, a fourteen-year-old may be more articulate than a six-year-old, but the latter may just as well be able to form an intelligent preference. This can be done only when the judge meets the child. The law is also that a child up to five years old is *ordinarily* to be with the mother.[24] Here, please know that this does not mean that the mother loses custody after child turns five: it just means that the issue of custody can be reviewed at that age and there would have to be very good reasons for a court to dislodge a child from the mother who has had custody for those five years.

A judge reminded me that once, while arguing for a father whose son was reluctant to meet him, I had told the court that a degree of firmness with children was necessary. Your positions are contradictory, the judge said, equating that incident with my insistence on interviewing children to find out their wishes about the divorce situation. I disagreed, saying that my position is that some interview is needed for a broad assessment on how the child is faring and how robustly she will handle a change in circumstances. It all depends on the facts and circumstances of each case. More than anywhere else, the idiosyncrasies of each member of the dramatis personae become important in custody matters. Even so, creating transparent and certain protocols for the management of cases will help a judge conclude the matter quickly and as much in the welfare of the child as possible. That is the least worst option.

~

The court will also need to record the conduct and demeanour of the parents, allowing for the fact that they may feel as powerless as their children. In a divorce court, someone else is in charge and thinks s/he knows better. Parents often have strong reactions to this unexpected powerlessness, and it often means a difficult time for the lawyer who has to manage the client and the court. We try to advise our clients from the beginning that litigation is a lot about perceptions and a careful demeanour earns goodwill of the court, and even the other side. But clients need to understand that the opposing party's conduct, which they may view as unconscionable, is not always deserving of the punishment that they would like to see imposed.

---

24. See p. 369: Section 6(a) of the Hindu Minority and Guardianship Act, 1956

A judge often has to reach within herself for empathy for the parents. I imagine this is not an easy exercise, because one cannot like every person and has to learn to transcend irrational dislikes (and intuitive likes) that could lead to prejudice. The court needs to avoid jumping to conclusions, even if they sometimes turn out to be true—there are machinating women who misuse the law and tutor children, just as there are fathers who fight for custody only to avoid child support payments or to intimidate the mother into giving up claims of maintenance and alimony in order to protect her child from stress of litigation.

Then there are clashing parenting styles that reverberate in a divorce court and affect the child. That is exactly what happened in a matter we settled recently.

Case study

Let's call the child Taploo. We were for the mother. The father was a macho movie cowboy type, who wanted the son to go a-huntin' an' fishin' an' shootin' with him. Taploo, on the other hand, was a quiet studious type who only wanted to be studyin'. He sang songs and wrote poetry, which the father thought was horrible for a little boy to do—how would he become a man? The father lost several opportunities to build a relationship with his son, because he would vilify the mother and berate Taploo as a mama's boy. Taploo had become utterly hostile to his father and protective of his mother, whom he had seen abused by his father. He absolutely refused to spend more than a few hours with his father. We insisted on those hours because I wanted the court to see that we were not withholding access unreasonably.

The divorce became messier after the mother put forward her financial claims, because the father decided to increase the pressure by claiming greater visitation rights, despite Taploo's reluctance to meet him. As the intensity of the litigation grew, Taploo was scared at first; then, after meeting too many judges, he became rebellious and finally refused to go to court. He became unruly in school and difficult for his mother, because he saw her as incapable of protecting him.

The father then made an offer in court that exposed his lack of true concern for his son: if his wife accepts less than her due for her financial claim, he said, I will not see my child. The judge could have dismissed the father's custody/visitation petition on that ground alone and then proceeded to adjudicate the wife's maintenance claim in accordance with her legal entitlement, but the court did not do that. Eventually, the mother accepted less money only to protect Taploo from the stress of the ongoing litigation.

The financial factor

This brings us to the next issue that a child has to confront: money. The court may say that finance is not a factor in custody matters,[25] but financial considerations may influence the children to choose one parent over the other. The courts therefore need to ensure that the amounts awarded as child support and maintenance to the mothers do not allow for the financial scales to be tilted unevenly against them. This is a mother's nightmare.

A client saw me looking at her children playing in my office and said, 'They are cute now. I hate to think I will lose them to a Maserati car.'

'Don't trivialize your upbringing or their love for you,' I said. But I understood exactly what she meant, having seen a number of painful choices made in court. Recently, a child left my client because she refused to buy him a pair of Nike shoes. Now that he is with his father, he has not found the courage to come back. On the other hand, maybe he does not want to come back. Maybe he actually wanted to be with his father and grabbed at a trivial quarrel about shoes for the courage to leave his mother.

I once saw a woman wandering outside court, disheveled and distraught, tearfully telling anyone who would listen that her son had chosen his father over her. 'He has been with me thirteen years and now he wants to go', she ached. Just then, I saw the father in a smart suit, walking with his son, who looked embarrassed but did not glance at his mother as he passed by. I wondered whether the boy could not bear to look back at his mother because he hated leaving her. I wondered whether the father had lured his son away from the mother with money. But it's equally possible that the son couldn't look at her because she may have been abusive or mean. The father's parenting style may have been more relaxed. Not better, but different.

Choosing one parent over the other is necessarily a painful process, but the equivocations and uncertainties can be reduced if both parents have the power to provide more or less equally for the child, and if the

25. Amit Beri v. Sheetal Beri, AIR 2006 All 267; Wazid Ali v. Rehana Anjum, AIR 2005 MP 141; Surabhai Ravi Kumar vs. State of Gujarat, AIR 2005 Guj 149; Gaurav Nagpal v. Sumedha Nagpal, AIR 2009 SC 557

matter of financial division is settled, the angst of the custody matter will also settle.

The law requires that a woman needs to be provided with adequate home and household expenses: but adequate never covers the extras, such as the father's ability to afford luxurious holidays and gifts. The mother's financial weakness could influence children to view her as weak and disempowered and hence, the lesser parent. Some children, like Taploo become protective of the mother as the weaker parent, but many children may feel moments of embarrassment or resentment towards her.

A professional photographer estranged from her very rich husband lived independently with her two children. The maintenance order had not come through and they were living with unaccustomed frugality. Though steadfast and loyal to their mother, they could not hide a twinge of embarrassment when they accompanied her to buy the first car she could afford—a non-air-conditioned Maruti 800. This is a stop-gap they told the salesman. Our father is going to give us his Pajero. It never happened.

Another father's idea of spending time with his little girl was to take her to a car show-room to buy an SUV for his six dogs. She had come to visit him in a three-wheeler because her mother could not afford a car. She has grown up sane, sober, balanced and charming, and has needed no tutoring to dislike her father. But that is not healthy for her either.

On the other hand, there is a little girl I know who has chosen her father just because she is happier with him. She complained that her mother never smiled, and did not really love her because she did not talk and listen to her, and gave her indifferent food. This little girl chose the richness of taste and texture of life with her father. I understood that too.

The child's choice

Child rearing is a mountainous task for any of us. Even a grudging acknowledgment from our children that, though we could have done better, we still did our best, would be a distinguished accolade marking us as competent parents. But how does even the most experienced parent—or the most erudite scholar of child welfare—objectively decide what's best without making moral or value judgments? This question stresses a judge applying any law but it is particularly so in the matter of children.

In 1893, the English court of appeal[26] in the case of McGrath held that welfare is not just about money and physical comfort, but also the moral and religious welfare of the child. It also held that the bond of

---

26. In Re McGrath, [1893] 1 Ch. 143

affection cannot be disregarded. Two decades later, in Mrs Annie Besant vs. G. Narayaniah[27], the Madras High Court used the McGrath ruling to decide a battle for the custody of two brothers, Krishna and Nitya.

Mrs Annie Besant, president of the Theosophical Society, saw in the boys the potential to be vehicles for a great spirit. She approached their father, who initially consented to them being taken to England, but later changed his mind and sought their return. The father also alleged that the boys had been exposed to 'unnatural conduct' by one encumbered with the unfortunate name of Mr Leadbeater, a senior office-bearer in the Theosophical Society.

The Madras High Court bench, comprising two English judges, ruled in favour of the father. The court acknowledged that the father had been induced to consent to send the boys with Annie Besant by a promise of an education at Oxford University. Yet, it found that the welfare of any child lay without doubt with its parents, and to hold otherwise should be only in extreme cases.

> 'A man may be in narrow circumstances, he may be negligent, injudicious and faulty as the father of minors; he may be a person from whom the discreet, the intelligent and the well disposed, exercising a private judgment, would wish his children to be, for their sakes and his own, removed; he may be all this without rendering himself liable to judicial interference, and in the main it is for obvious reasons well that it should be so. Before this jurisdiction can be called into action between them, the Court must be satisfied, not only that it has the means of acting safely and efficiently, but also that the father has so conducted himself, or has shown himself to be a person of such a description, or is placed in such a position, as to render it, not merely better for the children, but essential to their safety or to their welfare, in some very serious and important respect, that his rights should be treated as lost or suspended—should be superseded or interfered with. If the word "essential" is too strong an expression, it is not much too strong.'

On the allegation of sexual abuse, the court found that the conduct may have been improper or unseemly but it was not 'unnatural' sex. On the issue of their spiritual future in the Theosophical Society, the judges said, 'A father may believe in the doctrine of reincarnation and may have given expression to that belief, but he may well be reluctant that the body of his son should be the medium.'

---

27. (1913)25MLJ661

The court thus ruled that Mrs Besant must return both boys to their parents in Madras. She challenged the ruling in the Privy Council and the Madras High Court's judgment was overturned on the reasoning that the High Court in England alone had jurisdiction over the matter, since the children by then were living there.[28] The children were interviewed by court order and stated that they did not want to return to India without completing the promised Oxford education.

The older boy, Krishna, became the great philosopher J. Krishnamurthi. One can only wonder what his life would have been had he returned to his father following the Madras High Court judgment. His younger brother, Nitya, died on board ship while the brothers were returning to India after completing their education. His death affected Krishnamurthi deeply. The education abroad and his travels left Krishnamurthy with no relationship or familiarity with his family. He eventually rejected the Theosophical Society as well.

To be plucked from family and thrown into an entirely alien environment is not the best thing to do to a child. Yes, it produced an important thinker, but his photographs show me a beautiful face behind which I think I see sadness. Did the experience scar him? Speaking for myself I agree with the sentiment of the Madras High Court judgment, but once the Privy Council interviewed the children and found that they wanted to finish their studies, to let them remain in England was undoubtedly the correct way forward, because it was a consultative process. Yet as recently as a few months ago, a mother refused to deal with her child's preference for her father and a particular lifestyle, saying she was too young to know about these things. She had removed her daughter from her home in another country and brought her to India, ostensibly for a holiday, and then told her that they could not return because the mother was choosing not to return. The child raged against the unfairness of not being consulted about such a fundamentally life-changing decision. The mother thought it was but natural that her daughter be with her and expected the unquestioning obedience that earlier generations gave to their parents. In a contrasting case, the mother in question returned to the foreign country and the unsettled marriage because the child could not settle in India. I was struck by the parallels between this and the story of the Urdu poet, Nida Fazli. In 1947, when he was nine years old, he chose

28. Annie Besant v. G. Narayaniah and J. Krishna Murti and J. Nityanananda, AIR 1914 PC 41

to stay in Delhi while his parents migrated to Pakistan. Fazli was able to choose and his choice was respected—therein lay the root of his great independence that created a poet. As was the case with Krishnamurthy and Nitya: they chose to finish their foreign education.

~

The approach to welfare is a vexed question. Indian courts still quote the Krishnamurthy judgment but 'moral and religious' welfare is a disturbingly wide and amorphous concept. The times should be moving to secular conceptions of welfare, that ask about affection, freedom, respect, education, health, a good diet, etc. but the moral position is difficult to get away from.

Here is an example, sadly not uncommon, of a moralistic tone based on gender stereotypes in custody matters: In about 1990, a custody matter was pending before a Division Bench comprising a lady and gentleman judge. The gentleman judge (senior) disappointingly predictable, expected 'milady' to meet us to explore resolutions. My forty-year-old client, mother of two teenage girls, came out of the judge's chambers shaking with anger. She had just been given a lecture by the judge on raising children, on the responsibility of women, on the importance of sacrifice for the children, on how she should not have had children if she was going to be so career-oriented. The judge dismissed us after giving us a smug account of the success stories of her progeny. I was upset as well. We had been reduced to two errant schoolgirls upbraided by a headmistress. Fortunately, the sheer volume of matrimonial litigation nowadays has constrained judges to be less simplistic while dealing with these matters.

Parental Alienation

The turning point in custody battles is persuading parents to agree to fair co-parenting plans. Both have strongly ingrained resistances to the idea of cooperating with a person who they see as an adversary. A woman might feel, 'Why should he be allowed to treat me badly and have equal time with the children?' So, she treats the children as her security and her revenge, by refusing to share the parenting experience. On the other side, alpha-male conditioning makes men think of 'losing' litigation to a wife as emasculating. It is this competitive instinct that seems to prompt many to seek that siblings be split up between the parents.

No one ever admits to misusing parental power to influence children, though we all know it happens, even unwittingly. Each parent tries to co-opt the child to their view of the matter. Delays in establishing meaningful co-parenting arrangements during the divorce process result in the children feeling distant from the other parent, which increases the probability of tutoring, brainwashing, or programming against the other parent. Tutoring can be reversed with conversation and time, while brainwashing, as more intensive, is difficult to neutralize and once the child is programmed against the other parent, the damage could be irreversible.[29]

Psychologists and therapists have coined many words and phrases to describe the problem but the most common phrase that now encapsulates a child tutored, brainwashed or programmed is 'Parental Alienation Syndrome.' This could manifest through various symptoms, such as hostility or 'mirroring'—when children mirror the custodial parent for approval to ensure their own safety. The reading list at the end of this chapter is for those who are interested in a more detailed study.

A case of tutoring

H came from a loving, close-knit family. They had several flourishing businesses. H and W had an arranged marriage. A son, S was born and W returned to her parental home with him when he was about seven years old. She then refused to let H or his parents meet the son. A year later, they came to see me. I told them it was difficult to neutralize the ancient 'mother and child' socialization. Fathers rarely get custody unless the mother is found unfit in some extreme form. I also warned them that children were often victims of alienation programs against the other parent by the custodial parent. Even so, H and his family were confident that their child would retain his affection for them. I thought it was a lot to expect from a seven year old, but they instructed me to file for custody.

The judge ordered that S be produced in court to meet the father. On the date of hearing, my cynical self was prepared for the frustration of a no-show or an indifferent or hostile child if he did show up. I was not prepared for the delight of watching S run to his father, shouting 'Papa!' He hugged his grandparents and settled himself on his father's lap. The judge noted this in her file. The Court allowed H to take S out for the day. The meeting went well and we moved another application for a regular visitation pattern.

---

29. See Clawar and Rivlin, *Children Held Hostage: Dealing with programmed and brainwashed children*, pp. 7-9 for details about these distinctions.

By the time this came to court, there was a new judge who asked to meet S again. S was a different person this time round: he would not look at his father and refused to let go of his mother. After that, we had to fight hard for every access order. During arguments about child support and alimony, their lawyer would tell the court how rich my clients were. (We were willing to pay child and spouse support, but my client did not agree to the amount W wanted.) Any chance of a quick settlement was stymied by constant references to my clients' alleged wealth and lifestyle, which the opposing lawyers used to paint them as a dissolute family with lots of money that they were unfairly denying to the mother of their child.

The matter went back and forth. Finally, we got an order allowing for the child to be with us over a weekend. After spending time with his father, the child refused to return to the mother. Then when he was persuaded to go to the mother, he refused to come to the father. Basically, the little boy was confused about what he wanted: he loved both parents and was exhausted with the travel. In his mother's house, he was with loving grandparents and a gentle mother who let him alone. The activity in his father's house on the other hand, was more interesting.

During a visit with S by the mother at my office she gathered him in her arms in a bear hug and ran out of the office, followed by two bodyguards. I never thought I would do a movie-type chase. All of us stampeded down to her 'getaway' car. My court clerk heroically stood in front of the SUV while someone else pulled out the ignition key. The child was screaming. The mother dialed 100. The police arrived. My entire neighbourhood gathered and I saw suspicion in their eyes about the true nature of my work. Eventually, the child clung to his father and the mother had to let him go.

The next day in court, I was worried that the child would be too frightened to take a firm decision on what he really wanted. He might decide to go with his mother because, in any case, the travel was getting a bit much, and of course he loved his mother and did not like what had happened the day before. My client was beginning to worry because the child had begun resenting his regimen of discipline.

A golden Labrador called Shahji used to attend office with me. S loved him and just that day chose to ask his father for a puppy. Father and son got a puppy the same day. (This could be called bribery but giving children puppies is good for all concerned, I believe.) In court he hugged and kissed his mother and said he would spend the day with her, but wanted to return to his father's house to feed the puppy. The mother did have the choice of offering to take the puppy with the child for the weekend, but she did not.

The father discovered over the course of several visits that this child's ability at school was less than others of his age. Assessments revealed dyslexia and ADHD. The nearest remedial school for children with such special needs was in Delhi; there were none where the mother lived. I asked my client's mother whether she could bring up the child. She said she was happy to but did not want to separate her grandson from his mother.

Here is a rare case of true commitment to the welfare of the child in a custody battle. There would be no custody battles if that were always the case. The matter was settled out of court. The child lives with his father and spends vacations with his mother. The puppy is a big happy dog now.

Examples of brainwashing and programming

H and W were an amicably separated couple, with a son. Everything changed the day H suspected that W might be having an affair. Normally, she would collect the child from school. One day, he arrived half-an-hour earlier and whisked the child away from Delhi. For about two months, W was frozen in shock and took no legal action. She then felt strong enough to file a habeas corpus petition seeking to restore the child to her care. Habeas corpus petitions seek the freedom of the person illegally detained—it literally means 'produce the body'. The judges were reluctant to issue the writ. Can the father's custody of his own child be termed illegal[30] they asked? The answer is not self-evident,[31] but such petitions can be entertained where the comfortable care routines established with the primary care-giving parent are forcibly interrupted. The courts have been more inclined to entertain such petitions in cases of international abduction rather than domestic.

The son, C, was brought to court. He was the cutest image of his mother. Holding his father's hand in the corridor of the courthouse, he loudly said he did not want to meet his mother. The father triumphantly

---

30. Rama Prabha vs. the Inspector of Police and Ors. MANU/TN/3192/2011—'we are of the considered view that the child Vajra is not under the illegal custody of the father, who is a legal guardian. Further the child is also willing to go with her father and study at Saudi Arabia. Under the circumstances, we are of the considered view that there is no merit in this Habeas Corpus Petition and accordingly the same is dismissed.'

31. Habeas Corpus petitions not allowed in Sarita Sharma v. Sushil Sharma, (2000) 3 SCC 14

looked at me and said, 'He is saying he does not want to meet his mother.' C stubbornly refused to make eye contact with his mother. Eventually, with seeming reluctance, he sat on his mother's lap in the far corner of the visiting room. The mother read him a story and handed him his favourite stuffed toy that he had left behind.

H, with his mother and their lawyers, waited at the door of the visiting room, blue with holding their breaths. Slowly, some ice was broken and the visitation became meaningful. W was relieved, having held her baby in her lap and kissed him. It seemed she had managed to break through. We reported a satisfactory meeting to the judge and he adjourned the matter for another meeting.

At the next meeting, the child rushed at his mother, calling her a liar because she had told the judge that the previous meeting was good. Obviously, the brainwashing at home was intense and he was being programmed against his mother. His daddy and dadi had done this by chastising him for liking being with his mother. C turned his back to W and howled and screamed till everyone was scared he would be sick.

I went into the courtroom and told the judge about C calling his mother a liar. 'He is being affected seriously by their agenda of alienating him from the mother,' I said. The judge understood. He sent for the other side and spoke to them, saying that he noticed the blatant abuse of process and programming of the child.

The judge asked to meet C again: he came into the chambers and wept uncontrollably. I knew the little boy's tears came from bitter helpless rage rather than any complaint against the mother. He stopped crying when he was exhausted. The judges asked us to leave while they talked to the child alone. When we returned, the senior judge looked sternly at me and said that the child said his mother used to beat him.

'I do not think so,' I said, 'but I will ask.'

'Of course not,' said the mother. Even the judge did not really believe the allegation, I could see, but the eternal vague fear of 'What if?' was on his mind. He was too robust to cave in and came up with a brilliantly original and innovative solution that should be used more often.

'All right,' he told the other side. 'What if W is accompanied by her parents and niece during the overnight visitation?'

Baby C was sharp: he quickly said, 'My grandmother beats me too.'

'What about the grandfather?' countered the judge.

There was a silence. C had realized that he had carried the beating story too far. He then came up with the only statement that was clearly spontaneous: 'Nana shouts at papa.'

The judge smiled and said, 'Oh we don't care that he shouts at papa. Your papa can look after himself. We will make sure that no one shouts at you. Would you like to sit in the courtroom in my chair and pass an order right now?' There was a faint smile on the child's tear-stained face.

I have great affection for the judge since that day. Orders were passed that the child would be left at W's residence by H and her parents and niece would be present throughout.

W was delighted. She cleaned and decorated her house. There were welcome streamers and balloons. The dining table was laden with food cooked by W for her child. During an earlier court visitation, despite the trauma and tears, I had seen C eating with evident enjoyment the idlis his mother had cooked for him. How can a mother not get through to her child when she feeds him, I thought. But the tribulation was yet to begin.

At 8 p.m., W called to tell me the child had not eaten anything. I could not believe that six years of sole caregiving by a loving mother had been wiped out. But C refused to eat. The night passed. W washed and bathed her baby and they slept together but C did not eat the next morning either. W took C to a pediatrician. The doctor said she needed to meet the father as well. W then had to call the father, who arrived raging and indignant. He whisked the child away to a mental hospital to record C's statement. W only wanted that the father give the child something to eat before taking him to the hospital. To my knowledge, he was fed some biscuits.

W had won the case in court, but lost her child. H had lost the case in court, and though seemingly won the child, had really lost him as well. There is bound to be damage when a child is so hostile to his mother, whether by programming or otherwise: he has a traumatic time ahead while he resolves the conundrum of having rejected his mother, because his father told him to. The problem is that there is no clear mechanism to handle and reverse such damage.

My client continued to have unrealistic dreams about how she would soon get custody. I tried to say there was only so much a judge or I could do. Somewhere, the tone and tenor of all concerned may turn against the lawyer. Sadly, this type of exchange is common between family lawyers and their clients. We become the punching bag because we are seen as miracle people who refuse to use their wand—why are you not crying and raging with us, they want to know. This too is part of my brief and I have had to learn the humility to listen to such accusations without too much reaction.

Custody: The Process

The Supreme Court has ruled that a 'tutoring' parent is clearly not acting in the welfare of the child[32] and the estranged parent is thus given leave to file in the family court for change of custody. Though the sentiment behind the ruling cannot be faulted, the process of doing so is impractical. Here is a typical scenario, so that readers have a more realistic idea of the patience and painstaking effort involved in a custody battle.

A petition asking for custody of the child is prepared. Notice is issued and the other side is given response time. The documents and filings are complete for the trial to begin. But these basic procedures may have already taken more than a year.

Between the filing of the petition and the time it comes to trial, there are many applications moved under Section 12 of the Guardians and Wards Act[33] calling for interim arrangements pending the main case. Everything from vacations to school admissions to the mode of birthday celebrations are under Section 12. Most matters are settled before they reach trial because of sheer litigation exhaustion.[34]

The proceedings may require specialist reports and visitation arrangements to neutralize the tutoring of the child. Invariably, the reports are challenged and doctors cross-examined. The hearing dates are set for every other month, and whether there will be a hearing is uncertain till the day. After finally getting a date of hearing, the actual arguments may begin but perhaps are not completed for any number of reasons, the most frequent of which is an overburdened court. Considering the amount of over-work, it is amazing that something gets done at all—but it does.

A neglected aspect in custody battles is that the child's perspective of time is different from that of an adult. The run of time that an adult sees as finite might feel like forever for an unhappy child. Children, with their 'immediate and present' sense of time, are particularly anguished by protracted court proceedings. It hurts to see their spirit fading as they move into robotic survival mode to go through each painful day. It is difficult to explain to children separated from a beloved parent or a place by a custody order that is passed in their 'best interest', that they will 'soon' see them. But what is 'soon' to a child?

---

32. Ashish Ranjan vs. Anupama Tandon, (2010) 14 SCC 274

33. See p. 362: Section 12 of the Guardians and Wards Act: Power to make interlocutory order for production of minor and interim protection of person and property.

34. See other statutes dealing with children's issues in *Appendix*

'Tomorrow? Next week? Will we be together for Diwali? When will I see my dog? When can I come to my room? Where are my friends? I don't want to make new friends. Suppose, I can never go back?'

'I don't know, darling,' says the helpless parent and for the first time your child sees you without power and is scared about his/her own security without a protector.

Divorce battles take as blood money the basic parenting instinct to protect children from adult weaknesses. Many children end up ashamed of seeing their parents exposed in a divorce situation: over-anxious, over-sensitive, bullying, mean, obsessive, money-minded, miserly, manipulative, incorrect or dishonourable. Children end up learning lessons that are polar opposites to those taught in an intact home. They learn to seek approval by deception or by adopting a victim mentality. They learn to lie to exit from uncomfortable situations and avoid difficult questions.

On the other hand, when children tell the truth, they are frustrated by sceptical judges who, in turn, may only be trying to rule out the possibility of tutoring, while balancing what the children say they want with what the judge thinks is best for them.

~

One father's initial case was that W was immoral and, because of her affair, she could not be in charge of the child. I denied the charge of the affair but said that even if it were true it does not and cannot take away from W's competence as a mother.[35] The response of the lady judge was significant: 'Yes: but conduct is also to be a consideration eventually.'

True, the conduct of a parent is a necessary factor in deciding what is best for a child in custody applications, but only if she is a child abuser, alcoholic or drug addict, etc. It is interesting that a man's extramarital liaison is not viewed as hampering his fathering skills, yet the woman's chastity is important even to her mothering. Singleton L.J. said, 'I have yet to learn that the fact that a woman commits adultery prevents her in all circumstances from being a good mother'.[36]

The de-sexed mother is a well-known phenomenon and the subject of many studies. Sudhir Kakar calls it the Devdas Syndrome in the Indian context: men often want their wives to be like their mothers, and seek sexual satisfaction elsewhere. The schism is due to a failure in processing the idea of a mother as a sexual being.[37] If you want to argue that the child

---

35. Willoughby v. Willoughby 1951 Probate J 84, p. 192

36. *Ibid.*

37. Kakar, *Intimate Relations: Exploring Indian Sexuality*

is exposed to immorality through the idea of sex outside marriage, then the same standards should apply to both parents. While the husband's affair invites an indulgent nudge and wink as something that 'men do,' sexual expression by the wife makes her 'immoral.' Furthermore, how moral is black money spent on the child at a five-star hotel? Or lying under oath? Or being derisive of women? Or expressing caste, gender and religion-based biases?

Contempt and custody

Increasingly, parties are invoking the contempt jurisdiction of the High Court to decree when custody orders are not complied with. The legal defense against this is that the alleged contempt was neither willful nor deliberate.[38]

The Supreme Court, while ruling that 'tutoring' a child may amount to contempt of court, has also observed that no purpose will be served by sending the contemnor (in this case mother) to jail.[39] Brainwashing of the child by the custodial parent is a common allegation—often with reason—but all custodial parents have to deal with the presumption of brainwashing. The truth is that often, despite the parents' best efforts to persuade the children to meet the other parent, many children do not want to confront difficult, complex and intensely emotional issues, particularly when they have witnessed verbal and physical abuse.

~

To make Family Court orders more effective, it has become common, in divorces by mutual consent, to record undertakings by the parties that they will adhere to the terms of their agreement.

In one case[40], the second motion of divorce[41] was resisted because the wife was not comfortable with the custody arrangement. The Delhi High Court held her refusal to proceed with the divorce as contempt, because she had given an undertaking to sign the final divorce and had received some monetary advantage. The problematic aspect of this judgment is

38. David Jude v. Hannah Grace Jude, AIR 2003 SC 2925;

39. Ashish Ranjan vs. Anupama Tandon, (2010) 14 SCC 274; Thritie Hoshie Dolikuka v. Hoshiam Shavaksha Dolikuka, (1982) 2 SCC 577; Hadkinson vs. Hadkinson, [1952] 2 All ER 567;

40. Avneesh Sood vs. Tithi Sood, MANU/DE/2419/2012

41. The first motion of divorce by mutual consent is followed by a second motion after six months, which are treated as a cooling-off period.

that it dilutes the essence of the 'cooling-off' period between the first and the second motions of divorce as was noted by the Supreme Court in another case.[42] The Supreme Court had held that the parties have a right to change their minds.

In DKC vs. KC[43], the father acceded to the mother's abduction of their daughter from another country to India. They filed the first motion for divorce by mutual consent soon after he gave an undertaking that he would not take the child abroad on holiday till after the second motion of divorce. He violated this undertaking and admitted her in school abroad. The court found him guilty of contempt.

Through the proceedings, the judge met the child several times. He listened to her. He knew that she had expressed an unequivocal preference for the father. She was about seven years old and the judge found her to be intelligent beyond her years. Nevertheless, the court ordered that the child be returned to the mother 'forthwith'. The court did not want to be seen as rewarding child abduction, which is a serious offence.

Even so, the good judge tried hard to balance matters. The court gave liberty to the parties to approach the Family Court for variation of the court order. He also passed a supplementary order by oral application, by which he arranged for daily visitations by the father to the mother's house. He decreed that the child's cousin should spend two nights at the house to ensure that she settled in and the transition was not too brutal; the judge could see that it would be so. Regrettably, this supplementary order remains unreported as an important precedent for empathetic dealing with child-related matters within the rigour of the law.

What will the child of KC and DKC think of the judge and justice, only time will tell. But I do know that the judge while passing the supplementary order told the child that he had kept in his drawer some drawings that she made for him.

It was a painful decision, the judge admits, but then quotes a rare Supreme Court judgment (almost an aberration amongst these matters) that 'some collateral damage'[44] had to be accepted in dealing with the bigger picture of the Court not being seen as rewarding unconscionable behaviour. As it happens, the matter settled and the child was returned to her father on freshly negotiated terms. But children are never supposed to

42. Surestha Devi vs. Om Prakash, (1991) 2 SCC 25,

43. 227 (2016) DLT 1

44. Arathi Bandi vs. Bandi Jagadrakshaka Rao and Ors., AIR 2014 SC 918

be collateral damage in a country that wants to treat the welfare principle as central!

~

Not an easy job, judging, I agree. However, the DKC v. KC judgment is problematic because the court did not accept *parens patria* in a case of contempt. But even while calling the *parens patriae* argument a 'red herring' the judge, in fact, acted within it, while ordering the supplementary arrangement until the child could be heard by a Family Court for variation of the custody arrangement.

My concern about the contempt jurisdiction in family law is that, where children are an issue, no order can ever be final, as has been held by the Supreme Court in Rosy Jacob's case.[45] The court thus needs to look at welfare as part of its contempt jurisdiction because an integral part of justice is compassion. The court would better uphold the majesty of the law by demonstrating that it can work for those who cannot represent themselves.

Perhaps one way to reduce the burden of invoking the contempt jurisdiction for implementing custody arrangements would be to have greater participation of children in their visitation agreements. A corollary to the maxim that hard cases make bad law, is that the cases suffer because sometimes judges do what they should not do: be like lawyers. 'The greatest of the arts of advocacy is reasoning from a conclusion—which is reverse of what judges should do, tempting though it may be'.[46]

Guardianship

Ms Hariharan[47] wanted to open a bank account for her child, but the manager refused to allow it without the signature of the father who, he said, is the child's guardian. Githa Hariharan went to court to challenge the Hindu Minority and Guardianship Act[48] under which a mother is guardian 'after' the father.

The obvious meaning is that the mother is the guardian after the death

45. Jacob v. Jacob, AIR 1973 SC 2090

46. Sir Stephen Sedley, 'Declining the Brief' in *Ashes and Sparks*. Quoted in Lady Hale gives the Fiona Woolf Lecture for the Women Lawyer's Division of the Law Society. *Women in the Judiciary*, 27 June 2014

47. Githa Hariharan and Anr. vs. RBI, (1999) 2 SCC 228; See also Ch. 2: Decoding Gender, p. 27.

48. Hindu Adoption and Maintenance Act, 1956

of the father.[49] Instead of striking down the provision as gender-biased, the court made a half-hearted effort at reading 'after' as 'in the absence of'. The court thus ruled that the mother is the guardian of the child, even in the father's life, if he is absent for any reason, including neglect. The ruling is a tentative gesture to mothers, but really gives them no meaningful rights that make them equal guardians.[50]

The Hariharan judgment does not translate into practical relief for mothers with estranged husbands. The mother still has to move a petition to be appointed the guardian of the person and/or property of the child. If she wants to get a form signed by the child's father, he can refuse to cooperate. She is still not the guardian, because he is neither dead nor absent nor neglectful, but is only cussed and uncooperative.[51]

Custody and guardianship are different: a caregiver need not be a guardian, but needs the smooth exercise of guardianship rights to be able to do the job of caregiving. These factors dilute what the law is supposed to be: shared access for parents who are required to collaborate as best as they can to bring up their child. Increasingly, we have complex documentation to take care of the eventuality of a parent suddenly turning recalcitrant, getting into the details of how passports are to be kept or how signatures and cooperation in procedural matters such as school admissions cannot be unreasonably withheld.

On custody and caregiving, the Hindu Guardianship and Minority Act says that a child under five years is 'normally' to be in the care of the mother.[52] Under the Shariat, the father is the guardian and should have custody of the child after seven years. This frightens many people who are wrongly led to believe by busybodies or quasi-legal persons that they will get custody after the child has reached a certain age. The courts, quite rightly, are reluctant to dislodge children just because of their age.[53]

Cross-border conflicts

Cross-border litigation is common in commercial issues, and various remedies have evolved to protect the rights and interests of the litigating

---

49. *Ibid*; See also Ch. 2: Decoding Gender, p. 27.

50. See p. 369: Section 6 of the Hindu Minority and Guardianship Act—Natural guardians of a Hindu minor

51. Shalu Nigam v. Regional Passport Office AIR 2016 Delhi 130

52. *Ibid*

53. Surjeet Singh vs. State & Another, 189(2012)DLT460

parties. Of such remedies, the anti-suit injunction is well known. The injunction enables the litigation to settle on a convenient forum for dispute resolution. The party suing in another jurisdiction can be restrained from doing so if s/he is amenable to the jurisdiction of both courts. This concept has been brought into the realm of family law and Indian courts are sometimes responsive to an anti-suit injunction that seeks to restrain the other spouse from proceeding with litigation in a foreign country.

The order does not restrain the other court, but the litigant, who is otherwise amenable to its jurisdiction for any number of reasons, including being a citizen of the country issuing the injunction, or if the marriage took place in the other jurisdiction, or if the foreign law is not in consonance with Indian law, or if the foreign order is oppressive to either parent or the children.[54] The first rule is that the party seeking the anti-suit injunction must not have submitted to the foreign jurisdiction. According to Dicey, a jurist:[55]

> 'The underlying principle is that jurisdiction is exercised when it is appropriate to avoid injustice, or, as it was once put, when foreign proceedings are "contrary to equity and good conscience"[56]...Although it is possible to identify certain categories of cases in which the jurisdiction has been exercised, the width and flexibility of equity are not to be undermined by categorization.[57]

While granting an anti-suit injunction to the wife in Singh vs. Taneja,[58] the court was concerned that she did not have a spouse visa, and in any case had not submitted to the jurisdiction of the US court. In another case, it was found that the wife was empowered enough to deal with the litigation abroad.[59]

Parental abduction across borders

The act of a parent fleeing with a child to another jurisdiction is called parental abduction. Many countries have signed The Hague Convention[60]

54. AIR 2002 SC 1796

55. Dicey & Morris, *Conflict of Laws*, p. 498

56. Carron Iron Co. vs. Maclaren (1885) 5 HLC 416, 439

57. Castanho vs. Brown and Root [1981]AC 557, 573

58. Harmeeta Singh vs. Rajat Taneja, 102(2003)DLT 822

59. Renu Judge v. Nanik Tirath Mulchandani 158(2009)DLT208

60. The Hague Convention of 25 October 1980 on the Civil Aspects of International Child Abduction

to deal with this problem and work together to ensure that the child is returned to the country of origin as quickly as possible. Under the Convention rules, the bereft parent must apply for return of the child to the original jurisdiction within one year of the abduction. The one-year period is a reasonable assessment for the time it takes for the child to settle into a new environment, after which it could be traumatic to uproot the child yet again.[61] The Convention also provides that no application for return of the child is to be allowed mechanically, without looking at the child welfare criterion. The court has the power to refuse to return the child to the country of origin in certain situations specified in the Convention.[62]

India is not a signatory to this Convention. Even so, there are cases where the Indian Supreme Court has sent abducting parents and their children back to the country they fled from, but the pattern of such rulings remains chaotic. The Law Commission, in its report 218[63] in the year 2009, has recommended that India sign the Convention. One of the reasons for this is that other countries will not allow travel permission to India for fear that children will not be returned. Regrettably, the reasoning is very superficial. However, the commission's report included a noteworthy comment:

> 'From the above, it can be observed that the Indian Courts while deciding cases pertaining to minor children have not followed a uniform pattern. There also is an absence of progressive development in the subject. If some matters are decided with prime importance placed on the welfare of the child, some are based on the technicalities of various provisions of law and jurisdictional tiffs. The reason cited for this can be the absence of any law that governs this aspect. This only will affect the condition, both physical and emotional, of the child, who is caught in the fire of shattered relationships.'

Women's groups in India have lobbied against the signing of the Convention because of the plight of many Indian women living abroad.

---

61. The application under the Hague Convention is disposed of within one to three months: See N. Lowe and V. Stephens, *The Timing of 1980 Hague Abduction Convention Applications: The 2011 Findings*, available at www.law.cf.ac.uk/newsandevents/elinks/1022_1363014635.pdf

62. See p. 392: Article 13 of the Hague Convention, available at https://www.hcch.net/en/instruments/conventions/full-text/?cid=24

63. http://lawcommissionofindia.nic.in/reports/report218.pdf

Indian women married to NRIs and living isolated lives cannot be in equal balance to their husbands, who participate in and are connected with the foreign world in a way that their wives are not. Many find themselves in a precarious, lonely situation, often housebound with a baby. They cannot afford to continue to live there and contest a legal battle. They need to return to the family fold for emotional, financial and infrastructural support that may not be available in a foreign country.[64]

Opposing principles: the child's welfare vs the offence of abduction

Before signing the Hague Convention, English courts had consistently maintained that the best interest of the child is the primary guiding principle, regardless of anything else. It must prevail, even when a child has been wrongly abducted by a parent. The precedent was set by Mckee vs. Mckee in 1951, where the English court refused to return the child to Ontario from where she had been abducted. As the child's welfare determined each case, the outcome could be different, with the child sometimes being returned and sometimes not.[65] Even in instances of children being returned to the country they were abducted from, the best interest principle was never compromised.[66] Though the UK signed the Convention in 1986, English courts have not jettisoned the welfare approach.

Till recently, Indian courts had three approaches to the situation, depending upon the facts of each case: 1) To decline the writ of habeas corpus asking for return of the child 2) to remand the matter to a trial court for detailed hearing on welfare of the child or 3) to summarily order the return of the child to the country s/he was abducted from.[67] Each approach was governed by the welfare principle. However, some recent Supreme Court judgments have tipped the balance in favour of returning the child to the country s/he was taken from, in deference to the principle of 'comity of courts'.[68] Regrettably this is often at the expense

64. See Kirti Singh, *Laws Relating to NRI Marriages and Their Impact on Women*, available at http://ncw.nic.in/ExpertCommitteePDFFiles/EC_NRIMarriages.pdf,

65. (1951) AC 352

66. Re J. (A child), [2004] 2 FLR 85

67. Dhanwanti Joshi vs. Madhav Unde (1998) 1 SCC 112

68. This is regarding the mutual respect/recognition that ought to exist between courts, as discussed on pp. 232-36. The precedent was set by Surya Vadanan vs. State of Tamil Nadu and Ors. (2015) 5 SCC 450

of the welfare principle. Here is the story of the precedents leading to this state of affairs.

~

The first question the court asks is whether the abducting parent has any legal proceedings against them in the foreign court. One would think that the matter would be relatively simple if there are none, but now there are some problematic exceptions that also grew around contradictory judgments on the 'ordinary residence' of the child being the place with jurisdiction to adjudicate on her welfare.[69] The terms, ordinary, habitual and domicile, are most used in the commercial and tax aspects of private international law. One can be ordinarily resident in a place without being habitually resident there and without claiming domicile in that place.

Let's take an example: I can decide to relocate tomorrow and so, in a day, my place of ordinary residence moves from Delhi to France. It is a matter of intention. A six-month-long rental of a cottage in the South of France makes me ordinarily resident there for that time.

Habitual residence, on the other hand, necessarily has tenure attached to it. The term ordinary residence used in the Guardians and Wards Act is in contrast to the UK family law statute, which requires a party to be a 'habitual' resident to invoke the jurisdiction of those courts.

This ordinary residence can develop to being a domicile (not dependent on citizenship) the day I decide that I will not return to India. Thus, it is also a matter of intention, in which case, it is only I who can articulate my intention. However, the other side can challenge my assertion by suggesting that I am saying so only to maintain a petition and thus, what I call my domicile has been artificially created by me.[70] There are a number of precedents for either position and now in some recent cases,[71] the Supreme Court has held that the issue of residence requires evidence

69. Mr Paul Mohinder Gahun vs. Mrs Selina Gahun, 130 (2006) DLT 524

70. Saket Varma vs. Shrutikeerti Khurana in the interest of Eleena Varma, in the District Court, 53rd Judicial District, Travis County, Texas Cause no. D-1-FM-11-002154

71. Ruchi Majoo vs. Sanjeev Majoo AIR 2011 SC 1952; Mst. Jagir Kaur & Anr. vs. Jaswant Singh AIR 1963 SC 1521; Kuldip Nayar & Ors. vs. Union of India 2006 7 SCC 1; Gaurav Nagpal vs. Sumedha Nagpal 2009 1 SCC 42; Surjeet Singh vs. State 189 2012 DLT 460; Dhanwanti Joshi vs. Madhav Unde 1998 1 SCC 112; Sarita Sharma vs. Sushil Sharma 2000 3 SCC 14; Dr V. Ravi Chandran vs. Union of India 2010 1 SCC 174; Chandrakala Menon vs. Capt. Vipin Menon AIR 1993 SC 2906

to be tendered in a trial, and is not just a question of law. (Frankly it never was and cannot be).

~

In one case[72], the single judge was upset with the subterfuge adopted by the wife in bringing her child to India for a holiday and then not returning. There are several instances of judges being upset at the subterfuge a wife uses to leave the foreign country and come to India. This approach lacks empathy for her predicament that required her to resort to an elaborate subterfuge to 'escape'. No estranged husband would have permitted a wife to return to India permanently with the child. While the spouse is entitled to the remedy of moving a writ of habeas corpus asking that the child be returned, the welfare principle should be applied to gauge which country is best suited to the child's needs, rather than any other consideration. While one understands the predicament of the court, ruling on the basis of the wife's actions alone basically punishes the child for the perceived misconduct of the parent.

I represented two runaway wives in the same court at about the same time, with a similar set of facts: both wives fled abusive marriages in foreign countries and returned to India with minor daughters. Upon arrival, they immediately filed for a divorce and sought protection of their custody of the child under the Guardians and Wards Act. In addition, they each filed an anti-suit injunction restraining the husbands from instituting proceedings in the foreign country. Both cases came up in the same court. That there were no foreign proceedings when they filed worked in their favours.

The foreign court, in both cases, later gave an ex-parte ruling in favour of the fathers, directing that the child not be removed from his custody or possession.

In one of the cases, the court had issued a restraint order against a breast-feeding mother, forbidding her from coming within 300 yards of the baby's residence and childcare facilities. Fortunately, the wife had left the US by the time this strange order was passed. It was served to her by e-mail. She had by then obtained an injunction from an Indian court restraining her husband from continuing with the foreign proceedings.

Her US lawyer advised her to return or she would suffer a default judgment, with custody being awarded to her husband. At the same time, the lawyer also warned of the possibility that once she returned, it was

72. Mr Paul Mohinder Gahun vs. Mrs Selina Gahun, 130 (2006) DLT 524

very likely that she would not be allowed to legally return to India with the child. He also advised that parental abduction was a criminal offence and, in all likelihood, warrants would be issued and executed against her. Understandably, she did not want to return. My advice was that the best interest of a breast-feeding baby was with the mother. 'There is no chance of an Indian court taking away such a small child from the mother or that they will in effect return the child to the foreign jurisdiction and thereby compel the mother to return as well,' I said, with pride and confidence at the time. I also told her that the US authorities could call for her extradition only the principle of duality by which such abduction was required to be a criminal offense in both countries, which it was not.[73] This matter was eventually settled by divorce by mutual consent.

In the other, the wife returned to the US, despite everyone being sceptical about the husband's intentions. Upon her return, she found that the violent abuse resumed. They are now in litigation there, and this time she is not able to come to India with the child. She is without family support and the maternal grandparents are in India, unable to meet their grandchild because she cannot come here and they cannot afford to go there.

~

Even so, these are the simple cases. Now we come to the complex cases where a parent abducts the child after having submitted to the jurisdiction of a foreign court.[74]

In all the early reported cases of child abduction in the 1980s, the Supreme Court ordered that the children be returned to the foreign jurisdiction from which they were abducted.[75] Though at first glance, all the judgments refer to respect for the comity of courts as the reason for ordering the return, a deeper reading and analysis of these judgments reveals a striking similarity in that the abducting parent was the father, who abducted the child from a working mother. Significantly, the fathers did not plead that they were fleeing from domestic violence and abuse, and the children were returned to the mother.

Then came a trend of abducting mothers, fleeing from abusive marriages. The courts favoured the mother in these cases as well. The first

73. See p. 375: Section 361 of the Indian Penal Code

74. Ms. Dorothy Thomas vs. Mr Rex Arul (2011) 6 MLJ 475

75. Elizabeth Dinshaw v. Arvand Dinshaw, AIR 1987 SC 3; Surinder Kaur Sandhu v. Harbax Singh Sandhu, AIR 1984 SC 1124

such reported case is of Sarita Sharma, who abducted her children to India in violation of orders issued by a US court.[76] Even though proceedings in the US had already begun, the Supreme Court refused to direct her return, saying:

> 'It will not be proper to be guided entirely by the fact that...Sarita has removed the children from the USA despite the order of the court of that country... The decree passed by the American court, though a relevant factor, cannot override the consideration of welfare of the minor children.'

From 2010, the Supreme Court began a new trend: that of returning children. The children in Aviral Mittal,[77] Ruchi Majoo,[78] Ravichandran[79] and Arathi Bandi[80] were all returned to foreign jurisdictions, though the court was careful to make suitable living arrangements and direct maintenance for the returning mother with the child.

In a recent ruling, the Surya Vadanan case,[81] the Supreme Court discussed the law in detail while ordering the abducting mother to return to the UK with the child, to enable the English court, as the court with the most 'intimate contact', to decide on their welfare.

The problematic part of this judgment is that it eliminates the welfare principle, by holding that while the best interests and welfare of the children were undoubtedly of paramount importance, 'it should be clearly understood that this is the final goal or the final objective to be achieved—it is not the beginning of the exercise but the end.' This 'the end justifies the means' philosophy is debatable in any context, but, with respect, here it does violence to the welfare principle itself.

The judgment has also set a precedent that the 'first strike' advantage is available to the person who gets the first substantive order in either jurisdiction. Though the abducting mother moved the Indian court first in the Surya Vadanan case, the UK court's substantive order came earlier. Thus, the father obtained the first strike advantage, despite not having been the first to file in any court. Frankly, given our systemic problem of delay, this interpretation puts our courts almost as non-starters. This

---

76. Sarita Sharma vs. Sushil A. Sharma, JT 2000 (2) S.C. 268
77. Shilpa Aggarwal vs. Aviral Mittal and Anr, (2010) 1 SCC 591
78. Ruchi Majoo vs. Sanjeev Majoo, AIR 2011 SC 1952
79. V. Ravi Chandran (Dr) (2) v. Union of India and Ors., (2010) 1 SCC 174
80. Arathi Bandi vs. Bandi Jagadrakshaka Rao and Ors., AIR 2014 SC 918
81. Surya Vadanan vs. State of Tamil Nadu and Ors., (2015) 5 SCC 450

ruling will cause immense pressure to and disadvantage Indian litigants, because our family courts are not able to give substantive relief quickly, given the over-load of cases they face.

Another uneasy implication of this judgment is that the first strike advantage is inconsistent with its own preference of giving priority to the court with the most intimate contact with the child. It is an inherent and uneasy contradiction that, if the mother had managed to get a substantive order from the family court in India, it would have prevailed against the UK court, despite the latter being the court with the most intimate contact with the child. These are technical and semantic ways to arrive at a decision, at the expense of the largeness and simplicity of the welfare principle.

On the question of the intimate contact itself, I submit that, for Indian children, Indian courts could also feasibly be ones with intimate contact, because of the strong cultural connection that most Indians maintain even when they live abroad. This is the nub of my position: the phrase 'close and intimate connection' in the context of a child has to be cultural as well, along with including the immediate environs of school, house and playmates. It may well be that a child living abroad is closely connected to an extended family in India and is as familiar with and happy in India as abroad. Also, when parents are estranged, one of the great advantages of this country is its wide family networks that hold and support the child and the fleeing mother.

It is also worth noting that the position of the courts is asymmetrical while dealing with international vs. inter-state abductions. Abducting mothers are now sent back to foreign lands, but in inter-state or inter-city abductions, the Supreme Court has not suggested that the close and intimate connection of the original court from whose jurisdiction the child has been removed should take priority. In fact, such intra-country abductions might have a more solid rationale to argue for return of the child, because the cultural differences are not insurmountable.

~

In this recent spate of judgments ordering the return of the children, the courts have referred to the Hague Convention as an implied benchmark for guiding principles. Yet the reference is incomplete without also looking at the fact that welfare remains central to the Hague Convention. In a case, the Delhi High Court chose to read the Hague Convention as a reference point but then did not apply the Convention fully. Thus, although the Convention provides for a one-year limitation to file an application seeking return of the child, the court accepted the husband's specious claim of not being able to file during this period because the wife had instituted some other civil and criminal proceedings against him. The court did not consider that if he could contest the wife's petitions with adequate legal representation, there was no reason he could not file his own. The court also chose to ignore the fact that the one-year limitation is not an administrative detail, but the period thought to be adequate for the child to develop new roots, that then should not be disturbed. In all the cases I have mentioned above, the children were ordered to be returned after more than two years.

~

The law is well settled on the fact that the welfare of the child is more important than anything else. It is central. It is all that is important. To use different words, such as primary instead of paramount, is a semantic exercise, to create a distinction without a meaningful difference. At best, a fine distinction can be made, saying that welfare is an amalgamation of factors: for the 'paramount' ones, the child alone is looked at, but once the child's needs are taken care of, parental rights and welfare can be looked at as 'primary' factors. Generally, however, courts have used the words paramount and primary interchangeably.[82] The appropriate word may also be 'primordial' which is used in Article 5(b) of the Convention of the Elimination of all Forms of Discrimination against Women 1979 (CEDAW).[83]

It is in the welfare of the child that s/he not be disturbed and that s/he have equal access to both parents. But the welfare of the parents is also important, so that they can be happy and secure in order to provide the love that nourishes the child and themselves. Admittedly, this is difficult in matters of international relocation.

~

Now we come to what the mother and child are being returned to. In all these judgments, the courts returned the children, while knowing that they could not in law compel the mothers to go back as well. Yet, such rulings amount to indirect pressure, because mothers will rarely abandon

82. Nil Ratan Kundu and Anr. vs. Abhijit Kundu 2008 (11) SCALE 437; Vikram Vir Vohra vs. Shalini Bhalla AIR 2010 SC 1675

83. Asha Bajpai, *Child Rights in India: Law, Policy and Practice*; See also p. 393: Article 5(b) of the Convention of the Elimination of all Forms of Discrimination against Women

the children. In none of the cases did the court enquire into the financial circumstance of the mother, or whether it would be safe for her to return to the foreign country. Often criminal cases may have been lodged against her in that country, but the courts have trustingly directed the husband to not press for coercive action against the wives. In the Surya Vadanan judgment,[84] the judge states that:

> 'We may add a word of caution here—merely because a parent has violated an order of a foreign court does not mean that that parent should be penalized for it. The conduct of the parent may certainly be taken into account for passing a final order, but that ought not to have a penalizing result.'

The judge has trusted that the foreign court will view the abduction as a 'mere' violation: but a mere expression of trust and hope may not affect the view of the foreign court. The returning parent surely faces hardship and uncertainty.

Where both parents are working abroad, they can deal with the situation in some ways; but when one is without a job or prospects, to insist that the jurisdiction remain with the foreign court is oppressive even for the child who will be dealing with a disoriented mother. After all, if Forum Conveniens[85] is a reasonable argument for commercial matters, why can it not be for the far more delicate and fragile situation of children who are victims in divorce battles? Surely there can be no doubt that the child's welfare lies with continuing with the care-giving parent. Tearing him or her away from that parent is more traumatic than uprooting from a place.

The mounting number of contradictory rulings have created uncertainty and so it is best that new rulings be confined to the facts of their cases, and should not in any way be read to dilute the welfare principle as central, primordial, primary, paramount and absolute. Based on the unique factual context of a case, it is better that the children sometimes return and sometimes stay.

While Indian courts seem to be wavering on the welfare principle in recent cases, subsuming it under the principle of comity of courts, or in deference to international conventions, or concern about the perceived misconduct of the mother, the US Supreme Court in a 2014 ruling has

---

84. Surya Vadanan vs. State of Tamil Nadu and Ors., (2015) 5 SCC 450

85. The court or forum most suitable for the ends of justice

asserted that notwithstanding the Hague Convention,[86] the one-year limitation for returning the child to the country s/he was abducted from is sacrosanct, even if the abducting parent goes into hiding for that one year and thereby stands rewarded for his/her misconduct. The clear message is that the welfare of the child is all that is important and that is not to be jettisoned in any circumstances.

~

The perception that family law has no rules and no law, and that the principle of best interest or welfare of the child is a general warm fuzzy feeling best left to bleeding hearts, has resulted in arbitrary judgments from limited personal perspectives. The other problem of many rulings is their tendency to indulge in dangerous gender generalizations.

The purpose of the legal system is to develop efficient methods of assessing the best interest of the child to serve her welfare. The child does not have an independent advocate or counselor. She may be vulnerable to tutoring by either or both parents; she may be heartbroken at the thought of having to choose between two beloved parents; she may be petrified about being alone with an abusive parent. She may be stressed at having to divide her time between both parents with no privacy for herself; she may feel completely ignored and misunderstood or not heard despite the clucking concern of noisy parents, lawyers, judges; she may feel exhausted and helpless with repeated interview calls to judges' chambers or because the judge has not heard her even once. She does not have the strength, wherewithal, language, confidence or status to demand to be counted.

The system can be harsh in its treatment of children who the law calls 'tender': There is no training in any law school on the ethics of dealing with children in a divorce battle. In none of the cases of international abduction were the children consulted whether they preferred to stay in India.[87] And yet, Article 12 of the Child Rights Convention, 1989,[88] to which India is a signatory, requires they be consulted. The municipal law requires that they be consulted. The *parens patriae* jurisdiction requires that they be consulted.

86. Lozano vs. Montoya Alvarez, 697 F. 3d 41

87. Dr V. Ravi Chandran vs. Union of India 2010 1 SCC 174; Shilpa Aggarwal vs. Aviral Mittal and Anr (2010) 1 SCC 591; Arathi Bandi vs. Bandi Jagadrakshaka Rao and Ors. AIR 2014 SC 918; Paul Mohinder Gahun v. Selina Gahun, 130 (2006) DLT 524

88. See Article 12, Convention on the Rights of the Child, available at http://www.ohchr.org/en/professionalinterest/pages/crc.aspx

The pendulum of rulings on custody matters has swung wildly and unpredictably to both extremes. The frustration of dealing with uncertain law propounded with certainty only for that moment, till a contrary ruling arrives, drove a senior lawyer[89] to tell off a Supreme Court judge in robust, fruity Bihari English, 'It is intriguing milud, how we, vairy aardinary liars,[90] become fountains of knaawledge when we go to that side of the bar!' It says a lot for the court, and the times, that the judges laughed!

Child Sexual Abuse Accusations in Divorce

An important part of child rights is protection from sexual abuse. Custody battles are sad, painful, troubling and stressful, but when allegations of sexual abuse come up, the matter turns horrific.

In 1995, the papers reported the story of a government servant called Jhakhu.[91] It was alleged that, during lunch hour, he would take his seven-year-old daughter to a hotel room where he would participate in group sex with colleagues. He would force his daughter to watch porn with them and put his finger in her vagina and they would all laugh while she cried. When confronted by his wife, he was unrepentant and infamously said that a mali has the first right to smell the flower he grows. He hanged himself before the trial concluded.

~

In 2003, John Mortimer wrote:

> 'We live, it seems in the age of pedophilia. The onset of this undoubted danger is a mystery to me. At boarding school we had the odd errant butler and some over-affectionate masters, but no one thought of the danger of being dragged into a strange car and ending up, perhaps dead, in the bracken.... In the 1950s and 1960s I did a large number of cases. Warring wives would make the most terrible allegations against their husbands, but I can't remember any charge of pedophilia. Now practically every case on the family division contains such allegations. They are, of course, easy to make and are included as a matter of course in American matrimonial cases. Should we believe that this horror emerged, like sex, at the time of the Beatles' first LP and grew with the encouragement of the internet?'[92]

---

89. The late S.P. Singh

90. Pun on our tendency to pronounce lawyers as liars

91. Smt. Sudesh Jhaku vs. K.C.J., 62 (1996) DLT 563

92. Mortimer, *Where There's a Will*

There are many cases of fathers, like the accused Jhakhu, abusing daughters, but what Mortimer observed in the UK in 2005 is beginning to be true of India, in that there are cases of loose allegations of child sexual abuse (CSA) made by vindictive parents. In this section, I will discuss the phenomenon of malicious or false allegations of child sexual abuse, which are a part of the sexual allegations in divorce (SAID) syndrome,[93] as well as the various ways in which law courts, judges and lawyers can deal with them. I will also briefly discuss the role of mental health and other experts, and the weightage given to their testimony, by the legal apparatus.

The allegation of sexual abuse is a genie that, once unleashed, acquires a life of its own. The concerned judges tend to err on the side of caution in what they see as protecting the child, while timid judges tend to develop biases and prejudices against the alleged abuser that are insurmountable. Either way, the lives of families caught in this allegation are devastated. To be clear, child sexual abuse by a parent does happen. Of course it does. Devastatingly often. All I say is that the allegation, like any other serious allegation, be weighed with care in a fair judicial process, and the filtration process should be efficient, so that interim visitation orders can be made without hesitation. To wait for the final order defeats the purpose as happened in the case below:

A possible malicious accusation

In the case of H vs W and their son (S) and daughter (D), I was acting for H. We tried to negotiate an out of court settlement and there was a comfortable discussion about co-parenting arrangements. The children were spending weekends with him anyhow. The problem arose when W began linking child visitation by the father with an extortionist financial settlement. Talks broke down and H was denied access to the children.

After litigation began, H went to the children's school a couple of times. They met him warmly and told him they loved him but did not want to upset their mother. While he was talking to them, the mother saw the children with their father and descended upon them with a rage that sent the children running from their father and into the school building.

W filed a thirty-page divorce petition, mainly alleging an extra-marital affair, but the children were mentioned in two paragraphs. He was careless with them she said: he watched porn, including paedophile sites. The porn

93. Blush & Ross, *Sexual Allegations in Divorce*, pp. 1-11; See also Wakefield and Underwage, *Sexual Abuse Allegations in Divorce and Custody Disputes*, pp. 451–468.

averment is common nowadays because of ubiquitous internet access. The plea is left as a bald statement to suggest depravity of mind. No judge has said that a necessary consequence of viewing or reading pornography is depraved conduct. In any case, pornography that objectifies women in a perverse way is often confused with other sexually explicit material viewed for pleasure, which is a fairly normal preoccupation at various stages of life.

An analysis of W's petition revealed that she had not pleaded any specifics, not even approximate dates, in contrast to the minute details she had furnished about the 'other lady'. The first allegation of sexual abuse was made against H only when he sought court-ordered vistiation. W did not explain why she did not take the plea earlier. H argued that the delay in making the sexual abuse allegation should at least raise suspicion, if not establish that it was an afterthought to prop up an otherwise bad case.

Courts are generous in condoning delays in amending pleas because such things are treated as a matter of mere procedure rather than substantive law. Procedure is described as handmaiden to the rule of justice. (I've just realized the gender inappropriateness of this cliché that I have parroted thoughtlessly over the years.) I argued that a delay in making a plea of such devastating magnitude, particularly when it amounted to setting up a new case, could not be indulged as 'mere' procedure. Substantive rights had accrued to H that should not be dislodged, particularly when W had omitted to plead the details of the sexual abuse. The judge did not deal with this argument.

W filed two medical reports to support her allegation. A certificate headed 'Not for Medico Legal Purposes' claimed that interviews with the children and W indicate sexual abuse. The other report made a general finding about sexual abuse without stating the clinical method of assessment to arrive at that horrific conclusion. The authors (both doctors) of the certificates chose to damn H without meeting him. An affidavit of a 'social worker' with unclear qualifications was also relied on to determine the state of mind of the daughter and it was concluded that she had been sexually abused. H argued that all reports were vague and thus inadmissible; in any case, the one titled 'Not for Medico Legal Purposes' should not have been accepted on record in court. Because we could not find a judgment of an Indian court as a suitable precedent, H cited an English judgment saying that in family matters courts should rely on expert opinions of persons who have wider and deeper experience than social workers.[94] H also cited a Delhi High Court judgment that distinguished sexual abuse from incompetent parenting.[95]

Yet the judge allowed the certificate to remain on record and relied on both reports without bothering to meet the 'specialist' authors. She interviewed the children but made no notes. I think this was a serious lapse. Given their heavy workload, judges should not expect themselves to remember the nuances of each chamber interview. Moreover, notes provide a continuity for the succeeding judge in case of a change of roster.

H's case was that the plea of child sexual abuse was vague and thus suspect and could not be sustained in the balance of probabilities given the delay in making it. As to the balance of probabilities, we argued that serious allegations required a higher standard of proof, given the possibility of serious damage to the life and reputation of a person wrongly accused.[96] W's best case was incompetent caregiving, which should not deny H access to the children. The children had a right to the opportunity of building a relationship with their father.

The case was at the interim stage of ordering visitation pending trial. The judge found some prima facie merit in the sexual abuse allegation but then went on to observe that it would still be in the interest of the children to meet their father. The court-ordered visitation was so heavily supervised and so infrequent that it rendered to nothing. W's conduct was difficult. H had wanted to send voluntary child support cheques and gifts to the house so the children should know he cared for them, but she denied them that knowledge by insisting on direct bank transfers into her account. Birthday gifts sent by courier were returned unopened.

Instead of ruling on the legal issues raised in the appeal about delay and probability and quality of certificates from 'experts', the High Court called a specialist for another opinion. The doctor gave a certificate saying he had talked to the entire family and it was best that the daughter not be exposed to her father as his assessment was that she had been sexually abused by him. The doctor's interview took place seven years after the last time the father had been alone with the children. There was nothing in the report about what either parent said: no mention that the father alleged that the mother had suffered sexual abuse as a child and thus was paranoid about the possibility of it, to the point of imagining it

---

94. Re A vs. B (1995) 3 FCR 389; Re N, (1996) 4 All. ER 225

95. Pavan Kumar Jha vs. Sapna Moudgil, MANU /DE/1136/2004,

96. Re: B (Children) [2008] UKHL 35; [2008] 2 FLR 141

and believing her untruths. All that is reported is the interview with the children (particularly daughter) who repeated verbatim what they had said in the two previous reports about a year earlier. The good doctor does not explain how he concludes that the consistency of the narrative establishes truth and not good tutoring by the mother. The High Court judge did not ask to meet the doctor either.

The law, even in criminal cases, is that medical opinions are not to be treated as determinative and conclusive. The court can consult experts and give their reports due consideration, but a judge is not expected to abdicate responsibility of a judgment by giving into the 'opinions' of the experts.

W's best case against H was incompetent parenting, which can always be rectified with checks and balances. Instead, he lost his children. What reparations could the court have given him if the charges had been found to be without basis? Nothing I guess. Just a feeling of vindication.

Realizing that even if he won this case, after challenging the report and cross-examining these so-called experts, it may be too little and too late, H has recently given up the fight for his honour and has embarked on his life without the children. I have to end this narrative by telling the reader that H feels his travails and anguish have made him strong, patient and caring—and have also given him a curious feeling of liberation. He counsels other parents now.

A sensitive judgment

In the Pawan Kumar case in front of the Delhi High Court,[97] the father alleged that his now eight-year-old child had witnessed as a two-year-old, his mother having sex with her paramour. This is within the definition of sexual abuse and quite rightly. The child had become sexually aware in an unhealthy and abnormal way.

The District Judge allowed the mother overnight visitation with her son after interviewing the child and observing that he had interacted well with his mother, even though a medical report had advised no contact with her. The judge ignored the report, saying that it was limited as it was based on the father's account of events and not on that of the child.

The husband challenged this order in the High Court. The High Court judge met the family in chambers and reduced the number of visitations and limited the timing to daylight hours. Even this modified order was

97. Pavan Kumar Jha vs. Sapna Moudgil, MANU/DE/1136/2004

not complied with. H said the child did not want to meet the mother and W said she was not allowed to meet the child. The matter went back to the High Court and came before a different judge. The ruling is extracted below:[98]

> '50. I find it very difficult to imagine, in the absence of anything to the contrary, that the Respondent (mother) who is a literate and articulate person would deliberately want to cause any anxiety, let alone any trauma, to A (child.) If her meetings with A have disturbed him to the point of traumatizing him, she would have at least sensed it, if not realized it during one of her several meetings with A. Since there is nothing to suggest otherwise, I have to proceed on the basis that the Respondent still has love and affection for A, as one would expect a mother to have. Keeping this in mind, I must give the benefit of doubt to the Respondent and conclude that she would not insist on meeting A if she had any reason to believe that the meetings would have an adverse impact on him. If her actions are bona fide, as they appear to be, her judgment must be respected, at least for the time being, and if her meetings do not cause any trauma to A, she should be permitted to meet him as frequently as possible. On the other hand, if the meetings traumatize A, the Respondent's maternal instincts would certainly be able to sense the trouble and persuade her to take remedial steps.
>
> '51. In the long run, even if it were assumed that the Respondent had any adulterous relationship, it would be necessary for her and for A to come to terms with other realities and complexities of human relationships. Ideally, both the parents should make a joint effort to achieve this. Unfortunately, this does not seem possible in the present case. Therefore, each parent should at least make an individual effort. Consequently, I think the Respondent should be permitted to meet A so as to enable him to develop into a better human being. According to the Petitioner, A is one of the brightest children in his class and is virtually a role model for other students. If this is so, I have no doubt that he can turn out to be even better if he is also allowed the company of his mother, at least until such time as A and the Respondent think it appropriate. If for some reason the relationship between them does not mature or it sours, I am confident the Respondent is intelligent enough to know what to do, in the best interests of A.'

The judgment is sensitive, robust, temperate and judicious but even then, the best W gets is daytime visits with her son, despite the trial judge

98. *Ibid*

ordering overnight unsupervised access. Contrast the socialization of the author of this judgment to the judge who observed, in a case discussed earlier, that a lady's extramarital affair could affect the outcome of custody because of the 'morality' issue.[99] Nevertheless, it is sobering to reflect that, though the allegations were discounted substantially, the mother lost ground consistently because, when the sexual abuse allegation is flung, some of it sticks.

Mental health experts and the law[100]

In the Satish Mehra case, the couple lived in New York. The husband alleged that his wife was suffering from psychotic disorders and asked for custody of the children. She then alleged sexual abuse of the daughter, which was dismissed as unfounded by the New York police after investigation.

The litigation moved to India. The husband had some access to his children based on a ruling of shared visitation by the court in New York. The wife again filed a criminal complaint against her husband, alleging that he had sexually assaulted their daughter in his South Delhi bungalow during a visitation. A charge sheet was filed indicting the husband and a criminal trial was to begin based on this complaint. He challenged the filing of the charge sheet but the High Court held against him.

The Supreme Court found in favour of the husband and quashed proceedings. The findings of the Supreme Court were based on the unrealistic nature and the timings of the pleas, made at a belated stage. The court also found the wife to be of a vengeful set of mind, out to punish her husband for wrongs she perceived as having been done to her.

~

The Satish Mehra judgment is valuable for the observations made on the nature of interviews of the children and the insidious power of suggestion. There is a real problem of damage done to children who have to 'remember' with the help of 'experts'. Here we come to the interplay between mental health experts and judges. When the interplay is harmonious, we reach the nub of the matter. The problem is that, in India, there are no rules of judicial interplay in the space between an allegation as a legal plea and a doctor's opinion. Mental health experts have begun exercising undue power in what is and must be retained as an exclusive

99. See p. 222

100. Satish Mehra vs. Delhi Administration, (1996) 9 SCC 766

judicial domain, where judges weigh the balance with a sagacity that is unique to their training if not temperament.

Courts need to be, and indeed are, receptive to assistance and advice from mental health experts on how to break through to children or dissolve ego-ridden family conundrums. But judges need to be accountable for justice being served, instead of submitting in unquestioning deference to experts. An example is the Pawan Kumar case discussed above, where the judge had the emotional and intellectual strength to evaluate expert advice as an indicator, but not let it solely determine the legal outcome.[101]

Recognizing this problem, the Children and Families Act 2014 (UK)[102] bars instructions to an expert for advice without the leave of the court. If such evidence is obtained, it is inadmissible unless the court rules specifically on its admissibility. Professional opinions obtained even after the court process has begun are to be used only as aids and not to determine the judgment. We also need to remember that no professional opinion is infallible and even judges and lawyers regret judgments and opinions they have made in the past.

The possible and irreparable damage that inept mental health experts can cause is the subject of a study by Dr Elizabeth Loftus and Katherine Ketchum.[103] They claim that though many emotional and behavioural disorders are rooted in repressed memories, the process of unearthing them is dangerous because therapists can plant ideas and thoughts that emerge as repressed memories under therapy. The authors compare repressed memory to a Wikipedia page that can be accessed by anyone to add information.

Let me tell you my personal 'memory': The dhobi sits on his haunches, counting the clothes for laundry. I see him gesture at my mother with fingers bundled into a threatening fist. Frightened, my mother steps back and I run to cling to her. I still remember it. At about age nine, I reminded my mother of it. She looked shocked and bewildered and said 'No'. I remember saying that I could not decide whether this was a dream or true. 'It's a dream,' my mother said firmly.

Consider another: my children allege that one day I forgot them at my

101. Pavan Kumar Jha vs. Sapna Moudgil, MANU/DE/1136/2004

102. Section 13, Children and Families Act, 2014, available at http://www.legislation.gov.uk/ukpga/2014/6/pdfs/ukpga_20140006_en.pdf

103. Loftus and Ketcham, *The Myth of Repressed Memory: False Memories and Allegations of Sexual Abuse*

parents' house. I said it's impossible—and in any case my parents also do not remember any such incident. One child may have mentioned anxiety about being left behind, but both lived out the story they had built around their fear of abandonment.

~

Satish Mehra's case was a criminal trial where the prosecution failed to prove its case beyond reasonable doubt. The standard of proof is less in matrimonial proceedings as they are civil proceedings, but given the life-changing effect such an allegation can have on the person accused of this heinous offense, the standard of proof should certainly be higher.

Over the years, with the increasing number of sexual abuse allegations, I have become alert to subtle insinuations and can smell the veiled demon in the petition that I know will be made to jump out if things get difficult for the other side. I call this a 'malodorous pleading' even though there is no such phrase in formal legal terms.

Blush and Ross have studied the pattern of false allegations in the SAID (Sexual Allegations in Divorce) syndrome and described some typical characteristics.[104] Such accusations are made only after separation or legal action and reveal unresolved family dysfunctionalities. The report noted that the allegations are almost always by the custodial parent. It went on to say that the female accusing parent is often a hysterical or borderline personality or is angry, defensive and justifying. The male parent accused is generally passive, nurturing and lacks 'macho' instincts. The report also had a thought-provoking discussion about revenge as a motive for allegations of sexual abuse. The modus operandi is that the mother takes the child to an 'expert' who confirms abuse and identifies the father as the perpetrator. The court reacts by limiting or terminating visitation. I may mention that the reports in two matters that I dealt with on behalf of the father were furnished by the same doctor who, I am constrained to conclude, is either lazy or incompetent or dishonest, because the wording of both certificates is almost identical.

In a recent matter, W produced a certificate to show her daughter's discomfort with/aversion to the father, carefully couched to develop into a case of CSA should the need arise. Such certificates are unimpressive, besides being unethical and unprofessional. The authors are always engaged by the accuser. Even in cases where the court has sought assistance, their findings are invariably pro-accusation. There is almost

---

104. Blush & Ross, *Sexual Allegations in Divorce*, pp. 1-11; See also Wakefield and Underwage, *Sexual Abuse Allegations in Divorce and Custody Disputes*, pp. 451–468.

never a description of the interview protocol to justify any conclusion. In this case, it was a malodorous pleading. We wrote to the doctor demanding an explanation; he then replied that it was common for girls that age to be uncomfortable with their fathers, establishing thereby that the discomfort pleaded based on that certificate was not due to some dark interaction, but a normal part of the father and daughter's evolving relationship.

My conversations with some psychologists in Delhi revealed their blissful ignorance of the existence of any protocols of assessment for child sexual abuse. I managed, with the help of Upasana Garnaik,[105] to access a wealth of material that I have mentioned in the bibliography to help us develop our own guidelines on this subject.

1. Cases of false accusations need to be recorded for us to develop accurate statistics.
2. Motives of the parties must be mentioned. For example, it is significant that many such allegations are made in ongoing litigation rather than forming the basis of the first complaint.
3. Besides the child, both parents need to be interviewed. Caregivers, schoolteachers, friends and their parents are valuable sources as well.
4. The adult accuser needs to be psychologically evaluated for paranoia and hypersensitivity.
5. The interviews with all, particularly the child, need to be in the free narrative form and held in comfortable surroundings.
6. Detailed case notes of interviews must be made available on court record.

~

In 2012, Parliament enacted the Protection of Children from Sexual Offences Act,[106] focused on the crime of sexual assault or aggravated sexual assault. Allegations in many divorce petitions do not have the courage to reach the mark of a clear accusation of abuse under the act. Their vagueness about 'inappropriate' touch requires careful consideration to protect against false accusations. A distance must be maintained between inappropriate or uninhibited behavior and actual sexual offence.

I listen to mothers getting stressed when fathers want to bathe their children or if they enjoy physical proximity with their daughters: it is difficult to explain that it is not ugly if the surrounding circumstances

105. Upasana Garnaik, Assistant Professor, Jindal Global Law School.

106. http://wcd.nic.in/childact/childprotection31072012.pdf

indicate a normal relationship. It is also difficult to suggest that if a son's physical proximity with his mother well into the teenage years is not misunderstood, why should a close father-daughter relationship be viewed with restraint and suspicion? I know of a little girl who told her father that she did not want him to bathe her any longer because she wanted her privacy and that was that. She did not have to say it again. But the fact that he may have bathed her in the past does not make him a 'sick man'. In one case, the other side pleaded passionately to protect a daughter from her father who would kiss her on the lips. Such personal moral perspectives wreak havoc in court, besides disrespecting a cultural ethos that may be far more tactile than in other homes: nothing wrong with that.

The times are sensitive and dangerous because an attitude of unhealthy repression about sexual matters has resulted in an over-sexualized society. This has led to grotesque symptoms of perversion. In many cases the accusing parent may have a propensity to sexualize ordinary contact and reduced ability to see the difference between 'inappropriate', 'intrusive' and 'sexual'. Where do you draw the line? To protect our children, we make them aware of their sexual being, with lessons on good touch and bad touch when they are just in kindergarten. It pained me to look into the clear unblinking eyes of my own two, as I explained that if they ever felt uncomfortable, they must step back confidently, even if it seemed silly to do that.

Yet, I knew in my mind that all discomfort is not necessarily due to 'inappropriate' touch. It could be due to dislike for the person or even a bad smell. I remember not wanting to be close to a particular teacher because she smelt of mothballs and sweat and I loved sitting on the lap of another teacher because she was always layered in perfumes that took me to a world of luxury. The child needs to be allowed to develop her own instinct on when to step back, without a great palaver made when and if she does.

Conclusion

Now that we are nearing the end of the discussion about children, I need to point out that judgments of our courts that I have mentioned in this chapter (and most others that are passed) will discuss the problems of the parents, their circumstances, their conduct and the story that brought things to this pass. They are not about the child.

One study[107] interviewed children of divorce and concluded that marriage usually has three versions: those of each parent and that of the child. The authors found that children almost never feel heard and do not believe that adults, including their parents, have their best interests at heart. The study suggests that a ceasefire for the sake of the children is not a solution either, because children remain aware of something amiss and the silence of that missing thing could create barriers in the child's own psyche, resulting in a 'feeling of numbness'.

My opinions on children and custody are derived from my experiences as a family lawyer, as a parent, and as a person who loves children. The last cannot be presumed. Many people might love children, but all do not perceive them as citizens with rights equal to those of adults, but requiring greater protection because of their helplessness. The opinions of children must be respected, even when we know that the child may change her mind—just as adults do. And often, they must be left alone, as you might remember wanting to be left alone as a child and even as an adult.

In 1927, Judge Lindsey, an American judge, suggested that an agreement to a no-fault divorce should not be upheld once children arrive.[108] This is clearly a very hard task for most people. The only parent who I have seen able to handle the problem of a bitter custody battle with exemplary humility and patience has been the mother in the case of Baby C[109] who, regardless of the hostility and the humiliation that was meted out to her, stayed within her child's vision for a few hours almost every day. Quietly and surely, she was making a powerful impact on the mind of the child who was not confident enough to walk across the room and give her a hug.

A child I know lived with her divorced mother and visited the father on the weekends. At the age of sixteen, the young girl said that she did not really mind that her parents had divorced because she knows them as individuals now and likes them the way they are. Yes, it would have been different if they were together, but she is not going to think about it because it was not to be.

She could be this serene, because both parents chose to deal with her as a person, without denigrating the other. They loved her more than their mutual differences. That's all it takes. But she is an unusual child

---

107. Wallerstein et al, *The Unexpected Legacy of Divorce*

108. Ben B. Lindsey and Wainwright Evans, *Companionate Marriage*, p. 81

109. See pp. 218-20

with an unusual set of parents. We still don't know whether she has any angst as a child of divorce, but at least we know she has the sagacity and wisdom to deal with her demons.

Another child said, 'I know Kaka (father) and Amma (mother) can't be friends, but as mama and papa they can make it work.' At the end of the day, that is all we can do for our children. We can't be perfect. We have to tell them that they are uppermost in our minds and we have to demonstrate this love sincerely, to make sure they believe us. This has to be communicated, not just to our own children, but to every child we meet. Then only will there be a generation of people who can deal with our messy legacy without cynicism and bitterness.

8. PRIVACY

A few months ago, I got a call from a friend. She had accidentally picked up her husband's cell phone and found inappropriate messages from some woman. 'I wish I had not seen the phone,' she said sadly. She was also angry: 'It's my own husband's phone! Why should I not see it?' She emphasized 'my' and 'own'.

'What if he rifled through your private things?' I asked.

'I have nothing to hide,' she replied.

I began to say that was not the point, but stopped because I could not pinpoint the limit of privacy in a marriage. Of course there should be no secrets, and of course adultery is wrong, but surely something can be just yours alone—phone, computer, space? Surely some conversations can be private? We have all done that—'Don't tell anyone, not even your husband, OK?'

Nothing was the same in my friend's life after the message. Their marriage might survive; it might even get better; but it will never be the way it was a moment before she saw the messages.

~

Is individual privacy a reasonable expectation in a family? It is a moot question, given the interconnectedness of family life in India as a rule. The power of silence and solitude as food for the soul and a calming balm on fevered society has not been fully appreciated in everyday Indian life, although we are the land that gave the world yoga and meditation techniques. Given this, what expectations can we have of privacy? Dr Dhawan[1] says that privacy is a grandiose word and brings in the baggage of the law and state and so on. Perhaps, he suggests, autonomy is a better word.

Autonomy means personal liberty and freedom of the will from external control.[2] Privacy, on the other hand, is the state of being withdrawn from the society of others: seclusion—'Listening winds overhear my privacies spoken aloud'.[3] While autonomy can exist without privacy, privacy cannot exist without autonomy. But what about privacy—from the other and from the state, which should not compel me to be with the other?

~

1. Dr Rajeev Dhawan, Senior Advocate, Supreme Court of India

2. http://www.oxforddictionaries.com/definition/english/autonomy

3. Maya Angelou, 'Love Letter' in *Maya Angelou: The Complete Poetry*

Marriage itself may be a loss of some autonomy because it is defined as a joining together of two beings. Complete autonomous control over earnings is also compromised in a marriage where the needs of the family must prevail over personal indulgences. The two people involved do not have the same experience of marriage, however: Since men have power, it is women who lose autonomy.

Autonomy has been used frequently in the feminist context to assert a woman's control over her body. The current law is that a married woman does not have autonomy over her body. The survival of the law of restitution of conjugal rights indicates there is no autonomy in marriage. That marital rape is not an offence similarly indicates lack of autonomy over her body.

Privacy seems a luxury, given that women have not even negotiated autonomy over their bodies within a marriage. Nevertheless, as we move towards increasing urbanization, nuclear families and women's empowerment, the idea of privacy as a legal right is taking root, and though it finds no mention as a separate legal right in the Constitution, Indian courts are beginning to read it in Article 21 that guarantees life and liberty as a quality and meaningful right.[4]

The law of privacy evolved from an essay written by Samuel D. Warren and Louis D. Brandeis complaining of breach of privacy by the press: 'The press is overstepping in every direction the obvious bounds of propriety and decency.' They defined the right to privacy as 'the right to be let alone'.[5] The law, as can be seen, began from and has developed about the right of the individual and family against the state or the press. Brandeis, later as Justice of the US Supreme Court, gave a dissenting opinion in the Olmstead case,[6] holding that evidence obtained by the

4. In 1954, an eight-judge bench in the case of M.P. Sharma and Ors. v. Satish Chandra, District Magistrate, Delhi, AIR 1954 SC 300 stated that there is no right to privacy although subsequent smaller benches of the Supreme Court have held it to be a part of Article 21 of the Constitution; See Kharak Singh v. State of U.P., AIR 1963 SC 1295; See also J. Subba Rao's minority opinion; Gobind v. State of Madhya Pradesh, AIR 1975 SC 1378

5. Samuel D. Warren and Louis D. Brandeis, 'The Right to Privacy' in *Harvard Law Review*, Vol. 4, No. 5 (15 December 1890), pp. 193-220

6. Olmstead v. United States, 277 U.S. 438: The petitioners were accused of unlawfully possessing, transporting and importing intoxicating liquors and therefore the question before the court was whether private telephone conversations could be used as evidence.

government through wire-tapping was illegal: 'The greatest dangers to liberty lurk in insidious encroachment by men of zeal, well-meaning but without understanding'.

~

The right to privacy within the family is a different matter altogether. It is about protection against intrusions by the other members of the family. As in all family law, the law of privacy in the home comes into play only when the family is disintegrating.

Given the cramped living quarters of the majority of the citizens of this country, an argument about privacy in the family home may sound pompous and seem irrelevant, but privacy exists in every degree. It can also apply to the right of a daughter-in-law to protect her possessions in her own cupboard or her space from a snooping mother-in-law who wants to check whether she has had her monthly period. It is a burning issue for a growing number of people who are able to afford larger living spaces. Calling for the right of an individual to have privacy does not of course mean that they have a licence to a secret life of betrayals that destroy the family. But, as a lifestyle, the expectation of an inviolable space is not unreasonable and it is not a bad thing to avoid too much togetherness which may be seen by some as irritating and intrusive. (Intrusions on the privacy of children may sometimes be necessary if the parents suspect drug use or secret drinking or misuse of the Internet, but for the most part we are discussing the adult members of a family).

Thus far, privacy is not a legal right, but a mutual need that the partners in the relationship must negotiate. The idea of one spouse having privacy from the other as a legal right is riddled with problems because the law will not enter places where it is not effective. It cannot enter a home because the privacy of the family as a unit is itself a legal right.

Though privacy between spouses is not a legal right, it can be argued that the brutal invasion of it could constitute the matrimonial offence of cruelty. However, this is invariably a question of degrees. Marital rape, for example, is not a criminal offence but can be used as a ground for divorce, subject to the problematic caveat of performing a marital duty.[7] Can invasion of privacy by a spouse who does not understand your need for privacy be a ground for divorce? It's too fine a point to have by itself, unless it is supported by behaviour that is intrusive to the point of becoming the matrimonial fault of cruelty.

---

7. See Ch. 3: Love, Sex and Marriage, pp. 64-66.

Of course privacy as mutual respect is a good quality that can sustain a marriage. Thus, a more apt description would be that privacy is a privilege: most often it is a choice made by the respecter of privacy or it is an attractive personality trait in many people who are non-intrusive by nature or personal belief. When it comes to the realm of belief, it could be said that privacy is a moral duty, but since it is not universal, it is only for those who believe in it as an ideology. Whatever the reason: belief or personality, it is a valuable privilege and when it is misused by the recipient, the licensor of privilege is hurt more by his/her own sense of betrayal than the actual act of misuse.

That was the only explanation I could think of when a client of mine was angry with her estranged husband because she found that, apart from the faults she had stated in her petition, he had also been adulterous. I was puzzled by her attitude. 'You are already in litigation,' I said. 'Why are you hurt? Your marriage is over anyway.'

'We are fighting over other things, but this is about a time when I thought all was well,' she replied. Her sense of betrayal about that time past created fresh wounds now. A spiritual adviser could question the wisdom of my client's attitude; she was self-inflicting wounds in a war that was over, but the point may be that the war is never over.

For marriages that survive, to forgive the betrayal is easy. But to forgive absolutely is more difficult and for this the betrayer has to earn back the privilege of privacy. As a result, many marriages crumble even after forgiveness because the betrayed spouse, driven by suspicion and the fear of being betrayed again, puts pressure on the marriage by constant intrusions and checking on the betrayer.

A man said to me. 'I had an affair fifteen years ago. She said she forgave me and we tried again, but the last fifteen years have been hell because I can't seem to do enough for her. Now that offence has become her power to use over me; she says she forgives me but keeps blackmailing and making me feel guilty about it. I can't suffer a life sentence for the affair.' I agreed with him but also understood the wife—how do you distinguish between a reasonable belief that your spouse is betraying you again and sheer dread that if it has happened once, it can happen again? Many couples have walked that path and only some have managed peace.

Adultery is the more obvious betrayal, but it could be other things too: secret smoking or drinking; meeting friends that the other absolutely cannot stand; political betrayal by parlaying with the other side. Of course, what constitutes betrayal for one person can be used as a litmus test for the health of the marriage. I frankly would feel constrained if I had to accept even one of the above restrictions from a partner as a basis for marriage.

This question may be philosophical for an intact family but becomes crucial in a divorce proceeding.

Privacy in Divorce Proceedings

Once the couple is estranged, privacy is often the first casualty as the couple rips open the innards of the marriage to expose even benign confidences that may have been shared in happier times.

In such cases, it is not just a public washing of the dirty marriage linen, but poor conduct during the litigation to make it even dirtier. The home becomes a war zone and cell phones, e-mails, drawers, almirahs are all rifled for signs of a hidden financial or sexual life. Modern technology makes for easy intrusion and the electronic exposés of salacious or sordid details have become almost passé. Many litigants are advised by over-zealous relatives and advisers to use hidden devices to arrive at the truth. Apart from the human rights and surveillance issues, I believe that mutual fear and suspicion of hidden devices has a 'chilling effect' on productive dialogue. Moreover, evidence procured in this clandestine manner is often skewed; for example, when the intruder provokes the unsuspecting opponent to display uncharacteristic behaviour.

In a case, my client was W. During the course of litigation she continued to live in the same house as H. One late evening, H, a big burly man, barged into her bedroom accusing her of lying in her divorce petition: shocked and frightened, she blamed her lawyer's drafting. H was recording this conversation. Petitions are always based on written narratives by the client, but H's lawyer arrived in court waving the transcript of the conversation as if he had won the case. W claimed wrongful invasion of her privacy. Though the matter eventually settled because H was getting impatient, the privacy issue was never addressed by the court.

Evidence obtained by breaching privacy

Privacy is guaranteed under the US Constitution and the Human Rights Act, UK. Thus, evidence obtained by state intrusion into individual privacy is not admissible in those countries. An important doctrine emerges here: Under US law, the fruit of the poisoned tree is inedible. Here, the poisoned tree refers to the illegal means used, and the fruit is the evidence. Ergo, such evidence will not be admissible in court. Similarly, press intrusions into private lives have been held to be illegal, entitling the person to compensation for breach of privacy.

In India, the courts have also read the privacy of the individual as an important right in cases of breaches by press.[8] However, as to intrusions by state, the fruit of the poisonous tree is edible in India. This was affirmed in the Parliament bombing trial[9] as an important principle to deal with serious cases of crime and terror.

Coming to family law, the Family Courts Act, 1984 has diluted most rules of evidence by making admissible any evidence that may not otherwise have been permitted under the Evidence Act. In practice then, the fruit of poisoned tree is edible in Indian law, but whether this justifies bludgeoning the privacy of the estranged spouse has rarely been addressed explicitly.

For example, the Allahabad High Court has held that a personal diary was permitted to be relied on by a husband against the wife. There was no discussion on the privacy issue apart from a sentence that 'the plea of privileged communication is unavailable in divorce suit'.[10] The judgment relies on Section 122 of the Evidence Act that protects the privacy of the marital relationship against the world,[11] but deems that it does not apply when the couple is in proceedings against each other.

On the other hand, the Andhra Pradesh High Court has ruled that surreptitious taping of a spouse's conversation was an infringement of privacy and the recordings were not admissible in evidence even if true.[12]

Despite this rare ruling on privacy in the marital home, our courts tend to admit evidence obtained by one spouse by breaching the privacy of the other. The validity of the legal justification in cases of terror and bombs is a separate argument, but it is troubling that there are no more judgments like the one from Andhra Pradesh that respects spousal confidentiality and the privacy of the individual within the family.

~

8. R. Rajagopal alias R.R. Gopal and Another vs. State of Tamil Nadu and Others, AIR 1995 SC 264; Indu Jain vs. Forbes Incorporated, (2007) ILR 8 Delhi 9; Kharak Singh and Anr. v. State of U.P. and Ors. AIR 1963 SC 1295; People's Union for Civil Liberties v. UOI, AIR 1997 SC 568

9. State (N.C.T. of Delhi) v. Navjot Sandhu @ Afsan Guru [sic], AIR 2005 SC 3820

10. Dr Kiran Singh vs. Dr Shiv Kumar, 2014 (102) ALR 370

11. See p. 374: Section 122 of the Indian Evidence Act, 1872.

12. Rayala M. Bhuvaneswari vs. Nagaphanender Rayala, AIR 2008 AP 98; See also Shamsher Singh Verma vs. State of Haryana, MANU/SC/1345/2015

Confidentiality is a part of the law of privacy. During divorce proceedings, confidence is often breached and the person responsible seeks to justify it by saying that: a) they were constrained to resort to self-help to obtain documents that the other side concealed or lied about; b) it was needed to establish a case of adultery; c) exposing past secrets gives them an upper hand psychologically in the ongoing vicious litigation.

As far as the first reason is concerned, the courts have to rely on financial information volunteered on affidavit even though they correctly assume that most people will not make a full and frank disclosure of their assets[13] even in a statement under oath. So, litigants ferret out documents about the other side and judges don't bother with the breach of confidence required to obtain them. The problem of the lying affidavit is serious in India because the offence of perjury does not invite meaningful consequences other than a perfunctory rap on the knuckles, if at all.

The legal remedy for deception and concealment is for a court to issue seize and search orders which ensures that assets are not hidden or dissipated, or evidence wrongly destroyed or concealed. Unfortunately such orders are not obtained with ease and efficiency, particularly from the lower courts, thus constraining parties to resort to self-help.

In the UK, the rules around uncovering documents on the financial status of parties are called the Hildebrand rules[14] and are discussed by Ward LJ in White vs. Withers LLP and Dearle:[15]

> 'It may be appropriate to summarise the Hildebrand rules...as follows. The family courts will not penalize the taking, copying and immediate return of documents but do not sanction the use of any force to obtain the documents, or the interception of documents or the retention of documents, nor...the removal of any hard disk recording documents electronically. The evidence contained in the documents, even those wrongfully taken, will be admitted in evidence because there is an overarching duty on the parties to give full and frank disclosure. The wrongful taking of documents may lead to findings of litigation misconduct or orders for costs.'

13. Vinod Dulerai Mehta v. Kanak Vinod Mehta, AIR 1990 Bom 120; Anupam Gupta v. Sumeet Gupta, CM(M) 1718/2004 (Delhi High Court)

14. Hildebrand vs. Hildebrand [1992] 1FLR 244; the husband had been to the wife's flat at Wallace Court surreptitiously on five occasions. He had taken photocopies of many documents obtained by him in the course of those visits (but returned after photocopying). The issues in that case were entirely related to disclosure.

15. White vs. Withers LLP and Dearle, [2010] 1 Flr 859, Para 37

The judgment discusses the matter of confidentiality. A bank statement, says the court, lying around the matrimonial house is not confidential, but to hack a computer lying in the house is a breach of confidentiality. This issue was again discussed in the Imerman case,[16] where the Hildebrand rules were held to be good law only to the extent that the spouse must disclose to the other that s/he has obtained unlawful access to information. For anything further, the court held that it could not sanction riding roughshod over established legal rights to permit the lawless procurement of documents.

~

In India, dealing with litigants lying under oath has become part of a day's work. However, a breach of confidence meant only to humiliate the other side is still unpalatable in most courts.

Historically, Duchess of Argyll versus Duke of Argyll[17] is the celebrated leading case on this aspect of confidentiality in a marriage. The couple was divorced due to the adultery of the duchess. After the divorce, the duke went to the press with an article about their married life: The duchess sought an injunction, saying that the article was in breach of confidentiality of communications made and confidences exchanged during happier days. She submitted that,

> 'Apart from explicit discussion, we naturally discovered many things about each other which, but for our close relationship we would not have done. These things were talked about and done on the implicit understanding that they were our secrets and that we allowed the one to discover them only because of the complete trust and mutual loyalty which obtained between us and created an absolute obligation of confidence.'

The court granted her the injunction observing,

> 'the duke does not say that he can disclose the matters because the plaintiff has already disclosed those same matters: but what he says is that the plaintiff has betrayed the marriage in some ways and so he should be free to betray it in others...the accumulation of the duke's breaches of the most intimate confidences in his article are to my mind of an altogether different order of perfidy.'

The court ruled that the deterioration of a marriage could not be treated as retrospective to undo the obligation to maintain the confidences of a happier past. It cited a precedent[18] with approval, saying that,

16. Imerman vs. Imerman [2010] EWCA Civ 908

17. Duchess of Argyll v. Duke of Argyll [1967] CH 302

18. Rumping v. Director of Public Prosecutions, [1962] 3 All ER 256

> 'It is not in my view just that adultery should have retrospective operation on a marriage and not only break the marriage for the future but nullify it for the past. The plaintiff's adultery, repugnant though it may be, should not in my view license the husband to broadcast unchecked the most intimate confidences of earlier and happier days.'

In more modern times,[19] a Florida court held evidence that the husband obtained by placing a wire-tapping device on the home telephone line as inadmissible, saying that it was breach of a reasonable expectation of privacy within the marital home.

~

In a recent case of mine, H filed the footage from concealed CCTV cameras to try and establish that W was mentally unsound. The judges of the Delhi High Court remarked that the recordings were not believable, since she had been clearly provoked to display an angry outburst, but did not comment on the invasion of privacy required to obtain the recordings. In another case, a wife revealed details of her sexual life with the husband to show him as perverse: she did not comment on why she participated in those acts for ten years. This nonchalance about the invasion of personal privacy is problematic: instinctively and intuitively one balks at the idea of vindictive litigation where personal confidences shared in happier times are used to embarrass the other side or threaten their case by using that information against them.

Similarly there may be a breach of confidentiality in accessing information to use in court. Whether the breach is in the manner of obtaining information is dependent upon each case. Contents in a computer lying in a common area may lose confidentiality if it is not password protected, but at the same time, as observed in the Immerman case, it is to be remembered that 'confidentiality is not dependent upon locks and keys.' In that case, the wife maintained against her husband the confidentiality of her personal diary, 'even though it was kept visible and unlocked on her dressing table.'[20]

On somewhat similar facts the Delhi High Court[21] held that taking the personal belongings of a spouse may amount to theft or criminal misappropriation:

19. Markham v. Markham, 272 So.2d 813 (1973)

20. Imerman v. Imerman [2010] EWCA Civ 908, para 88

21. Anil Bharadwaj and Others vs. State 1985(8)DRJ 75.

> 'there is no presumption of law that a wife and husband constitute one person in India for the purpose of criminal law. If the wife removing her husband's property from his house does so with dishonest intention, she is guilty of theft.'

An interesting analogy to this case is the nineteenth-century English case of Albert vs. Strange,[22] where Prince Albert and Queen Victoria made some etchings of their domestic life for their private pleasure. The material came into the hands of Mr Strange who denied having got them surreptitiously. Even so, the court restrained him from making public the etchings, saying that it was clearly the intention of the artists to have kept the etchings private and they are entitled to do so. This ruling was referred to by Brandeis and Warren in their article on privacy. The authors of the article claimed that the court had read the facts as limited to a property issue, whereas there was a deeper issue of privacy and breach of confidence that had not been addressed.

Surveillance and Privacy

About thirty years ago, although some well-known detective agencies existed, I had met only one private investigator who rejoiced in the work name of 'Phantom'. Dark glasses, trench coat with upturned collar and hat. 'Stereotype!' you will say with scorn, but he was all that a typical detective should be. He came to my office to meet a rich lady client who feared she would be murdered for her property and gave her tips that I find useful even today: if you feel you are being followed do a complete turn at a roundabout; if the follower stays, you are being followed. Since then, detective agencies have burgeoned and even movies have this advice, but I have never found a truly effective private investigator.

The following story is illustrative of the competence of most surveillance services. I got a desperate call from my client who hired surveillance services to watch his wife. The clever lady noticed the men tailing her and led them straight to the police station! I told him to stop this Perry Mason playacting. He disregarded my advice and engaged another private investigator. She caught the second set of detectives too and beat them up at a marketplace. He had to stop.

Recording devices are a different matter. The other day, I heard a recorded voice on my phone: 'Namaskar, we can give you a small chip that you can place anywhere in the house. When you call from your number

22. Prince Albert vs. Strange; ChD 8 Feb 1849

to anyone in the house, you will be able to hear all conversations and the *truth of your relationships*.' [emphasis mine]

Would I really want to know? I asked Mamta, who was dusting my desk, 'Would you buy such a thing?'

'Never,' she said firmly. 'There will be a Mahabharata in the house.'

But these devices are now easily available and almost every litigant wants to attend meetings with them. Some men want to place hidden cameras in the house to protect themselves from false cries of violence by wives, while women want to use devices to record abuse. Now there is a service available to 'sweep' premises for hidden cameras, cars for GPS devices and electronic gadgets for bugs. The question that few seem to ask though: Are they legal?

The law, as culled from Indian judgments earlier in the chapter, seems to be that evidence obtained by illegal means can be used in a trial,[23] though the person who has obtained the material in breach of legal rights may suffer separate legal consequences for damages, defamation and malicious prosecution that are all concomitant to and derive from the right to privacy. The practical truth is that these secondary actions are hardly ever maintained because both money and emotion is exhausted by then. Having said which, finding and using financial documents against the person hiding assets is certainly relevant, but the line has to be drawn at concealed cameras and recording devices to obtain private conversations, however angry.[24]

This is broadly in line with American law in most states. In an American case, one Leon Walker was set to go to trial for hacking his wife's computer because he suspected that she was having an affair. That his suspicion was correct gave him no reprieve from the offence of hacking.[25] Eventually all charges were dropped because it was found that the wife had been doing her own snooping as well.[26] Similarly, in the US, wiretapping or bugging a phone has been held to be intrusive, as is deliberate eavesdropping. However, to overhear a conversation by mistake is not: a husband overheard his wife talking to her lover on the phone. The window of the

23. Umesh Kumar vs. State of Andhra Pradesh, 2013(11)Scale28

24. PUCL vs. U.O.I, AIR 1997 SC 568

25. People of the State of Michigan vs. Leon Jermane Walker, Michigan Supreme Court, June 1 2012, 144639-40

26. 'All charges dropped against Rochester Hills man accused of reading wife's email without permission' in *The Oakland Press*, 19 July 2012.

room she was in was open and her voice carried to the yard where the husband was. He was allowed to depose on what he heard.[27]

The UK's position on privacy has already been explained earlier in the chapter. They take intrusions very seriously. Now a recent judgment has taken the matter to a new level where a UK court has restrained the media from reporting a divorce case with the names of the adulterer, etc, on the ground that the children of the adulterer and the couple would be disturbed.[28]

The exception to all of the above in the UK and US is the use of electronic surveillance to unmask cases of child abuse. Even so, the courts have advised weighing such matters in a careful balance instead of condoning privacy violations as a matter of mindless practice.

~

Returning to India, my associate, Upasana's research unearthed the 'Private Detective Agencies Bill', which was to be proposed for introduction in the Rajya Sabha in 2007. Clause 28 punishes the infringement of an individual's right of privacy with imprisonment up to six months, a fine of Rs. 50,000 and suspension or cancellation of licence. There was no definition of privacy and the bill was never presented.

Upasana also came across a bill drafted by the Centre for Internet and Society that recommends protection of personal data subject to considerations that the right to privacy is recognized as a fundamental human right by various international treaties to which India is a party, balanced with the need for public safety, good governance and delivery of services, at some cost of individual privacy.[29] Both documents are a useful starting point on an important debate that has been delayed too long.

Privacy Amongst Separated Spouses

Whether spouses can have a right to privacy within a seemingly intact marriage is the subject of the following case. H was rich enough to leave W no cause for complaint about finances. The social aspect too was taken care of, to some extent. They even made some public appearances together to the children's school and college, family events and so on. It was the sexual relationship that had ceased. H wanted to conduct a separate life, apart from financial and social formalities, so he moved out of the marital home, leaving her there with his extended family and children.

27. Mimms v. Mimms, 780 S.W.2d 739 (Tenn. Ct. App. 1989)

28. ETK vs. News Group Newspapers Ltd., [2011] EWCA Civ 439

29. Umesh Kumar vs. State of Andhra Pradesh, 2013(11)Scale28

H then filed for an injunction seeking an order against W to restrain her from entering his separate residence. The judge dismissed the case but H appealed. The court found[30] that the issue was related to marriage and thus the special enactment (the Hindu Marriage Act in this case) excluded the jurisdiction of the civil court from dealing with it. The judge found that H was trying to conduct a separate life, which if legally sanctioned, would effectively grant him a decree of judicial separation. H may not have been able to obtain such a decree through the usual route of filing a case, since that would require him to allege and prove not only that his wife was at fault, but also that he was not taking advantage of his wrong. The court held that the only remedy for H was divorce under the Hindu Marriage Act, and if he could not avail of it for any reason, civil law could not come to his aid. It did, however, make some observations on the merit of the matter: 'Public Policy considerations in India also appear to weigh against the Plaintiff's claim for privacy against his wife'.

The concept of the wife's right in the shared household was used to reinforce the court's opinion about no privacy in the marital home. In this case, H had walked out. The question is whether any action can be maintained against the left-behind spouse who decides to intrude into the private work and home life. In law, the wife has a right to live in the shared household or any alternative equivalent accommodation that the husband may provide for her. Once she obtains that, or has legally ousted him from the shared household, the mutual rights seem asymmetrical if she can barge into his separate residence but he can't into hers.

Unproven Interim Evidence

The current lack of clarity about the law pertaining to snooping and self-help becomes even more opaque when it comes to the submission of unproven evidence for granting interim orders. Unproven submissions admitted or even sighted by a judge at an interim stage can cause immense damage, unless of course it is prima facie clear that the evidence is not fabricated.

While judges are trained to be above clichés like no smoke without fire, etc., there is no doubt that they too, as much as anyone else, can be swayed by first impressions. More importantly, in developing its own procedure, the family court has to remain bound by its own rules. Some rules might seem pointlessly procedural, but in fact, these are substantive

30. 150 (2008) DLT 19

in ensuring that various rights remain protected by legal presumptions, and hence must not be set aside easily. Similarly, allowing the family court to develop its own procedure cannot mean that the family court is to resolve marital disputes outside a framework of law (which includes procedure). I heard a judge in the Supreme Court once joke: 'Oh we have practically set aside the rule about time limits for filing a defence. We are functioning like a panchayat.'[31] Everyone laughed (as everyone feels they must when a judge cracks a joke, however bad). But the family court was not meant to be a panchayat. The erosion of systems begins like this, with 'small' inroads into valuable rules of procedure made 'in the interest of justice'. By the time we notice the cumulative effect and begin to clamour for the protection of various 'rights', they have all evaporated.

I am thrilled to note that an important judgment of the Delhi High Court[32] on the issue of privacy in matrimonial matters has recently been made, which will hopefully ameliorate some of these problems:

> '30. Having now come across a number of cases of matrimonial and custody disputes, in the civil and criminal jurisdictions, the Court notes with concern that there is a growing trend amongst parties and their lawyers to readily disclose in the petitions, in the form of pleadings and documents, the most private and personal details of their clients and of the opposite parties, without a thought for the privacy implications, or even embarrassment potential, that it has. All too often no attempt is made to first seek the leave of the Court to tender the documents, be it in the form of private letters, notings, photographs, electronic evidence including video clips, text messages, chat details, emails, CCTV footage etc, the contents of which are of a private and personal nature. The Court has to consider if such documents are relevant to the case and how they should be presented, preserved and provided to the parties.
>
> '31. The Court considers it appropriate to issue the following directions to the Family Courts in Delhi, the parties and the lawyers, to be followed hereafter in the cases pending in those Courts:
>
> (i) Where a party in a case seeks to rely upon a document which in his or her assessment or the assessment of the party's lawyer is of a sensitive nature, viz., which contains details of a personal or private nature concerning a party or a person or their conduct, which when disclosed is likely to affect the right to privacy, or cause

31. In the context of interpretation of Order 8 about time limits for filing written statements

32. X v. Z, 2015 (151) DRJ 305

embarrassment, then such party and/or the lawyer of such party will first apply to the Court seeking leave to produce such document in a sealed cover. Till such time that leave is granted the contents of the said document shall not be extracted in the pleadings or a copy of the whole or part thereof enclosed with the petition. For this purpose a document would include any writing, private letters, notings, photographs, and documents in electronic form including video clips, text messages, chat details, emails, printed copies thereof, CCTV footage etc.

(ii) Whereupon a party applying under (i) above, or where any other party, or the Family Court on its own, comes across a document on record in the case which is prima facie of a sensitive nature, viz., which contains details of a personal or private nature concerning a party or a person or their conduct, which when disclosed is likely to affect the right to privacy, or cause embarrassment, the Family Court will pass appropriate orders concerning the said document including providing copies thereof to the parties, preserving the originals or copies as the case may be in a sealed cover, de-sealing for being produced during Court proceedings and re-sealing after the purpose for which they are directed to be produced is over.

(iii) The Family Court will also bind down by specific directions, the parties and their respective lawyers, and the Court staff regarding the making of copies, use, preservation and dissemination of such document with a view to maintaining its confidentiality. The Family Court can also pass necessary directions to specify the conditions upon which access would be permitted to such document by third parties.

(iv) The Family Court will endeavour to decide on the issues at (i) (ii) and (iii) above, without unnecessary delay, in accordance with law. The above directions are in the nature of broad guidelines and can be suitably modified and adapted/applied to a given situation by the Family Court. The Family Court will, however, at all times keep in view the requirements of protecting the rights to privacy and dignity of the parties and persons.

(v) The Family Court should as far as possible and practicable invoke the power under Section 11 of the Family Courts Act 1984 and hold the proceedings in camera. Where the circumstances so warrant, the Family Court may in the orders uploaded on the website or made available otherwise, suitably anonymize the names of the parties.

9. ON THE MISUSE OF GENDER-SPECIFIC LAWS

The Indian judicial system is seen as particularly prone to vengeful or misutlized litigation. A US State Department warning to Americans travelling to India states,

> 'since the police may arrest anyone who is accused of committing a crime (even if the allegation is frivolous in nature), the Indian criminal justice system is often used to escalate personal disagreements into criminal charges. This practice has been increasingly exploited by dissatisfied business partners, contractors, estranged spouses, or other persons with whom the US citizen has a disagreement, occasionally resulting in the jailing of US citizens pending resolution of their disputes.'[1]

Readers will note that 'estranged spouse' is only one possible category in which vendetta-type litigation is seen as common here. Vindictive litigants are prone to misusing any law and the legal system usually evolves to protect itself against misuse, not by doing away with the law, but by tightening procedure to filter frivolous litigation. Given our clogged legal system, which seems unable to protect victims of malicious prosecutions generally, the debate about the misuse of laws—which invariably focuses on the misuse of Section 498A[2] IPC and such criminal cases filed by wives—seems to miss the point. Or perhaps, it only too clearly reveals the level of social resentment about women-enabling legislation.

The benefits of the women-enabling legislations in criminal law far outweigh the pain and suffering of misuse and abuse of process generally. The law must remain. The way to deal with misuse of criminal law in matrimonial matters is no different from the way to deal with misuse of any law: careful and sharp investigations, robust but fair prosecutions, and balanced judgments delivered in an efficient timespan that punish false and malicious prosecutions heavily.

The Context

When Section 498A was promulgated, I was a cub lawyer with a trendy left liberal law chamber that also housed Shekhar, a quick-witted Malyali

---

1. Available at newdelhi.usembassy.gov/media/consularimages/acsnewsletterfall09.pdf

2. See p. 382: Section 498A. Husband or relative of husband of a woman subjecting her to cruelty

stenographer. Shekhar had been suspended from a government job for insubordination. Like all good Keralites, Shekhar bristled with legal rights I trod softly around, till I discovered his sense of humour. It was then easy to understand why a humourless government babu would mistake Shekhar's deadpan satire as rude and insubordinate.

One day, he handed me a sheet of paper on which was typed:

- We were married on [date].
- We have [x] number of children.
- Right from day one of marriage he troubled me.
- They demanded dowry and my father did the best he could, even though it was beyond his capacity.
- On [date] the entire family beat me because I did not get enough dowry…
- On [date] they beat me again. My father visited on [date] and they humiliated him.

Poker-faced, Shekhar told me that he would cyclostyle the document and I could just fill in the blanks for each woman complainant. I solemnly stood up to salute the singular courage of this literary endeavour in a feminist chamber.

Similarity in FIRs,[3] which often begin to sound much like Shekhar's standard form, is indeed disturbing, but it needs to be understood that what Shekhar standardized as fodder for his dark humour were the attitudes and customs that prevailed as common and popular. The similarity of complaints is that they all reflect disappointed expectations of transactional opportunities that celebrate gender inequality.

Many complaints seem patently false because we look at them from our own cultural perspective; we like to claim that we live in a milieu where dowry is 'not an issue'. The truth is that the problem of dowry does not always lie in the act of giving and taking—demand and reluctant supply—but attitudes that reflect and enact deep-rooted gender biases. Given that marriage has traditionally been about extending spheres of influence, it is not surprising that if not most, certainly many people

3. A First Information Report (FIR) is a written document prepared by police organizations when they receive information about the commission of a cognizable offence. It is generally a complaint lodged with the police by the victim of a cognizable offense or by someone on his or her behalf, but anyone can make such a report either orally or in writing to the police. Section 154 of Code of Criminal Procedure, 1973 deals with it.

expect some betterment from a valuable connection made by marriage. It may not be money itself, but opportunities that could translate to money, or influence that comes with some economic benefits. Even in the West, which claims to have transcended 'arranged' marriages and to believe in love, the advantages of 'marrying the boss' or the 'boss's daughter' are well known and the expectation remains that if a 'brilliant' match that helps up the social ladder can't be made, it should at least be a 'sensible' one that does not drop social status. This, incidentally, is not to say that love marriages reduce the problem for women: the practice is that many love matches too retain the customary trappings of monetary exchanges.

On this issue, most families are almost never what they seem to be. Treat the following as true of most of North India and certainly of Delhi. After families agree to the marriage, the standard questions are 'what's your budget? What are you giving your daughter? What car will you give?' followed by the standard demands: Wedding should be at a five-star venue; the barat is to be received with 'respect' and here is a list of the boy's relatives who have to be 'respected'. In a case I did for W, despite the high intensity and frequency with which the word 'respect' was buzzed into the heads of the bride's parents, it still took a while for the straightforward, simple couple to realize that to receive the barat with 'respect' did not mean just an elegant bow but the financial equivalent of a full body obeisance.

The milni ceremony is common in Punjab where corresponding male relatives of both families meet in a ceremonial bear hug and the girl's relative hands a gift to his counterpart. In the Sikh Punjab that I know, the charming remnant of the milni custom is a loi or a large shawl. Today there will also be an 'envelope' and other goodies, but the loi is a must, maybe due to the North Indian cold and the martial tradition of the hardy Sikhs on horseback. The light and flexible shawl provided warmth while riding with a gun or sleeping on the ground under a tree.

Traditionally, the girl was carried away on a palki, but the modern equivalent is the car bought by her father, into which her dowry, jewellery and clothes are packed. One groom had the good sense to feel some embarrassment about the naked avarice that dowry customs feed. So, he chose not to drive off in the car gifted by his father-in in-law but send for it the next day. I know another story where the car was not collected by the groom because he thought it below his 'standard'.

The next transaction is at the daughter's arrival to the marital family fold. Brides are expected to hand over their jewellery to the mother-in-law, ostensibly for safekeeping. Any desire to keep the jewellery with herself may be considered an insult, because it demonstrates mistrust and an unseemly assertion of independence.

After the wedding, every auspicious event, festival and birth is marked by gifts and money given to the groom and his family by the bride's parents. Obviously, not all of these can be counted as dowry, under the strict technical meaning of the term, but they point to the underlying feeling and philosophy of the marriage equation that gives rise to dowry. This is that we, the parents of this daughter, are most grateful that you have taken charge of her and we will do our best to ensure that she is not a financial burden to you. This carries on till the weddings of the next generation where the maternal family is expected to make the heaviest cash gift.

This insidious evil custom seeps through every class. Women suffer the most for it, as for them, the social security of being in a marriage is even more important than the financial. How likely is this, I thought, when coming across a reported case of a woman lawyer being brutalized by her lawyer husband and his family. They beat her with sticks and a belt, vilified and humiliated her, and she continued to suffer for the sake of 'her matrimonial life'.[4] I was repulsed by the idea and could not really believe that an empowered woman was allowing this to happen to her. But I had to rethink my initial scepticism when I met another young lawyer who also faced the consistent and persistent erosion of her persona by the family-in-law. She continued to suffer, believing that it was she who was failing them by not being subservient enough.

It is not difficult to guess that the lack of self-esteem at home, even amongst career women, is a problem deeper than the lack of individual self-confidence. Women fight a difficult battle every single day to retain their integrity and confidence against the shocking misogyny of their workplace: they look for comfort in their homes and become even more vulnerable when they don't find it there.

~

As the problem of violence and dowry demands increased, The Dowry Prohibition Act (1961) made the giving and taking of dowry a criminal offence, though voluntary wedding gifts listed under the signature or thumb impressions of the couple were exempted. The act is inert and passive. In 2012 there were 7,455 prosecutions and 673 convictions. I

4. Raj Kumar Khanna vs. State, 95 (2002) DLT 147

have never seen the list the act mandates, and the dowry problem still rages.

Long prior to this legislation, many regional customs served the same purpose as the lists required under the act, but these good protective customs have been jettisoned. As a child, I have a memory of a room in the wedding house glowing with the splendour of jewellery and poshak of the daj and vari displayed on velvet cushions. The older pieces of jewellery were wrapped in delicious stories recounted to us by aunts and old family retainers. The exhibition would then be listed in the handwriting of the mother of the bride and a member of the family-in-law. This custom is now dismissed as unfashionable and rustic by city-wallahs and I too found it gauche and garish till the wisdom of the signed list and display protocol struck me recently. A woman client claimed that her mother-in-law sent no vari to her parental home, but gave her jewellery on the day of the wedding reception party, only to take it back the same evening. Of course, this was difficult to prove.

On the Misuse of 498A

Soon after Section 498A was enacted, there was an outburst of apprehension that scheming vindictive families of the girl would misuse the law to extort settlements. Over time, many courts noticed and commented that indeed there was such a problem.[5] False complaints were filed against the husband and even the extended family was roped in to mount pressure. In a case, acting for H, I told W's lawyer, 'You have given my clients the moral handle they were looking for, by roping in the entire family. Now they are going to fight fiercely for their honour.' He thought for a moment and said, 'but I would have no case, without all of them in the fray.'

Yes, these laws are misused—just as all laws are. The bane of this country is the abuse of power by the new feudal lords—politicians, and the influential—to settle scores. So common is this that I am not in the least surprised that politicians across party fronts are united in their position that not only an accusation but even conviction of a criminal offence should not (while an appeal is pending) bar them from contesting elections, even if they are in jail at the time. The problem is that while a politician can use jail time as a career opportunity by becoming a martyr to a hazy cause, ordinary people view incarceration as causing irreversible

5. Preeti Gupta & Anr. vs. State of Jharkhand, 2010 (7) SCC 667; Smt. Sangeeta Kalra vs. State, 138 (2007) DLT 535; Savita Devi vs. Ramesh Chand, 2003 Cri LJ 2759

social damage. This is what makes 498A fearsome. Any ordinary family who has the misfortune of having a son in a bad marriage is vulnerable.

Even so, it is important not to let the misuse argument create scepticism about the cause of women that is benefited by this section acting as a deterrent against atrocities. The Supreme Court has discussed the danger of presuming misuse of 498A and advised effective filtration systems of robust police investigation to discard false complaints.[6]

Why is S. 498A misused?

Though I have appeared for many unfortunate men and their families who have suffered these complaints, let me consider a genuinely aggrieved woman: a young bride spends days and nights missing her parents' home and looks to her husband to support and protect her from overbearing intrusion by his family. Her effort at negotiating intimacy with her husband and acceptance into the family is a complex process: She must not be too independent; must not talk too much. Frequent conversations with her parents are called interference. She must excel in the kitchen. They magnanimously 'let' her work, but long hours in office are frowned upon. Her desire to go to parties is shocking; her desire to meet friends without her husband is suspect. If the first year goes by with no 'news', she is unworthy, as her basic purpose of child-bearing is not being realized. A lot is forgiven when a baby arrives; a lot more if she bears a son, but there never is a time when she is entirely without blame. Even without dowry demands or physical abuse, a family-in-law can radiate enough disapproval to create a painfully unhappy girl.

Such girls suffered silently and helplessly in the past. Now that they have legal remedies it is possible that they resort to these tactics fuelled by feelings of anger, disappointment and betrayal. Compound that with the desperation of such a girl being told that the end of a marriage is the death of her life, and her rage when she is invariably told that she should think of her 'fault' in this—maybe she did not 'adjust' enough.

I am only suggesting possibilities, but of course there is no one complete explanation. There never can be; the clients (husband or wife) always tell their story with conviction, but we need to be aware that often the truth is embellished by them. There is always a shade of extra or special pleading and we have to listen carefully for the true note in the clamour. As we work through such opaque situations towards fair resolutions, the client's

6. Sushil Kumar Sharma vs. Union of India (UOI) and Ors. AIR 2005 SC 3100

conduct exposes the lies s/he speaks. Let me explain how. While I write this, the anticipatory bail of a client (H) has been rejected in Bombay. The wife sent joyful messages to her friends in Delhi asking them to spread the word. To me, her happiness exposed her as shallow and vindictive: he was not a murderer. Her best case was that he was cruel because he ignored and demeaned her and he kept back her jewellery. That would certainly not be served better by his being denied bail.

Yet, upon careful thought, I did manage to understand a woman who felt slighted by her family-in-law and was now gleeful about them having to attend to her. I could not take that away.

I am not claiming to be more virtuous than her: I do dislike some people and do admit to slight malicious pleasure when they are troubled. But the lawyer in me knows how wrong a case can be, how trumped up, how lethal it is to be framed by accusations cooked in malice. When and if I see true retributive justice, I have never felt joyous, but am almost always sickened by the price of obtaining it and the cause that led to it. One can never feel glee.

How to deal with misuse is not to scrap 498A but to treat perjury as a serious offence. In a country where we have to shriek to be heard, it is no surprise that people tell lies for a day in court. Lies and crassness are the domain of public discourse and not limited to 498A.

False Charges

Police ineptitude and collusion with a woman's powerful father resulted in one of my friends being picked up on a false charge of Section 498A. He spent four nights in jail and it ended his career in a large financial consultancy.

He was arrested on a Friday. The wife used his credit card to buy a plane ticket to reach the UK that same night and approached the UK court saying her husband was a criminal. She obtained custody of the child and possession of his house in London. The matter carried on for a few years till my friend collapsed and gave her the house and patiently waited for the child to learn the truth.

Today he is married again to a strong, compassionate woman but she told me that he had great difficulty in telling her he had been to Tihar Jail. His apprehension of being misunderstood was not misplaced because my friend had lived through the inevitable caustic jibes of easy and cheap aphorisms like there can be no smoke without fire or that it takes both hands to clap, etc. These dreadful phrases have insidiously worked at destroying that marvellous principle called presumption of innocence, the value of which can only be understood by a lawyer or one wrongly accused.

A cautionary case

The intent to misuse can easily be prevented by intelligent investigators who can filter false complaints. Consider the following case where the husband and family could have been saved with a stronger, unbiased investigation and a bold judge.

I will break down a criminal complaint to analyse whether an offence under Section 498A should have been merited, even an FIR being lodged. The specifications were:

1. That the hotel bills for the honeymoon were paid by him from the cash gifts that they had received from the guests at the wedding.
2. Her jewellery, including stridhan and dowry articles, entrusted to her husband, mother-in-law and father-in-law at the time of the marriage at Delhi, had been misappropriated by the husband, mother-in-law, father-in-law and other family; it had not been returned.
3. She was subjected to cruelty on the pretext of not bringing sufficient dowry.
4. There was a fraud committed on her: She was not told that the husband suffered from depression.
5. He started pressuring her father for a partnership in the business.
6. On one occasion, he slapped her three times and pulled her hair.
7. He used to hit her till she was blue.
8. They wanted to take the child away from her.
9. He is an incompetent and careless father.
10. She still wanted to 'save the marriage' and the husband apologized and said he would 'mend his ways' but did not. (This is possible, but the argument is often used to condone delays in making complaints and so needs to be looked in the context of the timeliness of the complaint and what subsequent act prompted the initiation of proceedings.)
11. He 'assaulted' her brother for no rhyme or reason.
12. 'I almost became unconscious with the repeated uncontrolled physical beatings. I consulted various counsellors, a priest and psychiatrist and relationship specialist'.

Some of these are patently irrelevant: who pays for the hotel bills is as much a factor of social gender roles as of control over money. The husband's fitness to be a father is clearly not a matter of legal concern in this case.

Others indicate a breakdown of trust in the marriage, but not to the extent of a criminal offence. For example, the idea of him wanting a partnership in the family business was unlikely, since he was a successful professional, but not improbable. Even so, does an unpleasant conversation and disagreement become a criminal offence? Similarly, the point about depression may very well be true and full disclosure, particularly in an arranged marriage, should have been made to the wife—but how is it relevant to a criminal offence under Section 498A?

Another subset of accusations need to be taken seriously, but with a pinch of salt. For example, the overkill of including unnamed relatives and the father-in-law in stealing jewellery exposes the malice of the complaint and makes the entire allegation improbable. Similarly, the allegation that the in-laws wanted to take away the child is possible, especially as it was a boy, but the fact of the matter remained that the son was with her when the complaint was filed.

Finally, shorn of extraneous details, the matters of cruelty need to be addressed. Cruelty due to dowry demands is more than probable in any case, but the lack of detail is suspicious. As to the various assaults alleged upon her and her brother, no doctor is amongst those consulted and the worthy priests and psychiatrists are not named. When the police investigated, they should have asked for the names of psychiatrists and counsellors and verified her story about visits to them. They did not.

Much of the subsequent proceedings indicated biased or inept investigation, which we all know is at the centre of the rot in the criminal justice system. The Investigating Officer (IO) is normally a non-English-speaking person. As part of these proceedings, she filed a status report in fluent well-crafted English that mirrored the pleadings of the wife and the language of her posh lawyers. We suggested that the IO was not independent and also indicated some other lapses and contradictions to support our case but the High Court was not impressed.

Anticipatory bail to the husband's old parents was made contingent upon the son returning to India, which again created a hostage situation that is unfair to them. We could have challenged the order, but time was becoming of the essence and the family was getting stressed dealing with the underbelly of the workings of the legal system: the rage, malice, arbitrariness, hostility and suspicion.

My suggestion in such matters is that judges need to look up from their files and use some instinct in reading the demeanour of the persons before them and asking themselves: 'Who has drafted this report? Is it significant that the police status report is in language that is clearly beyond the vocabulary of the IO? Is it not likely that the IO is unfairly biased?' The assessment of the judges may be wrong, but they need to do this exercise. We lawyers do it as well.

While arguing in court, I once pointed out my client to a judge: who responded, 'Do you think I have X-ray vision? Why should I see him?' My humble tentative comment that demeanour should be noted earned a flickering, withering glance that my hapless client fought hard to counter without quailing.

Delays and denials of justice

In the Crime Against Women Cell, many complainants get impatient with what they see as the dilatory tactics of the husband. They then refuse dialogue and insist that FIRs be registered against the entire family-in-law. The husband, aged parents and married sisters living far away then scurry around for bail. The strategy is to undertake firefighting measures akin to a commando raid rather than a clear vision of what is required and needed. Thus, in civil cases: get the injunction and sit on it. Let the law take its course after that, which basically means for a long time. In criminal cases, get the bail and let the law take its own course after that, which basically means for such a long time that it may as well be forever. It is for this reason that a huge legal jurisprudence has developed around interim relief, rather than the legal outcomes of a trial.

~

In another case, H lived abroad and was called to participate in the investigation as a bail condition. He was worried about losing his job if his return was delayed. It was during a global recession and finance sector employees were particularly vulnerable in a cut-throat environment. I asked that the investigation be finished as quickly as possible because he only had a week off. The public prosecutor, smug and haloed like all prosecutors in the world, told me that I could not tell the police how to do their job. 'Your client is an accused after all,' he said 'and there is no reason why he should get special treatment only because he lives abroad.'

The prosecutor was somewhat within the margin of right, but an accused still retains the presumption of innocence and so deserves the treatment, consideration and accommodation that accompanies the presumption. But I held my peace, as is always sensible with prosecutors.

My client was due to return on the night of the 21st after attending the case that was listed on that day and I knew that the police were going to try and keep him hanging beyond that date.

To force some transparency of procedure, I advised my client to file an affidavit in court recounting the investigation. The substance was as follows:

> 'I informed the IO (Investigating Officer) of my arrival on the 14th. My counsel called the IO who asked him to come to A police station. When we reached there, we were told to go to B Police Chowki, and then we were asked to return to A. Finally the SHO (Station House Officer) met us and made inquiries about the cases pending between the families. This meeting was over in a few minutes.
>
> I was asked to come with sureties on the 20th. I said I was available all of the six days earlier and was the 20th not cutting it too fine, since I was scheduled to leave the next day. I was told that it is the convenience of the police that needed to be seen.
>
> When we reached on the 20th our presence was not marked. The SHO arrived late and asked us to come back with younger [!?!] sureties. [interjection mine]

When I insisted that the investigation be carried out, the SHO informed the counsel that it would be carried out by the 'Inspector Investigations' who was present at the police station at that time. The IO finally arrived at 1 p.m., and left immediately to get the requisite file. He returned at 2 p.m. By 2:20, the entire investigation was concluded. We were asked about the stridhan, and whether we had tried to settle the matter. The IO said that he would issue another notice under section 160 Cr. Pc for further investigation, but he would not record on my copy of the notice that my client was present for investigation. He had no other option but to accept (another) notice under section 160 Cr PC for investigation on 22nd (Sunday) for 11 a.m.

The 22nd date was given, despite my client saying that he was due to leave on the evening of the 21st. On the morning of the 21st, the judge read my client's affidavit and commented that the accused seemed to have been called on Sunday, 22nd, for no cause other than that he was due to leave a day earlier. The court allowed him to leave as scheduled and the Sunday investigation never happened.

~

H had to give up his life abroad because of a Red Corner Notice placed by Interpol on their website, under advice from the CBI, describing the husband as a fugitive wanted for prosecution and that he could be 'dangerous' and 'violent'. The notice mentioned that the alleged offences committed by him carried a punishment of ten years imprisonment.[7]

When this was challenged, the court observed, 'This must be an invention, [...] as far as IPC is concerned, the maximum punishment for offences under Section 498A & 406 of the IPC is up to three years imprisonment.'

The judgment quashing the Red Corner Notice came four years after it was challenged but the emotional cost cannot be calculated.

~

Feeling secure that there are now several checks and balances to counter hasty arrests, we sent two accused, the father and brother of the main accused, for their first meeting at the Crime Against Women Cell (CAWC which in this fast-forward abbreviated age is further abbreviated to a horrible CAW). Normally this is a preliminary procedure to get an overview of the case. The main accused, i.e. the husband, lived abroad. My clients were asked by the police officers to accompany them to the local police station. This they trustingly did without consulting us.

Once inside the station, the police would not let them leave till they called the main accused and asked him to withdraw the legal proceedings against his wife that he had validly instituted in the court of the foreign country he lived in.

~

In another case, drunken behaviour was alleged against someone whom I personally knew to be a teetotaler.

~

On the other hand, as this game is all about delaying or denying bail, I was pleasantly surprised when a wife's lawyer told me: please take bail; we don't want to waste time; I want you in trial. The husband settled.

~

The problem is not the law and the misuse of it but the skewed dynamics of its workings. This was driven home to me when a husband was refused bail by a court on the same day that it allowed bail to some builders of a construction project that collapsed, killing seventy-four people, three children amongst them.

---

7. Sumer Singh Salkan vs. Asstt. Director and Ors., (2010) ILR 6 Delhi 706, MANU/DE/1937/2010

Preventing Misuse

Criminal case salvos are generally fired in the intense heat of the inception of divorce proceedings. Judgments are replete with observations about the misuse of laws: strong observations against this malpractice;[8] warnings against it;[9] and, by the Supreme Court, blame placed equally on the lawyers.[10] Indeed, there were several tough rulings on the issue of how to deal with misuse.[11] The rationale behind the judgments was that vague omnibus type of complaints should be scrutinized with care and police should refrain from entertaining cases where the rules of the Dowry Prohibition Act, 1985[12] have not been complied with.

The High Courts began invoking their inherent powers to quash FIRs that did not make out a probable case.[13] The section and the law were in danger of being diluted till the Supreme Court restated the law and ruled

8. Savitri Devi vs. Ramesh Chand and Ors. 2003CriLJ2759

9. Manita Khurana vs. Indra Khurana, AIR 2010 Delhi 69

10. Preeti Gupta vs. State of Jharkhand, 2010 (7) SCC 667: 'The learned members have an enormous responsibility and obligation to ensure that the social fibre of family life is not ruined or demolished. They must ensure that exaggerated versions of small incidents should not be reflected in the criminal complaints. Majority of the complaints are filed either on their advice or with their concurrence. The learned members of the Bar who belong to a noble profession must maintain its noble traditions and should treat every complaint under section 498-A as a basic human problem and must make serious endeavour to help the parties in arriving at an amicable resolution of that human problem. They must discharge their abilities to ensure that social fibre, peace and tranquility of the society remains intact. The members of the Bar should also ensure that one complaint should not lead to multiple cases.'

11. Neera Singh vs. State, 138(2007) DLT 152: 'Now-a-days, exorbitant claims are made about the amount spent on marriage and other ceremonies and on dowry and gifts. In some cases claim is made of spending crores of rupees on dowry without disclosing the source of income and how funds flowed. I consider time has come that courts should insist upon disclosing source of such funds and verification of income from tax returns and police should insist upon the compliance of the Rules under Dowry Prohibition Act and should not entertain any complaint, if the rules have not been complied with.'

12. See p. 391: Rule 2 of The Dowry Prohibition Rules, 1985 (Maintenance of lists of presents to the bride and bridegroom)

13. Sangeeta Kalra vs. State, 138(2007)DLT 535: 'It is true while considering the quashing of criminal proceedings under Section 482 Cr.P.C., the Court should not embark upon an enquiry into the truthfulness of the allegations made by the

(Contd...)

that scope of misuse is no reason to invalidate a law. It disapproved of the activist comments by the High Courts on the issue of misuse, and said that such comments were more appropriate for workshops and seminars instead of judgments.[14]

To add to the filtration process to separate the truth from the lie as much as possible, government notifications have now made counselling a necessary prerequisite and an FIR is to be registered only when the possibilities for amicable resolution have failed. The Delhi High Court passed a series of guidelines for the police authorities to ensure protection from misuse of power to arrest at the behest of the complainant.[15]

Yes, there is misuse of enabling laws by women, but it is miniscule compared to the percentage of genuine cases. Also, often the complainant's cases are weakened due to incompetent or dishonest investigators of the police. As Indira Jaising notes, rather than being concerned about poor prosecutions, the court is more concerned about disgruntled wives.[16]

Misuse by men

The other side of the problem is the manipulation of the system by men who, as a gender, are stakeholders in a machismo-ridden police system. Many genuine cases are not registered for investigation. I have watched women pleading with the police that their complaints be registered. They are denied for a variety of reasons: they may be too poor, or just too ordinary or the wife of a very important or rich man.

While talking of misuse, please keep a sense of perspective about the frequency with which men manipulate the legal system and play out its

---

(Contd...)

complainant but where the charges are framed by the lower court without considering the material, with closed mind and charges amount to gross misuse of the criminal justice system and trial is an abuse it becomes the duty of the High Court to intervene in such cases, under Section 483 Cr.P.C. so that there is no miscarriage of justice and faith of people remains intact in the judicial system.' See also: Nidhi Kaushik vs. Union of India, MANU/DE/1306/2014 discussing a plethora of judgments on misuse.

14. Sushil Kumar Sharma vs. Union of India (UOI) and Ors. AIR 2005 SC 3100; See also: Sheoraj Singh Ahlawat & Ors vs. State of U.P., (2013) 11 SCC 476; Geeta vs. State of U.P., (2012) 10 SCC 741

15. Chander Bhan & Anr. vs. State, 151 (2008) DLT 691

16. Indira Jaising, 'Concern for the Dead, Condemnation for the Living' in *Economic and Political Weekly*, Vol-XLIX No. 30, 26 July 2014, p. 34

intrinsic delays in the legal system to financially exhaust their wives to submission. To protract proceedings, to make them expensive and tiring is also misuse. It is also misuse when false and frivolous cases are filed against women to embarrass them: she is accused of theft, abducting children or servants, stealing evidence, adultery with the chauffeur: cases against her family are registered so that it affects their business.

Conclusion

Courts have advised on methods of dealing with false cases. The investigations are not to be left unsupervised at lower level of police officers and all interviews with the complainant, accused and witnesses are to be recorded.[17] The reasons for registering FIRs must be noted and the details of the investigations given. Corroborating witness statements, for example from neighbours, may also be recorded as is done in any criminal investigations. But more is needed.

Maybe there could also be serious counselling by a pre-litigation mediation centre on the consequences of building false cases. Heavy costs and punishment for perjury would also be a deterrent.

A balanced perspective of an Indian 'woman' would also help—on the one hand, the Supreme Court makes the patronizing unbelievable statement that a woman can never lie[18] while on the other it believes that the only victims of vindictive litigation are husbands and their families! To lie and cheat and game the system is a human impulse and officers within the system have to learn how to sift and be committed to the cause of the important work they do. They are the life breath of civilization.

Once the system is cleaned of scope of manipulation, and we can say with confidence that it is unlikely that cheaters will prosper in court, we can return to the silly debate about whether laws should be diluted because they are being misused.

---

17. Arnesh Kumar v. State of Bihar, AIR 2014 SC 2756; Chander Bhan & Anr. vs. State, 151 (2008) DLT 691

18. Wahid Khan v. State of Madhya Pradesh, (2010) 2 SCC 9

10. THE UNIFORM CIVIL CODE

Article 44 of the Constitution says: 'The state shall endeavour to secure for the citizens a uniform civil code throughout the territory of India.' This is one of the Directive Principles of state policy in Part Four of the Constitution. Directive principles are just that: principles to help navigate governance towards an ideal state.

Presently, each community—Hindu,[1] Christian, Muslim, Parsi and Jewish is governed by its personal law that, even if codified, is nevertheless an amalgam of custom drawn from religion and culture. Tribals are also governed by their own customary laws. Personal laws have come to be treated by communities as part of their cultural identity, given that the laws have emerged and are closely intertwined with their society, which they believe is ordered by their religion. Thus, they are seen to determine much more than the legal rights they delineate.

Whether personal laws count as law within the meaning of Article 13 of the Constitution[2] is the vexed question currently. Some would argue that they do not, and so cannot have constitutional protection, while others claim that they do, and are a part of the right to a cultural and religious identity. Family law emanates from personal laws. A book on family law—on how the way it works is a reflection of society, even while it strives to move to the ideal—must necessarily encompass a discussion on the Uniform Civil Code (UCC), which is the constitutional aspect of this subject.

~

'Uniform' is often used interchangeably with 'common' when talking about the civil code, and therein lies the first problem. The difference is not merely semantic.[3] A uniform civil code envisages uniformity of laws amongst various communities relating to marriage, divorce and succession. A common civil code however, envisages one code for all.

1. The Hindu community includes Buddhists, Jains and Sikhs and any other community that is not Parsi or of Abrahamic origin, or a tribal community.

2. See p. 355; Article 13 Constitution of India: Laws inconsistent with or in derogation of the fundamental rights

3. Vasudha Dhagamwar, *Towards the Uniform Civil Code*, p. 71

The call for reforms to personal laws has mainly been in the context of women's rights. For example, women have rights in the properties of their husbands and fathers under Islamic law, but Hindu law only gave a woman partial rights in her father's share in his ancestral property in 1956 and equal rights in her father's coparcenary property were granted to her as late as 2005.[4] A Hindu person has absolute unfettered rights in self-acquired property. Hindu and secular marriage law subscribes to the separate property regime, which means that there is no inherent right in a spouse's property.

Islamic law gives no power to disinherit a family member, since the law defines the shares of each member of the family, and the ratio and manner of succession is defined as well, providing that no person can make a bequest of more than one third of their property. Even so, a Muslim has free right of gift or hiba. A Hindu on the other hand is free to bequeath or gift his/her entire property.

The power of free dealings in property erodes rights women may have in either community. Both communities have perpetuated patriarchy using the loophole of bequest or gift to benefit sons. In the same way, though Christian law allows for equal shares between sons and daughters, it too gives the owner complete power to transfer to sons by will or gift.

The differences between personal laws of each community also reflect their different approaches to family structures and degrees of consanguinity acceptable in a marriage. Forms and types of marriage are also the realm of personal law. Christian marriage law is monogamous; Hindu law made polygamy illegal only in 1956 and Islamic law in India continues to be polygamous.

While Islamic law considers relations with a woman who is not a wife as 'haram', classical Hindu law gave a woman living with a man rights of concubinage which were lost in codified Hindu law. The secular PWDV Act has developed some rights for live-in relationships that were trivialized by the Supreme Court when a judge referred to such a woman as a 'keep'.[5]...That damage fortunately was undone by a subsequent judgment of Indra Sarma v. V.K.V. Sarma,[6] which we will discuss later. Yet, a wife living in adultery loses her right of maintenance under all

4. Some states gave it earlier because succession is in the concurrent list of the Constitution.

5. D. Velusamy vs. D. Patchaiammal, AIR 2011 SC 479

6. Indra Sarma vs. V.K.V. Sarma, AIR 2014 SC 309

personal laws.[7] Hindus did not permit widows to remarry but that has never been an issue under Islamic law.

Personal laws also underpin the concept of marriage (and by extension, of divorce) in any community: Hindus, Christians and Parsis treat marriage as sacred, while under Islamic and Hebrew law it is contractual.[8]

Thus, contrary to what any religious fundamentalist may say, it is apparent that no personal law is superior to the other and all religions are patrilocal. Calls for reform thus cannot ignore the reforms required in the personal laws of all communities to achieve meaningful gender justice.

Reconciling Religious Rights with the UCC Directive

The Directive Principles of State Policy are non-justiciable rights and consequently not law. The idea was borrowed from the Irish Constitution. No law can be struck down on the ground that it does not further a Directive Principle, and thus no Directive can be enforced by court. [9]

The pivotal point is government reform can follow the Directives, but not at the expense of the basic structure of the Constitution, which is inviolable. The operative word in Article 44 is *endeavour.*

The debate is about the method of dovetailing UCC into any community without compromising its religious and cultural integrity.

The Supreme Court has developed the 'essential ingredients' doctrine to maintain freedom of religion even while stripping away regressive customs and rituals or redressing gender and caste biases.[10] The doctrine envisages an analysis of the religion, to arrive at the kernel of it, while discarding its regressive elements. Under this lens, while personal laws may have evolved from religion, it can be argued that they do not form an essential ingredient in the practice of any religion. Thus, there should be no problem in reforming them to be in consonance with the principles of gender equality and give force to the Directive to have the same laws for all, regardless of religion.

This is a reasonable position, but in practice it is a complex and delicate

7. Under Section 125(4) of the Cr.P.C., a wife loses her right of maintenance if she is living in adultery as opposed to adulterous act(s) under the classical law.

8. See Ch. 1: Marriage and Divorce Construct, p. 17

9. See p. 357: Article 37 of the Constitution of India; See also: Seervai, *Constitutional Law of India*

10. The Commissioner, Hindu Religious Endowments, Madras vs. Sri Lakshmindra Thirtha Swamiar of Sri Shirur Mutt, AIR 1954 SC 282

exercise, made much more difficult by those who have made the uniform civil code debate into an inflammable topic. Their relentless promotion of it is viewed by others as an overzealous commitment to the code. After all, why should the UCC directive (as also the ban on cow slaughter nowadays) be given preference over other Directive Principles?[11] Most importantly, there is no draft under discussion, though the Law Commission has been instructed to 'examine' the matter—the call for implementing a UCC that does not as yet exist seems highly premature.

As a result, feminists who would otherwise strongly favour a UCC are cautious about finding themselves on the same side as, for example, a Hindu right-wing proponent of a uniform civil code. The feminist position is in harmony with the constitutional basic structure, which indicates that a uniform civil code must not be imposed at the expense of giving up cultural pluralism. Most feminists understand that the rights of religious minorities are a fundamental part of the Constitution. Nivedita Menon, for example, strongly opposes the Hindu right's call for a uniform civil code in the following terms: 'talk of (UCC) has nothing to do with gender justice. It has entirely to do with a nationalist Hindu agenda and is right up there with the beef ban and the temple in Ayodhya'.[12]

The Hindu right has neglected to express any thoughtfulness in their call for the imposition of a uniform civil code to counter this position. Mr Vankaiah Naidu of the BJP has recently written an article by way of assurance to the Muslim community, quoting Gandhi to say that all religions must co-exist and a 'common' civil code will help 'gender justice'.[13] He does not explain why gender justice cannot be achieved by internal reform within each community. He cites only Muslim women who have been denied 'Qur'anic rights' and rights under the Indian Constitution. He complains as if patriarchal laws that need to be redressed only exist in the Muslim community. He does not acknowledge that Hindu law suffers many similar anomalies created by patriarchy, notwithstanding amendments to Hindu law, which are discussed later.

Thus, it cannot be emphasized enough that the UCC is not necessarily

11. I will not comment on the directive to ban cow slaughter because that takes the argument away from family law and even the welfare state.

12. Menon, 'It isn't about women' in *The Hindu*, 15 July 2016; Menon also says that the Portuguese (Goan) Civil Code should not be taken as the model for a UCC as it is not gender friendly and also has a lot of exceptions for Hindus only.

13. Naidu, 'Why not a Common Civil Code for All' in *The Hindu*, 16 July 2016

limited to having one code for all, but extends to reform in all communities. The UCC is about much more than politicians have even considered: it is about equality on every front that will dislocate power centres from perpetuating male control over generations. Simultaneously, the UCC debate has to be given a place that does not threaten the multiple religious influences and diverse personal laws that are unique to India.

The Historical Case for a Uniform Civil Code

Pre-Independence

As the British East India Company inched its way onto the subcontinent, it needed to create some rudimentary system of justice to manage the ruled and sustain its power amongst them. Thus, its focus was on codifying criminal and commerical law. In 1858, following the brutal suppression of the Revolt of 1857, Queen Victoria proclaimed India to be her direct dominion, saying:

> 'We know, and respect, the feelings of attachment with which the Natives of India regard the lands inherited by them from their Ancestors; and We desire to protect them in all rights connected therewith, subject to the equitable demands of the State; and we will that generally, in framing and administering the law, due regard be paid to the ancient rights and customs of India.'[14]

Following the proclamation, British settlement officers began recording various customs to create a source of law that could form the core of the new Anglo-Indian legal system. While trying to adapt Indian custom and law to fit into the colonial framework of law, the English judges filled gaps in their understanding of various laws in India with their idea of justice embodied in the common-law principle of 'Justice, Equity and Good Conscience' (JEGC). The resultant amalgam became a uniquely Indian common law.[15] However, marriage, succession and property rights were left to the 'personal' laws[16] of each community. Thereafter,

---

14. *Proclamation by the Queen to the Princes, Chiefs, and the People of India, 1858*, available at http://www.sdstate.edu/projectsouthasia/loader.cfm?csmodule=security/getfile&pageid=861653

15. Setalvad, *The Hamlyn Law Lectures On Common Law*, p. 18, 25

16. Balwant Rao v. Baji Rao, AIR 1921 Pc 59; The Collector of Madura vs. Mootoo Ramalinga Sathupathy, (1868) 20 Er 389; Neelkisto Deb Burmono vs. Beerchunder Thakoor, (1869) 20 Er 436

any reform-based legislation in the colonial period was at the behest of forward-thinking members of each community.[17]

The Indian Succession Act (1860, 1881 and 1925) covered Indian Christians,[18] Europeans and the British who lived in India. However, amalgamation of many legal concepts led to members of other communities also adopting certain aspects of these laws. This is apparent in the adoption of the idea of a will into codified Hindu law from English law—Hindu classical law was bound by the rights of the members of the joint family, and did not recognize wills, or even gifts of property. Even rights of alienation of joint property were limited to special circumstances of need and benefit of the entire family. Now, this concept is commonly used by men to make bequests to male heirs to the exclusion of daughters.

Muslims had lobbied for the Shariat Act in 1937 to unite followers of Islamic law and remove regional customs that they saw as contrary to Islamic tenets. However, rather than imposing the Shariat Act on all Muslims, the act allowed individual Muslim communities to opt whether to be governed by it. The Cutchee Memons, for example, did not opt for the Shariat till much later.

Hindu law continued to be entirely custom-based, with regional variations, except the instance of codification by the Princely State of Baroda. Hindu law was not codified for the country till 1956.[19] Thus, the Hindu Mitakshara and Dayabhaga laws of succession, followed in most of the north and the east, were unknown in Punjab, which was governed by customs around an agrarian society. B.S. Mann,[20] during the debate on Hindu Code Bill said, 'we do not know any Manu in the Punjab.' The matrilineal system in the south amongst the Nairs and Namboodris also had no connection with Manu.

To suit their needs for administrative purposes, the British introduced a criminal law and several civil statutes, such as The Evidence Act and The

17. Dhagamvar, *Towards the Uniform Civil Code*: 'Acts that were passed: Suttee Regulation, xxvii of 1829, Caste Disabilities Removal Act, 1850, Hindu Widow's Remarriage Act, 1856, The Hindu Gainful Employment Act, 1930, Muslim Personal Law (Shariat) Application Act, 1937, Dissolution of Muslim Marriages Act, 1939, Parsi Marriage and Divorce Act, 1936, Native Converts Marriage Dissolution Act, 1866, Indian Divorce Act, 1869, Indian Christian Marriage Act, 1872'

18. Mary Roy vs. State of Kerala, 1986 SCR (1) 371

19. Baroda Hindu Nibandh 1937 and the Gains of Learning Act, 1930.

20. See Ch. 2: Decoding Gender, p. 57

Contract Act. They however were concerned about disturbing religious sentiments and deep custom.

The other explanation for leaving personal laws untouched is that it suited the colonial powers to maintain distinct communities. Dr Romila Thapar argues that the colonial rulers scrambled together various religions to form a monolithic Hinduism and a monolithic Islam that confronted each other, which allowed them to maintain their hold on colonial power. This perception of the relationship between the two religions, Thapar says, was a 'departure from existing religious self-perceptions'.[21]

The unquestioning acceptance of these newly-created perceptions she argues, has led to a distorted perspective of who and what we are today and the consequent problem of fractured and confused identities. The imposition of a UCC on to a people still seething over post-colonial confused identities will only exacerbate rather than help the ailment.

Independence

The beginning of the freedom movement brought to the fore the varying perspectives and conflicting claims of India's diverse cultural identities. Gandhi and Ambedkar were powerful commentators on the problem of communal and caste identity faced by modern India, but with strong differences on how to deal with it.

Ambedkar's strategy was to fast-forward the nation's trajectory by killing the weeds of oppressive custom that abounded in the old social order. He warned that the process would be difficult, because India was not used to parliamentary democracy and Indians needed to be educated to meet its challenges. He wanted to use the freedom movement as a forum for that education, perhaps believing that the nation would be more responsive to reform across all communities while united against a common enemy.

Gandhi, on the other hand, was apprehensive that the focus of Ambedkar's movement could distract and delay from the actual gaining of freedom from British rule. He also had strong reservations about tampering with issues of religious identity in an already seething subcontinent.

The core reasons for the differences between Gandhi and Ambedkar were many. Scholars now are pointing to their different castes as an important reason.[22] Gandhi was an upper caste Hindu and Ambedkar,

---

21. Romila Thapar, *The Public Intellectual in India*, pp. xvi-xix, xxxiv

22. Arundhati Roy, 'The Doctor and the Saint' in *The Annihilation Of Caste*

a Dalit. Both men began their foray into politics with a train journey. Gandhi's train journey in South Africa is well known and he was a lawyer by then. Ambedkar's significant train journey was as a child, travelling with his brothers and sisters from Mahar to Goregaon to meet their father. They were carrying food cooked by their mother, but could not eat over the two-day journey because no one would give them water to drink with their meal.

Both Gandhi and Ambedkar studied law in the UK. Gandhi travelled as the son of a successful businessman, while Ambedkar went on a scholarship. From the UK, after completing his studies, Gandhi went on to South Africa where he developed the non-violent form of protest that he later used in India. Ambedkar returned to Bombay and set up a practice as an advocate for Dalit interests.

Gandhi arrived in India in 1914. As the momentum of the freedom movement accelerated under his charismatic influence (his worst critics cannot take that away from him), he developed a one-point agenda of freedom from British rule. He advised that all other caste and communal issues that were emerging in the simmering nation should be dealt with after the British left.

Gandhi's philosophy for the soon-to-be free India was to return to the village to discover her roots as a nation. His persona became that of a Mahatma, whose politics were fuelled by the common morality of all religions. Focus on the good in all religions and you will find they are the same,[23] he said: hence his favourite prayer, *Ishawar Allah tero naam, sabko sammati dey bhagwan*. He was against the caste system and was committed to Hindu reform, but all said and done, he was without a doubt a Hindu in thought and deed.

Ambedkar on the other hand, was emerging as a national hero who hated Hindus, but was not Muslim, Sikh, Christian, Jewish or Parsi. In 1928, he told the Simon Commission, 'It does not matter whether I call myself Hindu or non-Hindu, as long as I am outside the pale of the Hindu community.'[24] In 1935, he announced at a public forum: 'I will not die a Hindu'.[25] For the Congress, Ambedkar renouncing Hinduism was one thing, but the possibility of him leading by example mass conversions of lower-caste Ambedkarites to Islam was cause for high anxiety. Ambedkar eventually converted to Buddhism, along with many followers.

23. Long, *A Vision For Hinduism: Beyond Hindu Nationalism*, p. 114

24. Keer, *Dr Ambedkar: Life And Mission*, p. 118

25. Jadhav (Ed), *Ambedkar Speaks*, p. 275

Gandhi was assassinated in 1948. Ambedkar continued to steer the constituent assembly through the task of framing the Constitution.

~

The structure of the Constitution amalgamated the Westminster Parliament system and borrowed from the American Constitution to produce a unique framework of law—one that is great in its simple commitment to absolute values of equality, and complex in creating a legal system to maintain and sustain those values. History for the Constitution-makers was not an encumbrance, but a direction to follow the process of organic social change that allows for individual mobility to break through culture and class barriers, all the while strengthening democratic institutions.

At the constitutional assembly debate on a uniform civil code in 1948, Mr Naziruddin Ahmed sought to address the democratic process followed, by suggesting that a proviso be added to the Directive: 'Provided that the personal law of any community which has been guaranteed by the statute shall not be changed except with the previous approval of the community ascertained in such manner as the Union Legislature may determine by law.'[26] Mr Ahmed clarified that he did not wish to confine his remarks to the inconvenience felt by the Muslim community alone.[27]

Given the current furore on the issue of polygamy in Islam, it is relevant that prior to 1956, Hinduism too was polygamous, without a limit of four wives. Interestingly, Dr S.P. Mookherjee, who had left the Congress to form the right-wing nationalist party, the Bhartiya Jana Sangh, opposed monogamy amongst Hindus, saying: 'So far as monogamy is concerned, I shall support it with one reservation. Make it applicable to all citizens of India' He went on to say that the government would never pass a separate law about it because it '...dare not touch the Muslim community'. Clearly, for him, the reform's benefit to women was not the point; rather, it was a communal issue.

Dr Ambedkar was aware of the apprehension that minorities had about the UCC affecting their rights of cultural identity and wrote an assurance:

> 'I quite realize their feelings in the matter, but I think they have read rather too much into Article 35[28], which merely proposes that the State shall

26. See *Constituent Assembly of India Debates (Proceedings)*, Volume VII, available at http://164.100.47.132/lssnew/constituent/vol7p11.html

27. *Ibid*; See p. 365: Article 19 of the Constitution of India: Protection of certain rights regarding freedom of speech, etc.

28. See Article 31 in the Draft Constitution on the UCC

endeavour to secure a civil code for the citizens of the country. It does not say that after the Code is framed, the State shall enforce it upon all citizens merely because they are citizens.'

He recommended that it was possible that a future Parliament would make a provision to begin the implementation of the uniform civil code by making it voluntary, in the same way as the Shariat Act of 1937 was adopted:

> 'The law said that here is a Shariat law which should be applied to Mussulmans provided a Mussulman who wanted that he should be bound by the Shariat Act should go to an officer of the state, make a declaration that he is willing to be bound by it, and after he has made that declaration the law will bind him and his successors.'[29]

The following words encapsulate his position and present-day politicians would do well to remember them:

> 'Sovereignty is always limited, no matter even if you assert that it is unlimited, because sovereignty in the exercise of power must reconcile itself to the sentiments if different communities. No government can exercise its power in such a manner as to provoke the Muslim community to rise in rebellion. I think it would be a mad government if it did so. But that is a matter that relates to exercise of power but not the power itself.'[30]

~

One of the arguments often made is that if Hindus could accept changes to their personal laws, then why not the other communities. As always, the situation was much more complicated. The Hindu Code Bill had in fact been rejected as too radical, after which Ambedkar resigned.

Apart from its attempt to achieve some gender equality, there was concern around the definition of what constituted 'Hindu.' Non-Hindus (apart from Muslims, Christians, Jews and Parsis) were co-opted into mainstream Hindu law, as their religions did not prescribe special laws and, in any case, they shared a custom base with Hindus. Ambedkar's reasoning for this decision is instructive, as played out in this exchange:

> Dr Ambedkar: '...Now, it might be said that in making this Bill the Government has a political motive, namely, to absorb these non-descript people into the Hindu community so to say, by a side door. That is not our purpose at all, because you will see from the proviso what we are

---

29. Dr Ambedkar in Constituent Assembly of India Debates (Proceedings), Volume VII, available at http://164.100.47.132/lssnew/constituent/vol7p11.html

30. Tahir Mahmood, *Uniform Civil Code: Fictions and Facts*, p. 124

doing. The Hindu Code will apply to them only if it is proved that Hindu customs and Hindu usages are prevalent in that class; otherwise, they are free to do whatever they like…'

Professor Ranga: 'Can they opt themselves out?'

Dr Ambedkar: 'Once they have adopted the customs and so on, they are in; otherwise they are out. […] With regard to the question whether this Bill should apply to persons or communities other than Hindus in the strict sense of the word […] There are religions, which have as their part a legal system, which you cannot sever from those religions. There are religions, which have no legal system at all, which are just pure matters of creed. The peculiarity about the Hindu religion, as I understand it, is this, that it is the one religion, which has got a legal framework integrity associated with it. Now, it is very necessary to bear this thing in mind, because if one has a proper understanding of this, it would not be difficult to understand why Sikhs are brought under the Hindu religion, why Buddhists are brought under the Hindu religion and why Jains are brought under the Hindu religion. When the Buddha differed from the Vedic Brahmins, his difference was limited to matters of creed. The Buddha did not propound a separate legal system for his own followers; he left the legal system as it was, it may be that the legal system that then prevailed was a good system; that it had no blemishes and no faults. So, he did not direct his attention to making any changes in the legal system in consequence of the changes that he introduced in certain religious notions.'[31]

The Hindu Acts appropriated non-Hindus (Sikhs, Buddhists, Jains and all those who are not Muslims, Christians or tribals), thereby creating a false notion of a national majority. There are many Sikhs and Buddhists who want to be free of Hindu law.[32] B.S. Mann during the discussion on the Hindu Code Bill said, 'I am not a Hindu, I have never followed the Hindu law. I am constrained to say that this is a conversion law for Sikhs.'[33] Seventy years later, the Sikhs, Buddhists and Jains are protesting against this assimilation into Hindu Law, and now the political ramifications of a UCC are even more serious than before because India has regressed on the issue of communal politics.

---

31. http://www.ambedkar.org/ambcd/64b1.on%20the%20hindu%20code%20bill.htm.

32. Ambedkar's response to this criticism is mentioned later; See Birender Kaur vs. Union of India C.W.P. No. 18634 of 2011 challenging the inclusion of Sikhs under the term 'Hindus'.

33. http://www.ambedkar.org/ambcd/64b1.on%20the%20hindu%20code%20bill.htm.

Modern India

Analyzing this regressive turn, the economist Mueller notes that success in improving the welfare of India's population has led to increasing voter participation since Independence. Quoting Zakaria,[34] he says that increased voter participation has meant lower education levels on average, resulting in an India that

> 'has become less tolerant, less secular, less law-abiding, less liberal [...] India was a much better run and more liberal country during the early years of its democracy when voter turnouts were low than it is today with greater political participation.'[35]

The observation is incomplete in that the same can be said of the electorates of Mr Mueller's and Mr Zakaria's parts of the world, as is seen from the recent Brexit vote and the high anxiety about the next US president. Most of all, the observation underestimates the political acumen of the Indian voter. The recent Bihar elections have established that people want to vote for development without making a Faustian bargain at the cost of pandering to Hindu religious fundamentalism.

The problem in India is not the average voter, but the politicians. All of them. The new incumbents want a Hindu state, which is against the Constitution. But many, even from the old dispensation, and others who have lived in the corridors of power and occupied high office in every branch of the state, support this position and make muscular majoritarian statements... equivocal or not in various degrees, but always dangerous and manipulative. The difference is that the earlier facades have been ripped away. The choices are limited, but we carry on because the average voter of the sort that Mr Mueller and Mr Zakaria denigrate in a patronizing fashion exposes these shenanigans and insists on something more. An 'uneducated' man as perhaps pictured by Mr Zakaria and Mr Mueller may speak of the 'Ganga Jamuna' pluralistic tradition and culture of his social milieu.

Given the current political environment, an aggressive drive to promote a uniform civil code will be seen as an attempt to decimate the cultural and ethnic identities of minorities by inflaming the voter (who, however canny, may be prone to be illiberal if frightened by the bogey of the power of the minorities) towards a majoritarian attitude.

---

34. Fareed Zakaria, *The Future of Freedom: Illiberal Democracy at Home and Abroad*, p. 106

35. Dennis C. Mueller, *Reason, Religion And Democracy*, p. 259

Cultural diversity is unique to our history and one of the great achievements of our republic is that it has managed to sustain it thus far. The tidy egalitarianism that the uniform civil code seeks to achieve cannot be faulted as a vision, just as no fault can be found in any other Directive, such as legal aid, environment protection and so on. However, it is more practical to give priority to other Directives, like education, which in turn will prepare the nation for a uniform civil code.

Why Implement a UCC?

The arguments in favour of a uniform civil code are:

1. If the Hindus could adopt a common law in 1956, why can't the other communities do the same?
2. All women would benefit from the uniform civil code.

The fallacy of the first argument is apparent when you consider the following:

a) It is incorrect to say that Hindus have a common law. In 1956, the existing law in portions of North India was codified to form a compendium of four statutes that constitute codified Hindu law. It might be useful to consider that the bullying parochialism displayed by the northern states even against other Hindus in other parts of the country is what makes other minorities apprehensive about the agenda behind a uniform civil code.

b) In 1956, under Hindu law, equal inheritance rights in property did not guarantee daughters equal ownership of property because fathers retained the power to transfer their shares in coparcenary property to their sons by will or gift. The amendment of 2005, which makes women coparceners in joint family property, benefits only those women who are members of a joint Hindu family or families where there is coparcenary property. That is about 18 per cent of the Hindu families,[36] and so the amendment is inconsequential in the larger picture.

c) That Ambedkar's original bill was rejected indicates that it is not a spirit of reform that drove the Hindu Code Bill in 1956. According to Madhu Kishwar, Parliament eventually passed a watered-down version, in deference to the lobbies of the business

36. 'Several States in North India Cling on to Joint Families' in *The Hindu*, 16 March 2012

> community that wanted to mobilize land banks locked in various joint family claims by enabling individuals to liquidate property under the new law.[37] The same could well be said of the 2005 amendment, since that will also liquidate valuable assets when daughters ask for their rights in traditional homesteads.[38]

As to the second argument, the feminist view on the benefit to women from a UCC is more measured, because it is sensible to the ground reality that the backlash of imposing a uniform civil code on a restless nation divided on communal fronts will be horribly destructive. In fact, such a move will be playing into the hands of a vote-bank-building political strategy of polarizing the nation along communal lines.

~

The implementation of the UCC by Parliament has been difficult due to these counter-arguments, but political forces get an impetus from the judiciary each time it calls for the UCC. The Supreme Court has on several occasions called for a UCC even though it cannot insist that the government pass such a law.[39]

In the Sarla Mudgal case, the Supreme Court directed the government to file an affidavit stating the steps being taken to implement the uniform civil code. At the time, jurist H.M. Seervai commented that since the Directive Principles are not law, being unenforceable under Article 37, the judges were violating their oath to uphold the Constitution. 'This', he said, 'is all together apart from the difficulties which would be faced in introducing a uniform civil code amongst communities which are governed by widely different personal laws governing their civil rights.'[40]

In 2015, the Supreme Court ruled on an interpretation of the 2005 amendment of the Hindu Succession Act but ended its judgment by again directing that a Public Interest Litigation petition be filed on the matter of a uniform civil code.[41]

---

37. Kishwar, *Codified Hindu Law*, pp. 2145-2161

38. *Ibid*

39. Sarla Modgul vs. Union of India 1995 AIR 1531; Mohd. Ahmed Khan vs. Shah Bano Begum AIR 1985 SC 945; Agnes alias Kunjumol vs. Regeena Thomas 2011(1) Klt588; Jordan Dengdieh vs. S.S. Chopra, AIR 1985 SC AIR 935; State of Bombay vs. Narasu Appa Mali, AIR 1952 Bom 84

40. Seervai, *Constitutional Law of India*, p. 1923

41. Prakash vs. Phulvati, 2015(11)Scale643

What Seervai noted in 1995 continues to be the position now. The matter is one of identity, formed by custom and usage, which is a mixture of religion and culture. Religious and cultural freedom are both guaranteed under the Constitution. The gender aspect, which is actually what the UCC is supposed to be about, is just not allowed to have full play in any discourse.

From Courtrooms to Drawing Rooms

Any meaningful discussion on a new law must factor in *realpolitik* for it to be effective. Writing against the impositions of alien laws on an unprepared society, the nineteenth-century jurist Sauvigny wrote: 'Law is first developed by custom and popular faith, next by judicial decisions—everywhere, therefore, by internal silently operating powers, not by the arbitrary will of the law giver.'[42]

Doctors and lawyers dread drawing-room conversations about health and legal problems. The pressure is even more horrible when people want to harangue you about political generalities and expect you to sing for your supper with general 'gyaan' on the law around a political issue. I call it a harangue, because it is almost never a discussion where people are willing to look at other perspectives or say they have none and see where each perspective leads. These harangues are hysterical, emotional and wearisome. Television debates are the model.

I dread drawing rooms packed with serious people who want to change the country that very evening; this is what I call drawing-room politics disorder. Geographical proximity to Race Course Road deludes people in Delhi into thinking they are on intimate terms with power, and any discussion is largely governed by personal views on religion and gender rather than the politics of inclusiveness that are the cornerstone of the Constitution. Pompousness and hypocrisy may be easy to walk away from, but what fills one with misery and dread are callous, mindless statements that can be downright dangerous. The air smoulders with conspiracy theories, frustration and anger. Any discussion about a uniform civil code exemplifies all this.

At parties, feminists and other supporters of the uniform civil code, primed with the one drink too many, will pin me to the wall with accusations about all the bad things I represent, as a lawyer thriving on the untidy state of our personal laws. The feminist argument is that

42. https://www.britannica.com/biography/friedrich-karl-von-savigny

women of all communities should have equal rights, since gender equality must transcend all personal law, which is essentially as patriarchal as the religious orders it has sprung from. Interestingly, no political party has committed to dismantling patriarchy as such, even though the push for a uniform civil code is seemingly driven by the need to have better rights for women.

Others seem driven by a love of neatness and order. 'So many laws,' they say. 'What nonsense! We should all be equal and that's it. What's wrong with it? How nice and orderly if we could have a uniform civil code.' Their argument for a uniform civil code is that it is a desirable state of affairs to have predictable order, with one civil law for all communities, and the furtherance of the Directive Principles. This otherwise reasonable debate about the uniform civil code becomes dubious when you notice that other Directive Principles, that all will agree are laudable, do not become the subject of impassioned drawing-room debates, in this manner.

That there should be a uniform civil code where all personal laws give equal rights to all women is laudable, but the drawing-room debate is about the method of getting there. The method includes the timing. The current search for the true Hindutva culture generally suffers, if not a strong anti-Muslim bias, at least an unfair suspicion of Muslims. At present, the logic of seeking a uniform civil code seems nothing more than the idea that since Hindus have somewhat reformed their personal law, so must the minorities (read Muslims). This position indicates that there is a belief that Muslim women should have the same rights as Hindu women, but the proponents of this position choose to ignore that this approach does not have the support of Muslim women whose lot they want to ameliorate. The suspicion is that in pushing for a uniform civil code, the true motive is not to benefit women, but to eliminate the voice of the minorities.

'That is too much!' and 'very unfair', uniform civil code supporters may protest. But I will make good this statement by establishing that this view has infiltrated areas that must necessarily be secular spaces, as guaranteed by the Constitution. Even the Supreme Court has mostly commented on the need for a uniform civil code while ruling on the rights of Hindu women,[43] implying that other women would benefit from it as Hindu women are doing.

---

43. ABC vs. State (NCT Of Delhi), AIR 2015 SC 2569; Prakash and Ors. vs. Phulavati and Ors., 2015(11) Scale 643

To my drawing-room attackers, I say you have not thought through the danger of compromising on cultural and religious pluralism. I agree that all personal laws are biased against women, but I do not advocate achieving gender equality by imposing a uniform civil code at the expense of compromising democratic processes and the loss of cultural pluralism that so far has been the basic Indian ethos. 'We are not ready *yet*,' I say to both groups, trying to calm them down. 'It's not even seventy years since Independence. Festina lente—hurry slowly, as Amartya Sen says.[44] You will see that we are moving towards it, and we will move faster in that direction if you would focus on other things.' A natural consequence of greater education, for example, will be a greater inclination for all communities (not just the minorities) to introspect about matters of reform and gender equality.

Legal nuances of the UCC argument

We have established that a pro-Hindu (or often, an anti-Muslim) bias has infiltrated many areas that must remain liberal and secular circles as constitutionally sacrosanct. In any case, many occupying such spaces do not consider even the legal complexities of the problem. Consider the following observation by Justice Kuldip Singh in the Sarla Mudgal case:[45]

> 'Article 44 is based on the concept that there is no necessary connection between religion and personal law in a civilised society. Article 25 guarantees religious freedom whereas Article 44 seeks to divest religionfrom social relations and personal law. Marriage, succession and like matters of a secular character cannot be brought within the guarantee enshrined under Articles 25, 26 and 27. The personal law of the Hindus, such as relating to marriage, succession and the like have all a sacramental origin, in the same manner as in the case of the Muslims or the Christians. The Hindus along with Sikhs, Buddhists and Jains have forsaken their sentiments in the cause of the national unity and integration, some other communities would not, though the Constitution enjoins the establishment of a "common civil Code" for the whole of India.
>
> 'Those who preferred to remain in India after the Partition, fully knew that the Indian leaders did not believe in two-nation or three-nation theory and that in the Indian Republic there was to be only one Nation—Indian nation—and no community could claim to remain a separate entity on the

44. Amartya Sen, *The Idea of Justice*

45. AIR 1995 SC 1531

> basis of religion. It would be necessary to emphasize that the respective personal laws were permitted by the British to govern the matters relating to inheritance, marriages etc. only under the Regulations of 1781 framed by Warren Hastings. The Legislation—not religion—being the authority under which personal law was permitted to operate and is continuing to operate, the same can be superseded/supplemented by introducing a uniform civil code. In this view of the matter no community can oppose the introduction of uniform civil code for all the citizens in the territory of India.'

This idea, that one can trump religion with legislation, in the form of Warren Hastings' regulations, which can then be conveniently super substituted by a uniform civil code is misconceived and dangerous, given the complexity of Indian identities. Justice Kuldip Singh's judgment is problematic because it implies that everyone apart from the Hindus is anti-national. Given that the judgment is on the issue of bigamy it seems to also imply that the act of bigamy is anti-national. This resonates with an earlier judgment (in the Shah Bano case) where Muslim men are castigated for having a personal law that allows them what is seen as the sanction to discard women for no reason,[46] without noting that Hindu men also discard women. It thus communalizes a gender issue, and makes the position of women of both Hindu and Muslim communities even more precarious.

In the same case, (Sarla Mudgal) Justice Sahai, while agreeing with Justice Kuldip Singh, dissented on the reasoning. Please note that he does not use the phrase 'common civil code' as does Justice Kuldip Singh:

> 'The desirability of Uniform Code can hardly be doubted. But it can concretize only when social climate is properly built up by elite of this society; statesmen amongst leaders who instead of gaining personal mileage rise above and awaken the masses to accept the change.'

Interestingly, Justice Kuldip Singh seems to have changed his mind a year later in the Madhu Kishwar case.[47] She filed a case asking for equal rights for tribal women who were governed by patriarchal custom. Now, the court acknowledged that the tribal position is complex since custom varies from region to region. The judgment concludes:

> 'In face of these divisions and visible barricades put up by the sensitive tribal people valuing their own customs, traditions and usages, judicially

46. See Mohd. Ahmed Khan vs. Shah Bano Begum AIR 1985 SC 945

47. Madhu Kishwar and Others vs. State of Bihar and Others AIR 1996 SC 1864

> enforcing on them the principles of personal laws applicable to others on an elitist approach or on equality principle, by judicial activism, is a difficult and mind-boggling effort.'

There is no mention of the directive of a uniform civil code. At one place in the judgment, the judges say the Supreme Court is 'avowedly' apolitical. Finally, the court holds: 'Rules of succession are indeed susceptible of providing differential treatment, not necessarily equal. Non uniformities would not in all events violate Article 14.'

In the Lily Thomas case,[48] the Supreme Court stated that the direction in the Sarla Mudgal...asking the government to file affidavits 'indicating therein the steps taken and efforts made, by the government of India towards securing a Uniform Civil Code for the citizens of India' did not amount to 'any direction for the enactment of the Common Civil Code.'

~

In 2013, former justice Leila Seth wrote favouring the uniform civil code: 'I am not speaking as a Hindu, or an agnostic but as a woman'.[49] She, however, did not discuss the complexities of cultural pluralism unique to India, or the matter of fundamental rights. She also ignored the view of many feminists who are against implementing a uniform civil code at the present time, since it may mean aligning with the Hindu right. This point was forcefully made by the Anveshi Law Committee: 'We hold that the women's question cannot be separated from the notions of "democracy", "equality", "secularism", and "modernity" which are under contestation at present'.[50] The report criticized the women's movement in India as being on the same side as the Hindu right. Leading feminists strongly refuted this allegation, saying, 'there is a strange, almost magical fear about the power of words: if we talk of the same things as our opponents then we become them.'[51] They proceeded to lay out their stance as one committed to putting forward a proposal that seriously addresses questions of 'community, caste, gender and justice from a progressive, secular and feminist perspective.'[52]

---

48. Lily Thomas vs. Union of India, (2000) 6 Scc 224

49. Leila Seth, *Talking Of Justice*, p. 86

50. Anveshi Law Committee, 'Is Gender Justice only a Legal Issue? Political Stakes in UCC Debate', p. 453

51. Chhachhi et al, *UCC and Women's Movement*, p. 487

52. *Ibid.*, p. 488

Unfortunately, Justice Seth seemed not to have noticed any of these deeply thought-out careful positions when she said, 'we must depoliticize the question of the Uniform Civil Code'. This is to trivialize the meaning and import of the word political. It also ignores the reality that the development of law is an inherently political process, as she herself acknowledged, while saying, 'We cannot leave it only to the minority to raise the issue, for then we might wait forever, since it does not suit most men to give up their hold on women or any advantage that is already theirs.'...Apart from making the connection between law and political concerns clear, this suffers from inherently untenable assumptions that all men and minorities (read Muslims) would oppose a uniform civil code, but Hindus are ready and willing to dismantle patriarchy.

~

Another writer on the Constitution, Mr Durga Das Basu, even while acknowledging that Directive Principles are non-justiciable, proceeded to augment his position in favour of the uniform civil code by citing other non-justiciable portions of the Constitution, like clause (e) of Article 51A that requires the renunciation of practices derogatory to women. He denounced polygamy as the only practice derogatory to women. This was at a time when Hindu women did not have equal rights to property. Even now, wives do not have clear equal rights to marital property, but only a share in the form of maintenance as thought to be equitable by the court in each case. That marital rape is not an offence was also not considered by him as derogatory to women.

Even if we take up his claim that polygamy is derogatory, now that women in live-in relationships also have certain rights, to quote Salman Khurshid, 'four wives is not all right, but having four lovers is.'

This is not to suggest that Hindus should return to polygamy, but that the argument against it in this political environment is superficial. It is clear that marriage or 'living in' is not what derogates the dignity of women, but patriarchal and parochial attitudes towards women do—both of which Mr Basu suffers, given his cursory treatment of women's issues even while discussing the uniform civil code. While discussing the constitutional guarantee of equality before the law and equal rights in law he makes no specific reference to women.

Mr Basu proceeds to observe that in any other country a person opposing the uniform civil code would have lost his citizenship. He cites the Constitutions of China and the former USSR as examples. While saying all this, he forgot that the Directive Principles of State Policy are not law but guiding principles towards the ideal law. In any case, the comparison with China and the former USSR is a most unattractive inducement!

Hindu Law and the UCC

Democracy has survived here so far and we have a Parliament that we elect every five years. Religion and culture are integral components of identity in India, but the electoral strategy of politicians is based on the manipulation of identity politics to polarize communities. No politician has had the courage to view his role as someone who owes his constituents 'not his industry only, but his judgment; and he betrays, instead of serving you, if he sacrifices it to your opinion', as Edmund Burke said.[53] They prefer popular democracy rather than constitutional.

An example of political strategy at the cost of the law is when a politician loses an opportunity to show statesman-like leadership by mindlessly representing the reactionary elements of his constituency in Parliament. When the Jat khap panchayats seek an amendment in the Hindu Marriage Act to outlaw same-gotra marriages,[54] no one questions that politicians are 'pandering' to an unequivocally reactionary group, or points out that the majority community needs to introspect on the regressive elements in its cultural identity, just as Muslims are commonly advised to do. The politician representing the demands of the khaps needs to take equal responsibility for their shameful customary practices, whether these are honour killings and gang rapes as punishment for women asserting equal rights to land, or systemic caste and gender discrimination. This failure of courage to dissent from popular opinion is why lines of caste and community are deeper than ever before and the moderate elements within all communities are now afraid to speak up.

True introspection amongst *all* communities and not just one is what will result in progress. It is true that Hindu law has undergone major reform, but even progressive Hindus have not been able to divorce their religion from their law as completely as they expect the other communities to do. Despite many acts for Hindu reform, subtle catches in legislation ensure Hindu insularity from the true idea of secularism.

For example, though all matters of guardianship are well covered under the Guardians and Wards Act, 1890 there remains a separate

---

53. Edmund Burke, Speech to the Electors of Bristol, 3 November 1774

54. 'Sarv Khap demands ban on same "gotra" marriages' in *The Hindu*, 22 December 2014

Hindu Minority and Guardianship Act, 1956. In the same way, Section 19 of the Special Marriage Act, 1955 (the secular act), provides that a Hindu marrying a non-Hindu will be severed from the joint family.[55] Similarly, under Section 26 of the Hindu Succession Act, descendants of Hindus who convert to other religions are disqualified from inheriting property from any of their Hindu relatives unless they are Hindus when the succession opens.[56] Such disincentives for Hindus to marry outside the community are not replicated by other communities in their personal law statutes or in the secular law statutes that they may choose to opt for. The result is that while minorities are being exhorted to use secular enactments, Hindus are penalized if they want to, by severance from the joint family.[57] Hindus need to introspect about whether they too are willing to give up this 'separateness' and join the hotch-potch of equal succession regardless of conversion.

The matter is not just limited to those Hindus who wish to marry non-Hindus. A uniform civil code should make all Hindus think about whether they will stop treating marriage as sacred so that marital rape can become a criminal offence. Will they give up ceremony of kanyadaan that is at the root of the dowry problem?[58] Dowry, as per custom is still legal, unless it becomes extortionist—a relative term. Will they give up pativrata as the embodiment of womanhood and allow meaningful gender equality, instead of cosmetic changes that seem to have been made more for property mobilization than a regard for women? Conversely, if Hindus want to hew strongly to tradition, will they give up the practice of making wills, which was not part of their ancient law but brought in as a convenient device?

The parochial aspect of the matter is apparent from the customary laws of the south that had better rights for women but were given up when the 1956 Hindu Code Acts homogenized the laws of the country. Even so, disparity remains within Hindu Law, because personal laws are Entry 5 of the concurrent list of the Constitution, and thus different states have differed from or adapted central legislation to suit their unique cultural

---

55. See p. 389: Sections 19 to 21 of the Special Marriage Act

56. See p. 389: Section 26 of the Special Marriage Act: Convert's Descendants Disqualified.

57. See p. 389: Section 21a. of the Special Marriage Act: Special Provision in Certain Cases.

58. See Ch. 5: Property; p. 134, 154

ethos. For example, notwithstanding the Central Hindu Acts, Kerala under the communist regime abolished joint families.[59] Andhra Pradesh, Tamil Nadu, Maharashtra and Karnataka had made women coparceners in Hindu undivided families by 2000, though Parliament passed the Act only in 2005.[60]

In this political environment, a uniform civil code will amount to an imposition that compromises democratic values and pushes even the moderate amongst the minorities to adopt outmoded identities as a defense mechanism against times they perceive as dangerous. My understanding is that when the leaders of the majority community claim that they alone represent 'nationalists', minorities feel pushed to the wall. This then justifies them gathering every custom, practice and ritual, which they might have otherwise jettisoned, as a shield against the majority onslaught. The power of the communal divide in this manner is apparent: the anti-Sikh riots of 1984 transformed many of my urbane and moderate Sikh cousins from sahajdhari to keshdhari. To have achieved a Hindu-Sikh divide is a rare political feat, marvellous in its callous and inept mis-governance, but it is no surprise that the reaction was an assertion of cultural identity. Personal laws are part of this identity and the desperate fight to maintain them as a defence against communal majoritarianism leaves no time or space for minority communities to work on social reform and progress within their community.

Tanika Sarkar[61] has analyzed this problem and quotes Charles Taylor, recommending that to ensure thriving cultural pluralism, minorities need greater assistance than for mere survival. They need to be allowed the freedom of individual choices within the community.

~

Here is where the judiciary has played a sterling role. Contrary to the admonishments and impatience for the uniform civil code that the Supreme Court has sometimes exhibited, there is also sage advice from the same court:

59. The Joint Family System (Abolition) Act, 1975

60. Hindu Succession (Andhra Pradesh Amendment) Act, 1986, The Hindu Succession (Tamil Nadu Amendment) Act, 1989, The Hindu Succession (Karnataka Amendment) Act, 1994, The Hindu Succession (Maharashtra Amendment) Act, 1994

61. Sarkar, *Hindu Wife, Hindu Nation: Community, Religion, And Cultural Nationalism*, p. 247

In 1958, the Supreme Court[62] ruled, 'It is thus that the genius of India has been able to unity in diversity by assimilating the best of all creeds and cultures. Our Constitution accordingly recognizes our sacred obligations to the minorities'.

In 1974, it said:[63] 'The question of minority rights is a very sensitive and delicate one and there are no compelling or coercive considerations which would justify this Court in over-ruling its previous decisions and reducing the content of the right given to the minorities.'

In 2005, the Supreme Court observed: 'The only qualification for citizenship is a person's birth in India. We have to develop such enlightened citizenship where each citizen of whatever religion or language is more concerned about his duties and responsibilities to protect rights of the other group than asserting his own rights. The Constitutional goal is to develop citizenship in which everyone enjoys full fundamental freedoms of religion, faith and worship and no one is apprehensive of encroachment of his rights by others in minority or majority.'[64]

The judicial trend has been to uphold the fundamental right to practice religion, even while exercising its powers to strike down those portions of personal laws that are clearly unconstitutional. The Supreme Court has developed the 'essential practices' doctrine to help a fair balance between religion and illegal practices. The question the judges ask is 'What practice is core to the religion?'[65] Even in the course of this exercise, the court held in Krishna Singh v. Mathura Ahir[66] that a personal law could not be challenged as violating the constitutional guarantee of equality.

Islamic Law and the Demand for UCC

The first public debate about a uniform civil code was in 1985 with the Shah Bano case.[67] Abandoned by her barrister, Shah Bano sought maintenance for herself and her four children under Section 125 of the

62. In Re: The Kerala Education Bill, AIR 1958 SC 956

63. The Ahmedabad St. Xavier's College Society vs. State of Gujarat, AIR 1974 SC 1389

64. Bal Patil and Anr. vs. Union Of India (UOI) and Ors., AIR 2005 SC 3172; See also: Shamima Farooqui vs. Shahid Khan, AIR 2015 SC 2025.

65. Chandu Sajan Patil and Ors. vs. Nyahalchand Panamchand, AIR 1950 Bom 192; Sastri Yagnapurushdasji and Ors. vs. Muldas Bhudardas Vaishya and Anr. (Satsangi Case) AIR 1966 SC 1119

66. AIR 1980 SC 707

67. Mohd. Ahmed Khan vs. Shah Bano Begum (1985) Scr (3) 844

Criminal Procedure Code (Cr.P.C.), which is common to all citizens. The husband said that as he had divorced Shah Bano according to Islamic personal law, Section 127(3) Cr.P.C.[68] protected him from any liability under Section 125 Cr.P.C.

Section 125 entitles all wives, (including those divorced), children and parents to claim maintenance from husbands and adult children to protect themselves from penury and destitution. Earlier there was a ceiling of the amount awarded up of Rs. 500 per month, but the ceiling was removed by amendment in 2001.[69] The idea is to provide for effective and speedy legal help, since disregard of orders under this Act invites penal consequences, unlike in civil law.

The exception to the generality of Section 125 is Section 127(3). This section provides that men who have paid maintenance under their personal laws are protected from a maintenance claim under Section 125. In 1978,[70] the Supreme Court had already given a liberal interpretation of Section 127(3) in Bai Tahira's case by saying that the exception could not benefit men if the court found payments under any personal law to be inadequate. This ruling was reaffirmed in 1980 in Fuzlunbi's case.[71]

This was the situation for all communities till 1985 when, in the Shah Bano case, Justices Fazal Ali and A. Varadrajan said that in their opinion the previous judgments of Bai Tahira and Fuzlunbi were in direct contravention of the plain meaning of the act and so the matter needed to be referred to a larger bench. The larger bench reiterated its earlier positions and held that women's maintenance under 125 was available to all communities. Mahar (dower or bride price), the larger bench said, could not be construed as maintenance, even under Islamic personal law. It would be unrealistic, the court said, to expect any woman to survive on the mahar amount, which was usually a mere token given as consideration and out of respect for the marriage. The court also found that the Islamic rule of providing maintenance only during the period of iddat[72] was no

68. See pp. 358-60: Section 127(3) of the Cr.P.C., which states that if the woman has been divorced by her husband, and received the maintenance amount under customary or personal law, the magistrate can cancel the maintenance order under Section 125.

69. The Code of Criminal Procedure (Amendment) Act, 2001 Act No. 50 of 2001

70. Bai Tahira vs. Ali Hussain Fidaalli Chothia and Anr., AIR 1979 SC 362

71. Fuzlunbi vs. K. Khader Vali and Anr., AIR 1980 SC 1730

72. The waiting period for a woman before she remarries after the death of her spouse or after a divorce. Its purpose is to ensure that the male parent of any offspring produced after the cessation of a nikah (marriage) would be known.

longer adequate. It referred to passages in the Holy Koran that a divorced wife must be protected from penury and treated with kindness, even if it requires maintenance beyond the iddat period. The husband could not possibly claim that the Prophet would approve of an old woman rendered destitute, said the judges.

The husband's counter-argument was that the Prophet's observation about maintenance beyond the iddat period is 'Mutta Queena': it is for those who are more pious and more God-fearing than the general run of Muslims like himself, he said. The court dismissed this as a shuffling plea, but regrettably spared him a severe castigation. It was a disappointingly moderate reaction to a legal plea that was diabolical in its hypocrisy.

The argument of interveners who claimed to be speaking on behalf of the Muslim community, that the woman must look to relatives, like nephews and cousins, to maintain herself was found to be facile and unrealistic. The court said:

> 'They took up an extreme position by displaying an unwarranted zeal to defeat the right to maintenance of women who are unable to maintain themselves. The written submissions of the All India Muslim Personal Law Board have gone to the length of asserting that it is irrelevant to inquire as how a Muslim divorcee should maintain herself'.[73]

It was scathing towards such interveners, saying:

> 'Instead of wasting their energies in exerting theological and political pressure in order to secure an "immunity" for their traditional personal law from the state legislative jurisdiction, the Muslim will do well to begin exploring and demonstrating how the **true Islamic laws, purged of their time-worn and anachronistic interpretations, can enrich the common civil code of India**'.[74] [emphasis mine]

Crucially, the court recognized that Islamic law could make significant contributions to a UCC (even though it call it a 'common' civil code). The comment was in the context of the observation that under Islamic law, mahar was negotiated by the bride's father to be encashed by the bride when divorced, but regardless of mahar, the Prophet enjoined that a destitute divorced wife must be maintained too. The fact that Muslim women in India have not been able to exercise these rights is the problem women face from all patriarchies, compounded by the marginalization of this minority community by every political party.

73. Mohd. Ahmed Khan vs. Shah Bano Begum (1985) Scr (3) 844

74. *Ibid.*

The court also pointed out the gender bias in both major Indian religions:

> 'Some questions which arise under the ordinary civil and criminal law are of a far-reaching significance to large segments of society which have been traditionally subjected to unjust treatment. Women are one such segment. *No stree swatantramarhati,* said Manu, the Lawgiver: The woman does not deserve independence. And, it is alleged that the "fatal point in Islam is the degradation of woman". To the Prophet is ascribed the statement, hopefully wrongly, that "woman was made from a crooked rib, and if you try to bend it straight, it will break; therefore, treat your wives kindly"'.

These comments were laudable and unobjectionable till the court made the following observation about men of the Muslim community:

> 'Does the Muslim Personal Law impose no obligation upon the husband to provide for the maintenance of his divorced wife? Undoubtedly, the Muslim husband enjoys the privilege of being able to discard his wife whenever he chooses to do so, for reasons good, bad or indifferent. Indeed, for no reason at all'.

And then, after all this solemn pontification and agonizing, the honourable judges proceeded to award Shah Bano a monthly maintenance of Rs. 179.20 from her husband's claimed monthly earnings of Rs. 5,000.

~

Many Muslims (read clergy) gathered in protest against the judgment. 'Who are you to rule on our personal law', they said. The problem ceased to be about Shah Bano, who eventually retracted and dropped her maintenance claim because she did not want it to be the cause of communal tension. The intensity of the outcry led to the passing of the Muslim Women (Protection of Rights on Divorce) Act 1986. It was criticized as retrograde towards Muslim women because it limited their rights to personal law, and as tainted by a timid appeasement policy for short-term political gain. A renowned jurist and lawyer, Danial Latifi, challenged this act[75] as contrary to the secular principles of the Constitution and its guarantee of equality, life and liberty. The Supreme Court disagreed and held that the act encoded the rationale contained in the Shah Bano case, which was essentially protection of Muslim women.

N.K.P. Salve, speaking in Parliament, highlighted that from the Privy Council in 1898 to 1980, it had been good law that Section 125

75. Danial Latifi vs. Union of India, (2001) 7 SCC 740

Cr.P.C. included Muslim women. It was the intemperate remarks from the judiciary about Muslim men that provoked a reaction from the community. He said:

> 'I really hope that the judges in future will realize that in all sensitive issues, they may deal with the law in the manner they want to but they must understand how much they are capable of being misunderstood. It is irreverential reference to the Holy Prophet and the irreverential reference to the Muslim religion that created all this trouble. Perhaps if those comments had not been made and if this rather unwarranted discussion on Article 44 had not come maybe, these (provisions) would have continued.'[76]

Having given this context, and made it clear that we as a nation called the criticism upon ourselves, it must be pointed out that the legislation of the much-maligned Act for Muslim women is not as unsound as its critics make it out to be. A closer reading of the act will reveal that there is scope to interpret it liberally, securing her a far greater entitlement to maintenance than under the Criminal Procedure Code, besides releasing her from the ceiling that existed at the time of Rs. 500 per month.[77] Section 3(2) of the act empowers the court to order maintenance where mahar and payment during iddat were found to be inadequate.[78]

It also needs to be said that despite the new Act for Maintenance of Muslim Women, many petitions by Muslim women continue to be entertained under 125 Cr.P.C., as before, with no objection from husbands calling upon the wives to avail themselves of this remedy. For example, Shamima Farooqui[79] in 2015 obtained relief under Section 125 Cr.P.C. with no discussion about the Special Act for Muslim women. Given that this is the case, you can see the Shah Bano issue was not about women as much as it was about the Muslim community.

~

The post-Shah Bano tension led to confusion even amongst the judiciary, causing one Khatoon Nisa[80] to suffer an unjust ruling by the Allahabad

---

76. Rajya Sabha debates on the Muslim Women (Protection Of Rights On Divorce) Bill, 8th May 1986, available at http://rsdebate.nic.in/bitstream/123456789/321497/1/pd_138_08051986_12_p221_p326_9.pdf#search=muslim

77. Menski, *Modern Indian Family Law*, p. 233

78. See p. 382: Section 3(2) of the Muslim Women (Protection from Divorce) Act.

79. Shamima Farooqui vs. Shahid Khan, AIR 2015 SC 2025

80. Khatoon Nisa vs. State of U.P. and Ors., 2002(6)SCALE165

High Court in 2002. Even while ruling against her as a divorced wife, the Allahabad Court could not resist extraneous remarks about Muslim men. Here is the story:

Under the Land Ceiling Act, holdings of agricultural land beyond the prescribed 'ceiling' were to be declared 'surplus' by the revenue authorities, who could then acquire the area for redistribution under various social welfare schemes. The act defines a family as consisting of husband, wife and minor children. Ergo, a divorced couple or children who had attained majority at the time of the act were not a family and thus could hold land independently.

Khatoon Nisa claimed a separate holding outside the purview of the Land Ceiling Act because she had received agricultural property as a divorce settlement under Islamic law. The revenue authorities disagreed, and proceeded to acquire her land saying there was no evidence of a divorce by court decree.

The Allahabad High Court upheld the decision of the revenue authorities.[81] Supporters of the High Court judgment say that the court was not convinced about the divorce and found it to be a collusive device, as had become the practice amongst many feudal families to continue to have larger land holdings than permissible under law. However, if this was the case, the court should have said so in its 232-paragraph-long judgment, but it did not. And yet, over many pages, the court sympathized with women and their ill-treatment quoting the poet Begum Anjum to say, *Talaq de rahe garoor au kahar ke saath: Mera shabab bhi lauta do mere mehar ke saath.*[82] It also quoted from the Koran and severely criticized the triple talaq method of divorce.

The reader breathlessly reads through the judgment, seeing it as a beautiful exposition for the cause of women—till it suddenly swerves direction and deprives Khatoon Nisa of her alimony, by concluding divorce by the method of triple talaq to be invalid. *Jab mian bibi razi, kya karega qazi* is what the court should have noticed. Both husband and wife agree that they are divorced. He says he pronounced triple talaq and she says yes he did. Triple talaq (in a particular form pronounced over three months) is a valid form of divorce, notwithstanding judicial disapproval or misunderstanding. Once divorced, Khatoon Nisa should have been,

81. Rahmat Ullah and Khatoon Nisa vs. State Of U.P. and Ors., II(1994)DMC64

82. You pronounce talaq with such arrogance, can you return my youth and beauty along with my mahar.

on a bare reading of the law, permitted to keep for herself the property she got from her husband as alimony, but the court disagreed.

The judgment is painfully bewildering besides being problematic. The court needed to see whether the Land Ceiling Act was valid. Then it had to see whether Khatoon Nisa was divorced. And if she was divorced according to the law as prevailed then, she must hold her land as separate property. That is all. The court held the act to be valid: so far so good. But then it exceeded its jurisdiction to worry about all Muslim women, and proceeded to analyze the validity and legality of the custom of divorce by triple talaq.

The court may not have liked the custom but it was legal at the time (and still is, though petitions have been moved in the Supreme Court challenging it.[83]) Here is a woman who could benefit from talaq (albeit through the triple utterance) but the court's problematic reasoning denied her that advantage. The tears shed for the plight of other divorced women, who had nothing to do with this case, seem to have blurred the fact that, in this particular case, Khatoon Nisa had actually got a very fine settlement and should have been allowed to keep it.

The Supreme Court upheld the judgment, even while expressing disapproval of the Allahabad High Court's analysis of triple talaq. The logical conclusion to its disapproval was to uphold the talaq and thus its consequent benefit to the lady but that did not follow.

~

It is instructive to note that all the courts in all three cases discussed so far (Sarla Mudgal, Shah Bano, Khatoon Nisa) cited law reform in Islamic countries to indicate that it was time for Islamic law to be reformed in India. Many Muslim academics and lawyers agree that Islamic law needs to be reformed, but scathing remarks about their religion, of which personal law is a part, are not going to help achieve that reform.

This patronizing attitude is made even worse when Hindus express martyr-like outrage about having reformed because they gave up polygamy in 1956. They need to remember that criminalizing polygamy has not improved the plight of Hindu women, and they need to reflect that Hindu reform as proclaimed has not been able to dismantle the caste system and oppressive patriarchy.

---

83. In the case of Shamim Ara v. State of U.P., AIR 2002 SC 3551, the SC ruled that triple talaq cannot be arbitrary or unreasonable; See also: Menon, 'It isn't about women' in *The Hindu*, 15 July 2016

The Directive for a uniform civil code has become tarnished because minorities suspect that a uniform civil code means a Hindu code by another name. Given the current political climate, many Hindus presume that it will indeed be so. Secularism requires equal respect for all faiths and this is done by not bringing any faith, including the Hindu faith, into the domain of governance. Even so, religion is a political matter because it is part of the politics of identity. I agree that this should not be the case, but we can transcend it only once we acknowledge that it is so.

~

One last example: the Supreme Court was asked to intercede by one Imrana, who was prohibited by a fatwa from returning to her husband because she had been raped by her father-in-law.[84] The Muslim personal law board stated that fatwas and Shariat courts were not parallel to the legal system, but simply for those who wanted to understand and be advised about Islamic law. The court ruled that nobody could prevent someone from taking or giving advice on religious law but advised:

> 'We would like to advise the dar Ul Qaza, or for that matter anybody not to give any response or issue fatwa concerning an individual unless asked for by the person involved or the person having direct interest in the matter... Fatwas touching upon the rights of an individual at the instance of rank strangers may cause irreparable damage and therefore, would be absolutely uncalled for. It shall be in violation of basic human rights. It cannot be used to punish innocent. No religion including Islam punishes the innocent. Religion cannot be allowed to be merciless to the victim. Faith cannot be used as dehumanising force'.[85]

The Future of the UCC

Justice Kuldip Singh's opinion that a uniform civil code is the inevitable consequence of the single-nation theory does not consider that the theory encompasses cultural pluralism within a political state. The issue is not about the single-nation theory, which seems to be a dig at minorities, but how to achieve gender equality.

Menski writes that in seeking uniformity, India is modelling itself on a Western model that is proving unworkable even in the West.[86] India has a sixty-nine-year-long successful experiment with multicultural democracy,

---

84. Vishwa Lochan Madan vs. Union of India, (2014) 7 SCC 707

85. *Ibid.*

86. Menski, *Modern Indian Family Law*, p. 368

encompassing a diversity built up over many centuries. It would be foolhardy to drop this shining achievement now, only because certain sections of society are getting impatient with the pace of the nation's progress and have been deluded to think that a uniform civil code will be meaningful without education, sanitation, environment protection and the other Directives of State Policy. This road to an ideal family law seems long and meandering. They seem to hold that family laws have nothing to do with religion and cultural identity, so let's clean it up with a marvellous new uniform civil code, jettisoning ancient outmoded custom—but please note that no one is willing to say that in the name of equality let's destroy *everything* to start all over again. No patriarchy, no religion, no borders. Indeed, true progress will be when every community in the nation (including Hindus) accept the due process of democracy and effect reforms fearlessly after introspection about what really constitutes their faith.

Economic development is not being impeded by the absence of a uniform civil code, but its imposition will certainly take us back seventy years because the seething emotional energy of divisive politics will be unleashed to destroy the culture of tolerance we have built over centuries.

Another reason that the uniform civil code is a difficult topic is because at present no one really knows what it is, what it will be and what it should be. Recently, on a television debate, someone exposed his absolute ignorance on the scope of the topic (as opposed to some ignorance, because we are all slightly challenged on the issue), by asking how it would affect funeral rites!

Perhaps the discussion could start with acknowledging some value in all personal laws. There are fair and gender-friendly portions of many personal laws that could be co-opted in the uniform civil code. For example, under Muslim law a bequest cannot exceed one-third of the testator's property. Similarly, Islam allows for pre-nuptial contracts and allows women to demand divorce by way of khula. The divorce system is not based on the fault theory, which requires the lengthy and tortuous procedure of a trial to assess fault. The problem is that Islamic patriarchy did not leave women with power to assert their rights, just as Hindu patriarchy erodes a woman's right to exercise control over her stridhan.

Because present *realpolitik* seems to be about serving the interests of political leaders rather than those of the country, the onerous task of grappling and reducing the hostile gaps of the old-new; majority-minority; left-right to a workable middle path has to be borne by the judiciary as a guardian of the Constitution. Judicial rulings are moving us as close to a uniform civil code as is possible without the formal imposition of such a code. Judicial pronouncements nudge minority communities to introspect on those parts of their personal laws that perpetuate inequality and so are unconstitutional. The Shah Bano and the Sarla Mudgal rulings are instances of this, notwithstanding the disparaging remarks about Muslim men. The judiciary has (mostly) been powerful in the role of educating society on constitutional values by admonishments, lectures (even if moralistic sometimes), or simply stating the law, while at the same time ensuring that judge-made law is not too much at variance with the prevailing socio-cultural ethos. It has encouraged a gradual evolution of change away from unconstitutional traditional positions. Justice Mathews explained the role of the judiciary in the following manner:[87]

> 'It is admitted that the custom must not be unreasonable or opposed to public policy. But the question is, unreasonable to whom? Is a custom which appears unreasonable to the judge be adjudged so or should he be guided by the prevailing *public opinion of the community in which the custom prevails?* [...] A judge may not set himself in opposition to a custom which is fully accepted by the community [...] but I think that the judge should not follow merely the mass opinion when it is clearly in error, but on the contrary he should direct it, not by laying down his own personal and isolated conceptions but by resting upon the opinion of the healthy elements of the population...thus the judge is not bound to heed even to the clearly held opinion of the greater majority of the community if he is satisfied that opinion is abhorrent to right-thinking people'.

It is only the Supreme Court that can cajole and convince all religions that gender-friendly legal systems do not impinge on their religious freedoms. It can try to convince upper-caste Hindus that the caste system is not a part of Hindu religion. It can rule to discard irrelevant or evil customs. Most importantly, the Supreme Court can do this over a series of rulings, on a case-by-case basis. To gratuitously call for the implementation of a uniform civil code causes alarm about its position on secularism. This is a slow onward process even though sometimes it has alarming downward spirals: an example is the recent reactionary judgment on the criminalization of homosexuality.[88]

---

87. Sheikriyammada Nalla Koya vs. Administrator, Union Territory of Laccadives, Minicoy and Amindivi Islands, Kozhikode, AIR 1967 KER 259

88. Suresh Kumar Koushal and Anr. vs. Naz Foundation & Ors., 2013(15)SCALE 55

This is not to ignore the efforts of the legislature. The Protection of Women from Domestic Violence Act and the Juvenile Justice Act are instances of a uniform civil code working to enable women in all communities.

~

The main obstacle to a uniform civil code is not because of the passions of the ordinary citizen, who may or may not be fiercely religious and think less of other religions, but due to the political capital that is obtained by stoking this feeling and raising the demon of organized communal violence. This is how (all) governments are eroding the deep cultural memory of inclusiveness. Even the term 'Vasudev Kutumb Kamb' has been appropriated by the Hindu right to imply that it means a Hindu nation where others may choose to reside as less than Hindu. What remains now as the popular phrase to describe true inclusiveness is 'Ganga-Jamuna tehzeeb', which was used very effectively in the recent Bihar elections.

Ambedkar's effort to release personal laws from the grasp of religion should have encouraged spiritual purity from the wellspring of every religion, which was otherwise getting poisoned by vested communal interests. He challenged custom as the symptom of perverse politics. While introducing the Hindu Code Bill, he observed that though old custom could not be removed immediately, the creation of new ones could be stopped. The old would then wither away. The same principle is central to Ambedkar's adoptive religion. The Buddhist practice of Vipassana admires dealing with karmic causality by a meditative discipline of non-activity that does not allow for new karmic consequences while the old wither away. Gadgil, a parliamentarian, described the process evocatively: 'Because this well was dug by my great-great-grandfather, and although the water of it saltish, I must drink it, Well, that is not my outlook.'[89]

Bold, blunt and straightforward, not used to the smooth shenanigans of politicians, Ambedkar said in March 1955, 'The Constitution was a wonderful temple we built for the Gods, but before they could be installed, the devils have taken possession'.[90] Ambedkar's comment was prescient and the ordinary citizen's cynicism about politics has stood validated many times over these past six decades.

Having said which, technology driven social media has enabled the

89. http://www.ambedkar.org/ambcd/64B2.On%20the%20Hindu%20Code%20Bill.htm

90. Kanahaiyalal Sharma, *Reconstitution of the Constitution of India*

average citizen to demand answers to difficult questions. Politicians are being prodded and pushed from their pyramid tops to expose them as absolutely insensitive to the nuances of freedom and equality. They do not have the language skills to articulate its problems, and so they embarrass us with their harried crude statements emanating from intellectual distortions and absence of conscience regarding their roles and responsibilities as leaders of the largest democracy in the world.

The barricades set up by ruthless political intrigue seem difficult to breach, but a new generation is open to persuasion. The idea of change within each community for greater gender equality is already emerging, along with the need for a religion that matches a modern fast-paced life and is unencumbered by outmoded customs and rituals and free of mindless prejudices and biases.

Since earning women have become an economic necessity for most households there is a gradual, albeit grudging, acceptance of women's space in the home and outside. We evolve towards a uniform civil code and a harmonious cultural assimilation of gender equality as we move to spirituality to take care of needs that earlier needed a heavier and more imposing religion. The journey requires patience and tolerance, two qualities essential to the health of any nation and both are in danger of being compromised by the imposition of an external code.

EPILOGUE

A grand patriarch and his two sons came to consult me. Both sons had troubled marriages. The patriarch spoke for both of them, seeming not to hear their interjections. The main problem was that the wives did not want to live in a joint family. I told them that I did not advise divorce because the children from both marriages were small, and even by the old patriarch's account, the problems the sons had with their respective wives did not seem insurmountable. A lot may have to do with their father, I thought, though I did not say so. In the silence that followed, the patriarch looked at me with veiled dislike and said, 'I guess women are now talking and we have to live with it.'

Afterwards, the person who had referred the patriarch to me rang me up to enquire what had exactly happened. 'He said he wants another lawyer who is not a woman's libber.' We both laughed at the phrase, quaint even in the seventies but in 2013 nothing short of outrageously incongruous.

That we are in a time warp should be apparent even from my account so far: an old couple, their sons, daughters-in-law and grandchildren all living together. To avoid confusion, I had to use the word patriarch. And he was: he wielded economic power; his age gave him a stature that commanded respect. His daughters-in-law were not toeing his line: their issue was not with their husbands but with him.

In my experience, one reason this family structure has survived is due to real-estate prices. The sons may be working, but they would not be able to buy a house of the size and address that their father owned, and they did not want to jeopardize their inheritance by crossing him. It was that simple. Why this is so in the twenty-first century is for the academics to answer. The economics of why a lot of real estate is beyond the reach of the average earner; the perpetuation of patriarchy; the inability of the young to break free from the tyranny of elders—explanations for all these lie in separate studies, but while they exist, the traditional forms of marriage continue.

All this is made more complicated by the fact that new forms are arising even alongside the old. Nothing is as predictable as the old order graciously passing on to give place to the new. The past, the new, the yet emerging, and even the future are all contained in a candid snapshot of the now. In this final essay, I talk about the future of family and marriage in the abstract, and conclude with some suggestions for anyone finding themselves in divorce proceedings.

THE FUTURE OF FAMILY AND MARRIAGE

It is all complicated and complex and disorderly and fascinating, but one thing is quite clear: more and more divorces are due to the discomfort of men around a woman with a voice. Susan Faludi described marriage as male propaganda against women's empowerment by creating an artificial 'need' for a man's protection.[1] The sad, lonely spinster is advertising hype by men to cover their own need for a 'homemaker', and as part of the campaign, men propagate a picture of the single woman as dull, dreary and non-sexual. Jessie Bernard's research is also in consonance with the Faludi position: men need marriage more than women, she says.[2]

In the past, women's liberation campaigns have generally acquiesced to this propaganda by not challenging the marriage hype but claiming equality within it. This is changing as women become less fearful of singlehood. Some UK- and US-based studies show that single women are happier than single men.[3] The factors at play for the women in such studies could well serve upper-middle-class working Indian women as well.

Empowered women are not generally the most eligible in the marriage market perhaps because men are intimidated by them. Their empowerment removes from women a quality that men prize highly: that of being docile. Men prefer 'homely' women rather than trying to understand or have patience for a woman's unshackled persona.

Conversely, it seems that women are victims of their own gender stereotyping when you consider that while money adds to the sexual allure and eligibility of a man, an independent and wealthy woman tends to reduce the pool of choice of men for herself to those who are at least equal to her in financial status because both she and her partner are likely to struggle with the gender stereotypes involved. That is one explanation for why many powerful, influential women are single. It may be by choice, or it may be a status that they have to live with, because they have not found a man who is not intimidated or resentful of their power and success.

---

1. Faludi, *Backlash: The Undeclared War Against American Women*, p. 26, p. 113

2. Bernard, *The Future of Marriage*, p. 21, p. 309

3. 'Single women over 60 happier than single men' in *The Telegraph*, 15 November 2007; Faludi, *Backlash: The Undeclared War Against American Women*, p. 31

But it is reasonable to assume that they would prefer marriage even if it means cutting their persona to the size of the marriage bed, which basically means carrying the home burden along with that of work: something that men just don't do. While writing this, I searched online for top corporate women and got a slew of sites, including stories in *Cosmopolitan* magazine about how they had careers and yet managed the home. That is not the life of top corporate men. The current story that comes to mind[4] is that of Indra Nooyi who returned home at 10 p.m. and went out to buy milk, even while her husband, who had returned at 8 p.m., rested. She tells of how her mother had told her that Indra was chief at work but at home was wife, mother, daughter-in-law and daughter. The story is typical, but what disturbed me was that there was no quarrel with her mother or her husband about this skewed idea. In the same interview, she recounts that her daughters may not consider her a good mother, without questioning the relevance of the stereotyped mother if you want to contribute to changing gender equations in a new world.

My assessment from various private conversations amongst educated upper-middle-class women is that while many may regret having given up their chance for independent careers, most are reluctant to break from wealth or social security to strike out alone. Many of them have also developed rhythms around their kitchens and children that they find difficult to interrupt, which too is all right as long as it was a free choice. The gender equation will truly change only when men are able to have the choice of being home-makers.

Popular perceptions of the roles of house husband and working woman are explored in the film *Ki and Ka* (2016). The film is superficial and irritating, but bold in having started a trend. That the house husband role is viewed as lesser than the working man is clear from the back story of the husband, who is a dilettante son of a rich father—this is what justifies his staying at home. The film *Abhimaan* (1973) continues to be the classic exploration of clashing husband-wife work egos. The end resolves in a rapprochement, but no clarity on whether the wife will resume her work as playback singer who proved to be far more popular than her rock-star husband. The film is based on the lives of the sitar maestro, late Pandit Ravi Shankar, and his wife, equally a maestro, Annapurna Devi. Their story is that he left her, even though she had vowed to have no further

---

4. Conor Friedersdorf, 'Why PepsiCo CEO Indra K. Nooyi Can't Have It All' in *The Atlantic*, 1 July 2014.

public performances after the audience judged her music, in their initial performances together, to be far more sophisticated and refined than his.

The Changing Face of Marriage

Women's rebellion against patriarchy has been the most powerful catalyst for social change in the last hundred years. Marriage is changing because the rebellion is succeeding. Bernard makes a fine distinction between the early nineteenth-century movement for women's 'emancipation', calling for legal equality, and the twentieth-century 'liberation' from psychological and political constraints of patriarchy.[5]

Women were shackled through their sexuality, and hence women's movements have focused on agency over their bodies. As the discourse is around sexuality, the backlash against the movement has been a greater repression on women's bodies, of which rape is the most violent symbol, along with sexual harassment, which can be as traumatic.

Popular films and literature have documented this sexual rebellion in the context of the home where it began, and which remains the most immediate witness of it. In classical literature, this new woman emerges in the wake of crumbling feudal societies and her story of rebellion was always a tragic one. For example, the unconventional lives of both Madame Bovary and Anna Karenina pushed them to suicide. Early Indian films, too, punished a woman's bid for independence in any matter, but more so in love and friendship. Meena Kumari is killed in *Sahib Bibi aur Ghulam* (1962) for an innocent friendship that was presumed to be inappropriate in the feudal structure. The assumption that a woman outside the home is somehow inappropriate was the subject of Ray's *Mahanagar* (1963). Arati is the only working woman in her middle-class Bengali neighbourhood. One day she takes the last bus home from office. As she walks home in the dark, neighbours step out to look at her with silent shock and disapproval. Some women look at her with envy and admiration, and the men with hatred and resentment, as they realize that times are changing and the power to earn money is no longer going to be their exclusive domain.

Swami (1977) broke from the punishment trend. Girish Karnad leads his wife into the home after she returns from her lover but she is passive and shocked and says that he is her swami and she is going to spend the rest of her life at his feet. She is clearly returning to a life of guilt and

5. Bernard, *The Future of Marriage*

remorse. The husband in *Yeh Nazdeekiyan* (1982) scurries back home to his caring wife because his girlfriend does not understand any of his housekeeping needs.

In films of that era, the idea reinforced is that marriage should be with a wife who is sane, homely and an appealing comfort, in contrast to a temperamental and demanding mistress. These films treated marriage as social bonds and women's sexuality became a metaphor for personal freedom. This approach was appropriate, considering that it is an expression of the freedom of men that illicit sex is 'something men do', but in the popular mindset, women who have sex outside marriage become hungry sexual animals who cannot be good mothers any longer. In court, many custody petitions are based on the woman's sexual 'immorality'.[6]

The happiest—and not coincidentally, the most unusual—film I saw of the free woman is *Katha* (1983), where Naseeruddin Shah marries Deepti Naval after her affair with his friend Farooque Shaikh. The film ends with them laughing behind closed doors as she leads him through the sexual play as the more experienced of the two.

After the 1970s, popular films with strong women protagonists were still nervous about giving her total power and so compromised with tame happily-ever-after endings of marital bliss. This continued with *Kabhi Alvida Naa Kehna* as late as 2006. Love strikes the peace of four good people and breaks two reasonably happy marriages. The lovers leave their respective spouses and the moral dilemma of opting out of marriage is resolved by a period of separation and loneliness before they earn their happy endings.

In contrast to films, theatre with its immediate connect and understanding of its audience does not suffer such hypocritical conservative morality because it has the intimate reach to persuade an audience to break intellectual boundaries which, many would say, is the true purpose of art. Even in 1972, women's sexuality was being explored in plays like Surender Verma's 'Surya ki Antim Kiran se Surya ki Pehli Kiran Tak'. An impotent king forces a lover of his choosing on his queen so she can produce an heir for the kingdom. The queen has her revenge by deciding to keep her lover and avoid pregnancy. She knows the king will not interfere for fear of public knowledge of his impotency. Here, too,

6. That morality is still lurking, as discussed in Ch. 2: Decoding Gender, p. 27; See also Prabhati Mitra v. D.K. Mitra, 25 (1984) DLT 186: Justice Rohatgi quoting an English Judge in Willoughby v. Willoughby, 1951 P J 84 states that an adulterous mother could nevertheless be a good mother.

the boldness of the plot is somewhat diluted when we learn that the lover chosen for the Queen was in fact a childhood friend. Thus was avoided the moral issue of having sex with a complete stranger and liking it.

The rebellion of the postmodern woman is not sexual-centric any longer. Now she is moving to the next step of financial control of her earnings and the courage to claim a return from investment in marriage and be a parent, beyond simply caring for the physical needs of the children. The hit film *Queen* (2014) actually explored a woman rejecting marriage.[7] Rani, cocooned in a middle-class conservative Punjabi household, is jilted the day before her wedding. She goes alone on the Europe honeymoon. The trip transforms her into a sensitive, confident young woman who revels in the freedom of singleness. There is a lot of drinking, rock concerts and foreign men, including one she kisses. The audience loved it all. I was expecting a ban from some quarter and am delighted to have been proven wrong.

~

While the women's movement continues to challenge traditional marriage equations, in the past an important challenge was from the ideological left rebelling against the established social order. This has now lost force because of its fading political relevance, but is worth exploring.

From Marx and Engels in 1887 onwards, a pillar of the leftist argument against the feudal order was to declare family and marriage as petit bourgeois institutions. Great intellectuals, writers and artists explored life and love outside marriage or individual freedom within it. Many couples, such as Jean-Paul Sartre and Simone de Beauvoir, lived in their mutual love, which was yet open enough for either to enjoy the frisson of being joined by others, or to wade into the dangerous waters of full-blown sexual affairs.

The left liberal was the catalyst for newly independent India's literary and artistic renaissance, which peaked just before the Emergency. The challenge to marriage emerged from this left liberal environment that encouraged dissent, protest and rebellion against outmoded social norms as a right in a robust democracy. Some of the famous figures of this milieu were Nayantara Sehgal, who wrote of her love affair with the married E.N. Mangat Rai, while she herself was also married; Amrita Pritam and her unique relationships with Sahir Ludhianvi and her long-term companion,

---

7. *Arth* and *Paromita Ek Din* are both also unconventional movies. While *Arth* is similar to *Queen*, *Paromita Ek Din* also defies conventional norms.

Imroze; and the open secret of leftist politician George Fernandes's intimate life. There are also many undisputed stories of the unconventional lives of various film actors and directors like Kabir Bedi, Dharmendra and Hema Malini, Mahesh Bhatt, Guru Dutt and Waheeda Rehman, Raj Kapoor and Nargis, Dev Anand and Suraiyya. Strangely enough, the list stops after the 1980s, with a trend back to famous marriages and famous divorces, indicating the rise of the conservative right.

Having said which, many politicians have been happy to be single and have not felt the need to cultivate façades with a beaming hand-holding spouse. We have had single prime ministers (widowed or never married or living singly though married). Mrs Indira Gandhi's tumultuous marriage with Feroze Gandhi did not interfere with her political life as a Nehru daughter. Unlike in the West, the Indian media and public have displayed an inherent maturity in leaving alone the private lives of our leaders and public figures. The average citizen indulges the 'moral transgressions' of public figures, although many may not allow it in her/his own class since it lacks what s/he thinks is the necessary ingredient of wealth and influence.

Now, however an increasingly affluent middle-class has the strength to push back against traditional norms. The number of 'love marriages' are increasing, as are premarital sex and live-in relationships. The average middle-class person is perforce becoming aware of various types of family and relationship structures, whether or not s/he accepts them. Simultaneously, as if for the first time worried about the sexual freedom of the few in the past becoming the choice of many, the state is pushing back to assert morality as an 'Indian' ethos.

The current example is the newspaper coverage of the video showing the AAP president with two different women at different times. It was salacious yellow journalism of the kind that our media had restrained itself from in the past. In an over-zealous and overly moralistic reaction, the party sacked the minister, even though consensual sexual intercourse is not a crime. Another party member who, as the middling voice of reason, questioned the extreme reaction to consensual sex has received a notice from the National Commission for Women (NCW) for an offence. I do not understand how he has humiliated women by discussing consensual sex, unless the NCW wants us to believe that their view is that consensual sex outside marriage is humiliating to women. The lack of reasonable feminist discourse in such institutions that are supposed to be committed to the cause of women should be a cause of concern, but that it seems not to be again indicates the institutionalization of the conservative right.

Hence, marriage, as the ultimate conservative institution, is clearly here for a long forseeable while, bolstered by the fact that family businesses and potential legacies of land and resources continue to be major inducements to stay in the family fold and maintain its conservative status quo.

~

Add to that, conservativism is rising as a reaction to the dizzying pace of a technologically driven life. All sections of society, including the highest, seem frozen in fear and anxiety about change. *Will I be able to keep up? I am not ready: I feel alien: I don't understand what's happening to the people around me. When did this happen? Where am I: who was I: do I still remain who I am?* Extend these anxieties to those who identify themselves predominantly with their caste, community and religion; extend them to those who feel they are guardians of 'Indian culture' and it is possible to make a guess at the reasons for the reactionary wave. Marriage reflects society and so the traditionalist ruing lack of forbearance and patience in the young (women particularly) does not see that it is unreasonable to expect someone to be patient with abuse. The reactionary elements are against premarital sex because, to preserve the institution of marriage and hence the social status quo, it is safer to have marriage as the only license for sex. Challenges to these norms are shouted out with many cries, amongst which 'anti–national' is the most deafening.

Another reason that could explain the reaction is that it is so much simpler to collapse into the mindset of the past, instead of working to create new ones to process fast change. So, the reactionary wave seeks to persuade Indians that national pride lies solely in the deeply conservative, traditional mores that make India a spiritual leader of the world. Their one-point agenda is to protect traditional society, even if by violent and brutal methods. They are alarmed by sexual liberation. Violence against women is the strongest symptom of this yearning for pre-modern patriarchy; it is not a coincidence that perceived moral and social transgressions are punished more brutally than ever before.

In 1996, I met a well-known actress at a dinner party who told me she was considering making a film based on a true story of a girl from Punjab who eloped with her lover. Her parents hired killers to murder her and the mother confirmed the identity of her daughter by speaking to her on the assassin's cell phone before he killed her. I returned home feeling heavy and restless. I knew of honour killings as family lore: a man hiring a killer to murder his wife's paramour or some such. But to kill your daughter? True, female infanticide is a gruesome reality, but to kill a daughter you have brought up? Since then, we are numb with the routine reportage of honour killings and are in danger of digesting this as a new reality.

~

Simultaneously, with and despite this reactionary movement, the notion of commitment in relationships is changing. It is not simply the sacrifice of the self to the family as Campbell said.[8] Commitment is now about the self, either entirely divorced from the family, or the evolving self within the family: this self-centric approach as a positive attribute, as opposed to a selfish one, is taken by women to evolve beyond traditional roles and by men who want to explore a life more than as a provider for the family.

So you have modern life on the back of traditional values, which is well, except when there is modernity on archaic values: Thus are created complex creatures of law, such as when courts hold that if a promise to marry in the future is reneged from, then consenting sexual intercourse in the past was rape.[9] This reason for redressal makes it difficult to talk about legal rights emerging in a 'live-in' relationship.

Notwithstanding this, the twenty-first century still belongs to the bold individuals with the potential to break through and go beyond state and state-defined ideas of family and marriage. The idea that marriage is to produce children is not absolute any longer. Many modern couples have decided that life can be rich and meaningful even without being a parent. Others are adopting children or having them by surrogacy (the new bill clamping this freedom will probably be challenged with interesting outcomes). Single persons are also free to adopt and so children of biological or adoptive single parents are not a novelty in upper-middle-class India.

Wider social interaction has led to different types of relationships. One may be loyal to the ex-spouse without a sexual relationship any longer: there may be commitment to children other than one's own: loyalty to lovers married elsewhere: that apart, consider commitment to help an impoverished friend: commitment to colleagues: commitment to your own profession: loyalty to values and ideas and a special relationship with

---

8. Campbell, *The Power of Myth*, p. 7

9. State of U.P. vs. Naushad, AIR 2014 SC 384: 'A woman's body is not a man's plaything and he cannot take advantage of it in order to satisfy his lust and desires by fooling a woman into consenting to sexual intercourse simply because he wants to indulge in it. The accused in this case has committed the vile act of rape and deserves to be suitably punished for it.'

those who share them: this is a new network beyond family emerging from the heterosexual core of a man and a woman.

Marriage: A Legal or Social Entity?

The next question is whether marriage is a matter for society or for the law. Family law witnesses the closest intertwining of law and society. The law follows social norms, even while moulding societal views by declaring what is legal and illegal.

The societal instinct seems to be that marriage is more for social respectability than legal recognition. The legal rights that emanate from the married status are tested only at the time of divorce, but social acceptance is immediate. Instances of society prevailing over law can be seen in cases under the Land Ceiling Act. Many couples opted to state that they were living together and were not legally married in order to keep larger land holdings as two separate individuals rather than as a family unit. Many couples have opted for social marriages instead of legal, in order to avoid bigamy prosecution.[10] Hence, for the average person, social perception and acceptance is of greater importance than the law, which is seen as sitting far away in various seats of government.

Right-wing Hindu puritans blame a Western-influenced 'immorality' for the rising rate of divorce, but marriage remains popular in the West, where recognition of same-sex marriages has endorsed the institution by taking it to a new level. Here is an interesting example of the connection between law and society. Ruth Vanita's beautiful book, *Same Sex Marriage in India,* deals with same-sex marriages as an accepted reality in Indian society much before the present day homophobic attitudes, which can be traced to colonial law.[11] Even today, there are priests who perform Hindu marriage rites between same-sex couples.

Those who were surprised by the Supreme Court judgment in the Naz Foundation case[12] as regressive and out of pace with the times, need to consider that since her independence, apart from a few exceptions, India enjoyed a left-centric government that allowed liberal thought to develop, till those leaders failed us with the Emergency. The left has also lost social and political space because of its inability to deal with the deep roots of religion and marriage in almost all sectors of Indian society. It seems

10. See Ch. 4: The Fault Grounds for Divorce, p. 87, on bigamy

11. Ruth Vanita, *Love's Rite: Same-Sex Marriage in India and the West*

12. Suresh Kumar Koushal v. Naz Foundation, (2014) 1 SCC 1

unable to understand that the average non-intellectual needs them for a reassuring dimension and context to their life which otherwise may seem horribly mundane or, even worse, meaningless.

Now, intellectual discourse has disintegrated to shrill rhetoric between ideologues because the present conservative government seems not to be represented by public intellectuals who could rationalize the conservative point of view.[13]

Notwithstanding the vacuum in intellectual discourse, the power of women and an individualized middle-class continues to grow and (hopefully) make it impossible in the long run for a conservative movement to pull us back to the traditional view of marriage and women and caste and class boundaries.

We are moving to something that futurologists are wary of predicting till the cloud of dust raised by fast change settles, but a reading of the past can indicate the trajectory that we are on.

Till British rule, Indian women had better gender rights than those available to English women, but subsequent events have taken the West closer to the goal of gender equality. Family law in the West is well developed to enable a fair balance of various interests in a way that would benefit us to study.

Indian judges are reluctant to cite Western case law in family matters because they think our problems are unique to our culture and thus cannot be resolved with Western models of resolution. The use of the word 'model' to describe a set of rules or guidelines to deal with a situation is problematic however: model implies an insular and insulated self-contained unit created by law, that is then imposed on society. Such models do not help a solution for two reasons: there can be no 'model' as a solution to a social problem: the wave of an idea must fan out as far as possible in society. The law and its interpretation is what gives force to the wave, along with education and gender awareness: in this way, it can be seen that gender equality and the fair sharing of wealth and responsibilities is not limited to a Western 'model' but is a wave emerging from a constitutional mandate that needs to wash over our social ethos.

We need not emulate the West, but their experience of family law and gender studies is important, even if only to enable us to reject some of their ideas with good reason. For example, we are clearly not ready for entirely gender-neutral European-style laws that remove protections for women

13. Ramachandra Guha, *Democrats and Dissenters*

and reduce their maintenance and alimony claims, because those women are expected to work to full capacity. While the philosophy is sound, the problem with the approach is that it still benefits the man more. A study found that the income of men increases by 25 per cent after divorce, while women get poorer. This approach amounts to regulated unfairness.[14]

Some years ago, a Swedish woman came to consult me. She, with their two small children, had accompanied her husband while his career took him to many different countries. When marital problems began during the Indian posting, he expected her to return to Sweden with the children.

He said he would pay some child support but she was expected to return to work. She would get nothing to compensate for her being off the job market for twelve years after the children arrived. This is the problem when an egalitarian socialist system claims to be beyond patriarchy, but family reality remains rooted in old-fashioned gender roles. She was impressed with the theory of not treating as equal those who are innately unequal. That was a time I was grateful for some of our non-mechanical, humane judges who carry on stoically through our scathing remarks about the judiciary.

As was feared in 1956, the divorce law has not killed the culture and institution of marriage; it has not even killed the Indian ethos, however you may define it. Rather, it has helped nudge society to evolve to changing gender norms, which should lead to equality and mutual respect unless the current violent reactionary intervention is allowed to prevail.

~

In all this talk of law and divorce, it would be churlish of me not to recognize the human need for love that is contained in marriage. As long as that need exists, marriage will be something more than just a socio-economic unit. It is a celebration of a life partner who you hope will be a soul mate. The economics should not take away from the beauty of its purpose: it is another matter that it does do so, because the commerce has become so overwhelming.

Marriage pomp and splendour is a huge industry that feeds the consumer. Destination weddings, fashionable party planners, theme parties, branded luxury goods, designer trousseaus, honeymooning and luxury travel are part of the commerce of marriage, which will ensure that it continues to be successfully advertised as the best thing for everyone. Twenty years ago, when we discussed alimony, marriage expenses for

14. Singh, *Separated and Divorced Women in India: Economic Rights and Entitlement*

children were a separate head. Now, education in foreign universities is another head of expense, but by no means does that mean that the marriage expenses have become more sensible. Parties leading up to the event are so extravagant that in the last six months I have come across two couples who called off their weddings because the parents could not agree on who was to foot the bill!

Living together

The debate about whether to live together or marry has yielded no clear answer. Some couples I know have lived together for a long time but could not last even a year in marriage. What changed? None of them are ever able to articulate it, but I gather that marriage creates an expectation that they will play the archetypal husband and wife, which neither wants to meet. It is easier to coexist as two individuals with separate back-stories than be in the boiling pot of spouse stereotypes.

Despite some social change, and perhaps because living together is still largely limited to a miniscule minority of the upper-to-middle, mostly professional class, society is still heavily inclined towards marriage. Many people who want children opt to marry because they don't want to risk children 'out of wedlock' for the sake of their political and social ideology. Life outside marriage is riddled with problematic legal consequences, mixed with moral judgments. The following story will illustrate what I mean:

I met a former client at a dinner party. She had been divorced for ten years. With visible pride and affection she introduced her lover and friend to me as her partner. They radiated a happiness that touched me. They had been together five years. Their long wait into middle age for a satisfying relationship looked to have been worthwhile. He had two children from his previous marriage, both of whom had distanced themselves from him, the pain of which shadowed their father's happiness in his new partner, but did not kill it as the sons might have selfishly wanted.

My friend called one night. Her lover was fast sinking to death.

'We had been meaning to get married but never got down to it. As far as I know he has not made a will. We never discussed such things. We thought we would grow old together.' I heard her tears. A week later, he died.

The children arrived to collect their legacy. She called me to ask whether she had any rights to his estate. Not on the face of it—under the Hindu

Succession Act, without a will, she was not entitled to anything, strictly speaking. If my friend had married his lover even just before he died, she would have had a legal entitlement that a committed relationship of five years did not give her.

I may have advised my friend some legal action had she been destitute with children to support. I told her, 'We could try litigating to say that your relationship is in the nature of marriage and thus you are entitled to be maintained from the estate. It is a long shot though and you don't really need maintenance for basic needs, do you?'

'Not at all,' she said, 'and it sounds dreadful asking in those terms.'

Fortunately, her late companion's mother was supportive of my friend and called her 'Bahu'. The mother of a Hindu dying intestate is an heir along with his children. This mother decided that she was going to transfer her share to the person who her son loved and who had made him happy.

A case can be argued for the legal rights of a woman who has lived with a man. However the law is unclear and confusing. The April 2015 verdict of Dhannulal v. Ganeshram[15] dealt with the dilemma faced by my friend, where she could have claimed presumption of marriage to inherit the estate of her live-in partner/husband. The court held that the presumption must be in favour of marriage and against concubinage.

~

The number of 'live-in' relationships is now large enough for judicial notice, but the spectrum of judicial reactions is too wide, leaving no clear trace of the legal position. The complex texture of the law allows for different strategies in each case. In 2013, the Supreme Court called for Parliament to 'ponder' and legislate on laws for women and children born from such relationships. 'Live-in relationship is neither a crime nor a sin',[16] said the court, but also later cautioned that the 'legislature of course cannot promote pre-marital sex'.[17] Recently, the Supreme Court upheld a Bombay High Court decision to grant maintenance rights to a woman who was living with a married man.[18] In contrast, the Delhi High Court has chosen to ignore the last testament of a man who was living with a woman, by holding that the estranged wife had constructive

---

15. Dhannulal and Ors. v. Ganeshram and Ors., 2015(4) SCALE 613

16. Indra Sarma v. V.K.V. Sharma, 2013 (14) SCALE 448

17. *Ibid*, para 61

18. X and Y v. Z, Family Court Appeal No. 117 of 2005 (Bombay High Court), decision affirmed in Z v. X, SLP (C) No. 12978-12979/2015

and legal possession of the property in India by virtue of her status as a wife.[19]

This problematic situation reflects conflicts within society and resistance to change. Judicial *obiter dicta* consists of generalizations about what is 'immoral' or blaming genuine rape cases on 'spoiled live-in relationships'[20] and the notion that 'women in such relationships need to be protected'.[21] A Session's Court Judge was reported on 17 January 2012, as saying that live-in relationships are an 'infamous Western cultural product... Traditionally speaking, live-in relationships were alien to our nation till late. Even today it is fad which is visible only in urban areas.'[22] The good judge was constrained to take judicial notice of live-in relationships and that Parliament needed to deal with the issue, but could not resist also saying 'despite all the developments granting a level of legal legitimacy to live-in relationship, it is largely perceived to be an immoral relation in our society.'[23] That the comments were unnecessary is borne out by the facts of the case in which they were made: a simple case of convicting an Indian woman who was found to have stabbed her Nigerian boyfriend.[24]

Such reasoning obfuscates the true reason that marriage is important in law for no reason other than because of the legal rights that flow from it. Thus marriage is not about morality but as a starting point to calculate legal rights: so important is this starting point that it was thought better to presume marriage of a man and woman who had lived together for a long period of time rather than wasting time proving whether they were really married or not.

This legal fiction of presumption of marriage is culled from two sections in the Indian Evidence Act 1872. Section 114 empowers the court to presume the existence of certain facts. Section 50 empowers the court to look at relationships as relevant to arrive at a conclusion: for example if the court has to arrive at a finding of a marriage, it would be reasonable

---

19. Marguerite Chawla v. Miss Kiran Abnashi Chawla & Anr, MANU/DE/2946/2015

20. 'Live-in relationship road to lifelong commitment: Court' in *The Times of India* 6 December 2013.

21. Indra Sarma v. V.K.V. Sarma, (2013)14 SCALE 448

22. 'Live-in relationship a fad, perceived as immoral: Court' on NDTV 17 January, 2012.

23. *Ibid*

24. Zarzoliani v. State, Tis Hazari Court, Delhi, FIR No. 174/2008, SC No. 32/2010

for it to see as relevant that the man and woman were treated by their friends as husband and wife. Based on these two sections and for the need to do social justice, the Privy Council in 1927 and again in 1929 held that 'the law presumes in favour of marriage and against concubinage, when a man and woman have cohabited continuously for a number of years'.[25]

This presumption is subject to the right to rebuttal by a person refuting the marriage. The standard of proof in the rebuttal is what is in question. The courts tended to look to morality by setting a high standard wherein sometimes proof of custom may fail in the technicalities of evidence.

In 1952, in a case from Punjab, the Supreme Court said: 'It should be recognized that many agricultural tribes in the Punjab are governed by a variety of customs which depart from the ordinary rules of Hindu and Mohammedan law'.[26] The court however held the couple to be not married because the marriage by customary rites was not proven. The court held that 'custom in order to be binding must derive its force from the fact that by long usage it has obtained the force of law'. In 1971,[27] the Supreme Court affirmed the law of presumption of marriage, but even so, it held that the marriage was not proven. It needed Justice Krishna Iyer to say in 1978 that the presumption of marriage, though rebuttable, was not easily dislodged: 'Law leans in favour of legitimacy and frowns upon bastardy'.[28]

The live-in relationship was the subject of a Supreme Court ruling in 1994, in the case of a couple living together when either or both were married to others.[29] The question was whether the presumption of marriage stands rebutted if it is established that the marriage could not be valid. The court answered in the negative and ruled in favour of one Pavayee, who was presumed to be the wife of the late Manthi, though admittedly she was legally married to another man, while Manthi was married to another woman. The court was firmly liberal and ignored (but did not rule upon) the argument that Pavayee was clearly in an adulterous liaison with Manthi and could not be rewarded with legal rights.

Yet, the very next case reported in the Supreme Court volume of that

---

25. Mohabbat Ali Khan v. Mohd. Ibrahim Khan, AIR 1929 PC 135; A. Dinohamy v. W.L. Balahamy AIR 1927 PC 185

26. Thakur Gokal Chand v. Parvin Kumari, AIR 1952 SC 231

27. Kochan Kani Kunjuraman Kani v. Mathevan Kani Sankaran Kani, AIR 1971 SC 1398

28. Badri Prasad vs. Dy. Director of Consolidation and Ors., AIR 1978 SC 1557

29. S.P.S. Balasubramanyam v. Suruttayan, AIR 1994 SC 133

year, with the same senior judge, held that one Surjit Kaur[30] could not benefit from the principle of presumptive marriage. What seems to have swayed the court was the unproven allegation that 'Surjit Kaur was in the habit of changing husbands frequently'. Surjit Kaur was denied her property claim granted by the will of Gulaba Singh whom, she said, she had married by the karewa custom. She even filed a Karewa Nama to establish that. The court ruled that she could not prove her marriage even though it accepted that they had been living together for a long time. The presumption of marriage that arises from long cohabitation was not given the attention that Pavayee of the previous case had received. The court veered in the opposite direction and ruled 'mere living as husband and wife does not, at any rate, confer the status of wife and husband'.

Menski launched a scathing attack on the contrast between the two judgments saying, 'Depriving women like Kaur of any right in their deceased husband's property means these women are forced back into the old pattern of looking for another man to support them'.[31]

In keeping with this legal position on presumptive marriages and the law cited earlier, as compared to current social trends on living outside formal marriages, the PWDVA (2005) protects the rights of a woman in a relationship 'like a marriage'. However, the Supreme Court held that the PWDVA did not draw upon this presumption to give protection to women who lived in a relationship 'in the nature of marriage'. When a woman lives with a married man, she can claim no protection under the PWDVA and the presumption of marriage would not be available to her.[32]

The ruling that a woman living with a married man cannot claim protection under the PWDVA also dilutes the pre-statute legal position. The court observed that alienation of affection is an intentional tort that cannot be rewarded with statutory protection.[33] This part of the ruling is interesting in order to develop the law of tort that the judges acknowledged is at a nascent stage yet.[34]

Then, in 2013, the court revisited the issue and held that a woman living with a married man was vulnerable and needs to have rights of

30. Surjit Kaur v. Garcha Singh, AIR 1994 SC 135, p. 136

31. Menski, *Modern Indian Family Law*, p. 35

32. D. Velusamy v. D. Patchaiammal, 2010 (10) SCC 469.

33. Indra Sarma v. V.K.V. Sarma, (2013)14 SCALE 448; Pinakin Mahipatray Rawal v. State of Gujarat, (2013) 10 SCC 48

34. Right, duty, breach, injury and damages

protection under the PWDVA. It therefore called for an amendment of the definition of Section 2(f).[35] In many subsequent cases, the Supreme Court has reverted to upholding the principle of presumptive marriage.[36]

The two cases of Pavayee and Surjit Kaur highlight the problem of wide judicial discretion, leading to contradictory judgments, unpredictable rulings and uncertain law. The brunt of uncertain law is felt acutely in family law. For example, it would give no solace to Surjit Kaur that her case may be an aberration. Lawyers, judges, parliamentarians and even academics, while describing the bigger picture of a law, tend to forget the stories of the individual's search for justice and the times when it fails him or her.

One reason that the position is confused is that the court still sees itself in a moral conundrum about marriage versus unmarried partnership. An analysis of past legislation for marriage reform and of the recently presented bills that there was no time to take up, indicates that Parliament will do no more than draw a big picture.[37] At the end of the day, it is up to the courts to add shade and colour to portray our rapidly changing society's mores accurately.

DIVORCE IN INDIA TODAY

The divorce rate in India is increasing by quantum leaps though it remains the lowest in the world.[38]

Nevertheless, my uncle Gen. M.S. Mann's story is still relevant. Systemic problems of delay, conflicting interpretations of law and confusing precedents intensify the difficulty of unravelling complex

35. See p. 384: Section 2(f) of the PWDVA

36 Sobha Hymavathi Devi v. Setti Gangadhara Swamy and Ors., AIR 2005 SC 800; Bharatha Matha and Anr. v. R. Vijaya Renganathan and Ors., AIR 2010 SC 2685; Chanmuniya v. Virendra Kumar Singh Kushwaha, 2010 (10) SCALE 602; Dhannulal and Ors. v. Ganeshram and Ors, AIR 2015 SC 2382; Dhananjay Mahapatra; See also: 'Children born of live-in relationships are legitimate, Supreme Court says' in *The Times of India*, 24 April 2014; See also: Uday Gupta v. Aysha & Anr, 2014(5)SCALE358

37. Marriage Laws (Amendment) Bill as introduced in the Rajya Sabha in 2010, available at http://www.prsindia.org/uploads/media/Marriage%20Laws/Marriage%20 Laws%20Bill%20as%20passed%20by%20RS.pdf See also: Marriage Laws (Amendment) Bill as passed by the Rajya Sabha in 2013, available at http://www. prsindia.org/uploads/media/Marriage%20Laws/Marriage%20Laws%20Bill%20 as%20passed%20by%20RS.pdf

38. https://sites.google.com/site/indiandivorcelaws/divorce-rate-in-india

socio-economic structures. While beneficial legislation for women has been passed, their social and financial weakness still obstructs them from fearlessly asserting their new rights. At other times, women tend to misuse enabling legislations to force settlements to avoid sluggish legal systems.

Nevertheless, arguably, the overarching view is that marriages are important and not to be discarded carelessly, particularly when there are children.

This view misses the point that making divorce easier will help marriage as an institution. It will also avoid the suspicion-riddled live-in relationship that those who are refused divorce are constrained to embark upon, as did the General. Quite often, divorce is filed when one of the married partners wants to marry again. Divorce has increased the number of marriages—those arranged at second shaadi.com are a new genre.

A well-considered divorce has liberated many from bitter lives in emotionally arid zones. Moving on, through the mess, what is still clear is that the balance is shifting. Divorce is still not a right, but courts seem more inclined to grant it, unless there are weighty reasons against it. In 2006, the Supreme Court[39] discussed the need to introduce irretrievable breakdown of marriage as a ground, quoting that the 71st Law Commission report of 1978 had recommended that divorces be made easier.

To say that divorce should not be easy because society should show commitment to marriage is problematic. Contentious divorces are not going to allow for clean severance and healthy reconstructed lives, which surely are valuable social goals.

Under the present fault theory regime, it is impossible to get a divorce when your spouse is good to you, but that is still not enough for you. Some may say it is immoral to cause pain to a good spouse; but something seems perverse when a person is denied a divorce because s/he is not unhappy enough or the other side is not cruel enough. And that is the fault theory in a nutshell. It seems more humane to ensure that the divorce is clean, with equitable financial divisions in the aftermath.

It would also be an oversimplification to say that divorce has killed, compromised or sullied the haven of family. Divorce courts have served as the best laboratory to study family and how the law can benefit it. The right to pursue happiness, satisfaction and emotional enrichment (of course in contrast to instant gratification) is not explicit in the Indian Constitution but it can be read as implied within the guarantee of right to

39. Naveen Kohli v. Neelu Kohli, (2006) 4 SCC 558

life, and awareness of this may help counter the superficial moral façade around the institution of marriage.[40]

The potential of new relationships after a divorce to broaden the concept of family is not studied enough because of the social awkwardness around a 'failed' relationship. But it does not have to be so. Here is a good example of changing family structures: An eighty-year-old lady was going for a major surgery in a few days. Her two sons, one settled in the US and another in Dubai, came to be with her at Delhi along with their wives and children. Till they arrived, the person who had been with her through tests and doctor's visits till the diagnosis was confirmed, was the ex-wife of the old lady's son in the US. It is she who had kept her ex-husband and brother in law informed about their mother. She was the pivot of the family gathering I attended. She sat near her ex-husband and their daughter. Her new husband and his daughter from his previous marriage were there too.

That may be the case in a very trendy upper-class family, you will think. That's what I thought too, till I saw a TV advertisement for bed linen: a young girl is with her middle-aged father helping him buy sheets and bedcovers. While he protests at the expense, she says with a sideways glance at an attractive middle-aged woman shopping nearby, 'Papa, divorce does not mean you have to be a saint.' Children seem to be more accepting of their parents' divorce and remarriage and perhaps, of them as sexual beings as well.

~

Predictably, anxious conservatives worry that 'Indian family values' are dying because of such 'modern' ideas, by which they mean Western lifestyles and women who do not 'adjust'. In doing so, they choose to be obtuse about the power of a modernizing India. Whether they like it or not, a growing middle-class population is focusing on their individual aspirations beyond and outside marriage: love beyond family ties, exploring alternative sexualities, an alternative career that is less lucrative for the family, but more satisfying for the person. There are also papers being written about polyamory building the new family, but they do not concern us as yet. These changes are breaking boundaries of the traditional family unit and divorce is needed to adapt to this change: to deny divorce is to deny change and that really serves no purpose because, as they say, the only unchanging thing is that change is inevitable. The supporters of

40. Locke, *An Essay Concerning Human Understanding*

marriage in fact need to allow for divorce, because if marriage is going to be viewed as life imprisonment, the emerging empowered may prefer not to marry at all, and that will not serve the conservative position either.

Conservatives feel bound to disapprove of divorce, which breaks what they see as a sacred bond. In fact even a new-age liberal may see marriage as, if not sacred, certainly a spiritual conjoining of two beings who subsume their independent egos to each other. The idea is ethically attractive, but only if it allows the partners, in all humility, to acknowledge mistakes of choice, in order to continue the spiritual journey of which marriage is one part. These explorations and mistakes are in the realm of the individual's private life and, at present, the law of our free state respects the right of the individual to realize its inner potential in its own way.

To realize individual potential is a struggle and by its very definition, struggle includes heartache and disappointment. To inflict a punishment of life imprisonment for disappointment may be disproportionate and also is antithetical to the idea of spiritual growth that personal relationships are supposed to help us with.

As a divorce lawyer, I have learned that deep friendships are magical and marvellous and worth working at and sacrificing the self for. They are ennobling and help soften life's hardships. A friend in a spouse is indeed a grace, but with changing social norms and mores, a spouse is only one option to maintain a life-long friendship. The conservative naysayers underestimate the deep feeling for community and family that will survive changing parameters of marriage, because it is their community and family that supports a person through heartache.

But change is inevitable and it is a waste of energy and emotion and a life to resist it. We have to accept the shifting gender balance within and outside marital relationships. Increased divorces are one symptom of this shifting balance and, from that position of acceptance, we watch the gender balance closely to help avoid it settling into another imbalance: the law has to ensure that it does not tip too much in favour of men who are still socially more powerful or that enabling legislation for women does not work against the rights of men.

My Advice to Clients Undergoing Divorce

At the time of your marriage, you probably did not think beyond the promise of romance. Despite the jokes about marriage being drudgery and the end of romance, you (and even the cynics) had hoped that you would create a valuable base on which to build a life. You surely did not think of your legal rights within your new family unit. Marriage is a bid for joy, with security and supported personal growth—which is why divorce is earth-shaking. It is the end of the life that you knew or had hoped for. Like your marriage, your divorce too will become a defining moment, with life events marked either 'before' or 'after' the divorce.

~

The realization that your marriage is breaking is intuitive: It begins as you sense a growing dread in yourself while returning home and it culminates the day you or your spouse decide, for any number of reasons, that 'this is enough'. The decision may be by either of you, but it ends a defining feature of both your lives as well as those of your children and perhaps some extended family as well.

Once either of you decide to end a marriage, you both, distraught, rummage amongst its ruins, for your belongings and children. At this point, someone should tell you that you need to look after yourself. Clinical studies categorize divorce as the highest stress category of personal catastrophe[41] that can trigger depression and suicide. You must acknowledge that you need help. You may visit a family elder for advice and support, or a counsellor; and sooner or later, you will need legal advice.

The Law and You

Your first visit to a divorce lawyer is the beginning of a journey that can be tumultuous, painful, exhilarating and liberating, but never simple. It is a frustrating journey because you are in a situation that you cannot influence entirely. You may wish to work with fresh vigour at the marriage, or you may want an easy, painless divorce, but your spouse may not want the marriage, or might seize the opportunity to highlight your faults and assert her/his rightness during the divorce process. You may say that this is irrational behaviour, but divorce is rarely governed by pure reason.

Even if both of you want the divorce, you still might not have an easy exit because, as a friend of mine said to me: 'It is easier to start something than to close it down.' He was talking about business but marriage too is

41. P.R. Amato, 'The consequences of divorce for adults and children' in *Journal of Marriage and Family* Vol. 62, No. 4 (Nov 2000), pp. 1269–87; See also Johnson and Wu J., 'An empirical test of crisis, social selection, and role explanations of the relationship between marital disruption and psychological distress: a pooled time-series analysis of four-wave panel data' in *Journal of Marriage and Family*, Vol. 64, No. 1 (Feb 2002) pp. 211–24.

as complex to close down, because of the investments made in it that now have to be unraveled and returned to the shareholders—the spouses and children. This is why long tenure marriages usually have deeper divorce reverberations.

As with any quarrel you may have had in the past, the pain of the divorce battle is heightened by the sense of righteousness of the one wronged. Both sides think they are right and feel justified in their actions, even as the righteous belief leads to a toxic mess. As counsel, we usually advise you against emotional knee-jerk reactions that often backfire and prefer that you move slowly with careful reflection and introspection.

Even after due consideration, every move has its own set of problems that have to be overcome to minimize collateral damage. You will get angry and frustrated with your lawyer, when s/he tells you to do nothing. You will want them to be aggressive and take action. Your lawyer however knows that masterly inactivity is also a strategy. I often tell my clients: 'Do you ever see the powerful flapping around? They move slowly and surely.' The counsel's advice to you comes from a mixture of lawyer's experience and gut instinct, but be prepared for a change in strategy as new circumstances unfold. The divorce battle is a dynamic situation that changes every day and yet it may also be frustratingly static for a long time. Dealing with these variations is part of case management.

One of the main things you need to learn during the divorce process is how to wait. This is more than just marking time or trying not to panic as court dates approach: you need to learn to look after yourself and live a full life between the hearing dates. That is not easy at all, I agree, but one particularly difficult factor is ultimately under your control: whether or not you view your divorce as a handicap. You have to learn to walk into a room alone and ignore the stares from those who may view your new single status as your personal failure.

I have asked myself whether the death of a spouse is better than the death of the marriage. The death of a spouse leaves a painful vacuum, but it is nature's work. As you fall apart, you have the empathy and support of your entire family and all your friends who help you reconstruct yourself. Divorce, on the other hand, has all of the grief, along with many elements of anger and bitterness that obstruct the grieving process. Your friends and family may be divided in opinion about which of you is right and thus you may not have their unconditional support. There can never be a clean break: you are always the ex-spouse, co-parent, co-owner of property.

You may never be entirely comfortable with that role but you will have to learn to live with it. In the aftermath of the divorce, meetings with your former spouse can cause strong reactions, including the physical symptoms of helpless grief and anger: palpitations and tears. You will need succour, but the legal process might actually exacerbate the grief, focusing as it does on the faults of the other side. Simmering in your bitterness and rage, you may feel that the other side has not been punished enough or that you have not received justice.

This is my effort to tell you that you have to teach yourself to live with many wrongs, even when you think you are absolutely and exclusively in the right.

You may have missed the dialogue of mutual respect in your marriage, but it would be useful to make it part of the divorce interaction, to create a different relationship with your soon-to-be-ex that allows for a peaceful coexistence, as co-parents for example.

~

Your divorce may be your first engagement with the law and you are likely to be disenchanted by an overwhelming and bewildering legal system that allows innumerable possible outcomes, many of which may seem unjust. Your lawyer has to help you realize that the system of justice suffers all the flaws, weaknesses and failings of the persons who created it and the people who dispense it. 'Out of timber so crooked as that from which man is made nothing entirely straight can be built'.[42]

A legal system cannot improve on human beings. It cannot change someone and make him or her better, or the person you would like him/her to be. The law is not going to undo life's unfairness and offer you a fresh fair deal. The law and its systems will not change your spouse at a core level and improve your marriage. It does not create better persons and parents. Any lawyer who tries to tell you otherwise is playing God. And the legal joke[43] is that the difference between God and a lawyer is that God does not think he is a lawyer.

During your battle, remember to distinguish between asserting your legal right and expecting your spouse to maintain a righteous moral conduct. The latter is an imperfect obligation that cannot be enforced in law. Individual or personal morality and the law are not the same things: although law claims to be rooted in a universal morality, society and hence judges are not always in agreement about the finer points of that universal

42. Immanuel Kant, *Idea for a General History with a Cosmopolitan Purpose*

43. Quoted in Sadakat Kadri, *The Trial: A history from Socrates to O.J. Simpson*

morality. For example, it can be argued that it is universally immoral to kill, hence the law forbids it; but sexual mores and personal lifestyle choices are relative morally and so judgments may vary on the issue.

This is worth thinking about, even in the course of married life and about relationships generally. The dividing line between appropriate, right and illegal behaviour is porous. A person given to illegal behaviour may have a robust family life. In contrast, inappropriate behaviour and morally wrong conduct, while not illegal, may create great stress on the marriage. It is my personal right to misbehave; be inappropriate; I may want to drink too much on my fiftieth birthday. But am I a bad parent or partner because of it? My family may think so, but not the law.

A shopaholic spouse or a miserly one may be unfair, but neither of the two irritating or even destructive traits is illegal. It is not illegal that the earning spouse does not save enough, or that she was denied the seven-star holiday because he bought a golf set instead without asking her. A flirtatious nature or undue self-absorption that leads to neglecting the inner and finer needs of the spouse are immoral for the suffering spouse, but the law will not help unless the behaviour grossly flouts the standards of 'inappropriate' that modern family law is beginning to take cognizance of.[44]

While living with your spouse, you may have boundaries which, when crossed, however unwittingly, are perceived as wronging you. He surprises you with a magenta painting of a nude woman leering on a sofa. He wants it on the drawing room wall. You will surely not say it is ugly if you still love him, but the way to live with it is an essay on life itself. The leering magenta woman may be the last straw. You don't have a place to cry any longer because when you go to the drawing room at night to think your thoughts, they are blurred by the luridness of the magenta. Regardless, the law will not make you feel better by rapping the spouse on the knuckles or punishing him/her for less than perfect behaviour. A thoughtful family grapples with these matters and tries to avoid possessive expectations, to allow for individual privacy and freedom. It is a careful, difficult balance: for example, an asexual close friendship outside marriage may be viewed as inappropriate by some couples, while others may think it necessary for the marriage.

While you are spending time figuring out how to live with the spouse

---

44. Lord Sumption, 'Family law at a distance'; Munby, *Law, Morality and Religion in the Family Courts*, pp. 131–139

and his/her bad taste, do not forget that this is the person you chose and some responsibility for that choice must be taken by you. If it was an arranged marriage, remember it is a risk you took.

Then there are serious matrimonial offences of unarguable cruelty, desertion and infidelity. Though the law should compensate you for the injury you have suffered, the malaise of the system is that retribution comes too little, too late and frankly sometimes not at all. Family law is about balancing the wear and tear of marriage, reprehensible behaviour and a marital offence. It is for you to maintain that fine line between personal liberty and gross illegality and to remember that the judge will not step in to check all the wrongs perceived by you.

Family law has moved from revering marriage as sacred, to acknowledging a more contractual arrangement, because sacredness cannot obliterate the individual's right to exit the wedlock for just cause. The post-modern divorce law the world over, is now moving to a better appreciation of the right of a person to undo the mistake of an unfortunate choice of partner and seek fulfillment in a new relationship. Indian law does not seem to have kept up, except in cases where the Supreme Court has dissolved marriages using its extraordinary power under Article 142[45] of the Constitution. This however could be viewed by the lower courts as a signal to exercise the margin of discretion while appreciating evidence to dissolve a marriage where finance and children are not at serious issue.

In your engagement with the law, you will learn the bitter lesson that the presence of laws is not enough to ensure that they will be complied with and most people tend to break the law if they can get away with it. This is why courts and lawyers have to be vigilant and active and sensitive to maintaining the integrity of the rule of law.

~

Let us look to how legal systems developed. We today have a Constitution, the basic structure of which is immutable and it guarantees such human rights and liberties that are basic to a democratic system. The Directive Principles of state policy define the ideal that a state evolves towards, much like a plant growing towards the sun.

As civilizations advanced, laws were enacted to make illegal certain acts that had obtained social and legal sanction of custom. Sati, oppressive caste systems, child marriage, dowry, violence against women and Manu's misogynist views on women were all customary law. The written law has

45. See p. 357: Article 142, Constitution of India

changed but the problems of society that still chooses to govern itself by ugly custom remain.

The relationship between society and law is symbiotic: law reflects prevailing social norms even while providing the ideal towards which to nudge society. They work together and yet also against each other and in that case, not only must the law prevail but it also has to ensure the mechanism by which it must prevail.

In your case, as a litigant and as a part of society, you will see and sense your complex relationship with the law. You and your case are a part of the evolution of law as legal processes grapple with trying to create a society based on equality and respect for the individual, even while working to be cohesive.

Mediation

The resolution of family disputes by mediation is a demanding subject that has now become an integral part of the family law system. Despite its advantages, pre-litigation mediation has not become mandatory, though it is ordered as a matter of course at the commencement of litigation.

Mediators are not judges and are trained to restrain themselves from being judgmental. Many judges could benefit from such training as well. Some mediators have been a pleasure to deal with. Their empathy edged with firmness commands the confidence of both parties. Their commitment is noble. Most of their work is pro bono and they take time out of very busy schedules as successful lawyers to spend hours dealing with people whose pain is difficult to manage.

It is useful to highlight some problems of the mediation system while it is still developing. The training mediators undergo needs to be more rigorous to dilute their individual cultural personas which must not interfere with their ability to deal with cultural diversity. Some deeply regressive attitudes are still working against the current of change that is flooding family lives. Mediators who cannot understand and respect that change must not be allowed to mediate. A ghastly incident illustrates the dangers of such cases:

A man, his wife and their two brilliant daughters were caught in an ugly litigation. We were advising the wife and daughters. The older daughter was a scholarship student at an Ivy League university, who had recently figured on the Dean's List of meritorious students. She was outspoken and forthright and protective of her shy, school-going sister. Both had witnessed domestic violence and refused to talk to their father whom they saw as the unfair, unjust aggressor.

The mediator asked the older girl to spend time alone with her father. She refused. The mediator insisted and said that 'after all, he is your father and you must respect him as per our Indian culture'. She replied that he had performed no role in their lives worthy of being a father and she would have nothing to do with him. The mediator kept badgering her to meet her father till she could not keep her brave poise and sobbingly told the mediator that if she saw her father, she would slap him but did not want to demean herself by doing that. She called the mediator partisan.

The mediator lost his temper at her 'disrespectful' manner. This is certainly not 'our culture', he said. 'It is these attitudes that gets girls like you raped'. Then the younger daughter started crying while the tears of her older sister dried up in silent shock.

They called their mother who called my associate. This is my colleague's account: 'When I confronted the mediator, he admitted he said that but it was a "general" statement and not aimed at the daughters. He kept telling me that he could still speak to the father with regard to the terms of settlement that we had asked for.' We complained against the mediator to the Family Court judge. The judge agreed that the mediator should not have said what he did, but as far as we know, he remains on the panel of mediators. No action was taken against him.

Mediation as a single approach

Canada has developed a sophisticated system of lawyers working with their clients in a collaborative process, as opposed to adversarial litigation. It requires the lawyers to commit that they will not litigate. Julia Macfarlane writes in her paper on the experience of working collaboratively:[46]

> 'Spouses are an open book to one another, and the language of affidavits attacks all the vulnerabilities of the other. This is destructive between spouses as well as for children. Then an idiotic jerk of a judge who probably has an IQ of about 10 decides what should happen to this family.
>
> 'For many lawyers, watching their clients' distress compounded their own stress. Some described clients who had killed themselves, and many others talked about the impact of litigation (whether or not ultimately successful) on their clients' lives.'

---

46. Julie Macfarlane, *Experiences of Collaborative Law: Preliminary Results from the Collaborative Lawyering Research Project*, p. 191

In Canada, family lawyers choose either of these two approaches depending on which is more in consonance with their own personalities. In India, the collaborative approach does not seem possible as yet, because mediation protocol has not developed formal procedure or rules. Some would say that is a good thing, because formality kills the spirit of mediation. I agree to some extent, but some rules would be helpful. For example, financial disclosures and discovery processes in mediation would help drive realistic settlements pegged to legal entitlements, instead of a broad need-based approach. Those who fear that mediation may be used to discover documents which could eventually lead to litigation should be aware that now financial disclosures are the first set of court proceedings in most courts. It is thus practical to make fair disclosures at any forum and then be done with it.

At present, the mediator's role is that of a counsellor, telling the parties to 'move on' and settle for a 'little less' and so on. Mediation is thus often not an effective forum with the rich and powerful, who have the means to take a chance in litigation, banking on the uncertainty of its outcome. Nevertheless, even in its present nascent form, pre-litigation mediation remains a useful and strategic option, because it opens a back channel of dialogue and a 'vent' if matters go to court.

The downside is that mediation is vulnerable to misuse as a delaying tactic where there is no true intent to settle. Sometimes judges prefer to relegate complex matters to mediation and lawyers use the mediation route to avoid a potentially adverse ruling from a tough judge. But all said and done, the mediation process and its protocol of civility helps dialogue which, as we know, is at the end of it the only means to put any matter truly at rest.

Once litigation begins, the sabre-rattling and posturing makes settlement difficult. It is also difficult to rise above and ignore the barely veiled hostility that litigants have towards opposing lawyers and even judges. Many litigants and even their lawyers make loose personal allegations against the opposing side and their lawyers. Some lawyers seem to treat litigation as a game and the bad-mouthing is dismissed as 'sledging': learning to cultivate a Tendulkar-like serenity is a spiritual lesson that very few of us have completed. It all adds up to a very ugly battle in the trenches which even the most robust and seasoned lawyer is tempted to give up or turn away from—but that would amount to allowing the other side to succeed in their nefarious design of pushing you out of the battle.

Taking Heart

If you are a woman, then divorce is stressful because you have to re-evaluate your life in terms of finances and society, in that order. You also have to cope with the unhappiness and complaints of your children. They may turn against you and make you a scapegoat in their turmoil because children, like adults, look for someone to blame for their unhappiness, often the person they are closest to, or whom they perceive to be the most vulnerable—that may well be you.

The positive side is that your singleness is an opportunity for your growth as an individual without the context and restraint of a partner. It can be fulfilling and liberating to live alone. You could be an example to your children, particularly to a daughter, on the importance of self-esteem when you insist on mutual respect in your new relationships and do not look to a man for social and financial security. Your son could learn to respect, admire and enjoy strong women who have the courage to allow their men to cast off traditional male roles of being the only providers.

Love and marriage can happen again; maybe this time it will be for the sake of nothing other than the joy of a compatible companion. A word of caution however: don't make the mistake of looking to marriage as a panacea for your personal problems.

~

If you are a man, you are lucky (is that not always the case?) because gender ratios indicate that you remain eligible.

If the children are against you, please know that surveys and studies have shown that children invariably look for the estranged parent to identify and understand their provenance. Your child will eventually know your version of the truth. You may have suffered false charges of dowry harassment and domestic violence by vindictive women. Children will learn of that as well and that will be the time of reckoning for their mother.

To both parents, the mantra question should be: do I hate my spouse more than I love the children? You may want to consider being the way you want your children to be.

~

My advice to a distraught and grieving spouse is to develop activity which is individually fulfilling, and to try not to be a martyr to the cause of the divorce. You are not alone in your trauma. All divorcing couples grieve. Many are so shocked they can hardly talk; others can't stop talking. All have pain that they deal with differently. A healthy diet, exercise and rest are medicinal for all grief; modern medication and therapy are other useful supports.

Traumatic events, including bad partnership decisions and bitter divorces, can be a watershed for significant personal growth. If you agree with me that one of the purposes of living a meaningful life is personal growth, then you may agree that battling sadness achieves greater strength, much like many illnesses build immunity. Things could be worse: think of the loss of a child or terminal illness. This is divorce but it may well be a new beginning to a better future.

On a lighter note, always leave a courtroom smiling and happy. Don't allow the seeming good health and robustness of the other side to wreak havoc on your own mind. Have we missed something, my clients ask when they see the good cheer of the other side. Nothing, I say. Like you, they are also under legal advice to look happy. And yet, jokes apart, believe me, if you want revenge, the best revenge is to live well.

Don't expect the judge to eliminate the problem. S/he can only endeavour to minimize the impact of your problem. S/he can protect you from abuse, pass orders relating to finance and try to help the children. S/he will try to redress the balance of inequalities that are exposed at the time of divorce, and will try to order equitable sharing of money and time with children. This is the judge's mandate but remember judges and judgments are not ideal.

It may sound odd, but I say it without embarrassment, that the process of grappling with the philosophy of true justice versus the letter of the law has a spiritual by-product. Take heart that the effort is to improve systems: there are reform programs, therapy and counselling while judges philosophize and grapple and theorize about these matters. Take heart that there is a yearning to create institutions and systems that bring out the best in human beings. The sincere yearning to be better is an ideal enough.

FREQUENTLY ASKED QUESTIONS

This was originally a part of the Epilogue, but my editor insisted that it should be in this format. I do believe these are important things to consider, and I hope you will agree with me after you have read it. I have no complete answers to many of these questions, but I will try to address some of the most common ones.

Q: How do you begin the process?

A: One of the first questions I ask a person who comes to consult me is 'if the other person said sorry and really wanted the marriage to work, would you want to continue to try to fix it?'

The usual response is: but s/he will never say that.

Treat it as a fantasy situation, I insist: the answer, even if uncertain, is significant and could lead to the next question: name five good qualities of the estranged spouse.

The entire strategy of the litigation will unfold based on the answers to these two questions. I believe that aggressive litigation/intervention can begin only when there is a negative answer to the fantasy situation and despite the five good qualities.

My next question is, 'if you are certain to divorce, is there a chance of a dialogue towards a settlement initiated by family elders or mutual friends?' Since the family elder will know the person concerned, s/he can choose the particular 'family values' dialogue that will influence a decision to settle. But family elders now have less time and in any case no longer occupy the traditional position of absolute obedience or even respect. Many mutual friends want to avoid being dragged into the toxic mess of litigation and so prefer to stay away. The need of the hour is specialists trained in ethical standards that are not subjective.

Q: What do you think I should do?

A: Your call entirely! But here are a few caveats:

Don't become your case and inflict it on every hapless soul at every dinner party because, besides being a boring guest, you will also be confused by the contradictory (often inept) advice.

Don't get addicted to legal research on the Internet. The information overload on the Internet misleads one to think that there is enough to make an informed decision. Research is necessary to frame pertinent questions, so do just enough for that.

Take professional advice from lawyers and accountants and talk to some friends and family elders whose opinions you value and whom you trust will not thrive on conflict to inflate their own importance in your life. You don't need fuel but calm advice.

Q: You say maintenance orders are based on an assessment of lifestyle. What lifestyle is the benchmark? The one we lived together or the one based on my future earnings or those of my spouse.

A: It is based on the life you lived together, but what you earn later could be a factor if the order for maintenance is passed at a later date. This is why it is better to settle quickly, since earning graphs generally increase.

Q: The other side is really dangerous. Will I be able to handle it?

A: That's your lawyer's problem. Take heart that, without exception, every person at my table has said that about the other side.

Q: How long will it take?

A: It can take years. Before proceedings begin, the court will send you to mediation. Months can go by in that. If the mediators fail, the judge may try to mediate as well. Each judge will try to talk to the parties. This is time-consuming and the outcome is unpredictable.

Once proceedings begin and after pleadings are complete, many interim applications need to be decided; issues of maintenance and custody are primarily addressed. This, too, can take years. Matters move at a relaxed pace because courts generally are liberal in granting extensions of time for compliance with orders. This is frustrating, but the rationale to the liberal approach is that orders based on technical points of law are invariably overturned by the higher courts.

Q: How do I proceed with my life?

A: You must try to create a life that is as far as possible from the case. Focus on each day and make the most of it. Look for something truly elevating instead of making the case the focus of your very being. Don't expect too much from the system and if you do, be prepared to be very, very patient; very, very consistent; and still be prepared to be disappointed. Trials and court cases can go any which way, and justice has many facets: it is not just about you.

Q: When can I embark on a new relationship?

A: That is a tough one. Till the divorce, you are legally married and any other relationship will be viewed as adulterous. Of course, it is not sensible to stave off a new relationship and a chance of happiness because of endless divorce proceedings.

While it is true that a new relationship could hasten a settlement, my best advice is to exercise extreme caution and care. Better not to jump into another relationship without having severed this bond and recovered from it. We all know what happens to rebounds.

Q: What is the preferred route: mediation or litigation?

A: Mediation is better because, even if it may not heal, at least it does not wound, as contentious divorces are prone to do. I now routinely advise pre-litigation mediation. It has a reasonable success rate and, in case of failure, you will at least have managed to identify the areas of contest and perhaps even the psychology of it. This is an important exercise for resolution.

The different perspectives of each member of the family lead to many different, often contradictory, stories that need to be streamlined while looking for a resolution as a family. In litigation this is difficult because there is no process of harmonizing stories, and the scenario is further obscured by the clashing perspectives of lawyers and judges. Mediation helps a clearer picture to emerge for the parties, to enable them to outgrow the irrationality of their righteousness that may blind and embitter them.

Q: What is the ballpark figure to settle at? What is the norm?

A: There is no such figure. At the end of the day, the final figure is a combination of what you negotiate with the other side, what you need and what you want.

Q: Should I settle now?

A: That's a tough one. Your position is yours alone. A settlement requires a party settling for less than their ideal figure: that figure is somewhat pegged to what would be legally due in an ideal legal system. By this figure I mean that which the financially weaker (usually the wife) demands and that the financially stronger deems as reasonable.

Regrettably, a settlement, for both spouses, is often reached at great variance from their original position, after the realization that waiting for adjudication will take too long and, may not be worth it. This is the tragedy of the legal system failing the divorcing couple where the weaker party simply collapses under the strain of litigation or police harassment and thus 'drives' a settlement.

Judges could actually effect settlements by speedy dispensation of justice and quick orders instead of adjourning complex family issues with visible relief for mediation talks. Mediation cannot be the answer to bypass an overloaded legal system struggling with systemic problems.

~

There are many reasons why a person might not be willing to settle: The process of settling is complex because it is more than a paper transaction. There has to be closure within a person's mind and heart. The moment of settlement is not merely about the law. It is even deeper than ethics; it is about when you are ready to declare peace without feeling you have lost. No point in settling if you are going to be at war within yourself after that. A ceasefire or an armistice is never enough because it is difficult to live in uncertain peace in what is clearly a war zone.

Settlement talks require restraint even while refusing to allow free rein to a bully. Correct and inoffensive demeanour, conduct and protocol are essential for meaningful dialogue.

Move on with your life, the anguished man is told; use the alimony money and live well, the woman with the fat alimony offer is told. But the heart and the mind have to be willing to accept a peace offering from people tied to you with a toxic bond. How will you swallow your pride and shake hands with a person who has humiliated you and lied and cheated even in the course of litigation? I agree that sometimes even though it is practical, it seems immoral to accept an offer of settlement that is stinging in its unfairness and it seems wrong to not further pursue your rights.

A businessman worth thousands of crores offered my client a substantial alimony amount that would take care of her needs and wants, but he humiliated her by throwing it at her like an insult. She refused.

Another woman client had an alimony offer that can take a lifetime for an above average professional to earn, but she too refused because they wanted her to give up custody of her daughter. The family had got together and brainwashed the child into disliking the mother. She said she felt like she was selling her child.

A man refused to settle because his wife accused him of sexually abusing their daughter and he wanted to clear his name.

A man refused to settle because his wife lived in the matrimonial home worth several crores and then tried to reach for another property by blocking its sale. He could not tolerate the blatant greed and dishonesty.

Another man refused to settle because after spending two nights in jail on false charges of Section 498A he felt the worst was over and all he wanted now was to avenge the humiliation.

~

My advice is never to plug settlement avenues with offensive conduct. Remember the skill of the diplomat. Give the other side a face-saving exit because if you push them to the wall leaving no room for manoeuver, they will fight with renewed vigour. Don't let them have the moral high ground. The source of many types of violence is delusions of righteous rage.

The strategy has an ethical component, not to earn a halo but the practical and time-tested theory of ethical conduct earning good will and thus being sustainable in the long run. You might find that you get more eventually than what you settled for because of the ethical quality of the relationship that you negotiated during the dialogue.

The mood in settlement talks is complex because the grief of individuals watching their life unravel deserves respectful empathy. We, as lawyers, have to be careful with how we advise too. Sometimes my own client is exhausted and can't deal with the stress, while others are robust and angry and want the good fight to battle their cause against the injustice of their situation. A lot of this is based on trusting your lawyer. Sometimes settlements are fair and I jump at them, but some clients get suspicious when they think lawyers are pushing for settlements too hard. But timing is essential. Moments of closure emerge in a prevailing situation and can quickly submerge as well, like a particular wave in the flow of a river.

With difficult cases that can't be settled, we push for a court ruling and help create useful precedent. I sometimes have had to advise the practical route of walking away, because the battle is too fraught and uncertain. This advice is not easy even for me because it is disturbing to watch the perpetrator of horrific mental and physical crimes stroll out of the courtroom with a casual insouciance. The lesson I have learned is that divorce law is about the protection of the victim from cruelty, not about the punishment of the aggressor. This is a bitter lesson, and I agree that the matter seems unjust. It will be redressed only when finance and custody disputes are meaningfully close to legal principles and entitlements.

Now I share with you my most valuable lesson. While assessing a legal win do not forget that you can still feel defeated. The true lesson of the *Mahabharata* is not that the Pandavas were victorious, but that when their victory was obtained by breaking the rules, and justified by amorphous moral standards of past ill treatment, the aftermath of the war was emptiness, even if the cause was seen as morally and legally valid.

'Alas, having defeated the enemy, we ourselves have been defeated…this our victory is twined into defeat' (*Mahabharata*)[1] This sense of emptiness after years of litigation can be avoided by choosing a well-judged moment to settle.

Q: Why do you talk so much about ethics, protocol and demeanour in family law? It sounds pompous.

A: I might sound priggish, but ethics are an intrinsic part of a well lived life: and particularly important when family litigation is ultimately about the litigant's sense of right and wrong. This is always complex because there is no one reason behind any particular event. Rather than trying to get to a reason, it is better to deal with the current situation with restraint, and with respect for the law and its institutions, because that helps in checking the further deterioration of your bad situation.

In India this is a difficult exercise for most because our relationship with the law is not final, absolute and positive as in Abrahamic law. Hindu law developed around principles of sadachara (the usage of virtuous men) as contained in the Smritis and Dharmashastras: 'The secret of dharma is very deep. Follow the path traversed by the great'.[2] The process of arriving at dharma requires deep discourse and analysis of wise words. Varied texts allowed for widely divergent interpretations in different situations. A Shruti could say one thing and a Smriti another.[3] Such conflicts in the texts were to be interpreted by a sista, who is defined as one whose heart is free from worldly desires. Only those acts of sistas are to be held as dharma which have no (worldly or secular) cause (or motive).[4]

The role of the sista could be played by family elders or a panchayat, but this is liable to be self-serving. The panchayats are inclined to impose stringent laws to increase and maintain their hierarchical power.[5] The

1. In Gurcharan Das, *The Difficulty of Being Good*. That deserves another book that I hope I have the wits and strength to write some day. Every rule of war was broken by every Pandava to defeat the Kauravas: so does the moral high ground that started the war get muddied when the rules of war are broken.

2. See http://www.ambedkar.org/ambcd/64B4.On%20the%20Hindu%20Code%20Bill.htm

3. Gautam, *Shruti and Smriti: Some Issues in the Re-emergence of Indian Traditional Knowledge*

4. Kane, *History of the Dharmasastras*, Vol.III, p. 824

5. Uma Chakravarti, *Conceptualising Brahmanical Patriarchy in Early India: Gender, Caste, Class and State*, pp. 579-585

role of the sista was also performed by the king. 'The practice of duty having died out amongst mankind, actions at law (Vyavhara) have been introduced and the King has been appointed to decide them because he has the authority to punish'.[6] Vyavhara (a code of conduct) was mostly concerned with maintaining caste purity (hence upholding Brahmanical power) and male dynasties (hence imposing the subservience of women).[7]

For the thinking person, arriving at one's dharma at any time requires deep and rigorous intellectual introspection. The search for that ambiguous and equivocal recognition of dharma is the subject of the *Mahabharata,* where victory was with the seemingly righteous side, and yet their conduct during the war was often unrighteous. The *Mahabharata* is a dangerous lesson for modern society, where each person feels righteous about his/her personal cause, which, according to him/her, is above the law and rules of conduct.

A standard school lesson (particularly while studying Gandhi) is that a society of moral people is possible only when each one of us seek to grow in spiritual strength by being conscious of our human frailties. The very people who want to now reject the Western model of positive law as colonial trappings that have stifled our culture ignore that the great rishis and scriptures, as well as Gandhi, advised that the most difficult process of reaching one's true dharma is surmounting the tendency to lie and cheat.

In court, in the shadow of Gandhi's statues and photographs, I have mostly seen human frailty institutionalized instead of transcended. Thus, a person taking an oath in the name of 'God' is quite likely connecting with a private Ishtadevta indulgent of the transgressions of a favourite devotee.

As a nation we seem to live on a longitude and latitude of extremes where people have not learned the lessons of moderation, despite regular visits by saints every hundred years or so. Then about seventy years ago, we had a chance when diverse people with a wide variety of extreme ideas united on the one-point program of Independence. Instead of that moment becoming the moderating influence, it exposed our collective subconscious as violent, though we delude ourselves by claiming it as spiritual. This seething power lurking under a very thin skin is the weapon that our new oppressors (politicians and other stakeholders in economic and

---

6. *Journal of the Indian Law Institute* Volume 34, 1992, p. 523; See also http://archive.org/stream/publicadministra00banerich/publicadministra00banerich_djvu.txt

7. Uma Chakravarti, *Conceptualising Brahmanical Patriarchy in Early India: Gender, Caste, Class and State*, pp. 579-585

social power) are able to unleash and we are manipulated with sickening ease.

The Nehruvian model of governance, tending as it did to socialist secular policies required moderation, but today Nehru is being pilloried for social and political reasons. It can be argued that this is not the subject of my book, but family law is witnessing a change that society is unable to process fast enough, partly because it is not being allowed to by regressive forces, and partly because it does not have the inner mechanism to process it effectively. We are disintegrating into extremes that are worrying for families who want to live quietly and create a meaningful connect to the world. We seem to be moving in the opposite direction.

The best analogy is that we are in the throes of churning for amrit. In the legend, the scum floated to the surface first, but Shiva drank the poison and saved the world. In real life, the poisoned cup has to be drunk collectively by all those who want to commit to a system that processes social angst and delivers justice.

The most common questions and the most difficult to answer:

Q. From women: Why should he have everything? Get away cheap and have access to my kids?

Q. From men: Why should I reward her behaviour, her cruelty to my family?

A: To both, I can only ask you to focus on looking after yourself; the process of punishing the other will cause you much harassment and expense. The legal system will balance out fault somewhere and we all somehow, somewhere, live with our transgressions and punish ourselves for them or life does. I am not embarrassed to say this because I actually do not have all the answers and I do not believe anyone does.

Q: There is no God! There is no justice! Why?

A: It seems logical to think that, but I believe that both God and justice can be experienced more by instinct than understanding. We don't know the roads that are certain to lead to God and similarly there is no road that leads to complete justice, but the traveller seeking either of these marvellous intangible and yet powerful 'things' always finds something worthwhile.

APPENDIX OF LAWS

CONSTITUTION OF INDIA

13. (1) All laws in force in the territory of India immediately before the commencement of this Constitution, in so far as they are inconsistent with the provisions of this Part, shall, to the extent of such inconsistency, be void.

(2) The State shall not make any law which takes away or abridges the rights conferred by this Part and any law made in contravention of this clause shall, to the extent of the contravention, be void.

(3) In this article, unless the context otherwise requires,—

(a) 'law' includes any Ordinance, order, bye-law, rule, regulation, notification, custom or usage having in the territory of India the force of law;

(b) 'laws in force' includes laws passed or made by a Legislature or other competent authority in the territory of India before the commencement of this Constitution and not previously repealed, notwithstanding that any such law or any part thereof may not be then in operation either at all or in particular areas.

(4) Nothing in this article shall apply to any amendment of this Constitution made under article 368.

14. The State shall not deny to any person equality before the law or the equal protection of the laws within the territory of India.

15. (1) The State shall not discriminate against any citizen on grounds only of religion, race, caste, sex, place of birth or any of them.

(2) No citizen shall, on grounds only of religion, race, caste, sex, place of birth or any of them, be subject to any disability, liability, restriction or condition with regard to—

(a) access to shops, public restaurants, hotels and places of public entertainment; or

(b) the use of wells, tanks, bathing ghats, roads and places of public resort maintained wholly or partly out of State funds or dedicated to the use of the general public.

(3) Nothing in this article shall prevent the State from making any special provision for women and children.

(4) Nothing in this article or in clause (2) of article 29 shall prevent the State from making any special provision for the advancement of any socially and educationally backward classes of citizens or for the Scheduled Castes and the Scheduled Tribes.

(5) Nothing in this article or in sub-clause (g) of clause (1) of article 19 shall prevent the State from making any special provision, by law, for the advancement of any socially and educationally backward classes of citizens or for the Scheduled Castes or the Scheduled Tribes in so far as such

special provisions relate to their admission to educational institutions including private educational institutions, whether aided or unaided by the State, other than the minority educational institutions referred to in clause (1) of article 30.

19. (1) All citizens shall have the right—
   (a) to freedom of speech and expression;
   (b) to assemble peaceably and without arms;
   (c) to form associations or unions or co-operative societies;
   (d) to move freely throughout the territory of India;
   (e) to reside and settle in any part of the territory of India; and

(2) Nothing in sub-clause (a) of clause (1) shall affect the operation of any existing law, or prevent the State from making any law, in so far as such law imposes reasonable restrictions on the exercise of the right conferred by the said sub-clause in the interests of the sovereignty and integrity of India, the security of the State, friendly relations with foreign States, public order, decency or morality, or in relation to contempt of court, defamation or incitement to an offence.

(3) Nothing in sub-clause (b) of the said clause shall affect the operation of any existing law in so far as it imposes, or prevent the State from making any law imposing, in the interests of 5[the sovereignty and integrity of India or] public order, reasonable restrictions on the exercise of the right conferred by the said sub-clause.

(4) Nothing in sub-clause (c) of the said clause shall affect the operation of any existing law in so far as it imposes, or prevent the State from making any law imposing, in the interests of the sovereignty and integrity of India or public order or morality, reasonable restrictions on the exercise of the right conferred by the said sub-clause.

(5) Nothing in sub-clauses (d) and (e) of the said clause shall affect the operation of any existing law in so far as it imposes, or prevent the State from making any law imposing, reasonable restrictions on the exercise of any of the rights conferred by the said sub-clauses either in the interests of the general public or for the protection of the interests of any Scheduled Tribe.

(6) Nothing in sub-clause (g) of the said clause shall affect the operation of any existing law in so far as it imposes, or prevent the State from making any law imposing, in the interests of the general public, reasonable restrictions on the exercise of the right conferred by the said sub-clause, and, in particular, nothing in the said sub-clause shall affect the operation of any existing law in so far as it relates to, or prevent the State from making any law relating to—

   (i) the professional or technical qualifications necessary for practising any profession or carrying on any occupation, trade or business, or
   (ii) the carrying on by the State, or by a corporation owned or controlled by the State, of any trade, business, industry or service, whether to the exclusion, complete or partial, of citizens or otherwise.

21. No person shall be deprived of his life or personal liberty except according to procedure established by law.
37. The provisions contained in this Part shall not be enforceable by any court, but the principles therein laid down are nevertheless fundamental in the governance of the country and it shall be the duty of the State to apply these principles in making laws.
44. The State shall endeavour to secure for the citizens a uniform civil code throughout the territory of India.

Article 51A. It shall be the duty of every citizen of India—

(a) to abide by the Constitution and respect its ideals and institutions, the National Flag and the National Anthem;
(b) to cherish and follow the noble ideals which inspired our national struggle for freedom;
(c) to uphold and protect the sovereignty, unity and integrity of India;
(d) to defend the country and render national service when called upon to do so;
(e) to promote harmony and the spirit of common brotherhood amongst all the people of India transcending religious, linguistic and regional or sectional diversities; to renounce practices derogatory to the dignity of women;
(f) to value and preserve the rich heritage of our composite culture;
(g) to protect and improve the natural environment including forests, lakes, rivers and wild life, and to have compassion for living creatures;
(h) to develop the scientific temper, humanism and the spirit of inquiry and reform;
(i) to safeguard public property and to abjure violence;
(j) to strive towards excellence in all spheres of individual and collective activity so that the nation constantly rises to higher levels of endeavour and achievement;
(k) who is a parent or guardian to provide opportunities for education to his child or, as the case may be, ward between the age of six and fourteen years.

Article 142

(1) The Supreme Court in the exercise of its jurisdiction may pass such decree or make such order as is necessary for doing complete justice in any cause or matter pending before it, and any decree so passed or order so made shall be enforceable throughout the territory of India in such manner as may be prescribed by or under any law made by Parliament and, until provision in that behalf is so made, in such manner as the President may by order prescribe.
(2) Subject to the provisions of any law made in this behalf by Parliament, the Supreme Court shall, as respects the whole of the territory of India, have all and every power to make any order for the purpose of securing the attendance of any person, the discovery or production of any documents, or the investigation or punishment of any contempt of itself.

INDIAN STATUTES

Army Act, 1950

90. Deductions from pay and allowances of officers.

The following penal deductions may be made from the pay and allowances of an officer, that is to say,

(i) any sum required by order of the Central Government or any prescribed officers to be paid for the maintenance of his wife or his legitimate or illegitimate child or towards the cost of any relief given by the said Government to the said wife or child.

193. Prescribed officer under sections 90(i) and 91(i)—The prescribed officer shall be the Chief of the Army Staff or the officer commanding the Army.

Benami Transactions Act, 1988

3. Prohibition of benami transactions—
   (1) No person shall enter into any benami transaction.
   (2) Nothing in sub-section (1) shall apply to the purchase of property by any person in the name of his wife or unmarried daughter and it shall be presumed, unless the contrary is proved, that the said property had been purchased for the benefit of the wife of the unmarried daughter.

Criminal Procedure Code, 1973

125. Order for maintenance of wives, children and parents.
   (1) If any person having sufficient means neglects or refuses to maintain—
      (a) his wife, unable to maintain herself, or
      (b) his legitimate or illegitimate minor child, whether married or not, unable to maintain itself, or
      (c) his legitimate or illegitimate child (not being a married daughter) who has attained majority, where such child is, by reason of any physical or mental abnormality or injury unable to maintain itself, or
      (d) his father or mother, unable to maintain himself or herself, a Magistrate of the first class may, upon proof of such neglect or refusal, order such person to make a monthly allowance for the maintenance of his wife or such child, father or mother, at such monthly rate not exceeding five hundred rupees in the whole, as such Magistrate thinks fit, and to pay the same to such person as the Magistrate may from time to time direct: Provided that the Magistrate may order the father of a minor female child referred to in clause (b) to make such allowance, until she attains her majority, if the Magistrate is satisfied that the husband of such minor female child, if married, is not possessed of sufficient means.

   Explanation—For the purposes of this chapter
      (a) 'minor' means a person who, under the provisions of the Indian Majority Act, 1875 (9 of 1875); is deemed not to have attained his majority;

(b) 'wife' includes a woman who has been divorced by, or has obtained a divorce from, her husband and has not remarried.

(2) Such allowance shall be payable from the date of the order, or, if so ordered, from the date of the application for maintenance.

(3) If any person so ordered fails without sufficient cause to comply with the order, any such Magistrate may, for every breach of the order, issue a warrant for levying the amount due in the manner provided for levying fines, and may sentence such person, for the whole or any part of each month's allowances remaining unpaid after the execution of the warrant, to imprisonment for a term which may extend to one month or until payment if sooner made:

Provided that no warrant shall be issued for the recovery of any amount due under this section unless application be made to the Court to levy such amount within a period of one year from the date on which it became due: Provided further that if such person offers to maintain his wife on condition of her living with him, and she refuses to live with him, such Magistrate may consider any grounds of refusal stated by her, and may make an order under this section notwithstanding such offer, if he is satisfied that there is just ground for so doing.

Explanation. If a husband has contracted marriage with another woman or keeps a mistress, it shall be considered to be just ground for his wife's refusal to live with him.

(4) No wife shall be entitled to receive an allowance from her husband under this section if she is living in adultery, or if, without any sufficient reason, she refuses to live with her husband, or if they are living separately by mutual consent.

(5) On proof that any wife in whose favour an order has been made under this section is living in adultery, or that without sufficient reason she refuses to live with her husband, or that they are living separately by mutual consent, the Magistrate shall cancel the order.

127. Alteration in allowance.

(1) On proof of a change in the circumstances of any person, receiving, under section 125 a monthly allowance, or ordered under the same section to pay a monthly allowance to his wife, child, father or mother, as case may be, the Magistrate may make such alteration in the allowance he thinks fit: Provided that if he increases the allowance, the monthly rate of five hundred rupees in the whole shall not be exceeded.

(2) Where it appears to the Magistrate that, in consequence of any decision of a competent Civil Court, any order made under section 125 should be cancelled or varied, he shall cancel the order or, as the case may be, vary the same accordingly.

(3) Where any order has been made under section 125 in favour of a woman who has been divorced by, or has obtained a divorce from, her husband, the Magistrate shall, if he is satisfied that—

(a) the woman has, after the date of such divorce, remarried, cancel such order as from the date of her remarriage;

(b) the woman has been divorced by her husband and that she has received, whether before or after the date of the said order, the whole of the sum which, under any customary or personal law applicable to the parties, was payable on such divorce, cancel such order,—

(i) in the case where, such sum was paid before such order, from the date on Which such order was made,

(ii) in any other case, from the date of expiry of the period, if any, for which maintenance has been actually paid by the husband by the woman;

(c) the woman has obtained a divorce from her husband and that she had voluntarily surrendered her rights to maintenance after her divorce, cancel the order from the date thereof.

(4) At the time of making any decree for the recovery of any maintenance or dowry by any person, to whom a monthly allowance has been ordered to be paid under section 125, the Civil Court shall take into account the sum which has been paid to, or recovered by, such person as monthly allowance in pursuance of the said order.

154. Information in cognizable cases.

(1) Every information relating to the commission of a cognizable offence, if given orally to an officer in charge of a police station, shall be reduced to writing by him or under his direction, and be read Over to the informant; and every such information, whether given in writing or reduced to writing as aforesaid, shall be signed by the person giving it, and the substance thereof shall be entered in a book to be kept by such officer in such form as the State Government may prescribe in this behalf.

(2) A copy of the information as recorded under sub-section (1) shall be given forthwith, free of cost, to the informant.

(3) Any person aggrieved by a refusal on the part of an officer in charge of a police station to record the information referred to in sub-section (1) may send the substance of such information, in writing and by post, to the Superintendent of Police concerned who, if satisfied that such information discloses the commission of a cognizable offence, shall either investigate the case himself or direct an investigation to be made by any police officer subordinate to him, in the manner provided by this Code, and such officer shall have all the powers of an officer in charge of the police station in relation to that offence.

482. Saving of inherent powers of High Court.

Nothing in this Code shall be deemed to limit or affect the inherent powers of the High Court to make such orders as may be necessary to give effect to any order under this Code, or to prevent abuse of the process of any Court or otherwise to secure the ends of justice.

483. Duty of High Court to exercise continuous superintendence over Courts of Judicial Magistrates

Every High Court shall so exercise its superintendence over the Courts of Judicial Magistrates subordinate to it as to ensure that there is an expeditious and proper disposal of cases by such Magistrates.

Divorce Act, 1869

(The Indian Divorce Act, 1869 came to be known as the 'Divorce Act' after the 2001 amendment)

10A. Dissolution of marriage by mutual consent.

(1) Subject to the provisions of this Act and the rules made thereunder, a petition for dissolution of marriage may be presented to the District Court by both the parties to a marriage together, whether such marriage was solemnized before or after the commencement of the Indian Divorce (Amendment) Act, 2001, on the ground that they have been living separately for a period of two years or more, that they have not been able to live together and they have mutually agreed that the marriage should be dissolved.

(2) On the motion of both the parties made not earlier than six months after the date of presentation of the petition referred to in sub-section (1) and not later than eighteen months after the said date, if the petition is not withdrawn by both the parties in the meantime, the Court shall, on being satisfied, after hearing the parties and making such inquiry, as it thinks fit, that a marriage has been solemnized and that the averments in the petition are true, pass a decree declaring the marriage to be dissolved with effect from the date of decree.

40. Inquiry into existence of ante-nuptial or post-nuptial settlements.

The District Court may, before passing a decree for dissolution of the marriage or a decree of nullity of marriage, inquire into the existence of ante-nuptial or post-nuptial settlements made on the parties whose marriage is the subject of the decree, and may make such orders, with reference to the application of the whole or a portion of the property settled, whether for the benefit of the husband or the wife, or of the children (if any) of the marriage, or of both children and parents, as to the Court seems fit: Provided that the Court shall not make any order for the benefit of the parents or either of them at the expense of the children.

Family Courts Act, 1984

10. Procedure generally—

(1) Subject to the other provisions of this Act and rules, the provisions of the Code of Civil Procedure, 1908 (5 of 1908), and of any other law for the time being in force shall apply to the suits and proceedings other than the proceedings under Chapter IX of the Code of Criminal Procedure, 1973 (2 of 1974), before a Family Court and for the purpose of the said provisions of the Code, a Family Court shall be deemed to be a Civil Court and shall have all the powers of such Court.

(2) Subject to the other provisions of this Act and the rules, the provisions of the Code of Criminal Procedure, 1973 (2 of 1974), or the rules made

thereunder, shall apply to the proceedings under Chapter IX of the Code before a Family Court.

(3) Nothing in sub-section (1) or sub-section (2) shall prevent a Family Court from laying down its own procedure with a view to arrive at a settlement in respect of the subject-matter of the suit or proceedings or at the truth of the facts alleged by the one party and denied by the other.

Guardians and Wards Act, 1980

12. Power to make interlocutory order for production of minor and interim protection of person and property—
    (1) The court may direct that the person, if any, having the custody of the minor, shall produce him or cause him to be produced at such place and time and before such person as it appoints, and may make such order for the temporary custody and protection of the person or property of the minor as it thinks proper.
    (2) If the minor is a female who ought not to be compelled to appear in public, the direction under sub-section (1) for her production shall require her to be produced in accordance with the customs and manners of the country.
    (3) Nothing in this section shall authorize—
        (a) the court to place a female minor in the temporary custody of a person claiming to be her guardian on the ground of his being her husband, unless she is already in his custody with the consent of her parents, if any, or
        (b) any person to whom the temporary custody and protection of the property of a minor is entrusted to dispossess otherwise than by due course of law any person in possession of any of the property.
17. Matter to be considered by the Court in appointing guardian.
    (1) In appointing or declaring the guardian of a minor, the Court shall, subject to the provisions of this section, be guided by what, consistently with the law to which the minor is subject, appears in the circumstances to be for the welfare of the minor.
    (2) In considering what will be for the welfare of the minor, the Courts shall have regard to the age, sex and religion of the minor, the character and capacity of the proposed guardian and his nearness of kin to the minor, the wishes, if any, of a deceased parent, and any existing or previous relations of the proposed guardian with the minor or his property.
    (3) If the minor is old enough to form an intelligent preference, the Court may consider that preference.
    (5) The Court shall not appoint or declare any person to be a guardian against his will.

Other Statutes Dealing with Children's Issues

i. Child Labour (Prohibition and Regulation) Act, 1986
ii. Juvenile Justice (Care and Protection of Children) Act, 2000

iii. Prohibition of Child Marriage Act, 2006
iv. Protection of Children from Sexual Offences Act, 2012
v. Right of Children to Free and Compulsory Education Act, 2009

Hindu Adoptions and Maintenance Act 1956

4. Overriding effect of Act
Save as otherwise expressly provided in this Act,—
(a) any text, rule or interpretation of Hindu law or any custom or usage as part of that law in force immediately before the commencement of this Act shall cease to have effect with respect to any matter for which provision is made in this Act;
(b) any other law in force immediately before the commencement of this Act shall cease to apply to Hindus insofar as it is inconsistent with any of the provisions contained in this Act.

18. Maintenance of wife
(1) Subject to the provisions of this section, a Hindu wife, whether married before or after the commencement of this Act, shall be entitled to be maintained by her husband during her lifetime.
(2) A Hindu wife shall be entitled to live separately from her husband without forfeiting her claim to maintenance—
(a) if he is guilty of desertion, that is to say, of abandoning her without reasonable cause and without her consent or against her wish, or of willfully neglecting her;
(b) if he has treated her with such cruelty as to cause a reasonable apprehension in her mind that it will be harmful or injurious to live with her husband;
(c) if he is suffering from a virulent form of leprosy;
(d) if he has any other wife living;
(e) if he keeps a concubine in the same house in which his wife is living or habitually resides with a concubine elsewhere;
(f) if he has ceased to be a Hindu by conversion to another religion;
(g) if there is any other cause justifying her living separately.
(3) A Hindu wife shall not be entitled to separate residence and maintenance from her husband if she is unchaste or ceases to be a Hindu by conversion to another religion.

19. Maintenance of widowed daughter-in-law
(1) A Hindu wife, whether married before or after the commencement of this Act, shall be entitled to be maintained after the death of her husband by her father-in-law:
PROVIDED and to the extent that she is unable to maintain herself out of her own earnings or other property or, where she has no property of her own, is unable to obtain maintenance—
(a) from the estate of her husband or her father or mother, or
(b) from her son or daughter, if any, or his or her estate.

(2) Any obligation under sub-section (1) shall not be enforceable if the father-in law has not the means to do so from any coparcenary property in his possession out of which the daughter-in-law has not obtained any share, and any such obligation shall cease on the re-marriage of the daughter-in-law.

Hindu Marriage Act, 1955

5. Condition for a Hindu Marriage—

A marriage may be solemnized between any two Hindus, if the following conditions are fulfilled, namely:

(i) neither party has a spouse living at the time of the marriage; (ii) at the time of the marriage, neither party—

(a) is incapable of giving a valid consent of it in consequence of unsoundness of mind; or

(b) though capable of giving a valid consent has been suffering from mental disorder of such a kind or to such an extent as to be unfit for marriage and the procreation of children; or

(c) has been subject to recurrent attacks of insanity or epilepsy;

(iii) the bridegroom has completed the age of twenty one years and the bride the age of eighteen years at the time of the marriage;

(iv) the parties are not within the degrees of prohibited relationship unless the custom or usage governing each of them permits of a marriage between the two;

(v) the parties are not sapindas of each other, unless the custom or usage governing each of them permits of a marriage between the two;

9. Restitution of conjugal rights—When either the husband or the wife has, without reasonable excuse, withdrawn from the society of the other, the aggrieved party may apply, by petition to the district court, for restitution of conjugal rights and the court, on being satisfied of the truth of the statements made in such petition and that there is no legal ground why the application should not be granted, may decree restitution of conjugal rights accordingly Explanation: Where a question arises whether there has been reasonable excuse for withdrawal from the society, the burden of proving reasonable excuse shall be on the person who has withdrawn from the society.

11. Nullity of marriage and divorce: Void marriages—

Any marriage solemnized after the commencement of this Act shall be null and void and may, on a petition presented by either party thereto, against the other party be so declared by a decree of nullity if it contravenes any one of the conditions specified in clauses (i), (iv) and (v), Section 5.

12. Voidable Marriages.

(1) Any marriage solemnized, whether before or after the commencement of this Act, shall be voidable and may be annulled by a decree of nullity on any of the following grounds, namely:

(a) that the marriage has not been consummated owing to the impotency of the respondent; or

(b) that the marriage is in contravention of the condition specified in clause (ii) of Section 5; or

(c) that the consent of the petitioner, or where the consent of the guardian in marriage of the petitioner was required under Section 5 as it stood immediately before the commencement of the Child Marriage Restraint (Amendment) Act, 1978, the consent of such guardian was obtained by force or by fraud as to the nature of the ceremony or as to any material fact or circumstance concerning the respondent; or

(d) that the respondent was at the time of the marriage pregnant by some person other than the petitioner.

(2) Notwithstanding anything contained in sub-section (1), no petition for annulling a marriage—

(a) on the ground specified in clause (c) of sub-section (1) shall be entertained if—

(i) the petition is presented more than one year after the force had ceased to operate or, as the case may be, the fraud had been discovered ; or

(ii) the petitioner has, with his or her full consent, lived with the other party to the marriage as husband or wife after the force had ceased to operate or, as the case may be, the fraud had been discovered;

(b) on the ground specified in clause (d) of sub-section (1) shall be entertained unless the court is satisfied—

(i) that the petitioner was at the time of the marriage ignorant of the facts alleged;

(ii) that proceedings have been instituted in the case of a marriage solemnized before the commencement of this Act within one year of such commencement and in the case of marriages solemnized after such commencement within one year from the date of the marriage; and

(iii) that marital intercourse with the consent of the petitioner has not taken place since the discovery by the petitioner of the existence of the said ground.

13. Divorce—

(1) Any marriage solemnized, whether before or after the commencement of the Act, may, on a petition presented by either the husband or the wife, be dissolved by a decree of divorce on the ground that the other party-

(i) has, after the solemnization of the marriage had voluntary sexual intercourse with any person other than his or her spouse; or

(ia) has, after the solemnization of the marriage, treated the petitioner with cruelty; or

(ib) has deserted the petitioner for a continuous period of not less than two years immediately preceding the presentation of the petition; or

(ii) has ceased to be a Hindu by conversion to another religion; or

(iii) has been incurably of unsound mind, or has suffering continuously or intermittently from mental disorder of such a kind and to such an extent that the petitioner cannot reasonably be expected to live with the respondent.

Explanation: In this clause:

(a) the expression 'mental disorder' means mental illness, arrested or incomplete development of mind, psychopathic disorder or any other disorder or disability of mind and include schizophrenia;

(b) the expression 'psychopathic disorder' means a persistent disorder or disability of mind (whether or not including sub-normality of intelligence) which results in abnormally aggressive or seriously irresponsible conduct on the part of the other party and whether or not it requires or is susceptible to medical treatment; or

(iv) has been suffering from a virulent and incurable form of leprosy; or

(v) has been suffering from veneral disease in a communicable form; or

(vi) has renounced the world by entering any religious order; or

(vii) has not been heard of as being alive for a period of seven years or more by those persons who would naturally have heard of it, had that party been alive;

Explanation—In this sub-section, the expression 'desertion' means the desertion of the petitioner by the other party to the marriage without reasonable cause and without the consent or against the wish of such party, and includes the willful neglect of the petitioner by the other party to the marriage, and its grammatical variations and cognate expression shall be construed accordingly.

(1-A) Either party to a marriage, whether solemnized before or after the commencement of this Act, may also present a petition for the dissolution of the marriage by a decree of divorce on the ground—

(i) that there has been no resumption of cohabitation as between the parties to the marriage for a period of one year or upwards after the passing of a decree for judicial separation in a proceeding to which they were parties; or

(ii) that there has been no restitution of conjugal rights as between the parties to the marriage for a period of one year or upward after the passing of a decree of restitution of conjugal rights in a proceeding to which they were parties.

(2) A wife may also present a petition for the dissolution of her marriage by a decree of divorce on the ground—

(i) in the case of any marriage solemnized before the commencement of this Act, that the husband had married again before the commencement or that any other wife of the husband married before such commencement was alive at the time of the solemnization of the marriage of the petitioner:

Provided that in either case the other wife is alive at the time of the presentation of the petition;

(ii) that the husband has, since the solemnization of the marriage, been guilty of rape, sodomy or bestiality; or

(iii) that in a suit under Section 18 of the Hindu Adoptions and Maintenance Act, (78 of 1956), or in a proceeding under Section 125 of the Code of Criminal Procedure, 1973, (Act 2 of 1974) or under corresponding Section 488 of the Code of Criminal Procedure, (5 of 1898), a decree or order, as the case may be, has been passed against the husband awarding maintenance to the wife notwithstanding that she was living apart and that since the passing of such decree or order, cohabitation between the parties has not been resumed for one year or upwards; or

(iv) that her marriage (whether consummated or not) was solemnized before she attained the age of fifteen years and she has repudiated the marriage after attaining that age but before attaining the age of eighteen years. Explanation. This clause applies whether the marriage was solemnized before or after the commencement of the Marriage Law (Amendment) Act, 1976.

13-B. Divorce by mutual consent—

(1) Subject to the provisions of this Act a petition for dissolution of marriage by a decree of divorce may be presented to the District Court by both the parties to a marriage together, whether such marriage was solemnized before or after the commencement of the Marriage Laws (Amendment) Act, 1976, on the ground that they have been living separately for a period of one year or more, that they have not been able to live together and that they have mutually agreed that the marriage should be dissolved.

(2) On the motion of both the parties made earlier than six months after the date of the presentation of the petition referred to in sub-section (1) and not later than eighteen months after the said date, if the petition is not withdrawn in the mean time, the Court shall, on being satisfied, after hearing the parties and after making such inquiry as it thinks fit, that a marriage has been solemnized and that the averments in the petition are true, pass a decree of divorce declaring the marriage to be dissolved with effect from the date of the decree.

17. Punishment of Bigamy—Any marriage between two Hindus solemnized after the commencement of this Act is void if at the date of such marriage either party had a husband or wife living; and the provisions of Sections 494 and 495 of the Indian Penal Code (45 of 1860) shall apply accordingly.

23. Decree in proceedings—

(1) In any proceeding under this Act, whether defended or not, if the Court is satisfied that—

(a) any of the grounds for granting relief exists and the petitioner except in cases where the relief is sought by him on the grounds specified in sub-clause (a), sub-clause (b) and sub-clause (c) of clause (ii) of Section 5 is not any way taking advantage of his or her own wrong or disability for the purpose of such relief, and

(b) where the ground of the petition is the ground specified in clause (i) of sub-section (1) of Section 13, the petitioner has not in any manner been accessory to or connived at or condoned the act or acts complained of, or where the ground or the petition is cruelty the petitioner has not in any manner condoned the cruelty, and

(bb) when a divorce is sought on the ground of mutual consent, such consent has not been obtained by force, fraud or undue influence, and

(c) the petition not being a petition presented under section 11 is not presented or prosecuted in collusion with the respondent, and

(d) there has not been any unnecessary or improper delay in instituting the proceeding, and

(e) there is no other legal ground why relief should not be granted, then, and in such a case, but not otherwise, the court shall decree such relief accordingly.

(2) Before proceeding to grant any relief under this Act, it shall be the duty of the Court in the first instance, in every case where it is possible so to do consistently with the nature and circumstances of the case, to make every endeavour to bring about a reconciliation between the parties:
Provided that nothing contained in this sub-section shall apply to any proceeding wherein relief is sought on any of the grounds specified in clause (ii), clause (iii), clause (iv), clause (v), clause (vi) or clause (vii), of sub-section (1) of Section 13.

(3) For the purpose of aiding the Court in bringing about such reconciliation, the court may, if the parties so desire or if the Court thinks it just and proper so to do adjourn the proceedings for a reasonable period not exceeding fifteen days and refer the matter to any person named by the parties in this behalf or to any person nominated by the Court if the parties fail to name any person, with directions to report to the Court as to whether reconciliation can be and has been effected and the court shall in disposing of the proceeding have due regard to the report.

(4) In every case where a marriage is dissolved by a decree of divorce, the court passing the decree shall give a copy thereof free of cost to each of the parties.

24. Maintenance pendente lite and expenses of proceedings—
Where in any proceeding under this Act it appears to the Court that either the wife or the husband, as the case may be, has no independent income sufficient for her or his support and the necessary expenses of the proceeding, it may, on the application of the wife or the husband, order the respondent to pay the petitioner the expenses of the proceeding such sum as, having regard to the petitioner's own income and the income of the respondent, it may seem to the Court to be reasonable.

25. Permanent alimony and maintenance—

(1) Any court exercising jurisdiction under this Act may, at the time of passing any decree or at any time subsequent thereto, on application made to it for the purposes by either the wife or the husband, as the case

may be, order that the respondent shall pay to the applicant for her or his maintenance and support such gross sum or such monthly or periodical sum for a term not exceeding the life of the applicant as, having regard to the respondent's own income and other property of the applicant, the conduct of the parties and other circumstances of the case, it may seem to the Court to be just, and any such payment may be secured, if necessary, by a charge on the immoveable property of the respondent.

(2) If the Court is satisfied that there is a change in the circumstances of either party at any time after it has made an order under sub-section (1), it may at the instance of either party, vary, modify or rescind any such order in such manner as the court may deem just.

(3) If the Court is satisfied that the party in whose favour an order has been made under this Section has re-married or, if such party is the wife, that she has not remained chaste or if such party is the husband, that he has had sexual intercourse with any woman outside wedlock, it may at the instance of the other party vary, modify or rescind any such order in such manner as the court may deem just.

26. Custody of children—

In any proceeding under this Act, the Court may, from time to time, pass such interim orders and make such provisions in the decree as it may deem just and proper with respect to the custody, maintenance and education of minor children, consistently with their wishes, wherever possible, and may, after the decree, upon application by petition for the purpose, make from time to time, all such orders and provisions with respect to the custody, maintenance and education of such children as might have been made by such decree or interim orders in case the proceedings for obtaining such decree were still pending, and the Court may also from time to time revoke, suspend or vary any such orders and provisions previously made.

Hindu Minority and Guardianship Act, 1956

6. Natural guardians of a Hindu minor—

The natural guardians of a Hindu, minor, in respect of the minor's person as well as in respect of the minor's property (excluding his or her undivided interest in joint family property), are:

(a) in the case of a boy or an unmarried girl—the father, and after him, the mother: provided that the custody of a minor who has not completed the age of five years shall ordinarily be with the mother;

(b) in the case of an illegitimate boy or an illegitimate unmarried girl—the mother, and after her, the father;

(c) in the case of a married girl—the husband;

Provided that no person shall be entitled to act as the natural guardian of a minor under the provisions of this section—

(a) if he has ceased to be a Hindu, or

(b) if he has completely and finally renounced the world by becoming a hermit (vanaprastha) or an ascetic (yati or sanyasi)

Explanation—In this section, the expressions 'father' and 'mother' do not include a step-father and a step-mother.

Hindu Succession Act, 1956

6. Devolution of interest in coparcenary property

(1) On and from the commencement of the Hindu Succession (Amendment) Act, 2005, in a Joint Hindu family governed by the Mitakshara law, the daughter of a coparcener shall,

(a) by birth become a coparcener in her own right in the same manner as the son;

(b) have the same rights in the coparcenary property as she would have had if she had been a son;

(c) be subject to the same liabilities in respect of the said coparcenary property as that of a son, and any reference to a Hindu Mitakshara coparcener shall be deemed to include a reference to a daughter of a coparcener:

Provided that nothing contained in this sub-section shall affect or invalidate any disposition or alienation including any partition or testamentary disposition of property which had taken place before the 20th day of December, 2004.

(2) Any property to which a female Hindu becomes entitled by virtue of sub-section (1) shall be held by her with the incidents of coparcenary ownership and shall be regarded, notwithstanding anything contained in this Act, or any other law for the time being in force, as property capable of being disposed of by her by testamentary disposition.

(3) Where a Hindu dies after the commencement of the Hindu Succession (Amendment) Act, 2005, his interest in the property of a Joint Hindu family governed by the Mitakshara law, shall devolve by testamentary or intestate succession, as the case may be, under this Act and not by survivorship, and the coparcenary property shall be deemed to have been divided as if a partition had taken place and,

(a) the daughter is allotted the same share as is allotted to a son;

(b) the share of the pre-deceased son or a pre-deceased daughter, as they would have got had they been alive at the time of partition, shall be allotted to the surviving child of such predeceased son or of such pre-deceased daughter; and

(c) the share of the pre-deceased child of a pre-deceased son or of a pre-deceased daughter, as such child would have got had he or she been alive at the time of the partition, shall be allotted to the child of such pre-deceased child of the pre-deceased son or a pre-deceased daughter, as the case may be.

Explanation—For the purposes of this sub-section, the interest of a Hindu Mitakshara coparcener shall be deemed to be the share in the property that would have been allotted to him if a partition of the property had taken place immediately before his death, irrespective of whether he was entitled to claim partition or not.

(4) After the commencement of the Hindu Succession (Amendment) Act, 2005, no court shall recognise any right to proceed against a son, grandson or great-grandson for the recovery of any debt due from his father, grandfather or great-grandfather solely on the ground of the pious obligation under the Hindu law, of such son, grandson or great-grandson to discharge any such debt: Provided that in the case of any debt contracted before the commencement of the Hindu Succession (Amendment) Act, 2005, nothing contained in this sub-section shall affect—

(a) the right of any creditor to proceed against the son, grandson or great-grandson, as the case may be; or

(b) any alienation made in respect of or in satisfaction of, any such debt, and any such right or alienation shall be enforceable under the rule of pious obligation in the same manner and to the same extent as it would have been enforceable as if the Hindu Succession (Amendment) Act, 2005 had not been enacted.

Explanation—For the purposes of clause (a), the expression 'son', 'grandson' or 'great-grandson' shall be deemed to refer to the son, grandson or great-grandson, as the case may be, who was born or adopted prior to the commencement of the Hindu Succession (Amendment) Act, 2005.

(5) Nothing contained in this section shall apply to a partition, which has been effected before the 20th day of December, 2004. Explanation—For the purposes of this section 'partition' means any partition made by execution of a deed of partition duly registered under the Registration Act, 1908 (16 of 1908) or partition effected by a decree of a court.

[Section 6 before the Hindu Succession (Amendment) Act 2005 reads as follows:

6. Devolution of interest of coparcenary property

When a male Hindu dies after the commencement of this Act, having at the time of his death an interest in a Mitakshara coparcenary property, his interest in the property shall devolve by survivorship upon the surviving members of the coparcenary and not in accordance with this Act:

PROVIDED that, if the deceased had left him surviving a female relative specified in class I of the Schedule or a male relative specified in that class who claims through such female relative, the interest of the deceased in the Mitakshara coparcenary property shall devolve by testamentary or intestate succession, as the case may be, under this Act and not by survivorship.

Explanation I: For the purposes of this section, the interest of a Hindu Mitakshara coparcener shall be deemed to be the share in the property that would have been allotted to him if a partition of the property had taken place immediately before his death, irrespective of whether he was entitled to claim partition or not.

Explanation 2: Nothing contained in the proviso to this section shall be construed as enabling a person who has separated himself from the coparcenary before the death of the deceased or any of his heirs to claim on intestacy a share in the interest referred to therein.]

14. Property of a female Hindu to be her absolute property
    (1) Any property possessed by a female Hindu, whether acquired before or after the commencement of this Act, shall be held by her as full owner thereof and not as a limited owner. Explanation—In this sub-section, 'property' includes both movable and immovable property acquired by a female Hindu by inheritance or devise, or at a partition, or in lieu of maintenance or arrears of maintenance, or by gift from any person, whether a relative or not, before, at or after her marriage, or by her own skill or exertion, or by purchase or by prescription, or in any other manner whatsoever, and also any such property held by her as stridhana immediately before the commencement of this Act.
    (2) Nothing contained in sub-section (1) shall apply to any property acquired by way of gift or under a will or any other instrument or under a decree or order of a civil court or under an award where the terms of the gift, will or other instrument or the decree, order or award prescribe a restricted estate in such property.

23. Special provision respecting dwelling houses

Where a Hindu intestate has left surviving him or her both male and female heirs specified in class I of the Schedule and his or her property includes a dwelling-house wholly occupied by members of his or her family, then, notwithstanding anything contained in this Act, the right of any such female heir to claim partition of the dwelling-house shall not arise until the male heirs choose to divide their respective shares therein; but the female heir shall be entitled to a right of residence therein:

PROVIDED that where such female heir is a daughter, she shall be entitled to a right of residence in the dwelling-house only if she is unmarried or has been deserted by or has separated from her husband or is a widow.

26. Convert's descendants disqualified—

Where, before or after the commencement of this Act, a Hindu has ceased or ceases to be a Hindu by conversion to another religion, children born to him or her after such conversion and their descendants shall be disqualified from inheriting the property of any of their Hindu relatives, unless such children or descendants are Hindus at the time when the succession opens.

Indian Contract Act, 1872

2. Interpretation Clause—

...

(d) When, at the desire of the promisor, the promisee or any other person has done or abstained from doing, or does or abstains from doing, or promises to do or to abstain from doing, something, such act or abstinence or promise is called a consideration for the promise

...

25. Agreement without consideration, void, unless it is in writing and registered or is a promise to compensate for something done or is a promise to pay a debt barred by limitation law—An agreement made without consideration is void, unless—
    (1) it is expressed in writing and registered under the law for the time being in force for the registration of documents, and is made on account of natural love and affection between parties standing in a near relation to each other; or unless,
    (2) it is a promise to compensate, wholly or in part, a person who has already voluntarily done something for the promisor, or something which the promisor was legally compellable to do; or unless,
    (3) it is a promise, made in writing and signed by the person to be charged therewith or by his agent generally or specially authorised in that behalf, to pay wholly or in part debt of which the creditor might have enforced payment but for the law for the limitation of suits. In any of these cases, such an agreement is a contract.

    Explanation 1—Nothing in this section shall affect the validity, as between the donor and donee, of any gift actually made.

    Explanation 2—An agreement to which the consent of the promisor is freely given is not void merely because the consideration is inadequate; but the inadequacy of the consideration may be taken into account by the Court in determining the question whether the consent of the promisor was freely given.
27. Agreement in restraint of trade, void,

    Every agreement by which anyone is restrained from exercising a lawful profession, trade or business of any kind, is to that extent void.

    Exception 1—Saving of agreement not to carry on business of which good will is sold—One who sells the goodwill of a business may agree with the buyer to refrain from carrying on a similar business, within specified local limits, so long as the buyer, or any person deriving title to the goodwill from him, carries on a like business therein, provided that such limits appear to the court reasonable, regard being had to the nature of the business.

Indian Divorce Act, 1869

7. Court to act on principles of English Divorce Court

    Subject to the provisions contained in this Act, the High Courts and District Courts shall, in all suits and proceedings hereunder, act and give relief on principles and rules which, in the opinion of the said Courts, are as nearly as may be conformable to the principles and rules on which the Court for Divorce and Matrimonial Causes in England for the time being acts and gives relief: PROVIDED that nothing in this section shall deprive the said courts of jurisdiction in a case where the parties to a marriage professed the Christian religion at the time of the occurrence of the facts on which the claim to relief is founded.

40. Inquiry into existence of ante-nuptial or post-nuptial settlements
The High Court, after a decree absolute for dissolution of marriage, or a decree of nullity of marriage, and the District Court, after its decree for dissolution of marriage or of nullity of marriage has been confirmed, may inquire into the existence of ante-nuptial or post-nuptial settlements made on the parties whose marriage is the subject of the decree, and may make such orders, with reference to the application of the whole or a portion of the property settled, whether for the benefit of the husband or the wife, or the children (if any) of the marriage, or of both children and parents, as to the court seems fit:
PROVIDED that the court shall not make any order for the benefit of the parents or either of them at the expense of the children.

Indian Evidence Act, 1860

113A. Presumption as to abetment of suicide by a married women
When the question is whether the commission of suicide by a woman had been abetted by her husband or any relative of her husband and it is shown that she had committed suicide within a period of seven years from the date of her marriage and that her husband or such relative of her husband had subjected her to cruelty, the court may presume, having regard to all the other circumstance s of the case, that such suicide had been abetted by her husband or by such relative of her husband.
Explanation—For the purposes of this section, 'cruelty' shall have the same meaning as in section 498 A of the Indian Panel Code (45 of 1860).

113B. Presumption as to dowry death
When the question is whether a person has committed the dowry death of a woman and it is shown that soon before her death such woman had been subjected by such person to cruelty or harassment for, or in connection with, any demand for dowry, the Court shall presume that such person had caused the dowry death.
Explanation—For the purposes of this section, 'dowry death' shall have the same meaning as in section 304B of the Indian Penal Code(45 of 1860).

114A. Presumption as to absence of consent in certain prosecutions for rape
In a prosecution for rape under clause (a), clause (b), clause (c), clause (d), clause (e), clause (j), clause (g), clause (h), clause (i), clause (j), clause (k), clause (f), clause (m) or clause (n) of sub-section (2) of section 376 of the Indian Penal Code, where sexual intercourse by the accused is proved and the question is whether it was without the consent of the woman alleged to have been raped and such woman states in her evidence before the court. That she did not consent, the court shall presume that she did not consent.
Explanation—In this section, 'sexual intercourse' shall mean any of the acts mentioned in clauses (a) to (d) of section 375 of the Indian Penal Code.

122. Communications during marriage—
No person who is or has been married, shall be compelled to disclose any

communication made to him during marriage by any person to whom he is or has been married; nor shall he be permitted to disclose any such communication, unless the person who made it, or his representative in interest, consents, except in suits between married persons, or proceedings in which one married person is prosecuted for any crime committed against the other.

Indian Penal Code, 1860

304B. Dowry death.

(1) Where the death of a woman is caused by any burns or bodily injury or occurs otherwise than under normal circumstances within seven years of her marriage and it is shown that soon before her death she was subjected to cruelty or harassment by her husband or any relative of her husband for, or in connection with, any demand for dowry, such death shall be called 'dowry death', and such husband or relative shall be deemed to have caused her death.

Explanation—For the purposes of this sub-section, 'dowry' shall have the same meaning as in section 2 of the Dowry Prohibition Act, 1961 (28 of 1961).

(2) Whoever commits dowry death shall be punished with imprisonment for a term which shall not be less than seven years but which may extend to imprisonment for life.

354. Assault or criminal force to woman with intent to outrage her modesty—

Whoever assaults or uses criminal force to any woman, intending to outrage or knowing it to be likely that he will there by outrage her modesty, shall be punished with imprisonment of either description for a term which shall not be less than one year but Which may extend to five years, and shall also be liable to fine.

361. Kidnapping from lawful guardianship—

Whoever takes or entices any minor under sixteen years of age if a male, or under eighteen years of age if a female, or any person of unsound mind, out of the keeping of the lawful guardian of such minor or person of unsound mind, without the consent of such guardian, is said to kidnap such minor or person from lawful guardianship.

Explanation—The words 'lawful guardian' in this section include any person lawfully entrusted with the care or custody of such minor or other person.

375. A man is said to commit 'rape' if he—

a. penetrates his penis, to any extent, into the vagina, mouth, urethra or anus of a woman or makes her to do so with him or any other person; or
b. inserts, to any extent, any object or a part of the body, not being the penis, into the vagina, the urethra or anus of a woman or makes her to do so with him or any other person; or
c. manipulates any part of the body of a woman so as to cause penetration into the vagina, urethra, anus or any part of body of such woman or makes her to do so with him or any other person; or

d. applies his mouth to the vagina, anus, urethra of a woman or makes her to do so with him or any other person, under the circumstances falling under any of the following seven descriptions:—First—Against her will. Secondly—Without her consent. Thirdly—With her consent, when her consent has been obtained by putting her or any person in whom she is interested, in fear of death or of hurt. Fourthly—With her consent, when the man knows that he is not her husband and that her consent is given because she believes that he is another man to whom she is or believes herself to be lawfully married. Fifthly—With her consent when, at the time of giving such consent, by reason of unsoundness of mind or intoxication or the administration by him personally or through another of any stupefying or unwholesome Substance, she is unable to understand the nature and consequences of that to which she gives consent. Sixthly—With or without her consent, when she is under eighteen years of age. Seventhly—When she is unable to communicate consent.

Explanation I—For the purposes of this section, 'vagina' shall also include labia majora.

Explanation 2—Consent means an unequivocal voluntary agreement when the woman by words, gestures or any form of verbal or non-verbal communication, communicates willingness to participate in the specific sexual act:

Provided that a woman who does not physically resist to the act of penetration shall not by the reason only of that fact, be regarded as consenting to the sexual activity.

Exception I—A medical procedure or intervention shall not onstitute rape.

Exception 2—Sexual intercourse or sexual acts by a man with his own wife, the wife not being under fifteen years of age, is not rape.

[The pre-amended S. 375 reads as follows:

375. Rape—

A man is said to commit 'rape' who, except in the case hereinafter excepted, has sexual intercourse with a woman under circumstances falling under any of the six following descriptions:—

(First)—Against her will.

(Secondly)—Without her consent.

(Thirdly)—With her consent, when her consent has been obtained by putting her or any person in whom she is interested in fear of death or of hurt.

(Fourthly)—With her consent, when the man knows that he is not her husband, and that her consent is given because she believes that he is another man to whom she is or believes herself to be lawfully married.

(Fifthly)—With her consent, when, at the time of giving such consent, by reason of unsoundness of mind or intoxication or the administration by him personally or through another of any stupefying or unwholesome substance, she is unable to understand the nature and consequences of that to which she gives consent.

(Sixthly)—With or without her consent, when she is under sixteen years of age.

Explanation—Penetration is sufficient to constitute the sexual intercourse necessary to the offence of rape.

(Exception)—Sexual intercourse by a man with his own wife, the wife not being under fifteen years of age, is not rape.]

376. Punishment for rape.

1. Whoever, except in the cases provided for in sub-section (2), commits rape, shall be punished with rigorous imprisonment of either description for a term which shall not he less than seven years, but which may extend to imprisonment for life, and shall also be liable to fine.
2. Whoever,—
    a. being a police officer, commits rape—
        i. within the limits of the police station to which such police officer is appointed; or
        ii. in the premises of any station house; or
        iii. on a woman in such police officer's custody or in the custody of a police officer subordinate to such police officer; or
    b. being a public servant, commits rape on a woman in such public servant's custody or in the custody of a public servant subordinate to such public servant; or
    c. being a member of the armed forces deployed in an area by the Central or a State Government commits rape in such area; or
    d. being on the management or on the staff of a jail, remand home or other place of custody established by or under any law for the time being in force or of a women's or children's institution, commits rape on any inmate of such jail, remand home, place or institution; or
    e. being on the management or on the staff of a hospital, commits rape on a woman in that hospital; or
    f. being a relative, guardian or teacher of, or a person in a position of trust or authority towards the woman, commits rape on such woman; or
    g. commits rape during communal or sectarian violence; or
    h. commits rape on a woman knowing her to be pregnant; or
    i. commits rape on a woman when she is under sixteen years of age; or
    j. commits rape on a woman incapable of giving consent; or
    k. being in a position of control or dominance over a woman, commits rape on such woman; or
    l. commits rape on a woman suffering from mental or physical disability; or
    m. while committing rape causes grievous bodily harm or maims or disfigures or endangers the life of a woman; or
    n. commits rape repeatedly on the same woman, shall be punished with rigorous imprisonment for a term which shall not be less than ten years, but which may extend to imprisonment for life, which shall mean imprisonment for the remainder of that person's natural life, and shall also be liable to fine.

Explanation—For the purposes of this sub-section,

a. 'armed forces' means the naval, military and air forces and includes any member of the Armed Forces constituted under any Jaw for the time being in force, including the paramilitary forces and any auxiliary forces that are under the control of the Central Government!, or the State Government;
b. 'hospital' means the precincts of the hospital and includes the precincts of any institution for the reception and treatment of persons during convalescence or of persons requiring medical attention or rehabilitation;
c. 'police officer' shall have the same meaning as assigned to the expression 'police' under the Police Act, 1861;
d. 'women's or children's institution' means an institution, whether called an orphanage or a home for neglected women or children or a widow's home or an institution called by any other name, which is established and maintained for the reception and care of women or children.

[The pre-amended S. 376 reads as follows:

376. Punishment for rape—

(1) Whoever, except in the cases provided for by sub-section (2), commits rape shall be punished with imprisonment of either description for a term which shall not be less than seven years but which may be for life or for a term which may extend to ten years and shall also be liable to fine unless the women raped is his own wife and is not under twelve years of age, in which cases, he shall be punished with imprisonment of either description for a term which may extend to two years or with fine or with both: Provided that the court may, for adequate and special reasons to be mentioned in the judgment, impose a sentence of imprisonment for a term of less than seven years.

(2) Whoever,—

(a) being a police officer commits rape—

(i) within the limits of the police station to which he is appointed; or

(ii) in the premises of any station house whether or not situated in the police station to which he is appointed; or

(iii) on a woman in his custody or in the custody of a police officer subordinate to him; or

(b) being a public servant, takes advantage of his official position and commits rape on a woman in his custody as such public servant or in the custody of a public servant subordinate to him; or

(c) being on the management or on the staff of a jail, remand home or other place of custody established by or under any law for the time being in force or of a woman's or children's institution takes advantage of his official position and commits rape on any inmate of such jail, remand home, place or institution; or

(d) being on the management or on the staff of a hospital, takes advantage of his official position and commits rape on a woman in that hospital; or

(e) commits rape on a woman knowing her to be pregnant; or

(f) commits rape on a woman when she is under twelve years of age; or

(g) commits gang rape, shall be punished with rigorous imprisonment for a term which shall not be less than ten years but which may be for life and shall also be liable to fine: Provided that the Court may, for adequate and special reasons to be mentioned in the judgment, impose a sentence of imprisonment of either description for a term of less than ten years.

Explanation 1—Where a woman is raped by one or more in a group of persons acting in furtherance of their common intention, each of the persons shall be deemed to have committed gang rape within the meaning of this sub-section.

Explanation 2—'Women's or children's institution' means an institution, whether called an orphanage or a home for neglected woman or children or a widows' home or by any other name, which is established and maintained for the reception and care of woman or children.

Explanation 3—'Hospital' means the precincts of the hospital and includes the precincts of any institution for the reception and treatment of persons during convalescence or of persons requiring medical attention or rehabilitation]

376A. Punishment for causing death or resulting in persistent vegetative state of victim.

Whoever, commits an offence punishable under sub-section (1) or sub-section (2) of section 376 and in the course of such commission inflicts an injury which causes the death of the woman or causes the woman to be in a persistent vegetative state, shall be punished with rigorous imprisonment for a term which shall not be less than twenty years, but which may extend to imprisonment for life, which shall mean imprisonment for the remainder of that person's natural life, or with death.

[The pre-amended S. 376A reads as follows:

376A. Intercourse by a man with his wife during separation—

Whoever has sexual intercourse with his own wife, who is living separately from him under a decree of separation or under any custom or usage without her consent shall be punished with imprisonment of either description for a term which may extend to two years and shall also be liable to fine.]

376B. Sexual intercourse by husband upon his wife during separation

Whoever has sexual intercourse with his own wife, who is living separately, whether under a decree of separation or otherwise, without her consent, shall be punished with imprisonment of either description for a term which shall not be less than two years but which may extend to seven years, and shall also be liable to fine.

Explanation—In this section, 'sexual intercourse' shall mean any of the acts mentioned in clauses (a) to (d) of section 375.

[The pre-amended S. 376B reads as follows:

376B. Intercourse by public servant with woman in his custody—

Whoever, being a public servant, takes advantage of his official position and induces or seduces, any woman, who is in his custody as such public servant or in the custody of a public servant subordinate to him, to have sexual intercourse with him, such sexual intercourse not amounting to the offence of rape, shall be punished with imprisonment of either description for a term which may extend to five years and shall also be liable to fine]

376C. Sexual intercourse by person in authority.

Whoever, being—

a. in a position of authority or in a fiduciary relationship; or
b. a public servant; or
c. superintendent or manager of a jail, remand home or other place of custody established by or under any law for the time being in force, or a women's or children's institution; or
d. on the management of a hospital or being on the staff of a hospital, abuses such position or fiduciary relationship to induce or seduce any woman either in his custody or under his charge or present in the premises to have sexual intercourse with him, such sexual intercourse not amounting to the offence of rape, shall be punished with rigorous imprisonment of either description for a term which shall not be less than five years, but which may extend to ten years, and shall also be liable to fine.

Explanation l—In this section, 'sexual intercourse' shall mean any of the acts mentioned in clauses (a) to (d) of section 375.

Explanation 2—For the purposes of this section, Explanation 1 to section 375 shall also be applicable.

Explanation 3—'Superintendent', in relation to a jail, remand home or other place of custody or a women's or children's institution, includes a person holding any other office in such jail, remand home, place or institution by virtue of which such person can exercise any authority or control over its inmates.

Explanation 4—The expressions 'hospital' and 'women's or children's institution' shall respectively have the same meaning as in Explanation to sub-section (2) of section 376.

[Pre-amended S. 376C reads as follows:

376C. Intercourse by superintendent of jail, remand home, etc—

Whoever, being the superintendent or manager of a jail, remand home or other place of custody established by or under any law for the time being in force or of a woman's or children's institution takes advantage of his official position and induces or seduces any female inmate of such jail, remand home, place or institution to have sexual intercourse with him, such sexual intercourse not amounting to the offence of rape, shall be punished with imprisonment of either description for a term which may extend to five years and shall also be liable to fine.

Explanation 1—'Superintendent' in relation to jail, remand home or other place of custody or a women's or children's institution includes a person holding any other office in such jail, remand home, place or institution by virtue of which he can exercise any authority or control over its inmates.

Explanation 2—The expression 'women's or children's institution' shall have the same meaning as in Explanation 2 to sub-section (2) of section 376.]

376D. Gang rape.

Where a woman is raped by one or more persons constituting a group or acting in furtherance of a common intention, each of those persons shall be deemed to have committed the offence of rape and shall be punished with rigorous imprisonment for a term which shall not be less than twenty years, but which may extend to life which shall mean imprisonment for the remainder of that person's natural life, and with fine:

Provided that such fine shall be just and reasonable to meet the medical expenses and rehabilitation of the victim:

Provided further that any fine imposed under this section shall be paid to the victim.

[The pre-amended S. 376D reads as follows:

376D. Intercourse by any member of the management or staff of a hospital with any woman in that hospital—

Whoever, being on the management of a hospital or being on the staff of a hospital takes advantage of his position and has sexual intercourse with any woman in that hospital, such sexual intercourse not amounting to the offence of rape, shall be punished with imprisonment of either description for a term which may extend to five years and shall also be liable to fine.

Explanation—The expression 'hospital' shall have the same meaning as in Explanation 3 to sub-section (2) of section 376.]

406. Punishment for criminal breach of trust—

Whoever commits criminal breach of trust shall be punished with imprisonment of either description for a term which may extend to three years, or with fine, or with both.

494. Marrying again during lifetime of husband or wife—

Whoever, having a husband or wife living, marries in any case in which such marriage is void by reason of its taking place during the life of such husband or wife, shall be punished with imprisonment of either description for a term which may extend to seven years, and shall also be liable to fine.

Exception—This section does not extend to any person whose marriage with such husband or wife has been declared void by a Court of competent jurisdiction, nor to any person who contracts a marriage during the life of a former husband or wife, if such husband or wife, at the time of the subsequent marriage, shall have been continually absent from such person for the space of seven years, and shall not have been heard of by such person as being alive within that time provided the person contracting such subsequent marriage shall, before such marriage takes place, inform the person with whom such marriage is contracted of the real state of facts so far as the same are within his or her knowledge.

495. Same offence with concealment of former marriage from person with whom subsequent marriage is contracted—
Whoever commits the offence defined in the last preceding section having concealed from the person with whom the subsequent marriage is contracted, the fact of the former marriage, shall be punished with imprisonment of either description for a term which may extend to ten years, and shall also be liable to fine.

497. Adultery—
Whoever has sexual intercourse with a person who is and whom he knows or has reason to believe to be the wife of another man, without the consent or connivance of that man, such sexual intercourse not amounting to the offence of rape, is guilty of the offence of adultery, and shall be punished with imprisonment of either description for a term which may extend to five years, or with fine, or with both. In such case the wife shall not be punishable as an abettor.

498A. Husband or relative of husband of a woman subjecting her to cruelty—
Whoever, being the husband or the relative of the husband of a woman, subjects such woman to cruelty shall be punished with imprisonment for a term which may extend to three years and shall also be liable to fine.
Explanation—For the purposes of this section, 'cruelty' means—(a) any willful conduct which is of such a nature as is likely to drive the woman to commit suicide or to cause grave injury or danger to life, limb or health (whether mental or physical) of the woman; or (b) harassment of the woman where such harassment is with a view to coercing her or any person related to her to meet any unlawful demand for any property or valuable security or is on account of failure by her or any person related to her to meet such demand.

Muslim Women (Protection of Rights on Divorce) Act, 1986

3. Mahr or other properties of Muslim woman to be given to her at the time of divorce.

(1) Notwithstanding anything contained in any other law for the time being in force, a divorced woman shall be entitled to—

(a) A reasonable and fair provision and maintenance to be made and paid to her within the iddat period by her former husband:

(b) Where she herself maintains the children born to her before or after her divorce, a reasonable and fair provision and maintenance to be made and paid by her former husband for a period of two years from the respective dates of birth of such children:

(c) An amount equal to the sum of mahr or dower agreed to be paid to her at her time of her marriage or at any time thereafter according to Muslim law; and

(d) All the properties given to her before or at the time of marriage or after the marriage by her relatives or friends or the husband or any relatives of the husband or his friends.

(2) Where a reasonable and fair provision and maintenance or the amount of mahr or dower due has not been made or paid or the properties referred to in clause (d) of sub-section (1) have not been delivered to a divorced woman on her divorce, she or any one duly authorised by her may, on her behalf, make an application to a Magistrate for an order for payment of such provision and maintenance, mahr or dower or the delivery of properties, as the case may be.

(3) Where an application has been made under sub-section (2) by a divorced woman the Magistrate may; if he is satisfied that—

(a) Her husband having sufficient means, has failed or neglected to make or pay her within the iddat period a reasonable and fair provision and maintenance for her and the children; or

(b) The amount equal to the sum of mahr or dower has not been paid or that the properties referred to in clause (d) of sub-section (1) have not been delivered to her, make an order, within one month of the date of the filing of the application, directing her former husband to pay such reasonable and fair provision and maintenance to the divorced woman as he may determine as fit and proper having regard to the needs of the divorced woman, the standard of life enjoyed by her during her marriage and the means of her former husband or, as the case may be, for the payment of such mahr or dower or the delivery of such properties referred to in clause (d) of sub-section (1) to the divorced woman:

Provided that if the Magistrate finds it impracticable to dispose of the application within the said period, he may, for reasons to be recorded by him dispose of the application after the said period.

(4) If any person against whom an order has been made under sub-section (3) fails without sufficient cause to comply with the order, the Magistrate may issue a warrant for levying the amount of maintenance or mahr or dower due in the manner provided for levying fines under the Code of Criminal Procedure, 1973 (2 of 1974) and may sentence such person, for the whole or part of any amount remaining unpaid after the execution of thc warrant, to imprisonment of a term which may extend to one year or until payment if sooner made, subject to such person being heard in defence and the said sentence being imposed according to the provisions of the said Code.

Prohibition of Child Marriage Act, 2006

3. (1) Every child marriage, whether solemnised before or after the commencement of this Act, shall be voidable at the option of the contracting party who was a child at the time of the marriage:

Provided that a petition for annulling a child marriage by a decree of nullity may be filed in the district court only by a contracting party to the marriage who was a child at the time of the marriage.

(2) If at the time of filing a petition, the petitioner is a minor, the petition may be filed through his or her guardian or next friend along with the Child Marriage Prohibition Officer.

(3) The petition under this section may be filed at any time but before the child filing the petition completes two years of attaining majority.

(4) While granting a decree of nullity under this section, the district court shall make an order directing both the parties to the marriage and their parents or their guardians to return to the other party, his or her parents or guardian, as the case may be, the money, valuables, ornaments and other gifts received on the occasion of the marriage by them from the other side, or an amount equal to the value of such valuables, ornaments, other gifts and money:

Provided that no order under this section shall be passed unless the concerned parties have been given notices to appear before the district court and show cause why such order should not be passed.

Protection of Women from Domestic Violence Act, 2005

2. Definitions—In this Act, unless the context otherwise requires—

(f) 'domestic relationship' means a relationship between two persons who live or have, at any point of time, lived together in a shared household, when they are related by consanguinity, marriage, or through a relationship in the nature of marriage, adoption or are family members living together as a joint family;

(s) 'shared household' means a household where the person aggrieved lives or at any stage has lived in a domestic relationship either singly or along with the respondent and includes such a household whether owned or tenanted either jointly by the aggrieved person and the respondent, or owned or tenanted by either of them in respect of which either the aggrieved person or the respondent or both jointly or singly have any right, title, interest or equity and includes such a household which may belong to the joint family of which the respondent is a member, irrespective of whether the respondent or the aggrieved person has any right, title or interest in the shared household;

3. Definition of domestic violence.

For the purposes of this Act, any act, omission or commission or conduct of the respondent shall constitute domestic violence in case it—

(a) harms or injures or endangers the health, safety, life, limb or well-being, whether mental or physical, of the aggrieved person or tends to do so and includes causing physical abuse, sexual abuse, verbal and emotional abuse and economic abuse; or

(b) harasses, harms, injures or endangers the aggrieved person with a view to coerce her or any other person related to her to meet any unlawful demand for any dowry or other property or valuable security;

or

(c) has the effect of threatening the aggrieved person or any person related to her by any conduct mentioned in clause (a) or clause (b); or

(d) otherwise injures or causes harm, whether physical or mental, to the aggrieved person.

Explanation I—For the purposes of this section—

(i) 'physical abuse' means any act or conduct which is of such a nature as to cause bodily pain, harm, or danger to life, limb, or health or impair the health or development of the aggrieved person and includes assault, criminal intimidation and criminal force;

(ii) 'sexual abuse' includes any conduct of a sexual nature that abuses, humiliates, degrades or otherwise violates the dignity of woman;

(iii) 'verbal and emotional abuse' includes—

(a) insults, ridicule, humiliation, name calling and insults or ridicule specially with regard to not having a child or a male child; and

(b) repeated threats to cause physical pain to any person in whom the aggrieved person is interested.

(iv) 'economic abuse' includes—

(a) deprivation of all or any economic or financial resources to which the aggrieved person is entitled under any law or custom whether payable under an order of a court or otherwise or which the aggrieved person requires out of necessity including, but not limited to, household necessities for the aggrieved person and her children, if any, stridhan, property, jointly or separately owned by the aggrieved person, payment of rental related to the shared household and maintenance;

(b) disposal of household effects, any alienation of assets whether movable or immovable, valuables, shares, securities, bonds and the like or other property in which the aggrieved person has an interest or is entitled to use by virtue of the domestic relationship or which may be reasonably required by the aggrieved person or her children or her stridhan or any other property jointly or separately held by the aggrieved person; and

(c) prohibition or restriction to continued access to resources or facilities which the aggrieved person is entitled to use or enjoy by virtue of the domestic relationship including access to the shared household.

Explanation II—For the purpose of determining whether any act, omission, commission or conduct of the respondent constitutes 'domestic violence' under this section, the overall facts and circumstances of the case shall be taken into consideration.

17. Right to reside in a shared household—

(1) Notwithstanding anything contained in any other law for the time being in force, every woman in a domestic relationship shall have the right to

reside in the shared household, whether or not she has any right, title or beneficial interest in the same.

(2) The aggrieved person shall not be evicted or excluded from the shared household or any part of it by the respondent save in accordance with the procedure established by law.

20. Monetary reliefs.

(1) While disposing of an application under sub-section (1) of section 12, the Magistrate may direct the respondent to pay monetary relief to meet the expenses incurred and losses suffered by the aggrieved person and any child of the aggrieved person as a result of the domestic violence and such relief may include, but not limited to,

(a) the loss of earnings;

(b) the medical expenses;

(c) the loss caused due to the destruction, damage or removal of any property from the control of the aggrieved person; and

(d) the maintenance for the aggrieved person as well as her children, if any, including an order under or in addition to an order of maintenance under section 125 of the Code of Criminal Procedure, 1973 (2 of 1974) or any other law for the time being in force.

(2) The monetary relief granted under this section shall be adequate, fair and reasonable and consistent with the standard of living to which the aggrieved person is accustomed.

(3) The Magistrate shall have the power to order an appropriate lump sum payment or monthly payments of maintenance, as the nature and circumstances of the case may require.

(4) The Magistrate shall send a copy of the order for monetary relief made under sub-section (1) to the parties to the application and to the in charge of the police station within the local limits of whose jurisdiction the respondent resides.

(5) The respondent shall pay the monetary relief granted to the aggrieved person within the period specified in the order under sub-section (1).

(6) Upon the failure on the part of the respondent to make payment in terms of the order under sub-section (1), the Magistrate may direct the employer or a debtor of the respondent, to directly pay to the aggrieved person or to deposit with the court a portion of the wages or salaries or debt due to or accrued to the credit of the respondent, which amount may be adjusted towards the monetary relief payable by the respondent.

22. Compensation orders—In addition to other reliefs as may be granted under this Act, the Magistrate may on an application being made by the aggrieved person, pass an order directing the respondent to pay compensation and damages for the injuries, including mental torture and emotional distress, caused by the acts of domestic violence committed by that respondent.

Registration Act, 1908

17. Documents of which registration is compulsory

(1) The following documents shall be registered, if the property to which they relate is situate in a district in which, and if they have been executed on or after the date on which, Act No. XVI of 1864, or the Indian Registration Act, 1866, or the Indian Registration Act, 1871, or the Indian Registration Act, 1877 or this Act came or comes into force, namely:

(a) instruments of gift of immovable property;

(b) other non-testamentary instruments which purport or operate to create, declare, assign, limit or extinguish, whether in present or in future, any right, title or interest, whether vested or contingent, of the value of one hundred rupees, and upwards, to or in immovable property;

(c) non-testamentary instruments which acknowledge the receipt or payment of any consideration on account of the creation, declaration, assignment, limitation or extinction of any such right, title or interest; and

(d) leases of immovable property from year to year, or for any term exceeding one year, or reserving a yearly rent;

(e) non-testamentary instruments transferring or assigning any decree or order of a court or any award when such decree or order or award purports or operates to create, declare, assign, limit or extinguish, whether in present or in future, any right, title or interest, whether vested or contingent, of the value of one hundred rupees and upwards, to or in immovable property:

PROVIDED that the State Government may, by order published in the Official Gazette, exempt from the operation of this sub-section any leases executed in any district, or part of a district, the terms granted by which do not exceed five years and the annual rent reserved by which do not exceed fifty rupees.

(2) Nothing in clauses (b) and (c) of sub-section (1) applies to—

(i) any composition-deed; or

(ii) any instrument relating to shares in a joint Stock Company, notwithstanding that the assets of such company consist in whole or in part of immovable property; or

(iii) any debenture issued by any such company and not creating, declaring, assigning, limiting or extinguishing any right, title or interest, to or in immovable property except insofar as it entitles the holder to the security afforded by a registered instrument whereby the company has mortgaged, conveyed or otherwise transferred the whole or part of its immovable property or any interest therein to trustees upon trust for the benefit of the holders of such debentures; or

(iv) any endorsement upon or transfer of any debenture issued by any such company; or

(v) any document not itself creating, declaring, assigning, limiting or extinguishing any right, title or interest of the value of one hundred rupees and upwards to or in immovable property, but merely creating a right to obtain another document which will, when executed, create, declare, assign, limit or extinguish any such right, title or interest; or

(vi) any decree or order of a court except a decree or order expressed to be made on a compromise and comprising immovable property other than that which is the subject-matter of the suit or proceeding; or

(vii) any grant of immovable property by government; or

(viii) any instrument of partition made by a revenue-officer; or

(ix) any order granting a loan or instrument of collateral security granted under the Land Improvement Act, 1871, or the Land Improvement Loans Act, 1883; or

(x) any order granting a loan under the Agriculturists Loans Act, 1884, or instrument for securing the repayment of a loan made under that Act; or

(xa) any order made under the Charitable Endowments Act, 1890, (6 of 1890) vesting any property in a Treasurer of Charitable Endowments or divesting any such treasurer of any property; or

(xi) any endorsement on a mortgage-deed acknowledging the payment of the whole or any part of the mortgage-money, and any other receipt for payment of money due under a mortgage when the receipt does not purport to extinguish the mortgage; or

(xii) any certificate of sale granted to the purchaser of any property sold by public auction by a civil or revenue-officer.

Explanation: A document purporting or operating to effect a contract for the sale of immovable property shall not be deemed to require or ever to have required registration by reason only of the fact that such document contains a recital of the payment of any earnest money or of the whole or any part of the purchase money.

(3) Authorities to adopt a son, executed after the 1st day of January, 1872, and not conferred by a will, shall also be registered.

Special Marriage Act, 1954

4. Conditions relating to solemnization of special marriages

Notwithstanding anything contained in any other law for the time being in force relating to be solemnization of marriages, a marriage between any tow persons may be solemnized under this Act, if at the time of the marriage the following conditions are fulfilled, namely:

(a) neither party has a spouse living;

(b) neither party—

(i) is incapable of giving a valid consent to it in consequence of unsoundness of mind; or

(ii) though capable of giving a valid consent, has been suffering from mental disorder of such a kind or to such an extent as to be unfit for marriage and the procreation of children; or

(iii) has been subject to recurrent attacks of insanity or epilepsy;

(c) the male has completed the age of twenty-one years and the female the age of eighteen years;

(d) the parties are not within the degrees of prohibited relationship

Provided that where a custom governing at least one of the parties permits of a marriage between them, such marriage may be solemnized, notwithstanding that they are within the degrees of prohibited relationship; and

(e) where the marriage is solemnized in the State of Jammu and Kashmir, both parties are citizens of India domiciled in the territories to which this Act extends.

Explanation—In this section, 'custom', in relation to a person belonging to any tribe, community, group or family, means any rule which the State Government may, by notification in the Official Gazette, specify in this behalf as applicable to members of that tribe, community, group or family :

Provided that no such notification shall be issue in relation to the members of any tribe, community, group or family, unless the State Government is satisfied—

(i) that such rule has been continuously and uniformly observed for a long time amongst those members;

(ii) that such rule is certain and not unreasonable or opposed to public policy; and

(iii) that such rule, if applicable only to a family, has not been discontinued by the family.

19. Effect of marriage on member of undivided family—

The marriage solemnized under this Act of any member of an undivided family who professes the Hindu, Buddhist, Sikh or Jaina religions shall be deemed to effect his severance from such family.

21A. Special provision in certain cases—Where the marriage is solemnized under this Act of any person who professes the Hindu, Buddhist, Sikh or Jaina religion with a person who professes the Hindu, Buddhist, Sikh or Jaina religion, section 19 and section 21 shall not apply and so much of section 20 as creates a disability shall also not apply.

26. Legitimacy of children of void and voidable marriages—

(1) Notwithstanding that a marriage is null and void under section 24, any child of such marriage who would have been legitimate if the marriage had been valid, shall be legitimate, whether such child is born before or after the commencement of the Marriage Laws (Amendment) Act, 1976 (68 of 1976), and whether or not a decree of nullity is granted in respect of that marriage under this Act and whether or not the marriage is held to be void otherwise than on a petition under this Act.

(2) Where a decree of nullity is granted in respect of a voidable marriage under section 25, any child begotten or conceived before the decree is made, who would have been the legitimate child of the parties to the marriage if at the date of the decree it has been dissolved instead of being annulled, shall be deemed to be their legitimate child notwithstanding the decree of nullity.

(3) Nothing contained in sub-section (1) or sub-section (2) shall be construed as conferring upon any child of a marriage which is null and void or which is annulled by a decree of nullity under section 25, any rights in or to the property of any person, other than the parents, in any case where, but for the passing of this Act, such child would have been incapable of possessing or acquiring any such rights by reason of not his being the legitimate child of his parents.

36. Alimony pendente lite

Where in any proceeding under Chapter V or Chapter VI it appears to the district court that the wife has no independent income sufficient for her support and the necessary expenses of the proceeding, it may, on the application of the wife, order the husband to pay to her the expenses of the proceeding, and weekly or monthly during the proceeding such sum as, having regard to the husband's income, it may seem to the court to be reasonable.

37. Permanent alimony and maintenance—

(1) Any court exercising jurisdiction under Chapter V or Chapter VI may, at the time of passing any decree or at any time subsequent to the decree, on application made to it for the purpose, order that the husband shall secure to the wife for her maintenance and support, if necessary, by a charge on the husband's property such gross sum or such monthly or periodical payment of money for a term not exceeding her life, as, having regard to her own property, if any, her husband's property and ability the conduct of the parties and other circumstances of the case, it may seem to the court to be just.

(2) If the district court is satisfied that there is a change in the circumstances of either party at any time after it has made an order under sub-section (1), it may, at the instance of either party, vary, modify or rescind any such order in such manner as it may seem to the court to be just.

(3) If the district court is satisfied that the wife in whose favour an order has been made under this section has re-married or is not leading a chaste life, it may, at the instance of the husband vary, modify or rescind any such order and in such manner as the court may deem just.

44. Punishment of bigamy

Every person whose marriage is solemnized under this Act and who, during the lifetime of his or her wife or husband, contracts any other marriage shall be subject to the penalties provided in section 494 and section 495 of the Indian penal Code, for the offence of marrying again during the lifetime of a husband or wife, and the marriage so contracted shall be void.

Muslim Personal Law (Shariat) Application Act, 1937

2. Application of Personal Law to Muslims

Notwithstanding any custom or usage to the contrary, in all questions (save questions relating to agricultural land) regarding intestate succession, special property of females, including personal property inherited or obtained under contract or gift or any other provision of Personal Law, marriage, dissolution of marriage, including talaq, ila, zihar, lian, khula and mubaraat, maintenance, dower guardianship, gifts, trusts and trust properties, and wakfs (other than charities and charitable institutions and charitable and religious endowments) the rule of decision in cases where the parties are Muslims shall be the Muslim Personal law (Shariat).

3. Power to make a declaration
   (1) Any person who satisfies the prescribed authority—
      (a) that he is a Muslim, and
      (b) that he is competent to contract within the meaning of section 11 of the Indian Contract Act, 1872, and
      (c) that he is a resident of the territories to which this Act extends may by declaration in the prescribed form and filed before the prescribed authority declare that he desires to obtain the benefit of 7 [the provisions of this section], and thereafter the provisions of section 2 shall apply to the declarant and all his minor children and their descendants as if in addition to the matters enumerated therein adoption, wills and legacies were also specified.
   (2) Where the prescribed authority refuses to accept a declaration under sub-section (1), the person desiring to make the same may appeal to such officer as the 8[State] Government may, if he is satisfied that the appellant is entitled to make the declaration, order the prescribed authority to accept the same.

RULES

Dowry Prohibition (Maintenance Of Lists Of Presents To The Bride And Bridegroom) Rules, 1985

2. Rules in accordance with which lists of presents are to be maintained:
   (1) The list of presents which are given at the time of the marriage to the bride shall be maintained by the bride.
   (2) The list of present which are given at the time of the marriage to the bridegroom shall be maintained by the bridegroom.

   Every list of presents referred to in sub-rule (1) or sub-rule (2)—
   a. shall be prepared at the time of the marriage or as soon as possible after the marriage:
   b. shall be in writing;
   c. shall contain—
      i. a brief description of each present;
      ii. the approximate value of the present;
      iii. the name of the person who has given the present; and
      iv. where the person giving the present is related to the bride or bridegroom, a description of such relationship;
   d. shall be signed by both the bride and the bridegroom.

   Explanation. 1—Where the bride is unable to sign, she may affix her thumb impression in lieu of her signature after having the list read out to her and obtaining the signature on the list, of the person who has so read out the particulars contained in the list.

Explanation 2—Where the bridegroom is unable to sign he may affix his thumb-impression in lieu of his signature after having the list read out to him and obtaining the signature on the list of the person who has so read out the particulars contained in the list.

(4) The bride or the bridegroom may, if she or he so desires, obtain on either or both of the lists referred to in sub-rule (1) or sub-rule (2) the signature or signatures of any relations of the bride or the bridegroom or of any other person or persons present at the time of the marriage.

INTERNATIONAL INSTRUMENTS

Convention on the Civil Aspects of International Child Abduction, 1980

Article 13

Notwithstanding the provisions of the preceding Article, the judicial or administrative authority of the requested State is not bound to order the return of the child if the person, institution or other body which opposes its return establishes that—*a)* the person, institution or other body having the care of the person of the child was not actually exercising the custody rights at the time of removal or retention, or had consented to or subsequently acquiesced in the removal or retention; or *b)* there is a grave risk that his or her return would expose the child to physical or psychological harm or otherwise place the child in an intolerable situation.

The judicial or administrative authority may also refuse to order the return of the child if it finds that the child objects to being returned and has attained an age and degree of maturity at which it is appropriate to take account of its views.

In considering the circumstances referred to in this Article, the judicial and administrative authorities shall take into account the information relating to the social background of the child provided by the Central Authority or other competent authority of the child's habitual residence.

Convention on the Rights of the Child, 1989

Article 12

1. States Parties shall assure to the child who is capable of forming his or her own views the right to express those views freely in all matters affecting the child, the views of the child being given due weight in accordance with the age and maturity of the child.
2. For this purpose, the child shall in particular be provided the opportunity to be heard in any judicial and administrative proceedings affecting the child, either directly, or through a representative or an appropriate body, in a manner consistent with the procedural rules of national law.

Convention to Eliminate of all forms of Discrimination against Women, 1979

5. States Parties shall take all appropriate measures:
   (a) To modify the social and cultural patterns of conduct of men and women, with a view to achieving the elimination of prejudices and customary and all other practices which are based on the idea of the inferiority or the superiority of either of the sexes or on stereotyped roles for men and women;
   (b) To ensure that family education includes a proper understanding of maternity as a social function and the recognition of the common responsibility of men and women in the upbringing and development of their children, it being understood that the interest of the children is the primordial consideration in all cases.

Universal Declaration of Human Rights, 1948

Article 25

(1) Everyone has the right to a standard of living adequate for the health and well-being of himself and of his family, including food, clothing, housing and medical care and necessary social services, and the right to security in the event of unemployment, sickness, disability, widowhood, old age or other lack of livelihood in circumstances beyond his control.

(2) Motherhood and childhood are entitled to special care and assistance. All children, whether born in or out of wedlock, shall enjoy the same social protection.

FOREIGN STATUTES

Children and Families Act, 2014

13. Control of expert evidence, and of assessments, in children proceedings
   (1) A person may not without the permission of the court instruct a person to provide expert evidence for use in children proceedings.
   (2) Where in contravention of sub-section (1) a person is instructed to provide expert evidence, evidence resulting from the instructions is inadmissible in children proceedings unless the court rules that it is admissible.
   (3) A person may not without the permission of the court cause a child to be medically or psychiatrically examined or otherwise assessed for the purposes of the provision of expert evidence in children proceedings.
   (4) Where in contravention of sub-section (3) a child is medically or psychiatrically examined or otherwise assessed, evidence resulting from the examination or other assessment is inadmissible in children proceedings unless the court rules that it is admissible.
   (5) In children proceedings, a person may not without the permission of the court put expert evidence (in any form) before the court.

(6) The court may give permission as mentioned in sub-section (1), (3) or (5) only if the court is of the opinion that the expert evidence is necessary to assist the court to resolve the proceedings justly.

(7) When deciding whether to give permission as mentioned in sub-section (1), (3) or (5) the court is to have regard in particular to—

(a) any impact which giving permission would be likely to have on the welfare of the children concerned, including in the case of permission as mentioned in sub-section (3) any impact which any examination or other assessment would be likely to have on the welfare of the child who would be examined or otherwise assessed,

(b) the issues to which the expert evidence would relate,

(c) the questions which the court would require the expert to answer,

(d) what other expert evidence is available (whether obtained before or after the start of proceedings),

(e) whether evidence could be given by another person on the matters on which the expert would give evidence,

(f) the impact which giving permission would be likely to have on the timetable for, and duration and conduct of, the proceedings,

(g) the cost of the expert evidence, and

(h) any matters prescribed by Family Procedure Rules.

(8) References in this section to providing expert evidence, or to putting expert evidence before a court, do not include references to—

(a) the provision or giving of evidence—

(i) by a person who is a member of the staff of a local authority or of an authorised applicant,

(ii) in proceedings to which the authority or authorised applicant is a party, and

(iii) in the course of the person's work for the authority or authorised applicant,

(b) the provision or giving of evidence—

(i) by a person within a description prescribed for the purposes of sub-section (1) of section 94 of the Adoption and Children Act 2002 (suitability for adoption etc.), and

(ii) about the matters mentioned in that sub-section,

(c) the provision or giving of evidence by an officer of the Children and Family Court Advisory and Support Service when acting in that capacity, or

(d) the provision or giving of evidence by a Welsh family proceedings officer (as defined by section 35(4) of the Children Act 2004) when acting in that capacity.

(9) In this section 'authorised applicant' means—

(a) the National Society for the Prevention of Cruelty to Children, or

(b) a person authorised by an order under section 31 of the Children Act 1989 to bring proceedings under that section; 'child' means a person under the age of 18; 'children proceedings' has such meaning as may be prescribed by Family Procedure Rules; 'the court', in relation to any children proceedings, means the court in which the proceedings are taking place; 'local authority'—

(a) in relation to England means—
  (i) a county council,
  (ii) a district council for an area for which there is no county council,
  (iii) a London borough council,
  (iv) the Common Council of the City of London, or
  (v) the Council of the Isles of Scilly, and
(b) in relation to Wales means a county council or a county borough council.

(10) The preceding provisions of this section are without prejudice to sections 75 and 76 of the Courts Act 2003 (power to make Family Procedure Rules).

(11) In section 38 of the Children Act 1989 (court's power to make interim care and supervision orders, and to give directions as to medical examination etc. of children) after sub-section (7) insert—

'(7A) A direction under sub-section (6) to the effect that there is to be a medical or psychiatric examination or other assessment of the child may be given only if the court is of the opinion that the examination or other assessment is necessary to assist the court to resolve the proceedings justly.

(7B) When deciding whether to give a direction under sub-section (6) to that effect the court is to have regard in particular to—

(a) any impact which any examination or other assessment would be likely to have on the welfare of the child, and any other impact which giving the direction would be likely to have on the welfare of the child,
(b) the issues with which the examination or other assessment would assist the court,
(c) the questions which the examination or other assessment would enable the court to answer,
(d) the evidence otherwise available,
(e) the impact which the direction would be likely to have on the timetable, duration and conduct of the proceedings,
(f) the cost of the examination or other assessment, and
(g) any matters prescribed by Family Procedure Rules.

REFERENCES

Abrams, Kerry. 2012. 'Marriage Fraud.' *California Law Review* 100 (1) pp.1-68.

Aggarwal, Bina. 1994. *A Field of One's Own: Gender and Land Rights in South Asia*. New York: University of Cambridge Press.

Agnes, Flavia. 2015. 'Liberating Hindu Women.' *Economic and Political Weekly* 50 (10) pp.14-17.

_____ 2012. 'His and Hers.' *Economic and Political Weekly* 47(17) pp.10-12.

_____ 2011a. *Family Laws and Constitutional Claims*. New Delhi: Oxford University Press.

_____ 2011b. *Marriage, Divorce and Matrimonial Litigation*. New Delhi: Oxford University Press.

_____ 2009. 'Conjugality, Property, Morality and Maintenance.' *Economic and Political Weekly* 44 (44) pp.58-64.

_____ 1995. 'Hindu Men, Monogamy and Uniform Civil Code.' *Economic and Political Weekly* 30 (50) pp.3238–44.

Agnes, Flavia, Chandra, Sudhir and Basu, Monmayee. 2011. *Women and Law in India*. New Delhi: Oxford University Press.

Ali, Syed Mohammad. 2004. *The Position of Women in Islam: A Progressive View*. Albany: State University of New York Press.

Alvarez, A. 1982. *Life After Marriage: Scenes from Divorce*. London: Macmillan.

Amato, P.R. 2000. 'The consequences of divorce for adults and children.' *Journal of Marriage and Family*. 62 (4) pp.1269–87.

Amar, Tanmay. 2005. 'Matrimonial Communications: Wedded to the irrational.' *Student Bar Review* 17 pp.59-72.

American Psychological, Association. 1995. 'Guidelines for Child Custody Evaluations in Divorce Proceedings.' *Family Law Quarterly* 29 (1) pp.51-62.

Amrita Chhachhi, Farida Khan, Gautam Navlakha, Kumkum Sangari, Neeraj Malik, Ritu Menon, Tanika Sarkar, Uma Chakravarti, Urvashi Butalia, and Zoya Hasan. 1988. 'UCC And Women's Movement.' *Economic and Political Weekly* 33 (9) pp.487-88.

Angelou, Maya. 1994. *The Complete Poetry*. New York: Random House.

Annhoff, Lee. 1990. *Battered Women as Survivors*. London: Routledge Publishers.

Anweshi Law Committee. 1997. 'Is Gender Justice Only a Legal Issue? Political Stakes in UCC Debate.' *Economic and Political Weekly* 32 (9) p.453.

Austen, Jane. 2010. *Sense and Sensibility*. New York: Harper Press.

Babu, S. Rajendra. 2002. 'Endowment Lecture on Gender Justice.' *Supreme Court Cases Journal* 5 (1).

Badran, Margot. 1995. *Feminists, Islam, and Nation: Gender and the making of modern Egypt*. Princeton: Princeton University Press.

Bajpai, Asha. 2006. *Child Rights in India: Law, Policy and Practice*. New Delhi: Oxford University Press.

Bala, N. and Schuman, J. 2000. 'Allegations of Sexual Abuse When Parents Have Separated.' *Canadian Family Law Quarterly* 17 pp.191-241.

Banerjee, Sikata. 2005. *Make Me a Man!* Albany: SUNY Press.

Barnett, Hilaire. 1997. *Sourcebook on Feminist Jurisprudence*. London: Cavendish Publishing Ltd.

Baron-Cohen, Simon. 2012. *The Science of Evil: On Empathy and the Origins of Cruelty*. New York: Basic Civitas Books.

Baxi, Pratiksha. 2014. *Public Secrets of Law: Rape Trials in India*. New Delhi: Oxford University Press.

Baxi, Upendra. 1986. 'Discipline, Repression and Legal Pluralism.' in *Legal Pluralism: Proceedings of the Canberra Law Workshop VII*, P. Sack and E. Minchin (ed.s), pp.51-61. Canberra: Australian National University.

Baxi, Upendra; Dhagamwar, Vasudha; Kelkar, Raghunath and Sarkar, Lotika. 'Open Letter to the Chief Justice of India.' http://pldindia.org/wp-content/uploads/2013/03/Open-Letter-to-CJI-in-the-Mathura-Rape-Case.pdf

Bayley, John. 1988. *Iris: A Memoir of Iris Murdoch*. London: Gerald Duckworth and Co. Ltd.

Beauvoir, Simone de; Translated by Borde, Constance and Malovany-Chevallier, Sheila. 1928. *The Second Sex*. London: Vintage Books.

Bedi, Rahul. 'Indira Gandhi's death remembered.' *BBC News*, November 1, 2009. http://news.bbc.co.uk/2/hi/south_asia/8306420.stm.

Bedi, Rajinder. 2010. *Ek Chadar Maili Si*. New Delhi: Full Circle Publishing.

Berlin, A. 2011. *The Oxford Dictionary of the Jewish Religion*. New York: Oxford University Press.

Bernard, Jessie. 1982. *The Future of Marriage*. New Haven: Yale University Press.

Béteille, André. 2006. *Ideology and Social Science*. New Delhi: Penguin Books.

Bhandare, Murlidhar C. 2010. *Struggle for Gender Justice: Justice Sunanda Bhandare Memorial Lectures*. New Delhi: Penguin India.

Bhattacharjee, A.M. 1996. *Matrimonial Laws and the Constitution*. Kolkata: Eastern Law House.

Bird, Roger and Burrows, David. 2009. *Child Maintenance: The New Law*. Bristol: Jordan Publishing Ltd.

Blankenhorn, David. 2007. *The Future of Marriage*. New York: Encounter Books.

Blush, G. L. and Ross, K. L. 1987. 'Sexual allegations in divorce: The SAID Syndrome.' *Conciliation Courts Review* 25 (1) pp.1-11.

Bono, Paola and Kemp, Sandra (Ed.). 1991. *Italian Feminist Thought: A Reader*. Oxford: Basil Blackwell Ltd.

Borchert, Christopher J. et al. 2015. 'Reasonable Expectations of Privacy Settings: Social Media and the Stored Communications Act.' *Duke Law and Technology Review* 13 (1) pp.36–65.

Bridgeman, Jo and Millns, Susan. 1998. *Feminist Perspective Law: Law's Engagement with the Female Body*. London: Sweet and Maxwell.

Bring, Margaret F. 1999. *Family Law in Action: A Reader*. Cincinnati: Anderson Publishing.

Brophy, Clare and Smart, Carol, (Eds.) *Women in Law: Explorations in Law, Family and Sexuality*. London: Routledge, 1985.

Burton, Frances. 2012. *Family Law*. New York: Routledge.

Butalia, Urvashi. 2000. *The Other Side of Silence: Voices from the Partition of India.* New Delhi: Penguin Books India.

Butler, Judith. 2004. *Undoing Gender.* New York: Routledge.

Cahn, Naomi R. 1998-1999. 'Models of Family Privacy.' *George Washington Law Review* 67 pp.1225-46.

Campbell, Joseph. 1991. *The Power of Myth.* New York: Anchor Books.

Carbone, June and Cahn, Naomi. 2014. *Marriage Markets: How Inequality is Remaking the American Family.* New York: Oxford University Press.

Carter, Terry and Gatland, Laura. 1997. "She Done Me Wrong': A Jury Agrees, awarding a jilted wife $1 million in an alienation of affection suit against the 'other woman'.' *American Bar Association Journal* 83 (10) p.24.

Chakravarti, Uma. 2013. *Gendering Caste Through a Feminist Lens.* Kolkata: Stree.

____ 1993. 'Conceptualising Brahmanical Patriarchy in Early India: Gender, Caste, Class and State.' *Economic and Political Weekly* 28 (14) pp.579-85.

Champappilly, Sebastian. 1994. 'Christian Law of Succession and Mary Roy's Case.' *Supreme Court Cases Journal* 4 (9).

Chandra, Sudhir. 2008. *Enslaved Daughters: Colonialism, Law and Women's Rights.* New Delhi: Oxford University Press.

Chiba, Masaji. 1993. 'Legal Pluralism in Sri Lankan Society: Toward a General Theory of Non-Western Law' *Journal of Legal Pluralism* (33) pp.197–212.

Child Rights Foundation. 2014. *Child Access and Custody Guidelines (approved by the Bombay High Court).* http://cja.gov.in/Important Instructions/Child Access and Custody Guidelines 01.06.2015.pdf.

Chowdhry, Prem. 1994. 'Widow Remarriage in Haryana: Law strengthens repressiveness of popular culture.' *Manushi* 82 pp.12-18.

Clawar, Stanley S. and Rivlin, Brynee. 1991. *Children Held Hostage: Dealing with Programmed and Brainwashed Children.* Chicago: American Bar Association.

Cohen, Jane Maslow. 1990. 'Feminism and Adaptive Heroinism: The Paradigm of Portia as a Means of Introduction.' *Tulsa Law Journal* 25 (4) pp.657-734.

Congreve, William. 1697. *The Mourning Bride.* London: The British Libray.

Cossman, Brenda and Kapur, Ratna. 1996. 'Bench-Marked by Hindu Right.' *Economic and Political Weekly* 31 (38) pp.2613-30.

Cottrell, Leonard. 1962. *Lost Worlds.* New York: American Heritage Publishing Co.

Daly, Mary. 1990. *The Metaethics of Radical Feminism.* Boston: Beacon Press.

Denning, Lord. 1980. *The Due Process of Law.* London: Butterworths.

_____ 1985. *The Family Story.* London: Butterworths.

Derrett, J. Duncan M. 1995. *Essays in Classical and Modern Hindu Law.* New Delhi: Universal Book Traders.

____ 1963. *Introduction to Modern Hindu Law*, New Delhi: Oxford University Press.

____ 1995. 'J.H. Nelson : A Forgotten Administrator-Historian of India' in *Essays in Classical and Modern Hindu Law*, Vol.II. New Delhi: Universal Book Traders.

Desai, A. and Muralidhar S. 2001. 'Public Interest Litigation: Potential and Problems' in *Supreme But Not Infallible: Essays in Honour of the Supreme Court*, B.N. Kirpal et. al. (ed.s) New Delhi: Oxford University Press.

Desouza, Peter Ronald. 2015. 'Politics of the Uniform Civil Code in India.' *Economic and Political Weekly* 50 (48) pp.50-57.

Dewar, John. 1992. *Law and the Family*. London: Butterworths.

Dhagamvar, Vasudha. 1989. *Towards the Uniform Civil Code*. Delhi: India Law Institute.

____ 2002. 'Invasion of Criminal Law by Religion, Custom and Family Law.' *Economic and Political Weekly* 38 (15) pp.1483-92.

Dhanda, Archana Parashar and Amita (Eds). 2008. *Redefining Family Law in India: Essays in Honour of B. Sivaramayya*. New Delhi: Routledge.

Dhavan, Rajeev. 1977. *The Supreme Court of India: A Socio-Legal Critique of its Juristic Techniques*. Bombay: N.M. Tripathi.

Dicey, A. and Morris John. 2012 *Conflict of Law*. London:Sweet and Maxwell.

Diduck, A. and Kaganas F. 2012. *Family Law, Gender and the State: Text, Cases and Material*. Oxford: Hart Publishing.

Doherty, Joshua. 2012 *Women's Representation in Judiciaries Worldwide: Arguments in Favour of Increasing the Gender Diversity on the Bench*. Washington: Institute for Global and International Studies. https://www.gwu.edu/~igis/assets/docs/working_papers/igis_wp2_ggp_wp1_doherty.pdf.

Donald R. Songer, Davis, Sue and Haire, Susan. 1994. 'A Reappraisal of Diversification in the Federal Courts: Gender Effects in the Courts of Appeals.' *Journal of Politics* 56 (2) pp.425-39.

Doniger, Wendy. 2013. *On Hinduism*. New Delhi: Aleph Book Company.

Doniger, Wendy and Kakar, Sudhir. 2002. *Kamasutra: A new, complete English translation of the Sanskrit text*. New York: Oxford University Press.

Dubler, Ariela R. 1998. 'Governing Through Contract: Common Law Marriage in the Nineteenth Century.' *The Yale Law Journal* 17 (5) pp.1885–1920.

Dubler, Ariela R. 2000. 'Wifely Behaviour: A Legal History of Acting Married.' *Columbia Law Review* 100 (4) pp.957-1021.

Eder, Steve and Valentino-Devries, Jennifer. 'A Spy-Gear Arms Race Transforms Modern Divorce.' *The Wall Street Journal*, October 6, 2012.

Eekelaar, John. 2006. *Family Law and Personal Life*. New York: Oxford University Press.

____ 1984. *Family Law and Social Policy*. London: Weidenfield and Nicolson.

Eekelaar, John and Maclean, Mavis. 1994. *A Reader on Family Law*. New York: Oxford University Press.

Eekelaar, John and Sarcevic, Petar (Eds). 1993. *Parenthood in Modern Society: Legal and Social Issues for the Twenty-First Century*. The Netherlands: Martinus Nijhoff Publishers.

Eekelaar, John M. and Katz, Sanford N. 1980. *Marriage and Cohabitation in Contemporary Societies: Areas of Legal, Social and Ethical Change*. Toronto: Butterworths.

Engels, Friedrich. 2004. *The Origin of the Family, Private Property and the State*. New South Wales: Resistance Books.

Epstein, Cynthia Fuchs. 1983. *Women in Law*. New York: Anchor Books.

Faludi, Susan. 1991. *Backlash: The Undeclared War Against American Women*. New York: Three Rivers Press.

____ 2000. *Stiffed: The Betrayal of the American Man*. New York: Harper Collins.

Federle, Katherine Hunt. 2013. *Children and the Law*. New York: Oxford University Press.

Fernandes, Leela. 2014. *Routledge Handbook of Gender in South Asia*. New York: Routledge.

Fernea, Elizabeth Warnock. 1998. *In Search of Islamic Feminism*. New York: Anchor Books.

Ferro, Gaetano; Lawson, Marcus and Murray, Sarah. 2010. 'Electronically Stored Information: What Matrimonial Lawyers and Computer Forensics Need to Know.' *Journal of the American Academy of Matrimonial Lawyers* 23 (1).

Fineman, Marta A. 1999. 'What Place for Family Privacy.' *George Washington Law Review* 67 p.1207.

Finkel, Eli J., Hui, Chin Mig, Carswell, Kathleen L. and Larson, Grace M. 2014. 'The Suffocation of Marriage: Climbing Mount Maslow Without Enough Oxygen.' *Psychological Inquiry* pp.1-41.

Forbes, Geraldine. 2012. *Women in Modern India*. Cambridge: Cambridge University Press.

Forbes, Stephanie. 2003. "Why Just Have One?': An Evaluation Of The Anti-Polygamy Laws Under The Establishment Clause.' *Houston Law Review* 39 p.1517.

Forster, E.M. 2002. *Aspects of the Novel*. New York: Rosetta Books

Freeman, Michael. 2007. *Understanding Family Law*. London: Sweet and Maxwell.

Friedman, Betty. 2001. *The Feminine Mystique*. New York: Norton Publishing.

Fromm, Erich. 1994. *Escape from Freedom*. New York: Henry Holt and Company.

____ 2006. *The Art of Loving*. New York: Harper Perennial Modern Classics.

Fyzee, A.A. 2011. *Outlines of Muhammadan Law*. New Delhi: Oxford University Press.

Galanter, Marc. 'Secularism: East and West.' in *Secularism and Its Critics*, Rajeev Bhargava (ed.). New Delhi: Oxford University Press, 1998.

Gangoli, Geetanjali. 2007. *Indian Feminisms: Law, Patriarchies and Violence in India*. Hampshire, UK: Ashgate Publishing.

Gardiner, Judith Kegan. 2002. *Masculinity Studies and Feminist Theory*. New York: Columbia University Press.

Garrity, Carla B. and Baris, Mitchell A. 1994. *Caught in the Middle: Protecting the Children of High-Conflict Divorce*. San Francisco: Jossey Bass Publishers.

Gautam, P.K. 'Shruti and Smriti: Some Issues in the Re-emergence of Indian Traditional Knowledge' available at http://www.idsa.in/issuebrief/ShrutiandSmriti_PKGautam_120213

Glick, S. J. 1992. 'Is your Spouse Taping your Telephone Calls?: Title III and Interspousal Electronic Surveillance.' *Catholic University Law Review* 41 (4) pp. 845-69.

Gibran, Kahlil. 1996. *The Prophet*. Hertfordshire: Wordsworth Editions Limited.

Goldstein, Gerard. September 2006. 'The Concepts of Habitual Residence and Ordinary Residence in Light of Quebec Civil Law, the Divorce Act and the Hague Conventions of 1980 and 1996' *Family Children and Youth Section*

Research Report. http://www.justice.gc.ca/eng/rp-pr/fl-lf/divorce/rhro_qc/pdf/rhro_qc.pdf

Goldstein, J, Freud, Anna and Solnitin, A. 1973. *Beyond the Best Interests of the Child*. New York: Free Press.

____ 1979. *Before the Best Interests of the Child*. New York: Free Press.

____ 1986. *The Best Interests of the Child*. New York: Free Press.

Greenberg, Judith G. 2003. 'Criminalizing Dowry Deaths: The Indian Experience.' *American University Journal of Gender Social Policy and Law* 11 (2) pp.801-45.

Greer, Germaine. 2008. *The Female Eunuch*. New York: Harper Perennial.

Guha, Ramachandra. 2016. *Democrats and Dissenters*. New Delhi: Penguin Random House India

Gupta, Apar. 2010. 'Balancing Online Privacy in India.' *The Indian Journal of Law and Technology* 6 pp.43-64.

Gupta, Monobina. 2009. *Marching Together: Resisting Dowry in India*. JAGORI. http://www.jagori.org/wp-content/uploads/2009/07/dowry_infopack.pdf

Hale, B. et al. *Family Law and Society Cases and Materials: Invincible Repugnance*. Oxford: Oxford University Press.

Hale, Lady Brenda. 'Women in the Judiciary.' Fiona Woolf Lecture for the Women Lawyer's Division of the Law Society, London, June 27, 2014. https://www.supremecourt.uk/docs/speech-140627.pdf

Hall, J.C. 1965. 'Husband and Wife, Confidential Communications.' *The Cambridge Law Journal* 23 (2) pp.219-22.

Hansen, Joseph, Redd, Evelyn and Waters, Mary. 2011. *Cosmetics, Fashions and the Exploitation of Women*. New York: Pathfinder Press.

Harari, Yuval Noah. 2011. *Sapien: A Brief History of Humankind*. London: Harvill Secker.

Hardy, Thomas. 1998. *The Mayor of Casterbridge*. Ware: Wordsworth Editions.

Hedrick, L. Kathryn and Gruber, Mark. 2001. 'Cybersex and Divorce: Interception of and Access to E-mail and Other Electronic Communications in the Marital Home.' *Journal of the American Academy of Matrimonial Lawyers* 17 pp.1-28.

Henkin, Louis. 'Privacy and Autonomy.' *Columbia Law Review* 74 (8), December 1974. pp.1410-33.

Herbert, A.P. 1934. *The Holy Deadlock*. London: Methuen Publishing.

Heredia, Rudolf C. 2015. 'Secularism in a Pluri-Religious Society: The Constitutional Vision.' *Economic and Political Weekly* 50 (14) pp.51-59.

____ 'Holding up Half the Sky: Reservations for Women in India.' *Economic and Political Weekly* 47(9) pp.51-60.

Herring, Jonathan. 2013. *Family Law*. Harlow: Pearson Education Ltd.

____ 2015. *Beginning Family Law*. New York: Routledge.

Herring, J; Probert, Rebecca and Gilmore, Stephen. 2012. *Great Debates: Family Law*. New York: Palgrave Macmillan.

Hite, Shere. 1995. *The Hite Report on the Family: Growing Up under Patriarchy*. New York: Grove Press.

Hobbshawn, Erich and Ranger, Terence. 1983. *The Invention of Traditions*. Cambridge: Cambridge University Press.

Hoggett, B. et. al. 1996. *The Family Law and Society: Cases and Material*. London: Butterworths.

Horner, Thomas M. and Guyer, Melvin J. 1991. 'Prediction, Prevention and Clinical Expertise in Child Custody Cases in which Allegations of Child Sexual Abuse Have Been Made.' *Family Law Quarterly* 25 (3) pp.381-409.

'India's Economy: One More Push.' *The Economist,* July 21, 2001.

Inglis, Ruth. 1982. *Must Divorce Hurt the Children*. London: Temple Smith Press.

Ismail, Shaik Mohammed. November 2013. 'A Critical Analysis on Telephone Tapping Conversation.' *Research Journal of Computer and Information Technology Sciences* 1 (6) pp.1-6.

Jadhav, Narendra (Ed). 2013. *Ambedkar Speaks*. New Delhi: Konark Publishers.

Jaffrelot, Christophe. 'Nehru and the Hindu Code Bill' *Outlook*. August 8, 2003.

Jain, Devaki and Sujaya, C.P. (Eds). 2015. *Indian Women: Contemporary Essays*. New Delhi: Publications Division, Ministry of Information and Broadcasting.

Jain, Pratibha. 2005. 'Balancing Minority Rights and Gender Justice: The Impact of Protecting Multiculturalism on Women's Rights in India.' *Berkeley Journal of International Law* 23 (1) pp.201-22.

Jaishankar, K. and Haldar D. 2004. 'Manusmriti: A Critique of the Criminal Justice Tenets in the Ancient Indian Hindu Code.' *ERCES Quarterly Review* 1(3) http://www.erces.com/journal/articles/archives/v03/v03_05.htm.

Jaising, Indira. 2014. 'Concern for the Dead, Condemnation for the Living.' *Economic and Political Weekly* 49 (30) pp.34-38.

____ 'Is this not what Section 354 is meant for, My Lord?' *The Indian Express*, December 16, 2013.

____ 2009. 'Bringing Rights Home: Review of the Campaign for a Law on Domestic Violence.' *Economic and Political Weekly* 44(44) pp.50-57.

____ 2000. 'Gender Justice and the Supreme Court.' in *Supreme But Not Infallible: Essays in Honour of the Supreme Court*, B.N. Kirpal et. al. (ed.s) New Delhi: Oxford University Press.

James N. Bow, Quinnell, Francella A., Zaroff, Mark and Assemany, Amy. 2002. 'Assessment of Sexual Abuse Allegations in Child Custody Cases.' *Professional Psychology: Research and Practice* 33 (6) pp.566–75.

Jamison, Kay Redfield. 1997. *An Unquiet Mind: A Memoir of Moods and Madness*. New York: Vintage Publishers.

Jenkins, Stephen P. 2008. *Marital Splits and Income Changes over the Longer Term*. University of Essex: Institute for Social and Economic Research.

John, Mary E. 2011. 'The Politics of Quotas and Women's Reservation Bill in India,' Centre for Women's Developmental Studies. http://www.cwds.ac.in/Politics of quotas and WRB-MJ-Ch.8.pdf.

Johnson, David and Wu, Jian. 2002. 'An empirical test of crisis, social selection, and role explanations of the relationship between marital disruption and psychological distress: a pooled time-series analysis of four-wave panel data.' *Journal of Marriage and Family* 64 (1) pp.211–24.

Kadar, S.A. 1998. *Muslim Law of Marriage and Succession*. Kolkata: Eastern Law House.

Kadri, Sadakat. 2006. *The Trial: A History from Socrates to O.J Simpson*. London: Harper Perennial.

Kakar, Sudhir. 1990. *Intimate Relations: Exploring Indian Sexuality*. Chicago: University of Chicago Press.

____ 1978. *The Inner World: A Psychoanalytic Study of Childhood and Society in India*. New Delhi: Oxford University Press.

____ 2007. *Indian Identity*. New Delhi: Penguin Books.

Kalter, Neil. 2006. *Growing Up With Divorce*. New York: Free Press.

Kane, P.V. 1941. *History of Dharmashastra*. Pune: Bhandarkar Oriental Research Institute Publishers.

Kant, Immanuel. 'Idea for a General History with a Cosmopolitan Purpose', quoted in *The Crooked Timber of Humanity: Chapters in the History of Ideas* by Isaiah Berlin. Princeton: Princeton University Press, 2016.

Kapur, Ratna. 2001. 'Sexcapades and the Law.' http://cscs.res.in/dataarchive/textfiles/textfile.2012-03-12.1317951631/file

Kapur, Ratna and Cossman, Brenda. 1996. *Subversive Sites: Feminist Engagements with Law in India*. New Delhi: Sage Publications.

'Karnal settlement report, 1892.' http://www.nidanaheights.net/images/Library/books/karnal-gazeetter-1892.pdf.

Karve, Irawati. 1968. *Kinship Organisation in India*. New Delhi: Asia Publishing House.

Kashyap, S.C. and Kashyap, A. 2012. *Indian Presidency: Constitution Law and Practice*, New Delhi: Universal Law Publishing.

Kaufold, M.A. 2004. 'Defining Misappropriation: The Spousal Duty of Loyalty and the Expectation of Benefit.' *Mercer Law Review* 55 (4) pp.1489-1503.

Kauffman, Linda, (Ed.) 1989. *Feminism and Institutions: Dialogues on Feminist Theory*. Oxford: Basil Blackwell.

Kaur, Ravinder and Palriwala, Rajni. 2014. *Marrying in South Asia: Shifting Concepts, Changing Practices in a Globalising World*. New Delhi: Orient Blackswan.

Kaushik, Susheela. 1993. *Women and Panchayat Raj*. New Delhi: Friedrich Ebert Stiftung.

Keer, Dhananjay. 2003. *Dr Ambedkar: Life And Mission*. Mumbai: Popular Prakashan.

Kennedy, Helena. 2005. *Eve was Framed: Women and British Justice*. London: Vintage Books.

Kenney, Sally J. 2012. 'Choosing Judges: A Bumpy Road To Women's Equality And A Long Way To Go.' *Michigan State Law Review* pp.1499-1528.

Khurshid, Salman. 2015. *At Home in India: The Muslim Saga*. New Delhi: Hay House India.

Kishwar, Madhu. 2013. *Off The Beaten Track: Rethinking Gender Justice For Indian Women*. New Delhi: Oxford University Press.

____ 2005. 'Strategies for Combating the Culture of Dowry and Domestic Violence in India.' http://www.un.org/womenwatch/daw/egm/vaw-gp-2005/docs/experts/kishwar.dowry.pdf.

____ 1998. 'Destined to fail: Inherent Flaws in the Anti-Dowry Legislation' *Manushi*. http://www.manushi-india.org/pdfs_issues/PDF%20Files%20148/MK%20Article%203-12.pdf?

____ 1994. 'Codified Hindu Law: Myth and Reality.' *Economic and Political Weekly* 29 (33) pp.2145-61.

____ 1986. 'Pro Women or Anti Muslim?: The Shah Bano Controversy.' *Manushi* (32) pp.4-13.

Krishnan, Jayanth K. et al. 2014. 'Grappling at the Grassroots: Access to Justice in India's Lower Tier.' *Harvard Human Rights Journal* 27.

Krishnaraj, Maithreyi. 2012. 'The Women's Movement in India: A Hundred Year History.' *Social Change* 42 (3) pp.325-33.

Kumar, Vijender. 2010. 'Irretrievable Breakdown of Marriage: Right of a Married Couple' *NALSAR Law Review*, 5 (1) pp.15-38.

Kumari, Ved. 2004. *The Juvenile Justice System in India: From Welfare to Rights*. New Delhi: Oxford University Press.

Lahoti, Rahul, Suchitra J.Y. and Swaminathan, Hema. 2016. 'Not in Her Name: Women's Property Ownership in India.' *Economic and Political Weekly* 51(5) pp.17-19.

Law Commission of India. 2009. *217th Report on Irretrievable Breakdown of Marriage*. http://lawcommissionofindia.nic.in/reports/report217.pdf

____ 1978. *71st Report on the Hindu Marriage Act*, 1955(1978). http://lawcommissionofindia.nic.in/51-100/Report71.pdf

Lee, Catherine M. and Bax, Karen. 'Children's Reactions to Parental Separation and Divorce'. *Paediatric Child Health*. 5(4) (2000) pp.217–218.

Lerner, Gerda. 1986. *The Creation of Patriarchy*. Oxford: Oxford University Press.

Lerner, Laurence. 1979. *Love and Marriage, Literature and its Social Context*. New York: St. Martin's Press Inc.

Leslie, Julia, (Ed.) 1991. *Roles and Rituals for Hindu Women*. London: Pinter Publishers.

Levesque, Roger J.R. 2008. *Child Maltreatment and the Law: Returning to First Principles*. New York: Springer.

Lindsey, Ben B. and Wainwright, Evans. 1927. *The Companionate Marriage*. New York: Ayer Co Pub.

Locke, John. 1689. *An Essay Concerning Human Understanding*. http://www.earlymoderntexts.com/assets/pdfs/locke1690book1.pdf

Loftus, Elizabeth, Ketcham, Katherine. 1996. *The Myth of Repressed Memory: False Memories and Allegations of Sexual Abuse*. New York: St. Martin's Griffin.

Long, Jeffery D. 2007. *A Vision For Hinduism: Beyond Hindu Nationalism*. New York: I.B. Tauris.

Lovell, Terry (Ed). 1990. *British Feminist Thought: A Reader*. Oxford: Basil Blackwell.

Macfarlane, Julie. 2004. 'Experiences of Collaborative Law: Preliminary Results from the Collaborative Lawyering Research Project 2004.' *Journal of Dispute Resolution* 2004(1) pp.180-226.

Maclean, Mavis. 2011. *Making Family Law*. Oxford: Hart Publishers.

Maclean, Mavis and Eekelaar, John. 2009. *Family Law Advocacy*. Portland: Hart Publishing.

Mahmood, Tahir. 2016. *Muslim Law in India and Abroad*. Gurgaon: Universal Law Publishing.

____ 1995. *Uniform Civil Code: Fictions and Facts*. New Delhi: India and Islam Research Council.

Maidement, Susan. 1984. *Child Custody and Divorce*. Sydney: Croom Helm.

____ 1981. 'Dipper v. Dipper: Custody Revisited.' *The Modern Law Review* 44 (3) pp.341-44.

Manohar, V. R. and Chitaley, W. W. 2014. *Hindu Law*. New Delhi: All India Reporter.

Masson, Judith; Bailer-Harris, Rebecca and Probert, Rebbeca. 2008. *Principles of Family Law*. London: Sweet and Maxwell.

Mause, Llyod de, (Ed.) 1995. *The History of Childhood*. New Jersey: Jason Aronson Inc.

Mckinnon, Catherine A. 1989. *Toward a Feminist Theory of the State*. Cambridge, MA: Harvard University Press.

McMullen, Judith G. 1992. 'Privacy, Family Autonomy, and the Maltreated Child.' *Marquette Law Review* 75 p.569.

Mead, Margaret. 2001. *Male and Female*. New York: Perennial.

Mehta, Rama. 1975. *Divorced Hindu Woman*. Delhi: Vikas Publishing House Pvt. Ltd.

Menon, Nivedita. 'It isn't about women.' *The Hindu* July 15, 2016 http://www.thehindu.com/opinion/lead/nivedita-menon-on-uniform-civil-code-it-isnt-about-women/article8850353.ece.

____ 2012. *Seeing like a Feminist*. New Delhi: Penguin India.

____ 2011. *Recovering Subversion: Feminist Politics Beyond the Law*. Ranikhet: Permanent Black.

Menski, Werner. 2008. 'The Uniform Civil Code Debate in Indian Law: New Developments and Changing Agenda.' *German Law Journal* 9 (03) pp.211-50.

____ 2004. 'From Dharma to Law and Back? Postmodern Hindu Law in a Global World.' *Heidelberg Papers in South Asian and Comparative Politics, Working Paper No. 20.*

____ 2001. *Modern Indian Family Law*. Richmond: Curzon Press.

Menski, Werner and Pearl, David. 1998. *Muslim Family Law*. London: Sweet and Maxwell.

Merwin, W.S. and Masson, J. Moussaief. 1977. *Sanskrit Love Poetry*. New York: Columbia University Press.

Millett, Kate. 2000. *Sexual Politics*. Chicago: University of Illinois Press.

Mody, Perveez. 2008. *The Intimate State: Love-Marriage and the Law in Delhi*. New Delhi: Routledge.

Morgan, Laura and Reich, Lewis B. 2010. 'The Individual's Right of Privacy in a Marriage.' *Journal of the American Academy of Matrimonial Lawyers* 23 (1) pp.111-29.

Mortimer, John. 2005. *Where There's a Will*. New York: Viking.

Mueller, Dennis C. 2009. *Reason, Religion and Democracy*. New York: Cambridge University Press.

Mulla, Dinshaw F. 2010. *Principles of Hindu Law*, 504. Delhi: Lexis Nexis Butterworths Wadhwa.

Mullally, Siobhan. 2004. 'Feminism and Multiculturalism Dilemmas in India: Revisiting the Shah Bano Case.' *Oxford Journal of Legal Studies* 24 (4) pp.671-92.

Munby, James. 2014. 'Law, Morality and Religion in the Family Courts' *Ecclesiastical Law Journal* 16 pp.131–39.

Nagarajan, V. 1992. *Evolution of Social Polity of Ancient India: From Manu to Kautilya*. Nagpur: Dattsons.

Nair, G.R. 2011. *Gender Justice under Indian Criminal Justice System*. Kolkata: Eastern Law House.

Nair, Nivedita. 2014. 'Scope of Mediation in Matrimonial Disputes in India.' *The National University of Advanced Legal Studies Law Journal* 8 pp.154-74.

Nandy, Ashis. 2012. 'Reconstructing Childhood: A Critique of the Ideology of Adulthood' in *Bonfire of Creeds*. New Delhi: Oxford University Press.

____ 'Science in Utopia: Equity, plurality and openness.' *India International Centre Quarterly* 28 (4) pp.91-101.

____ 1997. 'The Twilight of Certitudes: Secularism, Hindu Nationalism, and other Masks of Deculturation.' *Alternatives: Global, Local, Political* 22 (2) pp.157-76.

____ 1995. 'Secularism In Crisis:An Anti-Secularist Manifesto.' *India International Centre Quarterly* 22 (1) pp.35-64.

____ 1984. 'Culture, State And The Rediscovery Of Indian Politics.' *Economic and Political Weekly* 19 (49) pp.2078-83.

____ 1976. 'Woman versus Womanliness in India: An Essay in Cultural and Political Psychology.' *Psychoanalytic Review* 63 (2) pp.301-15.

Narain, Vrinda. 1965. *Gender and Community: Muslim Women's Rights in India*. Toronto: University of Toronto Press.

Nath, Sib. 1976. *Pulle Visre Lok*. Amritsar: Ravi Sahit Prakashan.

Neil, N.O. and Neil, G.O. 1984. *Open Marriage*. New York: M. Evans and Company.

Nelson, James Henry. 1881. *A Prospectus of the Scientific Study of the Hindu Law*. London: Kegan Paul and Co.

____ 1887. *Indian Usage and Judge-Made Law in Madras*. London: Kegan Paul and Co.

Newbigin, Eleanor. 2013. *The Hindu Family and the Emergence of Modern India: Law, Citizenship and Community*. New York: Cambridge University Press.

Norton, Caroline. 1982. *Caroline Norton's Defense: English Laws for Women in the Nineteenth Century*. Chicago: Chicago Review Press.

____ 1855. *A letter to the Queen on Lord Chancellor Cranworth's Marriage and Divorce Bill*. London: Longman, Brown, Green and Longmans.

O'Brien, John. 1846. 'A treatise on American military laws, and the practice of courts martial'. Philadephia: Lea and Blanchard.

Oldenburg, Veena. 2002. *Dowry Murder: Reinvestigating a Cultural Whodunnit*. New York: Penguin Books.

____ 2002. *Dowry Murder: The Imperial Origins of a Cultural Crime*. New York: Oxford University Press.

Olsen, Frances E., (Ed.) 1995. *Feminist Legal Theory*. Vol. I and II. New York: New York University Press.

Parliament of India, *Parliamentary Debates*, Vol. VIII, Part II, 6 February, 1951. pp.2473-83

Parwwen, Samina. 'Gender Quota: Travails of the Women Reservation Bill in India.' *International Organization of Scientific Research Journal of Humanities and Social Science* 19 (3 Ver IV) (2014). pp.98-103.

Peters, Anne and Schwenke, Heiner. 'Comparative Law beyond Post-Modernism.' *The International and Comparative Law Quarterly* 49 (4) (2000). pp.800-34.

Perry, George G. 1886. *History of Reformation in England*. London: Longmans, Green and Co.

Phadke, Shilpa. 'Women's Studies Reflects on the Women's Movement.' *Economic and Political Weekly* 38 (43) (2003). pp.4567–76.

Pinker, Steven. 2011. *The Better Angels of Our Nature: The Decline of Violence in History and its Causes*. New York: Penguin Books.

Prest, Charles, Mark Saunders, Stephen Wildblood, Claire Wills Goldingham (Eds). 2008. *Family Law Case Library*. Bristol: Jordan Publishing Ltd.

Queen Victoria. Proclamation by the Queen to the Princes, Chiefs, and the People of India, 1 November 1858. http://www.sdstate.edu/projectsouthasia/loader.cfm?csModule=security/getfileandPageID=861653.

Raitt, Fione E. 2007. 'Hearing Children in Family Law Proceedings: Can Judges make a Difference.' *Child and Family Law Quarterly* 19 (2) p.204.

Rao, Mamta. 2008. *Law Relating to Women and Children*. Lucknow: Eastern Book Company.

Rao, Nitya and Rurup, Luise (Eds). 1997. *A Just Right: Women's Ownership of Natural Resources and Livelihood Security*. New Delhi: Friedrich Ebert Stiftung Publishing.

Ratnaparkhi, M.S. 1997. *Uniform Civil Code: An Ignored Constitutional Imperative*. New Delhi: Atlantic Publishers and Distributors.

Rayden, William. 1979. *Rayden's Law and Practice in Divorce and Family Matters in All Courts*. London: Butterworths.

Redd, Evelyn. 2010. *Problems of Women's Liberation*. New York: Pathfinder Press.

Rege, Sharmila. 2013. *Against the Madness of Manu: B.R. Ambedkar's Writings on Brahmanical Patriarchy*. New Delhi: Navayana.

Richards, Janet Radcliffe. 1994. *The Sceptical Feminist: A Philosophical Enquiry*. London: Penguin.

Robert, Chester and Jane Streather. 'Cruelty in English Divorce: Some Empirical Findings.' *Journal of Marriage and Family* 34 (4) (1972). pp.706-12.

Roy, Arundhati. 2014. 'The Doctor And The Saint' in *Annihilation Of Caste* by B.R. Ambedkar. New Delhi: Navayana.

Russell, Bertrand. 2013. *Marriage and Morals*. London: Routledge Publications.

Sagade, Jaya; Jivan, Vedna and Forster, Christine. 2014. *Feminism in the Subcontinent and Beyond: Challenging laws, changing laws*. New Delhi: Eastern Book Company.

Sarkar, Lotika and Mazumdar, Vina. 2008. 'Dissenting Voices: Note of Dissent to Towards Equality, Report of the Committee on the Status of Women in India.

1974.' in *Reservations of Women*, Meena Dhanda (ed). New Delhi: Women Unlimited.

Sarkar, Tanika. 2001. *Hindu Wife, Hindu Nation: Community, Religion, and Cultural Nationalism*. New Delhi: Permanent Black.

Sarma, R. Naga Raja. 'Ethics of Divorce in Ancient India.' *International Journal of Ethics* 41 (3) (1931). pp.329-42.

Sathe, S.P. 'Uniform Civil Code: Implications of Supreme Court Intervention.' *Economic and Political Weekly* 30 (35) (1995). pp.2165-66.

Schopenhauer, Arthur. 2005. *On the Basis of Morality*. New York: Dover Publications Inc.

Schultz, Ulrike and Shaw, Gisela. 2013. *Gender and Judging*. Oxford: Hart Publishing.

Seervai, H.M. 2007. *Constitutional Law of India*. 4th ed. New Delhi: Universal Law Publishing.

Sehgal, Sangita Dhingra and Khurshid, Hasan. 2016. *Woman Know Thyself: Law Relating to Women in India*. Gurgaon: Universal Law Publishing.

Sen, Amartya. 2009. *The Idea of Justice*. London: Penguin Books.

Sen, Jhuma. 'Matrimonial Property Rights, Is India Ready for a Law?' *Manupatra* http://www.manupatra.co.in/newsline/articles/Upload/F2587F8B-1162-415A-8E76-6F4019530939.pdf.

Sen, Samita. *Toward a Feminist Politics? The Indian Women's Movement in Historical Perspective*. Policy Research Report On Gender And Development, Working Paper Series No. 9. http://unpan1.un.org/intradoc/groups/public/documents/apcity/unpan051009.pdf.

Seneca, Lucius Annaeus. 2010. *Morals: Of a Happy Life, Benefits, Anger and Clemency.* Charleston: Nabu Press.

Setalvad, M.C. 1960. *The Hamlyn Law Lectures On Common Law in India*. London: Stevens & Sons Limited.

Seth, Leila. 2014. *Talking Of Justice*. New Delhi: Aleph Book Company.

Shabbir, Mohammad. 'Analytical Positivism in Judicial Perspective: Some Reflections.' *Supreme Court Journal* 3 (1996). pp.46–51.

Shah, Prakash. 2005. *Legal Pluralism in Conflict: Coping with Cultural Diversity in Law*. London: Glasshouse Press.

Shanbagh, Vivek. 2016. *Ghachar, Ghochar*. Noida: Harper Perennial.

Shandilya, Akshay and Tiwari, Shaleen. 'NRI Marriages: The Evolving Societal Malaise in India.' *International Organization of Scientific Research Journal of Humanities and Social Sciences* 12 (6) (2013). pp.29-39.

Sharma, Kanahaiyalal. 2002. *Reconstitution of the Constitution of India*. New Delhi: Deep and Deep Publications.

Sharma, Kumud and Sujaya, C.P. 2012. *Towards Equality: Report of the Committee on the Status of Women in India*. New Delhi: CWDS.

Sharma, Swarna Kanta. 2014. *Divorce: Don't Break after Break Up*. New Delhi: Bukaholic Publications.

'Should Secular India have an Uniform Civil Code?' *The Telegraph Calcutta Club National Debate*. March 13, 2015. http://www.cse.iitk.ac.in/users/amit/other/debate0503.html/.

Showalter, Amanda. "What's Yours Is Mine': Inadvertent Disclosure of Electronically Stored Privileged Information in Divorce Litigation.' *Journal of the American Academy of Matrimonial Lawyers* 23 (2010). p.177.

Simmons, Christina. 2011. *Making Marriage Modern: Women's Sexuality from the Progessive Era to World War II*. New York: Oxford University Press.

Singh, Jagjivan. 2009. *Bibi Gurbachan Kaur Mann: Jeevan Katha*. Fategarh Sahib: Mata Gujri College.

Singh, Kirti. 'Laws Relating to NRI Marriages and Their Impact on Women.' http://ncw.nic.in/ExpertCommitteePDFFiles/EC_NRIMarriages.pdf.

____ 2013. *Separated and Divorced Women in India: Economic Rights and Entitlement*. New Delhi: Sage Publications IDRC.

Sivaramayya, B. 1999. *Matrimonial Property Law in India*. New Delhi: Oxford University Press.

Smith, Donald Eugene. 1967. *India as a Secular State*. Princeton: Princeton University Press.

Smith, Gayle Rosenwald and Abrahms, Sally. 2007. *What Every Woman Should Know About Divorce and Custody*. New York: Penguin USA.

Smith, Julia Llewellyn. 'Welcome to Maidenhead Britain's Capital of Infidelity.' *The Telegraph*, April 13 2014.

Sorabji, Richard. 2010. *Opening Doors: The Untold Story of Cornelia Sorabji*. New York: I.B. Tauris and Co.

South Asian Human Rights Documentation, Centre. 'Anti-Conversion Laws: Challenges to Secularism and Fundamental Rights.' *Economic and Political Weekly* 43 (2) (2008). pp.63-73.

Souza, E.D. and Silgardo M. 2012. *These My Words, The Penguin Book of Indian Poetry.* New Delhi: Penguin Books India.

Srinivasan, K. and James, K.S. 'The Golden Case: Stability of the Institution of Marriage in India.' *Economic and Political Weekly* 40 (13) (2015). pp.38-45.

Stedley, Stephen. 2011. "Declining the Brief', in *Ashes and Sparks*. Cambridge: Cambridge University Press. https://www.supremecourt.uk/docs/speech-140627.pdf.

Stiftung, Friedrich Ebert (Ed.) 1993. *Women in Politics: Forms and Processes*. New Delhi: Har Anand Publications.

Subramanian, Narendra. 2014. *Nation and Family: Personal Law, Cultural Pluralism and Gendered Citizenship in India*. Stanford: Stanford University Press.

____ 2010. 'Making Family and Nation: Hindu Marriage Law in Early Postcolonial India', *The Journal of Asian Studies* 69(3) pp.771–98.

Sudarshan, Ratna M., Swapna Mukhopadhyay, Kali for Women, and International Development Research Centre. 2003. *Tracking Gender Equity Under Economic Reforms: Continuity and Change in South Asia*. Ottawa: International Development Research Centre.

Sumption, Lord. 2016 'Family law at a distance', *Law, Morality and Religion* https://www.supremecourt.uk/docs/speech-160608.pdf.

Swaminathan, Padmini (Ed). 2012. *Women and Work: Readings on the Economy, Polity and Society*. New Delhi: Orient Blackswan.

Thapar, Romila. 2015. *The Public Intellectual in India*. New Delhi: Aleph Book Company.

____ 2014. *The Past as Present: Forging Contemporary Identities Through History*. New Delhi: Aleph Book Company.

____ 1989. 'Imagined Religious Communities? Ancient History and the Modern Search for a Hindu Identity.' *Modern Asian Studies* 23 (2) pp.209–31.

Trotsky, Leon. 2011. *Woman and the Family*. New York: Pathfinder Press.

Vanita, Ruth. 2005. *Love's Rite: Same-Sex Marriage in India and the West*. New York: Palgrave Macmillan.

Vivatvaraphol, Tai. 'Back to Basics: Determining a Child's Habitual Residence in International Child Abduction Cases Under the Hague Convention.' *Fordham Law Review* 77 (6) (2009). pp.3325–69.

Wakefield, Hollida and Underwage, Ralph. 'Sexual abuse allegations in divorce and custody disputes.' *Behavioral Sciences and the Law* 9 (4) (1991). pp.451-68.

Waldron, Kenneth H. and Joanis, David E. 'Understanding and Collaboratively Treating Parental Alienation Syndrome.' *American Journal of Family Law*. 10 (1996). pp.121-33.

Wallerstein, Judith; Julia, Lewis and Blakeslee, Sandra. 2000. *The Unexpected Legacy of Divorce*. New York: Hyperion.

Warren, Samuel D. and Brandeis, Louis D. 'The Right to Privacy.' *Harvard Law Review* 4 (5) (1890). pp.193-220.

Warshak, Richard A. 1992. *The Custody Revolution*. New York: Poseidon Press.

Westermarck, Edward. 1891. *The History of Human Marriage*. London: Macmillan and Co.

Williams, Joan. 2000. *Unbending Gender*. New York: Oxford University Press.

____ 2010. *Reshaping the Work-Family Debate*. Cambridge, MA: Harvard University Press.

Wilson, Robin Fretwell. 2006. *Reconceiving the Family*. New York: Cambridge University Press.

Wood, Cheri L. 'The Parental Alienation Syndrome: A Dangerous Aura of Reliability.' *Loyola of Los Angeles Law Review* 27 (4) (1994). pp.1367-1415.

Woolf, Virginia. 2000. *A Room of One's Own*. London: Penguin Books.

Zahava, Irene (Ed). 1996. *Feminism: The Third Generation in Fiction*. Boulder: Westview Press.

Zakaria, Fareed. 2003. *The Future of Freedom: Illiberal Democracy at Home and Abroad*. New York: W. W. Norton and Company.

Zelliot, Eleanor. 2013. *Ambedkar's World: The Making of Babasaheb and the Dalit Movement*. New Delhi: Navayana.

ACKNOWLEDGEMENTS

I acknowledge with gratitude the following persons who supported my endeavour:

Megnad Desai read each chapter as I wrote it: his feedback kept me going.

Rajeev Dhavan directed me to a mine of reading material: his input, particularly on the Uniform Civil Code, was invaluable.

Jasjit Purewal, gave me the title and important editorial input, particularly on the chapter on gender. Prosenjeet (Ronnie) Banerjee, Sushmita Dev and Sandeep Prabhakar read the first few chapters as I wrote them and encouraged me to keep going. Akhil Sibal's insightful and candid comments on the structure of the manuscript were important to me.

Ronnie patiently read the complete manuscript once again and his inputs were important in giving the book its final shape.

Sonal at The Book Shop read the manuscript and her perspective as a non-legal person was valuable.

My college friend Sara Ipe and I met after years and she promptly took charge of reading and critiquing as if she had never been away.

Kapil Sibal was patient and encouraging as I wrote and ran concepts by him. Nivedita Menon helped me immensely with the gender chapter, though I confess I did not take her advice to limit the comment to the law; some of the arguments consequently may seem obvious to a person widely read on the issue of gender, but I have tried to distil and simplify without hopefully being simplistic.

Aarushi Mahajan, law student NLUD (Delhi), was a great support while she interned with me.

Pradeep Krishen, Ganeve Rajkotia, Rachel Dwyer, Mahesh Mathai, Freyan Desai, Ravi Awasthi, N. Ranjay, Rebecca John, Binoo John: all read various chapters and critiqued them. Thank you.

I am grateful to Saumya Maheshwari who read the final draft and gave me sterling support in tidying it all up into a workable manuscript.

I thank Javed Gaya and Aruna Ghose, who read the early draft. Javed introduced me to Michael Dwyer who I am grateful to for reading the manuscript and directing me to my publisher, Ravi Singh. In one of those lovely coincidences, Aruna independently introduced me to Ravi.

Meeting Ravi brought the book to safe harbor. His reassuring manner and calm confident support was the incentive for the final push to completion.

My editor, Shalini Krishan, was marvelously patient, insightful and tough with inconsistencies in my arguments. She helped gather the material into a cohesive whole. Thank you.

Apart from those who actually read the manuscript and helped research, my office colleagues encouraged me by freeing me from routine work to the extent possible to work on the book: I thank Arpita Rai, Tanya Prasad, Chaitanya Puri, Vaibhav Vats, Ramakant Sharma, Ramanand Sahib, Brijesh Singh and Manmohan for their able support.

Ajay patiently typed out numerous drafts and Munendra Tiwari spent hours ordering and filing my research material.

And finally I thank, with folded hands, my colleague and friend Upasana Garnaik for her wise counsel, patient support, careful research, footnoting and editing. I believe this endeavour would have been very rocky and lonely without her.

My children, Adya and Tejas, encouraged me by reading some chapters, commenting on them and even challenging many positions that I took. As for all parents, having the active support of my children was a special delight.

INDEX